Women, Work, and Family in the Antebellum Mountain South

Wilma A. Dunaway breaks new ground to examine the race, class, and ethnic differences among antebellum Southern Appalachian women. Most women defied separate spheres of gender conventions to undertake agricultural and nonagricultural labors that were essential to family survival or community well-being. Unlike elite and middle-class females, Cherokee, black, and poor white women engaged in stigmatized labors and worked alongside males in cross-racial settings. To support their work portfolios, nonwhite and most poor white women constructed nonpatriarchal families that challenged cultural ideals of motherhood. Churches and courts inequitably regulated the sexual behaviors of these women and treated their households as aberrations that were not entitled to the legal privilege of family sanctity. Legal and religious officials sanctioned family breakups and the removal, indenturement, or enslavement of their children. Still, many women resisted patriarchal conventions through their work lives, family roles, and group activism.

For more than two decades, Wilma A. Dunaway worked in civil rights and public services organizations in the Appalachian region. At present, she is an associate professor in the School of Public and International Affairs at Virginia Polytechnic Institute and State University. Dunaway is a specialist in international slavery studies, Native American studies, Appalachian studies, and world-system analysis. Her dissertation about the incorporation of Southern Appalachia into the capitalist world economy was awarded a Wilson Fellowship and the Distinguished Dissertation Award from the American Sociological Association. She has won several awards for her previous three works on Appalachia and slavery, including two Weatherford Awards. Her interdisciplinary work has appeared in numerous history and social science journals.

Women, Work, and Family in the Antebellum Mountain South

WILMA A. DUNAWAY

Virginia Polytechnic Institute and State University

CAMBRIDGE
UNIVERSITY PRESS

CAMBRIDGE UNIVERSITY PRESS
Cambridge, New York, Melbourne, Madrid, Cape Town, Singapore, São Paulo, Delhi

Cambridge University Press
32 Avenue of the Americas, New York, NY 10013-2473, USA

www.cambridge.org
Information on this title: www.cambridge.org/9780521886192

First published 2008

Printed in the United States of America

A catalog record for this publication is available from the British Library.

Library of Congress Cataloging in Publication Data
Dunaway, Wilma A.
Women, work, and family in the antebellum mountain South/Wilma A. Dunaway.
    p.   cm.
Includes bibliographical references and index.
ISBN 978-0-521-88619-2 (hardback)
    1. Women – Appalachian Region, Southern – Social conditions.   2. Poor women – Appalachian
Region, Southern – History.   3. Minority women – Appalachian Region, Southern – History.
4. Women – Employment – Appalachian Region, Southern – History.   5. Sex Role –
Appalachian Region, Southern – History.   6. Family policy – Appalachian Region, Southern –
History.   I. Title.
HQ1438.A55D85   2008
305.48'96240975 – dc22   2007023441

ISBN   978-0-521-88619-2 hardback

Dedicated to

Professor Donald Armour Clelland

My Beloved Soulmate

who constantly reminds me that there is still

so much to interrogate, to discover, and to remember

that many would prefer to dismiss, to conceal, and to forget

and to

Betty Dunaway Farmer

My Best Friend and Loving Sister

whose hard work, resilience, and commitment

to our extended family echo the persistence

of the women I describe in this book

The companion Web site for this book is located at
http://scholar.lib.vt.edu/faculty_archives/appalachian_women/index.htm

Contents

Maps, Tables, and Figures

Maps

Tables

Figures

Acknowledgments

Without the invisible labor of many library staff, my complex research about such a large geographical area would not be possible. I am particularly grateful to the Interlibrary Loan staff at Virginia Tech for their persistence in securing hundreds of sources. Numerous library and archival staff at the libraries listed in my Bibliography have also been invaluable in helping me locate a diverse array of primary documents. I am also grateful to Pat Beaver, Loyal Jones, and Rickie Solinger for their useful comments and suggestions.

Archive Locator Codes

Following each unpublished manuscript in the notes and parenthetical citations, one of the following locator codes has been added to indentify the archive in which it is located.

ABH	American Baptist Historical Society
ADA	Alabama Department of Archives and History
ALC	Alice Lloyd College Library
ASU	Appalachian State University
DU	Duke University Library
EHU	Emory and Henry University Library
FHC	Family History Center, Church of Jesus Christ of the Latter Day Saints
FUA	Fisk University Library
GHC	Georgia Historical Commission
GSA	Georgia State Archives
HPL	Handley Public Library
HUL	Harvard University Library
IAT	Institute for Advanced Technology in the Humanities, University of Virginia
IHA	Indian Heritage Association
KDLA	Kentucky Department for Libraries and Archives
LJC	Lees Junior College Library
LOC	Library of Congress
MA	Moravian Archives
MSA	Maryland State Archives
NA	National Archives
NCDAH	North Carolina Department of Archives and History
NLC	Newberry Library
TROY	Troy State University
TSL	Tennessee State Library and Archives

UGA   University of Georgia Library
UKY   University of Kentucky Library
UNC   University of North Carolina Library
UTK   University of Tennessee Library
UVA   University of Virginia Library
VHS   Virginia Historical Society
VSL   Virginia State Library and Archives
WVU   West Virginia University Library

Women, Work, and Family in the Antebellum Mountain South

Introduction

> The history of Appalachia is a drama written largely about men.... Women have been extras, hidden behind quilts and sunbonnets in tradition-bound domestic roles that supported their husbands, sons, and fathers as they transformed the region and made its history.... Apart from a few, specific individuals, women's experiences and perceptions have been peripheral in the major works of Appalachian history.
>
> (Barbara Ellen Smith 1992, 5)

If, as Catherine Clinton (1994, 1) writes, southern women have been American history's half sisters, Appalachian women have been only *second-cousins-once-removed* in the country's regionally parochial history construction.[1] This study breaks new ground by investigating the multiethnic majority of females who resided in the Mountain South between 1700 and 1860. This geographically massive subregion of the U.S. Southeast was characterized by slavery amid a nonslaveholding majority, a large surplus of poor white landless laborers, and small Cherokee and free black populations. Consisting of 215 counties in six Upper South states and three Lower South states (see Map 1), this large land area was distinguished in the antebellum period by its diverse mix of nonslaveholding farms and enterprises, small plantations, active small town commerce and external trade, mixed farming, light manufacturing, and extractive industry (Dunaway 1996). On the one hand, the population of this region was diverse enough to permit comparative analysis of the racial, ethnic, and class cleavages among women. On the other hand, this region offers an unusual opportunity to explore the complex portfolio of women's economic activities and their challenges to patriarchal family constructs.

---

[1] For a survey of recent literature about Appalachian women, see Anglin (2000), Smith (1992), and Engelhardt (2003). Anglin (2002, 4–7) provides an overview of works since the late 1980s. For a review of pre-1990 scholarly and fictional depictions, see "Stereotypes about Appalachian Women," Web site.

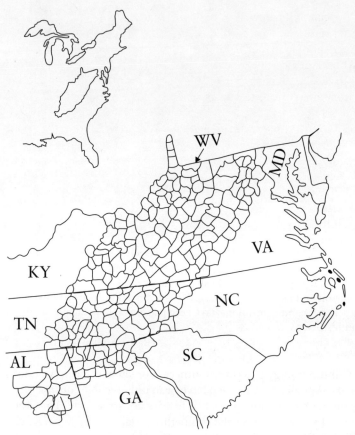

MAP 1. Where Is Southern Appalachia? 1860 county boundaries are shown. For a list of Appalachian counties, see the Web site.

For more than 30 years, writers have been calling attention to scholarly failure to produce revisionist analyses that attack a century of accumulated stereotypes about Appalachian females. Even though *Mountain Life and Work* first called attention to the historical distortions of Appalachian women in its 1974 "Special Women's Issue," this concern still resounds among regional female scholars in the contemporary era.[2] The task of analyzing the work and family life of antebellum females might be simpler if Appalachian women were totally absent from history writing, for then we could begin with a blank slate. However, the journey toward a meaningful analysis of Appalachian women is made more difficult by the need to overcome the burden of a century of out-dated assumptions about their character flaws and about their debilitating isolation in the separate sphere of their homes. Consequently, a revisionist analysis of Appalachian women must simultaneously overcome entrenched stereotypes

---

[2] The 1985 "Appalachian Women" special issue of *Now and Then* reiterated this critique.

and myths and convince other regional scholars that feminist analysis is both needed and appropriate. This revisionist research agenda is also complicated by male-dominated and male-privileging history production. As Pat Beaver (1999, xix) has observed, "Appalachian history has been constructed out of masculinist narratives." At the same time that "scholars have been working to discredit derogatory images of Appalachia," contends Sally Maggard (1986, 126), gender analysis remains "underdeveloped in Appalachian Studies," leaving stereotypes of women unquestioned. Barbara Ellen Smith (1999, 1) warns that researchers who attempt to investigate mountain women "must come to terms with implicitly gendered constructions of Appalachia and narratives of regional history that feature men as the determinant actors."[3] Even though history and social science production about Appalachian women has expanded over the last two decades, a majority of these new studies focus on the twentieth century. As Milton Ready (1991, 62) observes, "The most outstanding feature of Appalachian women in the nineteenth century is the fact that we know so little about them."

Conceptual Core of the Book

This study debunks popular mythology about Appalachian women and seeks to end historical silencing about their racial and ethnic diversity. Pat Beaver (1999, xvi) contends that "mythologized conventions of a static and homogeneous (white) society have dominated the literature on the southern Appalachian region." In fact, Indians and African-Americans are absent from the vast majority of the pages that have been written about Appalachia, an omission that transforms them into peoples without regional history. To obliterate nonwhites from regional history is perhaps the ultimate act of academic and journalistic racism, but there is a second pervasive regional myth that compounds the ideological denial of the presence of nonwhite Appalachians. Well before the Civil War, Lanman (1848, 314) acknowledged the presence of slavery in Southern Appalachia, but he described those slaves as "the happiest and most independent portion of the population." Such ideology pervaded the rhetoric of late nineteenth-century journalists, novelists, and clerics and is still predominant in popular regional mythology today. From within the region, early twentieth-century writers extolled the Anglo-Saxon heritage of Southern Appalachians who had not only kept out "foreign" elements but had "still more effectively ... excluded the negroes." Purportedly, "Appalachian America ha[d] received no foreign immigration" after the Revolutionary War. Consequently, "nowhere will be found purer Anglo-Saxon blood" (Semple 1901, 588). Carter Woodson (1916, 137, 147), African-American founder of the *Journal of Negro History*, embraced this

---

[3] Unfortunately, the recent *Encyclopedia of Appalachia* (Abramson and Haskell 2006) continues this scholarly marginalization of women. Out of 364,000 lines of text, women, gender, and feminism are allocated only 2,031 lines – or far less than 1 percent of the total coverage. Using the book's index, I counted the number of lines of text used for women and gender topics.

regional mythology, declaring Appalachians to be "more prejudiced against the slave holder than against the Negro."As Pudup, Billings, and Waller (1995, 112) observe, "The concept of Appalachia as a solid bastion of freedom and equality has been difficult to shake." That white Appalachians have themselves been "otherized" and "marginalized" by outsiders (Shapiro 1978; Williamson 1995) is not evidence that they must, therefore, have been less racist or less prejudiced than other southerners.

Second, I challenge the historical silencing that occurs when analysts reduce all women to a shared patriarchal position in subordination to white male elites. Indeed, there was no "common ground" between white and nonwhite women simply because they shared a "peculiarly female" reproductive capacity (Gwin 1985, 22, 39). It is unrealistic to conceptualize U.S. southern women as constructors of an interracial sisterhood "under the skin" that was grounded in shared biological aspects of reproduction and housework (Janiewski 1985, 7–12). Because women were so deeply differentiated by race, class, ethnicity, religion, and rural/urban divides, such a narrow approach cannot elucidate the lived experiences of the majority. Anne McClintock (1995, 6) reminds us that "the rational privileges of race all too often put white women in positions of decided – if borrowed – power, not only over colonized women but also over colonized men. As such, white women were not the hapless onlookers of empire but were ambiguously complicit both as colonizers and colonized, privileged and restricted, acted upon and acting." Poor white, nonwhite, and religious dissident females certainly did not share the same degree of access to political power, economic resources, and dominant culture as either elite slaveholding or middle-class white women. Nor did legal gender biases transform the lives of rural and urban females of different racial, ethnic, and class groupings into mirror images of one another. While they existed in the same slaveholding patriarchal system, antebellum southern women benefited from that system and were exploited and damaged by that system to vastly different degrees. Following the admonitions of minority feminists to avoid the pitfall of the notion of a "southern sisterhood," I have paid careful attention to the structural mechanisms through which affluent white women have benefited from the oppression of nonwhite minorities and have exploited poor white females and males.

I have made it my goal to make invisible Appalachian women visible, in all their class, racial, ethnic, and religious complexities. I concur with Trouillot (1995, 27–29) that we need to pay far more attention to marginalized peoples who have been silenced and erased from official history production. I am convinced that the way to accomplish that kind of more inclusive history is through the pursuit of *dialogic truth*, which, according to Immanuel Wallerstein (2000, 13), "assumes and thrives on the notion of a community of many voices and multiple perspectives." The path to dialogic truth "is through very intensive, often very emotional dialogue tempered by careful sifting of the evidence, in order to arrive at a multivoice, multiple perspective version of the truth." Consequently, I have heeded the advice of Jacquelyn Dowd Hall that "we need a historical practice…that releases multiple voices" (Bernhard et al. 1992, 15). In order to avoid reducing women to a homogeneous gendered category, I investigate the racial and ethnic schisms among women, as well as the class junctures that divided women of the same racial groupings. I also explore the intersections of race, ethnicity, class, and gender that often situated women in contradictory social and economic positions that placed their families and children at risk of public stigmatization and regulation. In addition, I have taken to heart the counsel of Hall that a truly "inclusive history of women" must be simultaneously multicultural, rather than isolating groups of women from one another (Bernhard et al. 1992, 16). For that reason, I analyze all the diverse racial, ethnic, and class groupings of Appalachian women, and I present them side by side within chapters so that similarities and differences are immediately rendered visible.

Moving beyond Separate Spheres Ideologies

Because they have made a blunder that Trouillot (1995, 27) describes as the production of history through the lens of a "conscious ideology" of dominant elites, U.S. women's historians have far too often engaged in academic legitimation of the racist, sexist gender ideologies of southern slaveholders and of affluent New Englanders by treating as factual representation of women's lives the separate spheres notions that are bound up in the "cult of true womanhood" (Boydston 1990, 1–29).[4] Even though the ghosts of separate spheres conceptualizations have not yet disappeared completely from recent scholarship, this framework has received increasing criticism in recent years (Warren 2006).[5] Glenna Matthews (1987, iii–xi) points out that this ideology is grounded in the assumption that the "housewife" is a manager of servants or slaves. Consequently, the ideal model depicted a lifestyle that was not affordable for the majority of white and nonwhite women (Kerber 1988).

Perhaps the most damning weakness of this ideology lies in its intellectual roots in popular notions about biological determinism. Antebellum U.S. intellectuals and southern elites were drawn to the work of the Lamarckian evolutionist Herbert Spencer (Perdue 1986, 56–67), touted by an 1864 *Atlantic Monthly* (14, 775–76) as "the scientific spirt of the age," whose "established principles" would "become the recognized basis of an improved society."[6] Highly respected American intellectuals termed Spencer "the most powerful thinker of our time," convinced that his writings were "far more fruitful and quickening here than in Europe" (Hofstadter 1944, 31). Spencer has been

---

[4] The term *cult of domesticity* is also used to refer to these antebellum gender conventions.

[5] It remains to be seen whether twenty-first-century scholars will toll the death bell for separate spheres since this framework remained popular with many feminists and U.S. women's historians throughout the 1990s (e.g., Osterud 1991; Mehaffey 1992, 131–32; Bernhard et al. 1992, 3).

[6] According to Coser (1977, 110), Spencer was heavily influenced by the ideas of Jean-Baptiste Lamarck, who popularized the notion of inheritance of social behaviors in Europe in the late eighteenth century. In turn, Spencer influenced the thinking of Charles Darwin (1859).

termed a "social Darwinist before Darwin" (Coser 1977, 90) because he argued
that there was a "natural hierarchy of human beings." In this natural order,
"there is no way from the lower forms of social life to the higher" except through
extremely slow evolution. That evolution was not unidirectional because the
person could be handicapped by the reemergence of a preceding lower evolu-
tionary stage. As a consequence, people at the bottom of the social hierarchy
often act from "principles at variance with those of modern man." Those anti-
social aberrations result from the exposure of lower human beings to environs
that cause them to develop "adaptive changes" that are suitable to their existence in their lower status, but at odds with civilized society. Unfortunately,
parents pass along these unsuitable adaptations of behavior and character to
their offspring. In short, one's societal subordination and status are determined
by one's biological past. Since "character is inherited," Spencer maintained,
"the children of the superior will prosper and increase more than the children
of the inferior." People are segregated by nature into distinct classes and orders,
and society should not intervene to alter the life chances of those on the lower
rungs. "When once you begin to interfere with the order of Nature," Spencer
(1851, 100, 102, 124, 157) contended, "there is no knowing where the result
will end." Because women and several racial groups are biologically endowed
with premodern tendencies, behaviors, and characters, they are dangerous to
societies that do not effect appropriate controls. Spencer insisted that society
"would have been better off" if many lower classes and racial groups and
nondomestic females "had never been born." He went so far as to question
whether society should "kill off certain classes of troublesome and bewildered
persons."

Spencer (1851, 194) laid the groundwork for separate spheres thinking when
he argued that women enjoy equality with males only among "the rudest [i.e.,
uncivilized] people" and that the truly civilized female exists only "in the domestic sphere." Those females who exist outside this appropriate sphere are "a
lower form" who are exhibiting social retardation caused by past or current
racial mixing. The purported evidence lay in the poverty and lack of acceptable social behaviors among poorer classes. "If women comprehended all that
is contained in the domestic sphere," Spencer contended, "they would ask no
other" (Blakemore 2000, 124). The resultant elite gender conventions romanti-
cized affluent women as the intergenerational bearers of societal ideals that they
shielded from corruption in the sanctity of their homes. In sharp contrast, those
elite standards accounted for the awkward presence of poor white women by
claiming they were inferior "racial throwbacks" who could not hope to achieve
the degree of "gentility" essential to the ideal woman. Nor could they ever be
"civilized" fully because their brains never developed beyond that of white male
infants (Vogt 1864), a biological deficiency that led to "character weaknesses"
that caused their poverty and ignorance.

Increasingly, writers are also calling into question the assumption that
by the midnineteenth century the cult of true womanhood (Boydston 1990,
1–29) was so culturally hegemonic that all women constructed their families and

constrained their work lives to meet these social ideals. On the one hand, it is not clear that separate spheres gender conventions "designated the values and code of behavior that predominated among the middle classes" (Harris 1985, 35). Several writers contend that alternative womanhood ideals had greater impact on the lives of a majority of middle-class white women. The gender conventions of "republican motherhood" (Kerber 1976) and the "farmwife ideal" (Hagler 1993) appeared in antebellum publications just about as frequently as separate spheres ideology, and these models depicted females working at income-earning endeavors outside and inside their households. The ideals of "evangelical womanhood" (Boylan 1978) and of the "real womanhood" survival ethic (Cogan 1989) also presented middle-class standards for females who were neither economically dependent upon husbands nor isolated from participation in solving the problems of their communities (Berg 1978; Cott and Pleck 1979, 555–78). If we are to move beyond historical silencing, we must recognize that there was class and racial struggle over gender conventions. While acknowledging the diversity of middle-class standards, we must also be cognizant that slaves (Cott and Pleck 1979, 298–310), Indians, poor whites, religious minorities, and free blacks (Horton 1986) developed their own gender conventions, even though they were demeaned by the nineteenth-century popular magazines that too many contemporary scholars privilege as evidence of widespread adherence to separate spheres ideology.

Despite recent challenges to claims about the cultural hegemony of separate spheres conventions, it is still important to test these notions against the realities that faced nineteenth-century Appalachian women. Perhaps to a greater extent than the females of any other U.S. region, Appalachian women have been repeatedly stigmatized by separate spheres thinking that represents some of the worst elements of antebellum *biological determinism* (Spencer 1851; Vogt 1864) and of its postbellum derivative, *social Darwinism* (Sumner 1963).[7] From the 1890s through the 1980s, yellow journalists and policymakers reduced their lives to that of illiterate mountain matriarchs who are menial victims of toil, of sexual promiscuity, and of a backward culture.[8] Writers have claimed that Appalachian women cannot overcome their poverty because they carry the debilitated genes of racial throwbacks who settled the region's frontiers (Fischer 1989).

Since 1980, revisionist regional writers have either not mentioned women at all or they have accepted uncritically the stereotype that women's roles were confined to the home (e.g., Waller 1988, 58).[9] In a period when so many feminist writers are questioning separate spheres assumptions, the recent *Encyclopedia of Appalachia* (Abramson and Haskell 2006, 170) reduces women to a

---

[7] For more extensive discussion, see "Legacy of Social Darwinism in Appalachian Scholarship," Web site.

[8] For a discussion of this literature, see "Stereotypes of Appalachian Women," Web site.

[9] Lewis, Johnson, and Askins (1978, 115) offered a short, low-key contradiction of separate spheres notions, but the only 1970s feminist challenge to this ideology was Kahn (1974).

racially and economically homogeneous group who are confined in their homes. According to the entry on gender roles:

Appalachian families generally follow traditional gender roles. Typically they consist of a provider father, a caregiving mother, and the couple's dependent children. Following this model, Appalachian households have been historically patriarchal with men serving as heads of households – owning land, directing production, controlling income use, and making decisions – while women act as loving nurturers to their husbands and children.

Repeating the rhetoric that was typical of the nineteenth-century cult of domesticity, the entry further generalizes that farm labor "was divided spatially. Mothers and daughters were primarily responsible for work done in the house and yard area; fathers and sons were responsible for crops and other chores beyond the house." Not only do such claims ignore the realities of the lives of Native American, enslaved, free black, and poor white females, but they also ignore the few revisionist works (e.g., Hall 1986; Seitz 1995; Anglin 2002) that have emerged about Appalachian women's work and community roles.

The Need to Capture the Complexity of Women's Work

It is in the analysis of women's work that U.S. women's history is probably weakest. Delfino and Gillespie (2002, 1) alert us to this void in the accumulated scholarship: "We know too little," they remind us, "about the work lives of ordinary women in the Old South.... Although the past two decades have witnessed an explosion of scholarship on southern women in the nineteenth century, much of this work has focused on the world of the plantation." However, the absence of scholarly attention is not the only problem. Conceptually, we need to stop being blinded by oversimplified stereotypes about women being trapped in housebound labors outside the reach of patriarchal market forces (Matthaei 1982), an idea that is a ghost of the separate spheres legacy. If we search only for unpaid and income-earning labors that were "manifestations of their private roles as housewives and mothers," we miss the real "dialectics of waged and unwaged labor" that characterize most women's resource accumulation (Collins and Gimenez 1990, 25–47). Zillah Eisenstein admonishes us to employ a "multigridded conceptualization" of women's work, taking into account differences of race, class, ethnicity, marital status, and religion (Hansen and Philipson 1990, 139–40). We must also stop assigning an overstated "rural isolation" to women (Anglin 2000, 82) that neither reflects the capacity of women to market commodities nor gives voice to those females who resided in or near towns. Because supervision and completion of back-breaking tasks are not the same thing, we need to recognize real gradations in the degree to which women worked hard and publicly at manual labor.

Finally, we must move away from the naive notion that all work done by women in households was *without* economic value and was *outside* the market. On the one hand, we need to investigate how women's work is "embedded, indeed hidden, within a gendered division of labor that allocated different tasks and status to women and men" (Smith 1999, 6). It is not enough, however, to search out "women's work" as a distinct category from "men's work." That can only lead us toward silencing and homogenization of much of women's work that is disguised behind class and racial junctures among women. An effective analysis of women's work, then, must examine "women's and men's differential access to and control over material resources" (Smith 1999, 8) alongside the structural inequalities that exist among females. On the other hand, we must take special care when analyzing the work done inside women's households, for some of that work is almost always aimed at the marketplace (Dunaway 2001).

To varying degrees depending on their class and racial positions, antebellum U.S. women engaged in a complex portfolio of agricultural and nonagricultural labors that included three types of unpaid labor and three types of paid labors:

- unpaid labors to sustain the household, clan, or family,
- unpaid labors associated with biological reproduction and child rearing,
- waged labor outside the household,
- business operation inside or outside the household,
- income-earning labors within the informal sector, and
- unpaid charitable or community work.

This diverse labor portfolio calls attention to three historical trends that are too often silenced. First, we cannot so cleanly separate women's household labors from work that is aimed at the external economic arena, for much income-earning activity occurs in the home, and women contribute significant "hidden labor" to male-dominated economic activities. Second, almost all rural women engaged in some nonagricultural labors from which they earned income. In order to capture much of the economically valuable work of women, we must pay attention to the conceptual importance of the *informal sector*, those non-waged, undocumented economic activities that result in the sale of commodities or services. Like females of today's poor countries, far more antebellum Appalachian women earned income from informal sector exchanges than from wages or from business entrepreneurship.

Therefore, I have attempted to document the diversity and complexity of women's labors – inside and outside their households. In the process of teasing out the diversity of women's paid and unpaid labors, I will call into question the separate spheres thesis that "both unmarried and married women did their primary work in households, in families" (Cott 1977, 26). Indeed, four historical realities of the everyday lives of a majority of Appalachian women stand as stark contradictions of "separate spheres" ideologies:

- the contributions of women's home-based labors to the market economy,
- participation of women in waged jobs, business or farm management, and cash earning outside their homes,

- the unpaid labors of women in community organizations, churches, and charities, and
- the high percentage of all women who lived outside marriages.

Female work was vital to both family and economy, and "the connections women forged between the household and economies were hydralike, shooting out in multiple directions" (Ryan 1981, 203). As I will show in subsequent chapters, it is historically misleading to dichotomize women's lives between a household sphere and the rest of the world, for the household is just as much a capitalist unit of production and reproduction as are the farm, the factory, and the marketplace. From a feminist standpoint, we need to be careful about broad use of the phrase *labor force*, which refers narrowly to waged occupations. Historically and worldwide today, women earn most of their income and generate household resources *outside* waged occupations (Dunaway 2001).

Moving Beyond Female as Victim

Gerda Lerner warns that women are not just acted upon by male-dominated history; they also make history by resisting inequality and oppression. "While inferior status and oppressive restraints were no doubt aspects of women's historical experience . . . the limitation of this approach is that it makes it appear either that women were largely passive or that, at the most, they reacted to male pressures or to the restraints of patriarchal society" (Cott 1992, 29). Barbara Ellen Smith (1999, 9) emphasizes that "it is a measure of lower-class women's 'subaltern' status that their gender subversions, negotiations, and rebellions have often been covert, indirect, and unrecorded." According to James Scott (1990, 136, xii), each subordinate group "creates, out of its ordeal, a 'hidden transcript' that represents a critique of power spoken behind the back of the dominant." Thus, I have searched out as many Appalachian women's hidden transcripts of everyday and organized resistance as I could find, and I have incorporated those actions throughout the book.

Research Questions, Methods of Research, and Sources

This study focuses on five research questions.

- Are nineteenth-century separate spheres ideologies accurate descriptors of women's work lives? Were these gender conventions culturally hegemonic, or was there class, racial and ethnic struggle over the scope of women's work and family roles?
- What were the racial, ethnic, and class junctures among women?
- What was the scope of women's agricultural and nonagricultural work, and how did this work vary across different racial, ethnic, and class groupings?
- When women's work conflicted with the elite gender conventions that were embedded in public statutes, what were the impacts on poor and nonwhite families, mothers, and children?

- Which groups of women were denied the ideals of motherhood and family that were advocated in the cult of true womanhood, and how was their work connected to those family disruptions?

To investigate these questions, I have triangulated hundreds of primary and archival sources with statistical analysis of samples drawn from public records. I have made a concerted effort to locate and include as many women's transcripts as possible, so I drew upon a wide array of archived manuscripts, missionary letters and journals, diaries, letters, the Appalachian Oral History Project (1977), the Tennessee archive collection of Civil War veteran questionnaires (Dyer and Moore 1985), the *Foxfire* collections (Wiggington 1972–85), emigrant narratives (e.g., Conway 1961, *Irish Immigrants* 2003), and slave narratives (e.g., Rawick 1972, 1977, 1979).[10] Because of the paucity of female sources in archival and published primary material, there are not as many women's voices in Part I (especially Chapter 1) as I would prefer. However, the scarcity of women's voices does not make Part I any less essential to understanding of the social and structural divisions among Appalachian females. Without this background about the race, ethnicity, and class divisions among women, readers would be unable to comprehend the complexities of women's work and family life that are analyzed in Part II. Should such a feminist book eliminate all background material that explains and describes the social structure of the historical era, simply because women did not "say it"? It would be a far easier world for feminist historians if we could find sufficient primary sources to permit women to speak for themselves on all our pages. But there is no such wide array of primary sources, especially for antebellum Appalachian women. It is not unusual for women's histories to find it necessary to include explanations that do not include women's voices, and I have approached this problem in the same way that most other feminist writers have been forced to deal with this formidable task. In this regard, I feel on safe (though not impossibly perfect) ground.

With respect to many patterns of women's lives, I am able to "fill in the gaps" caused by the lack of female narratives through analysis of gendered patterns that are evident in a large database of nearly 20,000 antebellum households drawn from Cherokee censuses, frontier county tax lists, and antebellum census manuscripts.[11] To acquire a rich reservoir of details about women and gender inequality, I drew five household samples from nineteenth-century census manuscripts for Appalachian counties.

- Sample 1: A systematic probability sample of 3,056 households drawn from the enumerator manuscripts for the 1860 Census of Population permitted me to draw generalizations about the socioeconomic characteristics, landownership, marketing, and female headship of both rural and town households.

---

[10] A detailed discussion of sources that provide women's voices is available at the Web site. A discussion and list of slave narratives is also posted at the Web site.

[11] Methods of sampling and statistical analysis are described at the Web site.

- Sample 2: A systematic probability sample of 3,447 farms drawn from the enumerator manuscripts for the 1860 Census of Agriculture permitted me to draw generalizations about the socioeconomic characteristics of female agricultural laborers and of farms operated by women, free blacks, and poor landless whites.
- Sample 3: A systematic probability sample of 1,200 free black Appalachian households drawn from the enumerator manuscripts for the 1860 Census of Population permitted me to draw generalizations about the characteristics of this group, including female headship and occupations.
- Sample 4: A systematic probability sample of 2,795 female-headed households drawn from the enumerator manuscripts for the 1860 Census of Population permitted me to examine the characteristics of these women and to compare their traits with those of the male-headed households in Sample 1.
- Sample 5: In order to examine how postbellum pregnancy decisions differed from the fertility patterns of enslaved women, I have drawn a systematic probability sample of 2,692 black Appalachian households from the 1870 Census of Population enumerator manuscripts.

In order to reserve as much space as possible for substantive analysis, I have posted at a permanent electronic archive an extensive discussion about research methods and about the primary sources that I have used to end historical silences about women. Even though West Virginia did not achieve statehood until 1863, the reader will find discussions of that area throughout the book, and those references are not a historical error. Because that area had the lowest incidence of enslavement and one of the highest rates of white impoverishment in the country, it is crucial to set it apart from the rest of Virginia. To ensure that my analysis would adequately represent conditions in this zone, I have separated out quantitative data and primary sources for those counties that became West Virginia during the Civil War.

Organization of the Book

Part I provides background necessary to understand the racial, ethnic, and class differences that circumscribed the lives of Appalachian women. While all females experienced gender discrimination, affluent white females benefited from the oppression of racial minorities and the poor. Nonwhite, ethnic minority, and poor white women confronted deeper levels of sexism, for they were trapped in the simultaneous intersections of gender with race, ethnicity, and/or class. Not only were Appalachian women constrained by the boundaries of their own ethnic, racial, or class groups, but they were also stigmatized or punished when they crossed ethnic and racial boundaries. In Chapter 1, I explore the ethnic and religious differences that prevented white Appalachian women from sharing a gendered sisterhood. In Chapters 2 and 3, I call into question the notion of a shared sisterhood among women by exploring the racism of whites toward Cherokee and black Appalachians. I also examine the resistance of those marginalized females against oppression. In Chapter 4, I address the degree to which class differences divided women of the same racial groups, and I examine class differences in gender conventions.

Part II explores the diversity of women's labors and examines the gendered costs to families associated with their work-related violations of domesticity conventions. On the one hand, a majority of women routinely ignored separate spheres ideals to undertake income-earning or extra-household labors that were essential to the survival of their families. On the other hand, the nature of a woman's productive labors – and the degree to which she engaged in menial work – were determined by her race, ethnicity, and/or class. In Chapters 5 and 6, I explore the agricultural and nonagricultural labors of women, pointing to the elastic demarcation between home and workplace. Before the Civil War, more than half of all U.S. women resided in poor households, and there was an even higher incidence of poverty in many Appalachian counties. For that reason, I focus on that majority of women who worked outside their household domains, often employed at manual labor or public occupations that the cult of true womanhood labeled "men's work." It was not just a woman's race that determined the nature of her work, for the class position of white women determined whether they would engage in manual labor or work alongside males in public income-earning activities. Primary sources make it very clear that poor white women frequently violated ethnic, racial, and gender proscriptions, as they tried desperately to accumulate survival resources for their households.

In Chapters 7 and 8, I examine the structural contradictions between a woman's reproductive labors and her income-producing work. By undertaking a diverse array of agricultural and nonagricultural labors, poor and nonwhite females challenged patriarchal family constructs. As a result, they resisted the separate spheres ideologies that southern elites embedded in public statutes and court systems. By concretizing separate spheres ideals into laws and court procedures, affluent classes legitimated disruptions of families and removal of children. In combination with her marginalized class or race position, a woman's publicly visible work attracted public regulation of her gender roles as mother and wife and delimited the degree of legal protection that she was provided against sexual exploitation and against disruption of her motherhood roles. Women who violated separate spheres ideals through their productive income-earning labors were stigmatized as "unfit mothers" in need of public regulation.

While a majority of antebellum women (including middle-class females) were not constrained by elite separate spheres ideologies when they made decisions about work, a female's race, class, or ethnic minority status determined whether she would engage in menial labors that stigmatized her as too far outside the cultural ideal of house-bound domesticity. Because of the similarities in their impoverished living conditions, poor white, African-American, and Cherokee women (i.e., the majority of antebellum southern females) engaged in similar agricultural and nonagricultural work that elites defined as the arenas of poor and enslaved males. As a result of their extra-household labor portfolios, these working women constructed nonpatriarchal families that challenged elite notions about racial divisions. Poor white and nonwhite females were socially and legally marginalized as "racial degenerates" who could not overcome their genetic weaknesses to achieve "civilized motherhood." Elite males used these proclaimed biological flaws to justify a legal system that violated separate spheres ideals about sanctity of family. On the one hand, poor and nonwhite women did not enjoy the same legal protections as affluent white women. On the other hand, courts treated their households as family aberrations too damaged to rear offspring, thereby legitimating the removal of children to be indentured or enslaved by affluent households. Still women did not acquiesce easily. They resisted separate spheres conventions in their everyday lives and through group activism.

To publish all the information about contextual background, sources, methods, and quantitative evidence would require far more space than is afforded to me here. In order to make those materials available to other researchers as quickly as possible, I have created a permanent electronic library archive. In order to shorten the original manuscript for publication, I have also stored several substantive discussions there that I did not have space to include here, including extensive discussions of women's work on Appalachian frontiers, pressures toward assimilation of diverse European ethnic groups, and stereotyping of Appalachian women in journalistic and scholarly accounts between the 1890s and 1980. Throughout the notes and in parenthetical citations, you will see references to sources that can be accessed at this Web site: http://scholar.lib.vt.edu/faculty_archives/appalachian_women/index.htm.

PART I

RACIAL, ETHNIC, AND CLASS DISJUNCTURES AMONG APPALACHIAN WOMEN

> There was no essential "Appalachian woman" but rather a profusion of socioeconomic, racial/ethnic, gendered, and legal statuses and/or circumstances.
>
> (Mary Anglin 2000, 82)

Because of their racial, ethnic, and class diversity, Appalachian women cannot be reduced to a single homogeneous group who shared the same gendered hierarchical space. At the time of the 1790 census, Euroamericans accounted for more than four-fifths of the population, and African-Americans composed another 11 percent (see Table 1). Even though indigenous Appalachians represented only 4 percent of the total regional population, they retained a visible presence in western North Carolina, southeast Tennessee, and northern Georgia. If we are to capture the lives of all Appalachian women, we cannot ignore the pivotal ways in which white Appalachian women benefited from the oppression of Appalachian men and women of color. Imperialism, civilizational arrogance, and racism were fundamental elements of the assimilation of Euroamericans in the process of becoming "white" Americans. Toward the beginning of the eighteenth century, there emerged "a marked tendency to promote a pride of race among the members of every class of white people; to be white and also to be free, combined the distinction of liberty" (Allen 1989, 185). The political, economic, and cultural privileges associated with white skin and the need for solidarity against nonwhite races spurred immigrants to categorize themselves first in terms of race and second in terms of their European ethnic heritage. The passage of a 1790 federal law cemented the unification of the new white American race by closing citizenship to all who were not Caucasian. Free white identity distanced immigrants from the low status of African-Americans and indigenous Americans, and "race became the primary badge of status" (Allen 1989, 186).

Even within their racial categories, however, women did not share a unified gendered space. Caucasian women were kept apart by rancorous ethnic and religious differences that reached back to their diverse European origins

TABLE I. *Race of Southern Appalachians, 1790–1860*

Appalachian Counties of	% White			% African-American			% Cherokee		
	1790	1820	1860	1790	1820	1860	1790	1820	1860
Alabama	——	83.8	77.6	——	9.8	22.0	95.0	6.4	0.4
Georgia	——	84.5	82.7	——	8.3	16.8	92.0	7.2	0.5
Kentucky	88.3	86.4	91.5	11.7	13.6	8.5	——	——	——
Maryland	89.3	80.6	87.6	10.7	19.4	12.4	——	——	——
North Carolina	78.1	79.1	84.8	8.1	14.1	13.8	14.8	6.8	1.4
South Carolina	91.3	76.6	78.0	8.7	23.4	22.0	——	——	——
Tennessee	84.1	88.9	87.5	7.9	9.9	12.2	8.0	1.2	0.3
Virginia	81.5	69.7	71.6	18.5	30.3	28.4	——	——	——
West Virginia	90.5	87.8	93.8	9.5	12.2	6.2	——	——	——
Region	85.0	79.0	84.0	10.6	19.3	15.7	4.4	1.7	0.3

Sources: U.S. Census Office (1791, 1821, 1863), Thornton (1990, 43, 49–50), *Report of the Indian Commissioner* (1884, li–liii).

(see Tables 2, 3, Web site). Women of color were also divided by ethnic differentiations that were grounded in skin color and degree of racial mixing with whites. Complicating matters, each racial group of Appalachian women was separated by complex class divisions that further exacerbated the degrees of inequality and discrimination they experienced because of their gender and their race. On the one hand, females were distinguished by their degrees of racial privilege or of racial exclusion. Females were polarized into sharply different racial groups, and there was no shared gender space that breached those racial barriers to enable women to coalesce around similar problems or grievances. On the other hand, shared racial identity did not unify females of the same color, for these groups of women were also set apart by status differentiations within these categories. In short, Appalachian women did not share the same subordinated gender position within the antebellum patriarchal system. In Chapters 1 through 4, I examine the sharp intersections of race, ethnicity, and class that forestalled the emergence of shared vantage points for Appalachian women. Where primary sources permit, I also explore women's resistance against patriarchal patterns and the ethnic and class struggles among women.

I

No Gendered Sisterhood

Ethnic and Religious Conflict among
Euroamerican Women

> Women, as wives and mothers, carried forward banners of strength and cultural
> identity. More often than not, within their cultures, they depended on each other
> for courage and support.... Across cultures, women were not the same.... They
> often did not know each other and did not want to. Bitterness and hostility fre-
> quently marked the interaction of the various cultures.... In their own eras, many
> women of all cultures resisted acknowledging the reality of their melding, denied
> the sameness of motherhood, the parallels of gender.
>
> (Anne Butler and Ona Siporin 1996, 120–22)

Antebellum Southern Appalachia was not an isolated egalitarian folk society.
Instead, this region was a reflection of the ethnic diversity and conflict that characterized transnational migration to the New World. As a European colony and
an emergent new country, the United States attracted a wide variety of immigrants, many of whom had long histories of interracial conflict in the contexts
from which they arrived. Europeans carried with them their ethnic enmities,
and those animosities reemerged when those groups came into contact with
one another in the New World. Moreover, ethnic intolerance among groups
persisted over time because second- and third-generation offspring were taught
about the European ethnic pasts of their parents, grandparents, and great-
grandparents. Because it was resettled by these uneasy, biased immigrants, antebellum Southern Appalachia could not be described as either having one unified
white culture or a singular ethnic ethos.

To as great an extent as is made possible by available primary sources, I will
present racial hatreds and interethnic prejudices and stereotypes through the
voices of immigrants. I caution readers to be critical of what those speakers
will say, for their words have been selected as evidence of *interracial intoler-*
ance – not as accurate cultural descriptors of any of the ethnic groups. Far
too many of the points of "evidence" presented by contemporary writers to
describe ethnic groups on American frontiers are nothing other than prejudices
and racial myths that were expressed by members of antagonistic ethnic groups

(e.g., McDonald and McDonald 1980, McWhiney 1988, Fischer 1989). It is crucial to avoid the historical error of treating the popular *repertoire of stereotypes* as empirical cultural descriptors. In reality, such dialogue (both positive and negative) is evidence only of *constructs of distance and difference* used by opposing groups to separate their own identities from ethnicities they considered to be inferior or inimical. Indeed, we can only correctly use such eighteenth- and nineteenth-century rhetoric as ideological barometers of the depth and longevity of interethnic bigotries in the New World. Unfortunately, female narratives are underrepresented in primary sources. On the one hand, male immigrants far outnumbered women, and migrating females were far more likely to be illiterate than men (Chickering 1848). On the other hand, religious denominations restricted women from playing visible public roles and limited coverage of them in public documents. Nevertheless, I have gleaned from primary sources as many women's transcripts as I could find, especially descriptions of their expressed intolerance of other ethnic groups and their resistance against patriarchal church procedures. In the sections that follow, I will explore

- interethnic biases among European immigrant groups,
- intolerance and conflict among religious denominations,
- persecution of religious minorities, and
- pressures toward religious assimilation.

In the final section, I examine women's resistance against patriarchal church policies.

Intolerance and Conflict among White Appalachian Ethnic Groups

Appalachian frontiers were a kaleidoscope of Euroamerican ethnic identities. Intergroup prejudices, stereotypes, and hostilities were commonplace, especially when there was intense competition over jobs, land, or religion (Wust 1969, 193). Because of the past history of British colonialism and racist oppression in Ireland, Celtic immigrants who originated from Ulster remained openly hostile toward English immigrants (whom they termed "Yankees"). Scotch-Irish immigrant John Caldwell hated the English for thinking of themselves as "a superior race of beings" (*Irish Immigrants* 2003, 632). William Thomas wrote to his Welsh parents that he was appalled that he had been unable to find any employment except "working on the canal with Englishmen." Indentured as a domestic servant in an English household, young Emily Jones complained that Yankee girls "are too ready to look down upon the clean, rosy-cheeked, hard-working Welsh girls.... They know no more about making a loaf of bread and a meal than a mule knows about knitting socks. All they are good for is to dress up and sit in a rocking chair reading novels and dreaming." Employers used both ethnicity and gender of immigrants as grounds for discrimination. English workers earned higher wages in all occupations, but female wages averaged only about half what males earned (Conway 1961, 60, 190).

According to Jackson (1993, 81, 86–87), bigotry toward Ulster immigrants was so extreme that "the Scotch-Irish reputation preceded their actual arrival, and made many established residents to be quite wary." English colonist William Byrd compared the entry into Virginia of large numbers of Scotch-Irish to invasion by the Goths and Vandals in ancient times. Another eighteenth-century English immigrant expressed alarm that "the number of white people in Virginia...[wa]s growing every day more numerous by the migration of the Irish." Fearing their presence because they "retained their distinctiveness,"one immigrant handbook warned that the Scotch-Irish were "spreading out more widely than any other ethnic group" (Burke 1777, 1: 112). Ignoring the thousands of landless poor of their own nationality, English immigrants accused the Scotch-Irish of squatting "on any spot of vacant land they can find." One land speculator claimed that "the settlement of five families from Ireland gives me more trouble than fifty of any other people." In western Maryland, English settlers complained that the Scotch-Irish had an "audacious and disorderly manner" that caused them to "crowd where they [we]re not wanted." While ideologically denying their own deadly frontier history toward indigenous Americans, English elites accused the Scotch-Irish of being "very rough" toward Indians (Hanna 1985, 63).

Another English writer was outraged by the ethnic "miscegenation" that was being introduced to the western Carolinas by the arrival of great numbers of indentured servants from Ireland. He worried that the "moral character" and "civilization" of earlier settlers were being "spoiled by an intercourse with the Scotch and Irish" (Thwaites 1904–7, 339). The Welsh were no less hostile toward the Scotch-Irish. After settling in West Virginia, John Williams wrote home that "the native white man of this state and adjoining states is about the most contemptible person on the face of the earth" (Conway 1961, 208).[1] Even some Quakers thought of the Scotch-Irish as "obnoxious being[s]" (*Irish Immigrants* 2003, 288). In language that provides us a small measure of his racial abhorrence, Anglican clergyman Charles Woodmason described the Scotch-Irish as "very poor owing to their extreme Indolence" and as "lazy, Sluttish, heathenish, hellish" (Jackson 1993, 86–87). When a British officer labeled east Tennessee and northern Georgia "barbarians, mongrels, and dregs of mankind" (Hsiung 1997, 20, 32), he was not applying those labels to them because they were American mountaineers. He was verbalizing stereotypes commonly applied by the English to the Irish and the Scotch-Irish.

As they traveled on the Appalachian frontiers in the eighteenth and early nineteenth centuries, English journalists misrepresented the diversity of the class positions and the homes of Scotch-Irish settlers. Overlooking the plantations and larger homes of wealthy and middle-class members of the ethnic group, one New England gentleman of English heritage pinpointed the "typical" dwelling

---

[1] By 1840, white Americans were using the phrase "native American" to distinguish recent immigrants from Euroamerican ethnic groups that had been settled in the country for more than a decade.

of the Scotch-Irish as "a miserable log house" that consisted of "but one room, two beds full of vermin, and not a single thing of any kind to eat or drink, six or seven children crying in the house, and two drunken Scotch neighbors, drinking, reeling, and smoking." According to another English traveler, the Scotch-Irish were "the most abject that, perhaps, ever peopled a Christian land.... Many of them cultivate no more land than will raise them corn and cabbages.... Their habitations are more wretched than can be conceived" (Bacot 1923, 692).

In a memoir for his children, James Patton, a wealthy western North Carolina merchant, assessed the difficulties that a Scotch-Irish immigrant faced. At the age of 28, Patton relocated to the United States and left his family in Ulster. Since their dialect differentiated them as members of an ethnic minority despised by the British, poor arrivals like him experienced employment and housing discrimination. Because of local bigotry, Patton was hired only for the lowest-paid, most back-breaking jobs, like "blowing rocks, digging wells," canal construction, and unskilled farm labor for which he never earned more than a few cents a day. He "soon discovered the difficulty of clothing himself decently and making money merely by hard labor." After three years, he "had very little more than when [he] landed" (*Irish Immigrants* 2003, 285–86, 345).

German emigrants to the United States "were a group separated by language and by their mores" from the English-speaking ethnic groups. Often concentrated together in small communities, they "aroused suspicion and prejudice" (Rippley 1976, 30). According to Wust (1969, 109), "the German who came to Virginia in the eighteenth century...came as a foreigner into an English colony." One English writer described Germans of the Virginia Valley as "quite indifferent about those who [we]re not of their race." One must be suspicious of that claim for he also incorrectly stereotyped them as "plodding, frugal persons who hoard their profits in hard money, entertain a great dislike to bank paper, and still a greater to the payment of taxes" (Featherstonhough 1844, 1: 18). Similarly, a French writer considered western Maryland Germans to be "good subjects, honest people, middling cultivators; but awkward, rude, uninformed and dirty" (La Rochefoucauld-Liancourt 1800, 2: 96–100). English-speaking Shenandoah Valley residents claimed that the "strongest passions" of their German neighbors were hatred of the Scotch-Irish and "love of beer" (Wayland 1957, 54). Supposedly, Germans loved "strong drink" and were "contentious through lawsuits." Tucker (1824, 49–54) thought German Appalachians were a "useful class of citizens" so long as they kept "in their place," which was to be "the dray-horse of society," their function limited to "that coarse but useful labour, which society requires." The English and more well-to-do Scotch-Irish stereotyped the German settler as "proverbial for his patient perseverance in his domestic arts" on a small farm (Kercheval 1833, 152–53). Despite the agrarian stereotype that is typically applied to them, German Appalachians were just about as frequently employed in artisan occupations, such as stonecutting, pottery manufacturing, clockmaking, silversmithing, and iron production (Wust 1969, 180–81).

With the same degree of racist bigotry that characterizes contemporary assaults on African-Americans, one Scotch-Irish settler wrote to European relatives in 1850 that his "neighborhood ha[d] rather gone back in a way" because a number of Germans were buying farms. Applying the ethnic label that was popular in his time, he ranted, "the Dutch will take over the country." John Caldwell described the tense relations between his own Scotch-Irish kin and neighboring Germans. "The descendants of the Dutch, are extremely cautious & jealous of Strangers" (*Irish Immigrants* 2003, 642). Kercheval (1833, 152–53) reiterated the common Scotch-Irish stereotype that most German women were "extremely slovenly, and their dwellings [we]re kept in the worst possible condition." Similarly, English and Celtic immigrants were repulsed by German foodways (Conway 1961, 50). From the perspective of the stigmatized minority group, some German women were equally shocked by the cultural differences between their households and those of the English and Scotch-Irish. One German wife wrote to her relatives that American women were "more free than in Europe." In her opinion, there were "few good housewives" in the United States because "the husbands let the wives become rulers of the house and they tend to control all household affairs" (Rippley 1976, 57).

German dialects attracted even greater bigotry than the Hiberno-English of the Scotch-Irish. While surveying lands in the Shenandoah Valley in 1748, George Washington (1892, 45) encountered "a great Company" of German settlers whom he described as "Ignorant" because "they would never speak English." The language of German Appalachians was disdainfully termed "dumb Dutch" or "slop-bucket Dutch" by English and Scotch-Irish neighbors who employed those terms indiscriminately for all Germans not fully assimilated. On the frontier of western North Carolina, the Scotch-Irish even objected to their ministers' baptizing or marrying recent German immigrants who did not yet have their own churches or congregations (Hooker 1953, 93). Even in those counties of western Maryland, West Virginia, and Appalachian Virginia that had sizable German populations (Wust 1969, 197), newspapers frequently published ethnic jokes or took anti-German positions in their editorials (e.g., *Cumberland Civilian*, 7 Dec. 1849; *Shepherdstown Register*, 5 and 26 Mar. 1856; *Virginia Free Press*, 24 May 1849, 14 Mar. 1850, 13 Dec. 1850). In most counties, there were also constraints against Germans' holding public office and participating on community committees. Even in counties with sizable German populations, members of this ethnic minority were excluded from the local vestry boards that managed county religious affairs (Johnson 1983, 31).

Though they were many fewer in number on Appalachian frontiers, the Welsh were despised by English and Scotch-Irish settlers. Employment agencies that recruited contract and indentured laborers in Wales often misled workers about the availability of work and about the ease with which they would be accepted. After immigrating in 1794, William Davies wrote home that the Welsh were having "hard times and scarcity. Men don't get things here without hard labor . . . and they must have good qualifications," which included English ethnic heritage. In 1817, David Jones wrote home to his wife that the American frontier was not welcoming for poor Welsh laborers, who were linguistically and religiously set apart from the dominant culture of the monied classes. "I do not want to drag you here because hundreds of people have come this year, pretty poor and with many children and who have no craft," he sadly lamented, adding that "the Welsh had a lot of trouble" acculturating "into the way of living in this country." Hugh Jones wrote home that he typically had no waged employment during the winter months, so he exchanged his labor for room and board in very menial conditions. He warned Welsh relatives not to emigrate because "wages are not as high as we had heard. . . . It is dangerous for anyone with money to buy land because it is difficult to know who has the right to sell"(Conway 1961, 58, 61–62, 66).

By the midnineteenth century, religious leaders were becoming increasingly fearful that "the Welsh language and Welsh culture would be completely lost unless measures were taken to ensure that Welsh emigration was concentrated into exclusive, compact Welsh settlements" of the sort that Congregational minister Samuel Roberts formed in 1856. In conjunction with William Bebb of Illinois, Roberts purchased 100,000 acres in east Tennessee, and two groups of settlers arrived in 1856 and 1857. "Almost immediately, they found that their title to much of the land was disputed, and a series of lawsuits rendered the settlement virtually stillborn." John Jones was one of the Welsh immigrants who settled with a small group in Scott County, Tennessee. They arrived to learn that the land agents could not be located, and someone else held title to their promised acreage. He wrote home to relatives that he wished he "had never heard of Tennessee." Without farms to support them, some of the new immigrants found jobs in railroad construction and mining. So long as they were needed as cheap laborers on the Virginia and East Tennessee Railway, Welsh immigrants were welcome. Once railroad construction ended, many local people were openly hostile and scapegoated foreigners as the cause of their unemployment. Jones advised a nephew who wanted to emigrate from Wales: "We must actually keep away from here parties who might have been useful" for the past railroad construction, but who are too poor to "start themselves" without such wages (Conway 1961, 114, 116–17).

At the same time that Celtic and German immigrants were demeaned by those of English descent, those ethnic minorities idealized their own kind as superior in intellect, civilization, economic progress, religion, and political prowess. Hiram James declared, "We the Welsh are greater in our morality than anyone" (Conway 1961, 50). Some Shenandoah Valley German immigrants considered themselves superior to the English in husbandry and in economic success. "While others indulge in idleness," Jacob Irion wrote home, "the Germans are reputed for their diligence and industry." John Schmucker was equally critical of his English and Scotch-Irish neighbors. "On a plantation on which ten English families were ruined," he wrote, "one German will get rich. Where English nabobs drive their slaves by the crack of the whip and grow poor, several German families thrive in abundance" (Kercheval 1833, 176).

Local communities were often politically divided between Germans and English-speaking ethnic groups. Almost all magistrates, sheriffs, and local officials were English (Wust 1969, 120). Little wonder that Shenandoah Valley Germans "had very little love for their countrymen, the English-talking Americans," or that they were "furious electioneers" when a German candidate was running for office (Featherstonhough 1844, 18–19). Until 1840, German Appalachians voted Democratic in contrast to the Whig leanings of their Scotch-Irish neighbors. Between 1816 and 1835, numerous Germans served in legislative and local offices, and "a command of the German language was patently an asset for a political candidate in large portions of the Shenandoah Valley and in Botetourt and Wythe Counties" (Wust 1969, 120). Ethnic differences are also reflected in the degree to which immigrants supported or opposed the Revolutionary War. Anglicans correctly accused many of the Protestants of "Instilling Democratical principles" against the state church and against "Subjection to Great Britain"(Hooker 1953, 111). However, none of the Appalachian ethnic groups uniformly supported independence from England. Appalachians of English, Scotch-Irish, and German ancestry were divided in their sympathies about decolonization. Presbyterians were split, Baptists tended to be anti-British, and many Methodists were pro-British. Even though a majority of the pacifist Friends, Mennonites, Moravians, and Brethren were anti-British, most of them refused to fight on religious grounds (Gaustad 1974, 179). Those few Quakers and pacifist Germans who fought in the Revolutionary War were almost always excommunicated from their congregations (Olmstead 1960, 203–8).

Racial bigotry, exacerbated by religious differences, sometimes triggered violent conflict. Between 1800 and 1830, Winchester, Virginia, experienced public conflicts among its "mixed population of Germans, Irish, a few English and Scotch." According to Kercheval (1833, 176), the Germans and Irish routinely created public disturbances on each other's religious holidays, "produc[ing] much disorder and many riots." Tensions also ran high enough in local communities to spark interpersonal violence. In one instance, ethnic loyalty and alcohol proved to be a tragic mix. One group of Scotch-Irish who were "assisting a distressed neighbour to repair a broken mill dam, became heated with liquor, unfortunately quarreled with a poor German about the honour of their respective countries, upon which a bustle ensued, and the consequence was, that the man died the next day" (*Proceedings* 1816, 39).

Ethnoreligious Conflict before 1820

According to Hofstra (1998, 1284–85), there was a "geopolitical and imperial" reason that Protestant dissidents were concentrated on the Appalachian frontiers of the Carolinas, Virginia, and Georgia. It was colonial policy to settle non-English European Protestants on the western U.S. frontiers in order to form buffer zones that would check French expansion, protect British settlements from Indians, and deter runaway slaves. Frontier contemporaries were aware

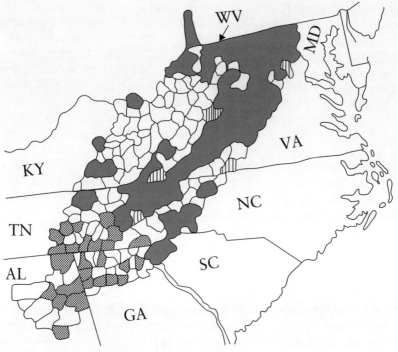

MAP 2. Presbyterianism in Southern Appalachia

■ Congregations from pre-1800 until 1850
▥ Pre-1800 congregations, but no 1850 congregations
▦ Congregations from post-1800 until 1850

Sources: U.S. Census Office (1854), Blethen and Wood (1998, 148), and Hanna (1985, iii–iv, 107–26). 1860 county boundaries are shown.

of their inferior status in the eyes of British descendants who had settled earlier along the coasts and in the Tidewater. One western Carolina settler observed that the older English settlements "consider'd the Back Country only as a Line of Outcasts they had plac'd there as a Barrier between them and the Indians" (Hooker 1953, 286n91). Because of that racist strategy, Southern Appalachia was populated by greater numbers of Scotch-Irish, Germans, and other religious minorities who had been persecuted in western Europe. Religious intolerance and conflict intensified after 1750 (Nolt 1996), and that growing disharmony coincided with the era in which several of the Appalachian frontiers opened for resettlement.

Despite the state-mandated Anglican Church in several Appalachian states, British religious customs did not predominate. Before 1800, the Scotch-Irish influence was evidenced by the presence of Presbyterian congregations in about one-third of the region's land area (see Map 2), those churches most heavily concentrated in Appalachian counties of Maryland, Virginia, and Tennessee.

Strikingly, only a few communities in east Kentucky, West Virginia, and western North Carolina had Presbyterian churches before 1800. Between 1800 and 1850, Presbyterian churches also opened in many of the remaining Appalachian counties of southeastern Tennessee, northern Georgia, and northern Alabama. In 1790 Maryland, Germans represented two-thirds of the population of Frederick County and one-third of the populations of Alleghany and Washington Counties.

In 1790 Virginia and West Virginia, Germans represented half or more of the settlers in Rockingham and Shenandoah Counties and two-fifths of the populations of Hardy, Harrison, Ohio, Pendleton, and Jefferson Counties. One-third of the populations of Augusta, Fauquier, Berkeley, and Greenbrier Counties and one-fifth of the settlers in Botetourt County were Germans. Before 1820, there were German churches in all western Maryland counties and in 21 Appalachian counties of Virginia (see Map 3). Germans immigrated into east Tennessee in the early 1800s, establishing churches in six counties, and the Moravians operated a mission for the Cherokees. By 1820, Lutherans formed a Tennessee Synod because Germans "had become so numerous in eastern and southern Tennessee" (Hill 1983, 295). Before 1820, there were also German churches in eight West Virginia counties; in Pickens County, South Carolina; and in eight east Kentucky counties. Between 1820 and 1850, German churches appeared in another six Appalachian counties of Virginia, West Virginia, Tennessee, and North Carolina (see Table 4, Web site).

Religious sects were deeply intolerant of one another, and sectarian conflicts were common in Appalachian communities. According to Mead and Hill (1985, 271), there was a "bewildering variety, a perplexing diversity" of denominations, separated by "great differences" in ethnic heritage. In short, "bitter sectarian competition" characterized religious activity on the late eighteenth- and early nineteenth-century frontiers (Hill 1983, 297). While a majority of Appalachians were *unchurched* on the frontiers and throughout most of the antebellum period (Finke and Stark 1992, 15), local communities were still the staging places for ethnoreligious animosities. In the western Carolinas, one Anglican minister was shocked that most of his "flock" were "Sectaries of various Denominations and Countries" (Hooker 1953, 85).

After the first U.S. Methodist congregation was established in Frederick County, Maryland, the Anglicans, Presbyterians, and Lutherans frequently jailed or assaulted their itinerant preachers. Even though both sects experienced repression, Presbyterians and Baptists were as antagonistic toward one another as they were toward the Anglicans (Hill 1983, 161–62). According to one contemporary, "the Antipathy that these two Sects bear each other, is astonishing. Wherefore, a Presbyterian would sooner marry ten of his children to members of the Church of England than one to a Baptist. The same from the Baptists as to the Presbyterians" (Hooker 1953, 80). One denomination rarely had anything positive to say about the other, as is the case with this description of the various sects on the western North Carolina frontier. "The Baptists are obstinate, illiterate, and grossly ignorant, the Methodists ignorant, censorious

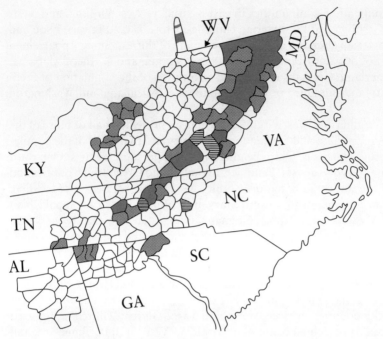

MAP 3. German Sects in Southern Appalachia

■ Pre-1820 congregations existed in 1850.

▨ Pre-1820 congregations and Moravian missionaries to the Cherokees had disappeared by 1850.

▤ Congregations established between 1820 and 1850

Sources: U.S. Census Office (1854), Faust (1927, 14–15, 264, 358–60), and Wust (1969, 133). 1860 county boundaries are shown.

and uncharitable, the Quakers, Rigid, but the Presbyterians are pretty moderate except here and there a Bigot or rigid Calvinist" (Saunders 1886, 6: 25).

Ethnoreligious differences led to intense conflict for two reasons. First, sectarian alignments followed the boundaries among ethnic groups, so religious intolerance stemmed initially from interracial bigotry. Second, intense conflict resulted because most denominations held ferociously that their "distinctive teachings were singularly authoritative" (Frantz 1976, 268). While it is not the intent of this study to examine in depth doctrinal points of difference, I would like to call attention to two ideological sore spots that intensified ethnoreligious frictions in Appalachian communities. The first major sectarian division emerged around revivalism. Because revivals and camp meetings involved lay preachers and multidenominational or unchurched crowds, Anglicans and many Presbyterians were critical of them. One Anglican missionary accused revival ministers of being nothing but "Ignorant Wretches, who can not write – who never read ten Pages in any Book, and can hardly read the Alphabet." In

FIGURE 1. Camp meetings were a threat to traditional denominations that feared loss of hierarchical control over local congregations and that opposed the use of uneducated lay religious leaders. Note the great numbers of women involved in a typical camp meeting. *Source:* Library of Congress.

the view of another Anglican cleric, these dissenter revivals were "calculated for private Entertainments . . . [and] often terminate[d] in Intemperance and Intoxication of both Sexes." Conservative Presbyterians considered revivals "Evil" because they were held "For all Classes of Villains, and the Vicious of both Sexes" (Gaustad 1974, 183, 181). In their organizational separatism, their worship and prayer, their daily dress, and their form of greeting, Bowman (1995, 86, 71) has noted, "Dunkers constructed real and symbolic fences between their own and the outside world." Convinced that "these societies believe in nothing at last," Dunkers "shunned" or "disowned" members who attended services or prayer meetings of other sects (Nead 1866, 55).

Despite public regulations and sectarian controversies, revivalism was widespread. Because there was a shortage of trained clergy (Levy 1991, 250 , the Baptists and Methodists depended heavily on revival meetings and lay preachers. An 1802 Methodist revival in Greene County, Tennessee, attracted loud criticism from Presbyterians because there was considerable "jumping, shouting, and jerking" throughout the services. Contemporary clerics claimed that the Presbyterians "were the aristocracy" while the revivalists represented "the poor" (Crawford 1980, 45–46). Even the Society of Friends was "in scorne called Quakers" by Old Side Presbyterians because their "meetings of worship in the evenings . . . were marked by profound religious experiences" in which participants were described as quaking and shaking (Pomfret 1951, 503, 511).

A second doctrinal point that led to community conflict was the nature of baptism. One Anglican cleric argued that public immersions "appl[ied] to the Passions, not to the Understanding of People" (Hill 1983, 226). Baptists disrupted nearby German churches that did not utilize similar practices. One Lutheran minister found "many immersionists (Baptists) in the audience" of a small Appalachian church. The Baptists "found [his] sermon so contrary" that "one of the company who carried a large club in his hand stepped up to the pulpit and interrupted [his] sermon." When Baptists preached that "the unbaptized" were "not Christians," Anglicans responded with ire. According to McLoughlin (1969, 721), "social prejudice against the Baptists reached the point where they were pointedly unwelcome in newly settled towns.... If they somehow got land, they were harassed until they left." Distinguished by traditional dress and opposition to many commercial activities, the German Baptist Brethren were disparagingly stereotyped the "Dunkers" or "Dunkards" to reflect their aggressive defense of complete immersion. The Brethren, in turn, condemned as "breeding grounds of 'popular' or 'nominal' Christianity' " those sects that did not practice immersion (Bowman 1995, 55, 69, 71). One Dunker leader termed the Mennonites "deteriorated Baptists" and the Anglicans and Presbyterians "worse than nothing."

Ethnoreligious conflicts did not stop at the boundaries between ethnic groups and denominations, for several of the sects were divided among themselves and were just about as antagonistic toward each other as they were toward outside denominations. By the early 1800s, "a series of social and political tensions had combined with ... religious forces to create irreconcilable differences between various factions in the churches" (Olmstead 1960, 295). It is not my purpose to record again the histories of their contentious politics, but two points are noteworthy. On the one hand, these doctrinal points of difference were not peculiar to Southern Appalachia. Instead, regional congregations reflected long-term religious views born in Europe and in the northern colonies. Institutionalized denominations in New England and Pennsylvania assigned missionaries and itinerant ministers to frontiers where there were few churches. On the other hand, congregations and their members were strong and vocal in their convictions, rigid enough in their positions to create permanent hostilities among neighbors. To demonstrate the depth of such splits and their potential impacts on small Appalachian communities, I will present only a few of the many possible specific cases. Originating from eighteenth-century revivalism in New England, the Separate Baptists were distinguished by their emotional, charismatic preaching and their appeals to the poor and working classes. When one of these sects emigrated from New England to western Virginia, they were not warmly received. Because the Regular Baptists "greeted [them] with hostility," they relocated three times. During an 1806 Shenandoah Valley camp meeting, Regular Baptists voted to excommunicate the charismatic minister who organized the services (Kercheval 1833, 66–67). One of the national schisms between Baptists occurred over "foreign missions," and that denominational division was reflected in Appalachian communities. In western Virginia, for example, about one-third of the congregations were antimission while the rest were not (Hill 1983, 338).

Nationally, Presbyterians were split between Old Side and New Side doctrinal positions that emerged in New York, New Jersey, and Pennsylvania. While New Side dissidents preferred preachers of Ulster heritage, Old Side adherents were more likely to have Scottish ties and to advocate a centrally controlled church structure that appointed educated clergy to local congregations. Such religious divides did not stay at an intellectual level; nor were these disagreements solely grounded in doctrinal debates that were free of ethnic bigotries (Olmstead 1960, 159–61). In eighteenth-century Augusta County, Virginia, for instance, the appointment of a Scotland-educated Old Side minister triggered conflict within a congregation that embraced a 60-mile area and "two Meeting houses." The minister had great difficulty "to hold them together their Disputes Rose so high." At the heart of the strife was the refusal of Old Side adherents and of the minister to protest against the state-supported Anglican Church, public religious taxation, and regulation of dissidents. Old Side supporters "rigidly sought . . . not to Give offence to ye Established Church, and Government." In addition to this significant point of ethnoreligious division, the minister was vociferously critical of lay preachers and of revivalism, and he regularly administered communion, an Anglican ritual that was deeply despised by Ulster Irish. New Side parishioners "look'd upon [him] as an opposer of ye work of God" and sought to realign the church with New Side itinerant ministers who "Speedily Came and thunder'd their New Gospel thro Every Corner of the Congregation." The minister's deriders were aggressive and subversive in their attempts to force his resignation. Hoping to "drive him away with Shame and Disgrace," New Side members charged him with causing the death of a neighbor's cattle through the use of witchcraft (*Irish Immigrants* 2003, 445–46, 390–93, 397).[2]

In the early nineteenth century, the split between Old Sides and New Sides was reflected geographically in Appalachian communities. The southwest Virginia Presbytery was divided so that most of the rural and frontier congregations in upper east Tennessee were New Side while congregations in and near the town of Abingdon were Old Side (Crawford 1980, 45). When New Side Presbyterian missionaries began to conduct revivals near Knoxville, Old Sider John Nevin stopped attending church because he thought it ungodly to rely on any minister other than Scottish-trained clergy. He was shocked by the "Jumping, Jerking, twitching, loud singing and shouting and clapping" at the meetings. Religious differences did not just embattle clergy or church members, for sectarian rivalries played out in community life. According to Nevin, there was a "realignment of local economic relationships according to whether merchants and customers supported or opposed the revivals or according to their membership in one or another of the many competing denominations and sects" (*Irish Immigrants* 2003, 606–7).

---

[2] Belief in witchcraft was not unusual on Appalachian frontiers (Doddridge 1824, 280–83).

Germans carried with them to Appalachian communities the ethnoreligious animosities of their European past, so they were just as intolerant of one another's churches as they were of English-speaking Protestants. In Germany, Lutherans had persecuted many of the same ethnic groups that migrated to Appalachia, so dissident German Protestants had historical reason to distrust Lutheran and German Reformed neighbors (Faust 1927, 53–72). Little wonder that western Maryland's prerevolutionary Lutheran churches voted to exclude Moravians and to permit only German Reformed neighbors to use their buildings (Hill 1983, 155–57). In Appalachian Virginia and West Virginia, small settlements were unified around specific sectarian identities. In Page County, Virginia, for example, German settlers "were almost exclusively of the Menonist persuasion; but few Lutherans or Calvinists settled among them" (Kercheval 1833, 61). In Appalachian counties of Maryland and Virginia, Lutherans were wary of German immigrants who arrived after 1820. In addition to the linguistic divisions among them, the different generations of Lutherans "were committed to a different style of faith." Recent arrivals criticized the circuit riders, revivals, and English services utilized by more Americanized Germans. There was also conflict over the use of wine in communion, for some of the new immigrants shunned the use of alcohol (Wust 1969, 195, 199, 124–26). Many Lutheran and Reformed Church adherents stereotyped the traditional speech, dress, and religious customs of dissident Protestant Germans as being "culturally only a trifle ahead of the Negroes" (Rippley 1976, 60). According to records of the Hebron Lutheran Church in Blue Ridge Virginia, the Brethren created "worries" and "gave rise to much quarreling and fighting" in the congregation (Huddle 1908, 42–43). In the view of more Americanized Lutherans, "the German Tunkers crept in and drew many into their net, greatly disturbing the peace" through their advocacy for lay preachers, revivalism, and water baptism (Rippley 1976, 56). Dunkers and Mennonites battled over religious issues such as dress, baptism, the Holy Kiss, and footwashing. Dunkers accused Mennonites of having "modernized too much" and of becoming too much like Americanized Baptists (Bowman 1995, 44). However, it was the issue of slavery that drove the widest schism between the German sects. While some Lutherans and German Reformed owned slaves and some congregations refused to condemn enslavement, the Mennonites, Dunkers, and Moravians remained antislavery (Sappington 1973, 173).

Discrimination against Protestant Dissidents and Disestablishment

Until well after the Revolutionary War, non-English Protestants were limited by state laws in their religious liberties because the Anglican Church was "the only established Religion" in the Carolinas, Georgia, and Virginia. In 1752, an Anglican minister expressed typical English prejudices toward religious dissenters on the western Carolina frontiers. From his ethnic vantage point, "there [we]re a very small number of Presbyterians, with some Quakers; and wherever these are, at least predominate, you shall never fail to find Immoralities and Disorders prevail." The same minister stereotyped the Scotch-Irish immigrants "upon and behind the Mountains of Virginia" as being too lazy to engage in any profitable employment, except "raising great Quantities of neat Cattle" in the forests (*Irish Immigrants* 2003, 61–63, 71n74). In similar fashion, a West Virginia Episcopalian clergyman admitted that "with the descendants of the Irish [he] had but little acquaintance, although [he] lived near them." That lack of interaction did not prevent him from espousing antagonistic bigotry toward Presbyterian immigrants, whom he labeled "mostly illiterate, rough in manner, and addicted to rude diversions of horse racing, wrestling, shooting, dancing" (Doddridge 1824, 135).

When Charles Woodmason preached in the Carolina backcountry in the mid-1700s, he encountered what he termed disdainfully a "Medley of Religions," which included Quakers, Dunkers, and Presbyterians, whom he described as "Heathens, Arians, and Hereticks" who were "as rude in their Manners as the Common Savages." He demeaned the Quakers, Presbyterians, and Dunkers as "concealed Papists" [Catholics] and labeled Baptists as "just so many Jesuits." In retaliation, the dissenters disrupted Woodmason's itinerary by "post[ing] a Paper, signifying, That the King having discovered the Popish Designs of . . . Romish Priests in disguise . . . had sent over Orders to suspend" all the Anglican ministers and to deport them back to England. The Anglican clergyman was particularly scathing in his intolerance of the "beggarly Irish Presbyterians," whom he termed "the Scum of the Earth and refuse of Mankind." Appearing in his wig and heavy woolen robes for summer church services, he looked out upon congregations of settlers who were attired in homespun cotton, linen, and flax that his London colleagues would think too uncivilized for church attendance. He was outraged that the women wore to church "Dresses almost as loose and Naked as the Indians." Even though he could "hardly bear the Weight of [his] Whig and Gown" in the summer heat, his prejudice did not subside, for he wrote to church officials that people attended services dressed barbarically, "the Women bareheaded, barelegged, and barefoot with only a thin Shift and under Petticoat." When western Carolina Scotch-Irish engaged in hymn singing after his services, the Anglican clergyman accused them of "Revelling, Drinking Singing Dancing and Whoring" (Hooker 1953, 47, 42, 45, 60–61, 56).

Colonial and postrevolutionary laws required every town to tax all inhabitants to fund the construction of a meetinghouse and the recruitment of an educated Anglican minister. In addition to their control over the church building and ministerial selection, Anglican vestries governed civil affairs, including tax levies, marriages, trade licenses, and care for the local poor (McLoughlin 1969, 721). Dissenters were prohibited from performing marriages, funerals, or baptisms, for which Anglicans collected fees, and they were required to register their meetinghouses and to take an oath of allegiance to the British. When legal cases involved Anglicans, dissenters were prohibited from serving on juries (Hooker 1953, 232). Even though Anglicans routinely employed nonresident circuit riders in the backcountry, it was illegal for dissenters to permit itinerant ministers to preach or to teach (Johnson 1983, 34). Like several other parts of the country (McLoughlin 1969), Appalachian frontiers were hotbeds for disestablishment activism against state-mandated religions. The Scotch-Irish were "in general adverse to the Church of England," and they disdained "establishment of the Church as oppressive" (Olmstead 1960, 214–15). They were equally intolerant of Scotland-educated Presbyterian ministers who integrated Anglican rituals into their services (Jackson 1993, 125), including the Lord's Prayer, English hymnals, and communion (Hooker 1953, 14, 44). The Scotch-Irish disrupted services and tried to make Anglican circuit riders as unwelcome as possible, and "Some Women" were more disruptive than the men. In one town, a missionary reported that "a large Body of People, 2/3 of them Presbyterians" disturbed the service by causing a fight with visiting Indians. On other occasions, the dissenters gave the cleric wrong directions, refused him food and shelter, scared away his horse, stole his church key, and started a pack of dogs fighting outside the church (Hooker 1953, 14, 44, 20, 22, 24–25, 30, 35, 39, 47, 45, 89).

Presbyterians were not the only dissenters who engaged in collective actions to challenge the state religion. In colonial Virginia, there were cases in which Baptists were branded or had their tongues burned with hot irons. Before the Revolutionary War, less than 1 percent of Virginians belonged to Baptist Congregations, and there were only about 30 churches. Persecution increased after 1768, when the General Assembly stopped licensing Baptist preachers. Because they would not "give bond and security not to preach in the county for one year," dozens of Baptist preachers were jailed (Little 1938, 38–42). Anglican vestrymen galloped horseback through river baptizings and disrupted public footwashings. During services, Anglican thugs attacked worshipers with horsewhips. Accustomed to a rigid, top-down church hierarchy and uniform dogma, Anglicans thought local selection of clergy, uneducated preachers, and internal sectarian divisions were the equivalent of "anarchy among the rabble" (Gaustad 1974, 183, 179–80). According to one Anglican cleric, the Baptists "Divide and Subdivide, Split into parties – Rail at and excommunicate one another – Turn out of Meetings, and receive into another." When the Baptists built a meetinghouse near his church, an Anglican minister harangued publicly that "the dissenting Tribe" were sexually licentious and infected with syphilis (Hooker 1953, 31, 42–43, 56, 60–61, 93, 95, 109).

In another community, dissenters demanded use of the publicly funded Anglican meetinghouse. To make their stand, "the Baptist Teacher entered" with his congregation "and began preaching when the [Anglican] Minister had ended." When a small settlement of Seventh Day Baptists moved near one of his parishes, the Anglican clergyman notified them that they were in violation of "the laws in force for due Observance of the Lords Day and sent to them to forbear Working." The Sabbatarians replied that "if [he] offer'd to come into their Parts for to preach they would give [him] Corporal Punishment." In retaliation for incidents like this one, Baptists "enter'd and partly tore down the Pulpit" in one Anglican church and "left their Excrements on the Communion Table"

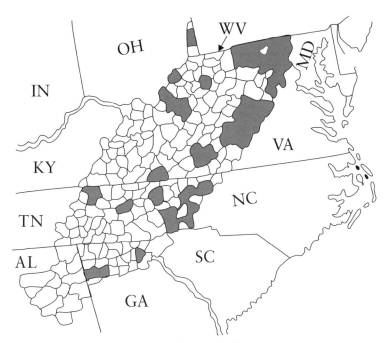

MAP 4. Anglican Heritage in Southern Appalachia

▨ Counties with Episcopalian congregations in 1850

Source: U.S. Census Office (1854). 1860 county boundaries are shown.

in another. They stopped construction of one meetinghouse, and "a Sett of Waggoners got round the Church with their Whips, and oblig'd the Minister to quit the Service" at another site. In violation of government regulations, Baptists routinely conducted clandestine baptizings, marriages, and funerals, collecting the fees, which were reserved to Anglicans (Hooker 1953, 47n40, 53, 46n40, 40–43).

Because they outnumbered the Presbyterians, the Baptists were more successful at harassing Anglicans until they abandoned their circuit services in some communities (Hooker 1953, 20). Terming themselves "Sons of Liberty," Carolina and Virginia Presbyterians flooded newspapers, public discourse, and politicians with repeated petitions in the 1760s. "We regard neither pope nor prince as head of the church," they announced in a 1768 pamphlet, "nor acknowledge that any Parliaments have power to enact articles of doctrine or forms of discipline or modes of worship or terms of church communion." In a 1772 petition, Blue Ridge Virginia dissenters decried "the illiberal treatment which a difference in religious sentiments... has produced." In 1780, a coalition of Virginia Baptists challenged their General Assembly to "consign to Oblivion all the Relicks of Religious Oppression." Dissenters rallied growing support with the motto "We are in the sure path to . . . *universal toleration* and *liberty of conscience*" (Bailyn 1965, 1: 162, 160n27, 161, 168).[3]

Opposition to the state church intensified after the Revolutionary War. In 1784, a convention of Anglicans lobbied the Virginia Assembly to establish a new Protestant Episcopal Church, which would retain "ownership and control of the property previously held by the established church." That act also mandated a publicly recognized sabbath, set civic days of prayer and fasting, defined *marriage* in biblical terms, and prohibited all ministers from holding public offices (Buckley 1995, 451). Dissenters attacked the Episcopalian incorporation act as "a Bitumen to Cement Church and State together" and saw it as another "foundation of Ecclesiastical Tyranny" (Gaustad 1974, 274). In 1785, Berkeley County, West Virginia, Presbyterians petitioned the Virginia state assembly to terminate taxation of non-Anglicans for support of the state church (Legislative Papers, VSL, 2 Sept. 1785). Collective resistance by the Presbyterians and Baptists was effective, for the Statute of Religious Freedom was passed in 1786. Despite the elimination of taxation and political repression of dissenters, Baptists and Presbyterians protested the continuing Episcopalian ownership of glebe lands that had been purchased with decades of public taxes (Buckley 1995, 452–56). In reaction to continuing public disgruntlement, the Virginia General Assembly passed a 1799 act that gradually confiscated and sold glebes, leaving Episcopalians in possession only of churches and cemeteries (Leyburn 1962, 285, 287). By 1800, most Episcopalian churches were "confined to Englishmen, generally of the privileged class," and there were few Appalachian congregations. By 1850, only 38, or less than one-fifth, of all Appalachian counties had functioning Episcopalian congregations, and most of them were concentrated in a handful of counties in western Maryland and in the Shenandoah Valley (see Map 4). Despite the decline of Episcopalian and Presbyterian congregations, elite Appalachians still linked class position to church membership. After experiencing loss of status when her husband left the Episcopalian fold, Mrs. William Hooper warned her daughter that "girls certainly make their way in the world and maintain a place in genteel society better as Presbyterians or Episcopalians than as baptists or methodists" (Hooper Papers, UNC, undated).

Protestant Persecution of Religious Minorities between 1780 and 1820

After the Revolutionary War, Protestant Appalachians directed intense prejudice toward several religious minorities. In addition to their religious, cultural, and linguistic differences, these nonconformist religious groups (see Map 5) took unpopular stands against war and slavery. In eight Appalachian counties of Virginia, two western Maryland counties, three West Virginia counties, three east Tennessee counties, and one western North Carolina county, the

---

[3] For a collection of petitions from dissident Appalachian Protestant congregations that were seeking permission to build churches, to license ministers, or to be relieved from taxes to support the state church, see "Early Virginia Religious Petitions," LOC.

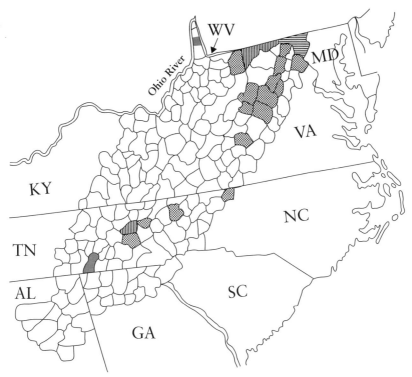

MAP 5. Appalachian Religious Minorities That Were Persecuted after 1840

▦ Pacifist sects: Quakers, Mennonites, Dunkers
▥ Catholics
▤ Catholics and pacifist sects
■ Jews

Source: U.S. Census Office (1854). 1860 county boundaries are shown.

Quakers, Mennonites, Moravians, and Brethren stood out because of their foreign dialects, their plain dress, their opposition to military service, and their
antislavery stands. Membership in Dunker congregations required converts to
be nonswearing, nonconformist to worldly ways, and unwilling to bear arms.
These sects refused to participate in political societies, opposed salaried ministers, and disdained certain forms of capitalist transaction and trade (Mead and
Hill 1985, 63, 65, 174). When an eighteenth-century surveyor encountered a
small settlement near Staunton, Virginia, he described the Dunkers as "an odd
set of people, who make it a matter of Religion not to Shave their beards, ly on
beds, or eat flesh. . . . The unmarried have no Property but live on a common
stock. . . . They keep their Sabbath on Saturday" (Fischer 1989, 437).

On the Appalachian frontiers, pacifists were suspected of treason if they
provided humanitarian aid to Indian groups. During the French and Indian
War in Preston County, West Virginia, militia commander George Washington

was angered that the Dunkers provided medical care to "Indians who [we]re wounded." Washington requested orders to arrest and jail the group because he "believe[d] they [we]re employed as spies, and [we]re useful to the French." Near Strasburg, Virginia, two Brethren attracted attention when they built a religious retreat on Massanutten Mountain. Because of their "queerness" and their periodic disappearances from the community, neighbors rumored that they were counterfeiting money or holding illegal Catholic masses (Fitzpatrick 1944, 1: 475, 2: 142–43). When Quakers and German pacifist sects challenged the established church through missionary work, they were often jailed.

In western Maryland and western Virginia, pacifists were accused of being pro-British during the Revolutionary War. Anglicans and most dissenter Protestants objected to the colonial policy of permitting conscientious objectors to refuse to serve in local militias (Bowman 1995, 39–41). One 1775 Appalachian petition demanded that pacifists pay fines and annual fees, and this approach subsequently became public policy (Gaustad 1974, 235). Even after they began to pay such fines, the pacifist groups were singled out for public violence and ridicule, were frequently jailed, or had their property confiscated by county courts that ignored the state law (Sappington 1973, 21, 30, 65–66, 71, 73–75, 77, 81). Again during the War of 1812, pacifists were jailed and lost property for refusing militia service, and these discriminatory practices continued throughout the antebellum period (Little 1938, 334–60).

Like the Anglicans, the Scotch-Irish stereotyped the Quakers as "a vile, licentious Pack" who were "unfit [for] the title of Christians." The first oppression of Quakers in Virginia occurred in 1690 when the general public was instructed to observe them carefully and report to officials their refusal to serve on militias and their convening of religious meetings. During the French and Indian War, Quakers were accused of receiving "strangers from other Governments" and of providing "a place of retreat" to Indians and French "after Mischief." One Quaker woman wrote home to England that her "station and connections" in an Appalachian community "made it very hard" because "language, fashions, customs" set her apart from the majority. In western North Carolina, Quakers were branded traitors because of their pacifism, harassed with quadruple taxes, and restricted from acquiring trade licenses (Renner 1974, 142–45). When the daughter of an Irish Quaker assisted her father in his western Carolina tavern, an Anglican minister publicly branded her "a very useful Piece of Goods...a raw ragged ignorant Girl fit for any Academy in Carnal Garden," accusing her of having "freely indulged" her sexual favors to "many Tasters," who had often "tapped her Barrel" (Hooker 1953, 46). From western Carolina, an Ulster Quaker peddler wrote to his Irish family that "Trade Rather Grows Better with me here." Still, he had decided to emigrate to Pennsylvania because he thought it too "Dangerous to Tarry Longer" (*Irish Immigrants* 2003, 534–36).

Protestant Persecution of Religious Minorities after 1820

By 1850, religious minorities represented about 15 percent of all church adherents in western Maryland and about 6 percent of all church adherents in

Appalachian Virginia. In east Tennessee, western North Carolina, and West Virginia, only about 1 percent of all church adherents were ethnoreligious minorities (see Table 4, Web site). The antislavery positions of the Quakers, Dunkers, and Mennonites set them apart and triggered harassment from their Appalachian neighbors (Drew 1856, 45). After 1830, public ordinances prohibited slaves from attending Quaker meetings, where they might be exposed to abolitionist notions or helped to escape (Drake 1950, 18). In western Carolina and northern Georgia, patrollers raided Moravian services looking for slaves (Hamilton 1971, 47). In the 1840s, Albemarle County Quakers were indicted for instructing blacks in their meetinghouses (Sappington 1973, 131–32). In 1846, a Mennonite pinpointed his group's unpopular dissidence in Appalachian counties. "Our doctrinal views and practices as a denomination are not well understood," he worried. "We can preach the Gospel to the poor, and they are ready to hear it. But there is one barrier between us and the wealthy classes . . . that barrier is African slavery." Two Dunker missionaries came face to face with the intensity of public reaction to their unpopular views. When they held services, few people attended, "not even the poor." One of them observed that they were "among a people largely opposed to the views and feelings of the Brethren on the slave question." Thus, their services "fearfully agitat[ed] the public mind" (ABCFM Annual Reports, HUL, 36, 93, 287).

In the early years of the Civil War, Quakers, Mennonites, and Dunkers were ridiculed in Appalachian newspapers and jailed after they refused to support the Confederate Army (Little 1938, 101–43). In response to 1862 petitions from Quakers, Dunkers, Mennonites, and Nazarenes in Botetourt, Roanoke, Franklin, and Rockingham Counties, Virginia, the Confederate government exempted the pacifists from military service, provided they "furnish substitutes or pay a tax of five hundred dollars each" (Sappington 1973, 30, 65–66, 71, 73–75, 77, 81). Local militias frequently refused to abide by the exemption act, sometimes kidnapping pacifists to try to force them into military service. Often county officials persecuted pacifists by charging them their exemption taxes several times. Some Mennonite farmers were impressed against their will to serve as teamsters and wagoners for the Confederate Army, and pacifist preachers were occasionally imprisoned. Through thefts and assaults, some neighbors expressed their resentment against the special status of pacifists. The frequency of farm burnings and murders caused hundreds of pro-Union pacifists to abandon their homes and escape to the North (Sanger and Hays 1907). Pacifist dissenters aided males to escape the Confederate draft through a network of safeway houses that moved them toward a hiding place at a mountain Mennonite church (Longenecker 2002, 179–82).

As we have previously seen, Protestant dissenters and Anglicans on Appalachian frontiers were staunchly anti-Catholic. When Catholic immigration to the United States increased dramatically after 1830, those earlier antagonisms were magnified. By far, the group of postrevolutionary immigrants to receive the most intense degree of discrimination and violence in the United States were the Irish and German Catholics who poured into the country in such great numbers after 1835. By 1850, when they constituted only 5 percent of the

FIGURE 2. Visible religious rituals, such as water baptizings and public footwashings, called public attention to religious minorities, such as the Dunkers depicted here. Because men and women participated together in violation of separate spheres conventions, other Protestants often stigmatized such religious dissidents as sexually licentious. *Source:* Nead (1866).

total population, Catholics were the third largest U.S. denomination, exceeded in number only by the Methodists and Baptists (Olmstead 1960, 321–22). In 1850, Catholic Appalachians were concentrated in the three western Maryland counties (see Map 5), and 1 of every 12 western Maryland church adherents was Catholic. Except for one congregation in Knoxville, Tennessee, no other Catholic churches were reported in 1850 Appalachian counties. However, census records do not provide a full accounting of this ethnic minority. Irish Catholic hucksters and peddlers were spotted in some Appalachian counties (*Janney's Virginia* 1978, 67). Even though there was no Catholic congregation in 1850 Wheeling, about half that town's white population was foreign-born, nearly one-third of them Irish and German (Fones-Wolf and Lewis 2002, 25).

There were frequent sightings of Irish Catholic laborers at Appalachian rail-road construction sites in the 1840s and 1850s (e.g., Buni 1969, 89n14), and numerous Catholics were employed by western Maryland iron manufactur-ers and coal mines (Harvey 1977). There were Catholic missions in Staunton, Charlottesville, Harrisonburg, Lexington, and Mountain Top to serve western Virginia's immigrant railroad workers (Turner 1948, 324–34). Even though a small church building had been erected in Staunton by 1851, a majority of the members of this "despised fellowship" met inconspicuously in homes (Longe-necker 2002, 85). Even though the census did not report any churches in those areas, large numbers of Irish Catholics worked as laborers in southeast Ten-nessee and northern Georgia to construct the Western and Atlantic Railroad (Takagi 1999, 146). Irish Catholics were recruited in large numbers to work on railroads in Lewis County and adjacent areas of West Virginia; in several Blue Ridge and southwestern Virginia counties; in the area around Asheville, North Carolina; in northwestern Georgia; and in parts of southeast Tennessee. While slaves composed a majority of the railroad labor force, Irish Catholics were assigned to the most hazardous work, such as mountain tunnel construction (Ambler 1964, 304; Maguire 1868, 333–34, 453, 627; Bickley 1852, 117–19).

Despite their low numbers in the region, there was widespread anti-Catholic sentiment. A recruitment letter to attract Irish Catholics into northwestern South Carolina warned that "the families who emigrate should settle in groups near each other" because they would be denied "social companionship" with the other inhabitants. In a letter to an east Tennessee newspaper, one Protes-tant boasted that he "considered it doing an honor to the deity to…shoot any Catholic he might meet" (Maguire 1868, 627, 333–40). It was impossible for middle-class Catholics to acquire fire insurance on their homes in Appalachian communities. When John McCue tried to insure the property of a railroad foreman, the company refused to endorse the policy for "one of the class of Irishmen," who frequently exhibited the propensity to "injure the whole world to effect an enemy, in feeling or in property" (McCue Papers, UVA, Box 2, 20 Nov. 1852).

One powerful indicator of the extent of anti-Catholicism can be found in the editorial policies of regional newspapers. In the 1840s and 1850s, news-papers in 34 Appalachian counties routinely published anti-Catholic editori-als, features, advertisements, and letters.[4] Like the Know Nothing Party and

---

4 The Appalachian anti-Catholic newspapers were the following: in Alabama: *Talladega Reporter*; in Georgia: *Dahlonega Sentinel, Rome Courier*; in Kentucky: *Ashland Kentuckian, Richmond Messenger*; in Maryland: *Cumberland Journal, Liberty Town Banner of Liberty*; in North Carolina: *Asheville Spectator*; in Tennessee: *Athens Post, Cleveland Herald, Greenville American, Kingston Gazetteer, Knoxville Register, Knoxville True Whig, Maryville East Tennessean, Sparta Times*; in Virginia: *Abingdon Virginian, Bath Enterprise, Buchanan Recorder, Charlottesville Advocate, Floyd Intelligencer, Lexington Gazette, Roanoke Republican, Staunton Republican, Staunton Spectator, Staunton True American, Warrenton Piedmont Whig, Wytheville Telegraph*; and in West Virginia: *Berkeley American, Charleston Free Press, Greenbrier Era, Hardy Whig, Kanawha Republican, Kanawha Valley Star, Morgan Enterprise, Morgantown Mirror*,

numerous American periodicals (Ignatiev 1995, 41), Appalachian newspapers routinely referred to Irish Catholics as "whitewashed Negroes" or as "niggers turned inside out"(*Kanawha Valley Star*, 10 Feb. 1857). "An Irishman builds him a turf stye," the *Shepherdstown Register* (26 Feb. 1850) claimed, "gets his fuel from the bogs, digs his patch of potatoes, and then lives upon them in idleness: like a true savage, he does not think it worth while to work that he may better himself." In east Kentucky, the *Richmond Messenger* (19 Mar. 1855) decried the immigration of "millions of papists and infidels into the American Protestant civilization." The *Abingdon Virginian* (28 July 1855) justified its anti-Catholicism as "resistance to religious intolerance and a rigid maintenance of the great principle of religious freedom."

For many Protestant dissenters, the influx of Catholics represented an even greater threat to their religious freedom than had the earlier Anglican Church. In 1840, the American Society to Promote the Principles of the Protestant Reformation emerged as a cross-denominational effort "to arouse Protestants to a proper sense of their duty in reference to the Romanists." Catholicism was perceived to be the "power and great authority of the Beast" while Protestantism was praised as "pure religion and undefiled." Appalachian Methodists, Presbyterians, Primitive Baptists, and Regular Baptists were most vocal against Catholics. As early as 1837, the Native American Association of Washington County, Virginia, petitioned Congress to amend the naturalization laws in order to curb Catholic emigration.[5] A mass meeting of 20,000 Protestants in Frederick County, Maryland, was treated to band music, barbeque, and an assortment of speeches against Catholics and other foreigners (Overdyke 1950, 237–38, 5, 145). Protestant immigrants arriving between 1830 and 1860 quickly embraced anti-Catholic mythology. Soon after arriving in the United States, Ezekiel Hughes wrote home to Wales that so many Catholics were pouring in that they would soon "bring this country under the trammels of Popery" (Conway 1961, 74).

An 1854 Wheeling, West Virginia, broadside (*Baltimore Sun*, 11 Jan. 1854) challenged "freemen" to rise up and "drive this monster back to his bloody master, the Pope" because Catholics were "not worthy to breathe American air." Even some German Appalachians believed that the Irish "st[oo]d nearer barbarism and brutality than civilization and humanity" (Gaustad 1974, 464). Many German Protestants defined the Irish as their "natural enemies" because they were "the truest guards of Popery" (Rippley 1976, 53). East Tennessee Methodist minister William G. "Parson" Brownlow, editor of the southern newspaper with the largest circulation, dedicated his *Knoxville True Whig* to halting "the Papal Conspiracy" (Overdyke 1950, 178, 231). Brownlow supported the nativist platform of the Know Nothing Party and repeatedly sounded

---

Parkersburg Gazette, Shepherdstown Register, Wheeling Gazette, Wheeling Intelligencer, and *Wheeling Times*. Most of these newspapers were also anti-German, especially anti-Semitic, in their editorials.

5 Note that this is an association of Euroamerican ethnic groups who are opposed to new immigrants.

the alarm that "the system of Popery . . . is injurious to the private morals of the civilized world; and if unchecked, will overturn the civil and religious liberties of the United States." In a continual flow of newspaper articles, books, pamphlets, and public appearances, the fiery Brownlow warned Protestants that they were quietly being overwhelmed by Irish Catholics and German Jews. The "foreign element," he harangued in one of his pamphlets, "is increasing in fearful ratio. . . . The majority of the civil and municipal offices of this government are today in the hands of Catholics and foreigners" (Brownlow 1856, 17).

It was in this era that the *ethnogenesis* of the U.S. "Scotch-Irish" identity occurred as a rallying cry to align Protestant and unchurched Americans against the "dangerous race" of Catholics. The term *Scotch-Irish* is an American ethnic invention that was rarely used before the massive influx of Irish Catholics in the 1840s (Blethen and Wood 1998, 1). At the peak of the racial antagonism toward arriving immigrants, many white Appalachians sought to dissociate themselves from Irish American Catholics, "by emphasizing, exaggerating, and if necessary even fabricating the ethnoreligious, cultural, and behavioral traits that purportedly and eternally distinguished all the 'Scotch-Irish,' regardless of social status, from all Irish Catholics" (Ignatiev 1995, 39).

Another indicator of regional anti-Catholic reaction was the expansion of the Know Nothing Party, which promised to resist foreign influences in order to preserve the United States for "none but native born Protestant citizens." Active in almost every Appalachian county, the party was especially strong in western North Carolina, western Maryland, and the Appalachian counties of Tennessee, Virginia, Georgia, and Alabama (Overdyke 1950, 38, 68–69, 76, 78, 80, 38, 252–54). The Know Nothings were so strong in western Virginia that there was a separate state council for the Appalachian counties – making Virginia the only state to have two organizational bodies for the party (Ambler 1964, 331). The *Abingdon Virginian* (23 Feb. 1856) told its readership that the Know Nothing Party was "the goddess of American Liberty" and the "torch of freedom" because its intent was to ensure that "Americans shall rule America." Even in small Appalachian towns without Catholic residents (like Loudon and Kingston, Tennessee, or Asheville, North Carolina), the Know Nothings captured local offices. When a Buncombe County, North Carolina, grand jury indicted Know Nothings for "binding men by secret oaths and trying to control the free voting of citizens," a friendly judge ruled "no action." Two newspapers publicized the anti-Catholic party line in east Kentucky, one bragging that through its circulation it would capture for the Know Nothings "the hardy mountaineers at their homes and firesides." West Virginia counties were very divided, with support for the Know Nothings strongest in the belt of former Whig counties. While there was not as much violence in Appalachia as in larger urban centers, there were racial hate crimes in every county with Catholic residents, churches, or itinerant workers. Despite the density of Catholics in western Maryland, newspapers in every county took anti-Catholic positions. There were instances of ethnic-based violence among laborers in western Maryland, western North Carolina, and several western Virginia counties (Hill 1983, 299,

160, 113; Fones-Wolf and Lewis 2002, 3–18; Buni 1969, 89n14). Even though there were few Catholics in the town, Knoxvillians engaged in several violent assaults against Catholics and against those who supported continuing foreign immigration.

Even though the census recorded Appalachian synagogues only in Wheeling, West Virginia, and Chattanooga, Tennessee (see Map 5), Jews were present in Beckley (Weiner and Reed 1996), Charleston (Meyer 1972), and Clarksburg, West Virginia (Weiner 1995, Shinedling 1963). Despite their small numbers, animosity toward Jews was widespread. The Know Nothings in Appalachian Virginia and Maryland warned against the immigrating Germans, who were portrayed as "dangerous abolitionists" (Faust 1927, 111). After the tiny Congress of the League of German Radicals met in Wheeling in 1852, Virginia Germans were accused of being "Red Republicans who intended to bring down the U.S. government" (Wust 1969, 209–14). In addition to calls for disenfranchisement of Germans, there were frequent attacks on their traditional festivities and meetings. The antiimmigrant platform of the Know Nothing Party warned Americans of the hidden threats of the German "Socialist Papists in disguise" (Hill 1983, 299). Even though there were so few Jews in Southern Appalachia, anti-Semitic prejudices and stereotypes were common. In Virginia, the "very dirty German Jews" were stigmatized as the "least valuable class" because they kept shops in alleyways that were "inhabited mainly by negroes" (Olmsted 1856, 51). According to Marvin Gullett (Transcript, ALC, 14), "the Jews were very much hated people" in east Kentucky because "they peddled goods."

Pressures toward Assimilation

Despite such long-running ethnic animosities, there were powerful economic, legal, linguistic, and cultural pressures on Euroamerican immigrants to assimilate.[6] Given the intensity of ethnoreligious conflict, how did the diverse denominations assimilate so fully that a majority of Appalachian church adherents – like all U.S. Caucasians – were Methodists and Baptists by 1850? The first explanation is that, like the entire United States, a majority of Appalachians were unchurched. In 1790, only 5 percent of the U.S. population were church members, denominational adherence rising to only one-third of citizens by 1850. Because there was a severe shortage of churches and ministers throughout the region, denominations merged services and shared buildings. Northern missionaries also facilitated ethnoreligious assimilation in the communities where they preached. Following the national trend, intermarriage across Appalachian denominational lines further widened the ranks of the Baptists and Methodists (Finke and Stark 1992, 12, 27, 29).

In addition, the class composition of Appalachian communities was a central factor in the breakdown of ethnoreligious conflict. Throughout the antebellum period, half or more of the region's whites were landless and poor, the vast

---

[6] For a more historically detailed discussion of assimilation, see the Web site.

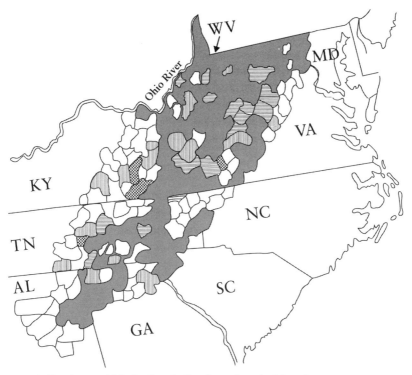

MAP 6. Baptists and Methodists in Southern Appalachia, 1850

☐ Counties in which a majority of church congregations were Baptist

■ Counties in which a majority of church congregations were Methodist

▨ Counties in which Baptists dominated, no Methodists

▤ Counties in which Methodists dominated, no Baptists

▥ Counties in which Baptists and Methodists were about even

Source: U.S. Census Office (1854). 1860 Appalachian county boundaries are shown.

majority of them illiterate (Dunaway 1996). There was an economic chasm separating working-class sects from denominations that appealed primarily to educated elite and middle-class families who could afford pew payments and annual subscription fees. Reliance on lay teachers, preachers, and missionaries; circuit riding ministers; revivals; and camp meetings allowed the Baptists and Methodists to capture great numbers of the illiterate, the unchurched, the poor, and those adherents to competing sects who had no church or minister in the geographical area. In sharp contrast, Anglicans and Presbyterians pushed for local laws to prohibit camp meetings and to fine or jail the leaders (Finke and Stark 1992, 7–12, 79–83, 98–105). In the last four decades of the antebellum period, the conflictual groups of the earlier decades changed and merged so extensively that the Baptists and Methodists were predominant (see Map 6).

Women's Resistance against Patriarchal Church Policies

Antebellum churches were dominated by male preachers, church boards, and teachers.[7] Even women's Sunday school classes and prayer meetings were led by males, and churches often segregated seating patterns by gender (Addington Transcript, EHU, 48; Bowman 1995, 55, 89). I have found no record of women voting in Appalachian churches, except among the Primitive Baptists and the Moravians (Smith and Wilson 1999, 65). "Let pious females be content," propounded *The Presbyterian*, "to walk and act in the sphere in which God has placed them" (Penfield 1977, 109–10).

However, the most publicly debasing gender biases resulted from the church discipline committees whose responsibility it was to police the behaviors of members and to bring public charges against transgressors. Whereas northern Baptists and Methodists ended such church trials in the early 1830s (Ryan 1979, 72), southern and Appalachian churches continued this practice throughout the antebellum period. Between 1800 and 1860, 31 Appalachian churches disciplined 792 members for disorderly conduct and sexual offenses (see Table 2). More than four-fifths of the females were charged with sexual offenses (including lewdness, licentiousness, adultery, fornication, and bastardy) while more than four-fifths of the males were charged with disorderly conduct (including blasphemy, drinking, profanity, fighting, and domestic violence). Women carried the burden of proof before male discipline committees. The Battle Run Baptist Church (VSL, 7 Mar. 1835) committee took its "divine task" very seriously. "From Eternity God chose out of the human family a certain definite number into everlasting life," the secretary recorded. Therefore, it was their duty as part of that special "elect" to discipline "the unholy." While Baptist congregations locally determined disciplinary codes, the Methodists and Presbyterians set national codes of church discipline (Sweet 1954, 110–19; Thompson 1963, 1: 77). Almost all denominations required their members to treat suspended or expelled offenders as outcasts. When a member was expelled, "there must be no familiarity, no social intercourse, no visitings to, or from him, nothing in short, that is expressive of ignorance at his conduct" (Green River Association, NCDAH, 5).

When the committee's recommended punishment of an offender went before the entire congregation, women did not have the right to defend themselves publicly, and their church sisters did not have the right to vote. In the cases I have scrutinized in church records, the male partners of women charged with sexual offenses were never identified, so churches placed solely on females the blame for violations of sex mores. Women did not always succumb easily to such public charges. In more than a third of the cases I have perused, committees noted that the female offenders were "acting defiant." In another 15 percent, the charged women withdrew from the congregations, their families protesting

---

[7] I perused manuscript minutes and records for 34 churches listed in the Bibliography under GSA, HPL, NCDAH, UNC, UVA, VHS, VSL, and WVU.

TABLE 2. *Baptist and Methodist Church Members Tried by Disciplining Committees, 1800–1850*

Part I. Offenses by Gender

Type of Offense	Males		Females		Total
	No.	%	No.	%	
Disorderly conduct	431	81.3	99	18.7	530
Sexual offenses	41	15.7	221	84.3	262
TOTAL	472	59.6	320	40.4	792

Part II. Church Sanctions against Offenders

Type of Sanction	Males		Females		Total
	No.	%	No.	%	
Warning/public citation	195	41.4	70	21.9	265
Suspended/probation	238	30.3	84	26.2	322
Expelled	39	28.3	166	51.9	205
TOTAL	472		320		792

Sources and notes: Analysis of manuscript minutes for 31 Baptist and Methodist churches listed in the bibliography under GSA, HPL, NCDAH, UNC, UVA, VHS, VSL, and WVU. Sexual offenses included lewdness, licentiousness, adultery, fornication, and bastardy. Disorderly conduct included blasphemy, drinking, profanity, fighting, and domestic violence.

that males should be held accountable for damage to daughters or wives. When Abba Mathews was summoned to the monthly meeting to answer to a charge that she had been sexually lewd, she did not attend. Five months later, she again refused to be tried and rebuffed the committee with "improper language" (Broad Run Church, VSL, 12 July, 9 Aug., and 13 Dec. 1828). When Sally Cornwall and Rachael Coatney were cited for drunkenness, they ignored the summons (Occoquam Church, VHS, 3 Aug. 1827, May 1831).

Women's Resistant Religious Roles before 1830
In the early 1800s, religious periodicals popularized the "cult of evangelical womanhood" as a reaction against separate spheres conventions that proscribed female religious labors. Publications of evangelical denominations challenged women to put their religious beliefs into action and condemned worldly preoccupation with balls, parties, and fashions (Kierner 1998, 148–58). The hardworking "pious housewife" was frequently contrasted with the "gadder" who wasted her life in "uselessness" (Groneman and Norton 1987, 23–29). Several Baptist and Methodist handbooks urged wives to prioritize religious duties over their domestic sphere (Loveland 1978, 462). With the aid of such religious

publications, women drew upon the ideals of "Evangelical Womanhood" to justify their calls for reform within their local congregations. For example, some suffragists pressured their churches to permit women to vote, arguing to male church boards that women's qualifications were represented in their abilities to teach Christian values to children and to raise church funds. At Pleasant Union Christian Church (UNC) and Broad Run Baptist Church (VHS), middle-class dissidents took a large segment of the female membership (and many of their supportive husbands) with them when they withdrew in protest of male board decisions against women's voting. In contrast, Moravian women could vote as members of the Elders Conference and were much more visible in their churches' economic activities than women in the vast majority of denominations (Smith and Wilson 1999, 65). Even though the Free Will Baptist General Conference ruled in 1830 that "women should be silent" in church decision making, some small Appalachian congregations ignored this proscription. Since they operated as small informal gatherings that met in homes, they had to rely on lay preachers from congregations that were mostly illiterate (Melder 1964, 76).

In the 31 Baptist and Methodist churches I studied, more than one-third of Sunday school teachers were women, many of them married. In addition, females routinely held their own gender-segregated prayer meetings, raised funds, and organized local missionary outreach to slaves. In contrast, the 1830s Sunday School Register for the West Liberty Presbyterian Church (WVU) listed several women's classes, all led by men. Three-fifths of revival and camp meeting converts were females, necessitating many women volunteers (Cott 1977, 159). Although Old Light Presbyterians and several other sects condemned the "practice of females praying with males" (Beecher and Nettleton 1828, 10), Methodist camp meetings routinely used women as exhorters and as counselors to new converts.[8]

Denominations that recruited members from all social classes were more likely to relax the barriers against public religious roles for women, and working-class congregations more often relied on lay female preachers. Out of necessity, denominations and sects that were opposed to educated clergy were more likely to utilize female church leaders, so there were more female preachers among Freewill Baptists, the Christians, and the New Light Methodists. Nationally between 1790 and 1840, hundreds of Free Will Baptist women had some experience with lay preaching (Melder 1964, 43, 61, 76, 92–93). Among the Baptists, Methodists, and Quakers, practices varied from one locale to another, but women in these denominations routinely led public prayers, exhorted sinners to repentance, and counseled new converts. Prior to 1830, when there was a shortage of churches and ministers in Southern Appalachia, more than 10 percent of Baptists and Christian preachers were probably women, most of whom were itinerant evangelists or circuit riders who traveled in the company of other

---

[8] The terms "Old Side" and "Old Light" were used interchangeably to refer to the traditional religious position within denominations, as were "New Side" and "New Light" to refer to the dissident position.

FIGURE 3. Female exhorters at Methodist camp meetings and gender-integrated public prayers excited critique from more traditional clergy whose congregations held separate services for men and women and reserved ministerial roles for males. *Source: Frank Leslie's Illustrated Newspaper* (September 1882).

females. One of the most famous female Methodist preachers of the 1830s was Luzene Chipman, who published a popular religious guide (Chipman 1852) and preached to large gender-mixed crowds in western and Piedmont North Carolina. Women were most publicly visible among Cumberland Presbyterians, who were concentrated in Southern Appalachia, and this sect was the first in the denomination to ordain female ministers (Penfield 1977, 109–10, 119).

Nationally, the more evangelical denominations contributed in a significant way toward widening the cultural boundaries of the women's prescribed religious sphere. Although there were restrictions on women's roles in denominations with a highly educated ministry and a clear structure of worship and church leadership, Methodists, New Lights, of all denominations, Free Will Baptists, Christians, Moravians, and Quakers often violated the kinds of gender norms advocated by supporters of "true womanhood" tenets (Billington 1985, 375). To more conservative denominations that interwove notions of female domesticity with church doctrine, white Methodist women "often seemed deviant, for they violated southern gender conventions in the service of their religion. . . . By speaking in public assemblies, aggressively proselytizing, and critiquing others' behavior, women assumed moral leadership previously reserved for men" (Coryell et al. 1998, 54–57). The spontaneity and exuberance of women who exposed their passions in public caused them to be accused of sexual lewdness, diabolical influences, witchcraft, or insanity. To stand their ground over religious convictions, women often challenged the church ties of husbands or fathers, thereby speeding assimilation. Conservative gentlemen who "had ridiculed the lowly evangelicals," observes Richard Rankin (1993, 48), "found themselves married to them" and likely to acquiesce to their wives' preferences.

Women's Less-Resistant Religious Roles after 1830

As the ideology of "separate spheres" became more entrenched among middle-class and elite Appalachians after 1830, intolerance increased toward females in public religious roles. The region's diminishing number of women preachers "were very conscious of being labelled as deviants," and "suggestions of sexual irregularities dogged their footsteps" (Sappington 1973, 135). Even though she was engaging in work that met the ideals of "Evangelical Womanhood" (Boylan 1978) and the "Moral Mother" (Block 1978), the female preacher clashed with those who grounded their Cult of True Womanhood in the Scriptures. Because she was ignoring the cultural boundaries between the gender-segregated separate spheres, an itinerant woman preacher or missionary was branded "a public spectacle" who was "sensation-seeking, crazy, hysterical," and "not religious at all," but driven by "financial greed" or "deliberate fraud" (Billington 1985). The Mennonites, Brethren, and Dunkers were ridiculed by other sects because they encouraged more active public roles for women. Many Blue Ridge Virginia Presbyterians, Baptists, and Methodists thought Brethren women were not much better than prostitutes when they traveled into adjacent counties "to preach to a hungry group of under-privileged folks" (Sappington 1973, 135). In this instance, separate spheres rhetoric disguised fears that these dissidents were engaged in abolitionism, a public sphere activity for which Quaker and Moravian women were deeply respected within their own religious groups. In fact, these dissident females were so far outside the mainstream of most white women's lives, they were viewed with hostility and would have rarely crossed the great divide that separated them from proslavery women. In 1832, the Georgia State Guard invaded the classroom of a female Moravian missionary because two black children were learning to read among the Cherokees (Hamilton 1971, 47). In east Kentucky, 60 vigilantes stormed a female-taught slave Sabbath school "armed with clubs and guns, and thus the Quaker school was dispersed never to meet again" (Drake 1950, 18).

Even though women were highly visible in church fund-raising, males made financial decisions for congregations (e.g., Reveille Church, VSL, 12, 22, 25; Shiloh Association, VSL, 26 Mar. 1852). The 1811 Presbyterian General Assembly acknowledged, "It has pleased God to excite pious women" to create, join, and lead associations that generated a high proportion of the funds needed for male-controlled charities (Penfield 1977, 110). Even though they could not lead their own classes or prayer meetings, the Ladies Sewing Society of Clarksburg Presbyterian Church (Browning Letter, WVU) organized a public fair "to liquidate a church debt." Between 1830 and 1850, women's missionary societies were the most common form of female voluntary associations. However, patriarchal church rules placed limits on the roles of missionary wives and independent female missionaries (Giele 1995).

By the 1840s, most southern denominations were frowning upon female-led prayer meetings in which there were no husbands present (Penfield 1977, 110). Still some women resisted and convened female meetings without male supervision (Bumpas Diary, UNC, 8; Capps Diary, VHS, 5 Nov. 1844; Davis Diary, UNC, 26 Aug. 1838). "It is good for us to meet together," thought one such organizer, because females were eager to discuss when they were in a gender-segregated meeting (Weisiger Diary, VHS, 4 May 1843, 11 Oct. 1845, 6 Oct. 1842). Women complained to husbands, to kinswomen, and to church boards that they could not discuss intimate women's issues in classes or meetings conducted by males (Lenoir Papers, UNC, 13 June 1849, 10 May 1858). "There are thoughts, doubts, suggestions which present themselves to my mind," one woman lamented. "If only I could *talk of them*. I think of our class leaders but there is in old Mr. Man no appreciation of the trials of a woman's nature" (Thomas Diary, DU, 4 June 1864).

Conclusion

Ethnic conflict drove deep divisions among Caucasian women. While all white Appalachian women were disadvantaged by the same paternalistic system, their degrees of privilege and of oppression within that system varied dramatically. All Euroamerican females were not "sisters under the skin" who confronted the paternalistic system at the same junctures or who were repressed in the same ways or to the same degree. There were deep schisms among the Euroamerican ethnic groups that arrived on Appalachian frontiers. By the 1830s, however, a majority of white Appalachians had assimilated, and there was less religious diversity in the region. However, a minority of females whose religious practices varied from the mainstream continued to be singled out for marginalization and persecution. These divisions made impossible the development of a gendered sisterhood that fostered women's networks or resistance against patriarchal institutions.

Even when they pushed the boundaries to seek more female-controlled activities, most Appalachian women did not challenge patriarchal church structures in which males voted and controlled the congregation's affairs. While many women pushed for female-controlled activities within patriarchal churches, they participated in creating and reproducing the patriarchal systems that subordinated them. Moreover, church denominations became more repressive toward woman after 1830, as cult of domesticity ideals were increasingly integrated into southern society. As a result, white women were visible in very few leadership roles, even when they struggled to eliminate sexist barriers in their own churches. As we will see in Chapters 2 and 3, Cherokee and black women held far more leadership roles in their communities, their religions were far less patriarchal, and they were pivotal to cultural persistence in ways that white women were not.

Paradoxically, however, these ethnically divided women shared a newly formed racial identity. Euroamerican women shared a structurally privileged racial position, and there was enormous pressure to assimilate toward racial solidarity. Because the evolution of the U.S. national identity was fueled by distinctions of color and race, European ethnic identities became far less central to white Appalachian women when they were juxtaposed against the subordination of peoples of color. Successive generations of immigrants evolved from stigmatized outsiders to become part of the white American race (Allen 1989, 1: 185). Racial membership as a "white"American provided women privileges denied to females of color. Despite ethnic differentiation among Euroamericans, the status of "white American" gave political, economic, and cultural privileges to all Caucasian women, including the right to be a citizen, the right to own property, and the capacity to derive benefits from the social and economic status of one's husband or father. As we will see in Chapters 2 and 3, *racial inequalities* quickly emerged as far more significant divisions among Southern Appalachians than the religious and ethnic differences that separated whites.

2

Not a Shared Patriarchal Space

Imperialism, Racism, and the Cultural Persistence of Indigenous Appalachian Women

> The place and power of Indian women, misunderstood by white soldiers, anthropologists, and reformers, remain shrouded for those outside Native American cultures....Legitimacy for [indigenous] women came out of established rights and expectations within their own culture....Somewhere in the history of America...rests a rich and layered account of Indian women that waits to be reclaimed.
> (Anne Butler and Ona Siporin 1996, 55–56)

Euroamerican settlers "otherized" into racial enemies those resistant indigenous people who had populated Appalachian frontiers for centuries. In 1775, a Staunton, Virginia, town ordinance claimed that whites had captured and now needed to fight to hold onto "this once-savage wilderness." That same year, Abingdon, Virginia, town officials alerted militias to white vulnerability. "We crossed the Atlantic," the town resolution announced, "and explored this uncultivated wilderness, bordering on many nations of savages" (Hagy 1896, 415–16). When they feared Indian attacks, English, Scotch-Irish, and Germans forgot their ethnic differences and worked together to build forts and man local militias (Jackson 1993, 112, 123–24). Euroamerican Appalachians identified themselves around two racial constructs. They rewrote the history of this geographical space to redefine themselves to be its true "natives," as opposed to the "uncivilized" Indians from whom they conquered "this empty wilderness" (McClintock 1995, 30–31; Jennings 1993, 73–74). They also defined themselves to be "free white Americans," who were "naturally" on a higher plane than *inferior* nonwhite Appalachians. These new racial identities emerged out of the historical shift from emphasis on *ethnicity* to a prioritizing of *race consciousness* as the primary criterion of inclusion in American peoplehood. While Euroamericans were divided by their ethnic hostilities, the social construction of "white American peoplehood" provided them the basis for solidarity (Ignatiev 1995). An Anglican cleric on the Carolina frontier urged whites to put aside their differences and unite against the threat of Indians. "There is an External Enemy near at Hand," he warned. "These are our *Indian* Neighbours. Common Prudence, and our Common Security, requires that We should live like Brethren in Unity, be it only to guard against any Dangers to our Lives and Properties as may arise from that Quarter" (Hooker 1953, 131, 93). In short, U.S. national identity was deeply rooted in white racialization of Indian savagery, and it was "determined by the white American's juxtaposition (and transposition) with the Native American," who was stereotyped as living in an uncivilized state of backwardness and barbarity (Gomez 1998, 11).

In the sections that follow, I will explore

- impacts of colonial racism and sexism on Cherokee women,
- racial conflict on postrevolutionary Cherokee frontiers,
- Cherokee resistance against white cultural domination, 1820–38, and
- ethnic cleansing of indigenous Appalachians.

Impacts of Colonial Racism and Sexism on Cherokee Women

In 1700, more than 11,000 Cherokees in 30 towns formed buffer zones that separated the British, French, and Spanish settlements in the North American Southeast (see Map 7). By 1710, the Europeans had claimed political preeminence over indigenous Appalachians and their territory, had secured indigenous markets for their trade commodities, and had transferred into indigenous villages a white settler class to supervise export production. Within less than 50 years, the Cherokees lost much of their economic and political autonomy and became dependent upon the commodities they obtained through trade with Europeans (Dunaway 1994b, 230–31). When colonists arrived, the Cherokees practiced a communal mode of sedentary agriculture, supplemented by hunting, fishing, and gathering. They "conceived of men and women as two radically different forms of humanity, and they consequently assigned to them contrasting roles in subsistence activities." Spring ground clearing and crop planting was the only major female-dominated activity in which Cherokee males were expected to assist (Hudson 1976, 258–59).

In addition to fishing and winter hunts, Cherokee males constructed and maintained village buildings, made and repaired tools, engaged in warfare and village protection against intruders, conducted the training of village boys, led rituals, and acted as village conjurers, priests, historians, and politicians. However, Cherokee communities depended heavily upon the economic production of women (Hudson 1976, 264–67). European travelers sang the praises of Cherokee females, who produced nearly one-third acre of corn per capita so that villages "abounded in every comfort of life" (Grant 1933, 38). In addition to their agricultural production, women gathered wood and tended fires; sewed clothing; collected wild berries, nuts, and herbs; filled the public granaries with emergency food supplies; preserved fruits, vegetables, and meats; organized meals for village ceremonies; cared for the ill; made baskets and other household items; and did all the work necessary to rear children and run households (*South Carolina Gazette*, 26 Oct. 1760; Williams 1927, 58; Fogelson 1990, 163). From scaffolds in the midst of their corn crops, older women and teenage

MAP 7. Rivalry for the Appalachians during the Colonial Period. English trading paths shown by dotted lines connected indigenous groups to four British coastal colonies. *Source:* Swanton (1946, 6–7, 430–31).

girls guarded the fields against birds and rodents. Even in the late eighteenth century, Adair observed that it was "a very rare thing to pass by those fields, without seeing them there at watch" (Adair 1775, 401, 408).

Gendered Impacts of the International Fur Trade

As trade dependency deepened between 1720 and 1750, villages attempted to meet debt obligations for European commodities by expanding deerskin exports. Consequently, the Cherokee economy was transformed into a *putting-out system* that required the redistribution of much of the village's collective labor to the fur trade. In a system that parallels sharecropping, traders advanced imported goods against the annual output of skins (Dunaway 1994b, 229). For example, a gun was priced at 30 dressed skins, a blanket at 14, a pistol at 20 (McDowell 1955, 104). Consequently, the Cherokees became "perennial debtors to the traders who staked them in their winter hunts" (Corkran 1962, 6). As households were reorganized around export activities, communal labor

FIGURE 4. From scaffolds in the midst of their corn crops, older women and teenage girls guarded the fields against birds and rodents. Their distance from the village made them especially vulnerable to slave raids and war parties. *Source:* Schoolcraft (1851–57, 3: 62).

arrangements were replaced by a new gender bifurcation of tasks. Men were exclusively engaged in export and diplomacy activities, leaving women responsible for most of the subsistence production (Adair 1775, 228).

This new division of labor disrupted production of survival essentials and intensified Cherokee reliance on expensive British commodities. As villages became dependent upon European imports purchased with male-controlled skins, women's workload intensified. Because hunting, external trade/diplomacy, and warfare occurred year-round, those activities siphoned Cherokee males away from the seasonal rhythm of subsistence production (Mooney 1900, 38–45). In addition to commercial hunting, males were employed to build European forts, to engage in slave raids, and to transport goods for traders (McDowell 1955, 272; McDowell 1958–72, 1: 195). The new emphasis upon hunting and warfare also necessitated greater male labor time for the production of weapons and canoes (Dunaway 1994b, 233). No longer were men periodically summoned to assist the females with spring planting. By the mid-1700s, British observers reported that the Cherokee "women alone do all the laborious tasks of agriculture" (Williams 1927, 68). Females also assumed greater responsibility for the village *gadugi*, a labor gang that tended the fields and garden lots of elderly or infirm members of the village (Fogelson and Kutsche 1961, 95). By the late 1700s, females also assisted with male fishing. The women scattered over the water their fermented concoction of horse chestnuts and roots. Once the fish were "inebriated" and floating on the surface, the males swam under water, "with their net stretched open." Simultaneously, "the women [we]re fishing ashore with coarse baskets, to catch the fish that escape[d] the nets" (Adair 1775, 424, 403–5).

In addition to their increased responsibility for subsistence production, Cherokee women became the invisible laborers of the deerskin trade. In the 1730s when males increased their annual deer kills, women joined the communal "fire surrounds." Nearly 300 people formed a three- to five-mile circle of moving fire to force deer into a smaller area where men could shoot greater numbers. Between November and March, women often accompanied men on hunts that might range as far as 300 miles from home villages (McDowell 1955, 104). Before horses were imported, women "travell[ed] fifteen or twenty miles a day . . . each woman carrying at least sixty and sometimes eighty weight at their back" (Catesby 1974, 1: ix). Females processed the hides to meet the stringent standards of the British Trade Commission. After the men skinned the animals and dressed the skins in a preliminary fashion, women removed the "Hoofs and Snouts, so detrimental to the leather" (McDowell 1958–72, 3: 586–87). The next female task "was to remove all the remaining flesh from the skin and dry it in the sun. Then they punched holes all around the skin and immersed it in water for two or three days. After this it was wrung dry and hung over an inclined log and all the hair was scraped off with a piece of flint set into the notched end of a stick" (Hudson 1976, 266–76).

During the second stage, women allocated more than a week's labor to tanning. After they soaked the skin in a mixture of water and pulverized deer brains, women pounded the skin to soften it and stretched it on a frame to dry again. Still female inputs were not complete. In the final stages, they smoked the hides over a shallow pit and repeatedly aired and checked them for maggots and mold (Hudson 1976, 266). Judging from the tedious work regimen that indigenous women followed to prepare skins for export to the Europeans, male hunting and killing required far less labor time than did female processing of the skins into exports that fueled British leather manufacturing. At the peak of the Charleston fur trade, Cherokee males were marketing 255,000 skins per year (Dunaway 1994b). Thus, village women must have invested more than one million labor hours annually to subsidize male export production.

Gender Bifurcation of Trade

During the late seventeenth century, women had engaged freely in long-distance trade between the Cherokees and other indigenous groups, and their exchanges of food, clothing, and decorative items were just as valued as male commodities (Hudson 1976). By 1720, the international fur trade stimulated a bifurcated system in which men dominated exchanges and diplomacy with Europeans while women's trade in crafts and agricultural produce was marginalized, eventually prohibited. Pushed out of the formalized export trade, Cherokee women marketed commodities they produced as an extension of their subsistence household duties. Through informal exchanges not regulated by the Charleston Trade Commission, they hawked their produce and crafts to whites. Cherokee women

FIGURE 5. As trade dependency deepened, the labor time of Cherokee women was redi-
rected to processing of deer skins for export. Here the woman is scraping the skin to
prepare it for drying in the sun. Notice the child in the cradleboard. *Source:* Library of
Congress.

peddled agricultural commodities in such numbers that British forts periodically had "the Appearance of a Market" (McDowell 1958–72, 2: 218, 121).
They were often described in military correspondence as cautious, shrewd bar-
gainers who sold only small surpluses. Because village survival depended on
their output, women placed high value on their food commodities. When forts
experienced shortages, they sold corn at such inflated prices that British officers reported they "could not afford it" (McDowell 1958–72, 3: 119, 301, 341,
344). In one instance, the Fort Loudon commandant reported to the British
Trade Commission that Cherokee women had begun "to grow very saving of
their corn" because they feared that the drought of the previous year might

be repeated in the next growing season. Once the women secured the needed supply of salt, they "immediately ceased to bring any more corn" (Adair 1775, 230). However, they were much less reluctant to dispose of chickens and hogs, which had been raised for marketing to Europeans (Smith 1987, 29–39).

In addition to their exchanges with nearby forts, Cherokee women traveled to European coastal settlements to market herbs and household crafts. Door to door and along the streets, females peddled ginseng, Indian pink, snakeroot, "very handsome carpets," turkey feather blankets, and colorful pottery (Carroll 1836, 2: 482; Bartram 1792, 53). Because the artisans modified indigenous designs to suit the tastes of their customers, Cherokee baskets were "highly esteemed" by British women "for domestic usefulness, beauty, and skilful variety." Unlike utilitarian containers, trade baskets had lids and were double-woven in nests of 8 or 10, each dyed and patterned "with a beautiful variety of pleasing figures" (Adair 1775, 388, 424–25; Hill 1996).

Lacking the status that Europeans assigned to male deerskins, female commodities were exchanged outside the networks of regulated trade. In an attempt to control Cherokee women, Europeans began to restrict their marketing. British commissioners prohibited traders from accepting women's baskets, pottery, and mats because these items were sold cheaper than manufactures imported from England (Sellers 1934, 121). When one village trader petitioned for permission to sell Cherokee baskets in Charleston, the commissioners rejected his plan, noting that "such a License w[ould] infringe the Trade" in imported manufactures. By the 1730s, the British had established a pass system to decrease the peddling by women in the streets of Charleston and Savannah (McDowell 1955, 126–28, 132, 201). Because outlying Virginia and Carolina forts were dependent on Cherokee women for foodstuffs, soldiers were permitted to continue their informal purchases (Williams 1927, 91). However, fort garrisons were instructed not to substitute indigenous crafts for manufactured household goods (McDowell 1958–72, 2: 137–39, 150). Because deerskins were essential to the emergent leather industry of western Europe, England prohibited the flow of deerskins from British colonies to any locations except London and Bristol (Dunaway 1994b, 227). In contrast, the trading companies identified many female commodities as economic threats because they competed with European manufactured goods. Consequently, British restrictions on women's informal trade deepened village dependence on the male-dominated fur trade.

The Male Role in Economic Dependency

As the fur trade expanded, Cherokee villages were "deindustrialized" because indigenous crafts were displaced by European commodities. Commercial hunting, population declines, and frequent warfare resulted in lowered production of those agricultural and craft outputs that were essential to the survival of the villages. By the mid-1700s, the British claimed that the Cherokees "by reason of our supplying them so cheap with every sort of goods, have forgotten the chief part of their ancient mechanical skill, so as not to be well able now, at least for some years, to live independent of us" (McDowell 1955, 104; McDowell

1958–72, 1: 255, 3: 344). By 1725, a new generation of young Cherokees had "been brougt up after another Manner than their forefathers," and their head warriors taught them that "they could not live without the English" (Williams 1928, 112, 77–78). Once males terminated their traditional salt manufacturing, Cherokee women were compelled to exchange their precious corn for that expensive import. In addition, Cherokee males broadened their consumption of European commodities. In archaeological digs of Cherokee sites, male luxury goods appear much more often than women's items (Smith 1987). Preparation of body paint disappeared after males began to substitute great quantities of vermillion, a Dutch import priced at 16 dressed deerskins per pound (Smith and Williams 1978). Many males replaced female-produced clothing with "a shirt of the English make" and "a large mantle or match-coat" (Williams 1927, 76–77). Indigenous tobacco was replaced by a West Indian variety (Sellers 1934, 186). To demonstrate their new economic status, many Cherokee males had "vast quantities of all sorts of goods buried with them which [wa]s a great advantage to the merchants of South Carolina" (Longe 1969, 26).

Because consumption of manufactured goods was relatively inelastic, British traders identified a commodity that would be in constant demand. Introduced to Cherokee men by 1700, rum became the trade good that deepened dependency upon deerskin exporting. A bottle of rum was expensively priced at one dressed skin (McDowell 1955, 104). Ironically, that rum had its origins in West Indian molasses that the British secured in exchange for Indian slaves (Rivers 1856: 66–72). Many white traders carried "very little Goods" other than alcohol and frequently cheated Indians out of their entire season of deerskins (Williams 1927, 77). Even though women resisted the alteration of community customs, they could not escape the trade dependency that male economic decisions entailed. Cherokee village debts rapidly ballooned as a result of male rum addiction, horse stealing, and luxury-good consumption (Jacobs 1954, 35).

Debt Peonage and Economic Disempowerment of Women
The average European trading company received a 500 to 600 percent profit on deerskins, yet the Cherokees "roamed the forests almost as employees of a trading system built around the faraway demands of European society" (Corkran 1962, 6). On average between 1699 and 1715, the Cherokees exported to Charleston 54,000 deerskins per year (Williams 1927, 87, 163–64, 76–77; Jacobs 1954, 35; Longe 1969, 26; Salley 1928–47, 1: 188). In 1711, however, the accumulated debt was nearly 100,000 skins per year – almost twice their average output (Crane 1929, 110–12, 165–67). By the 1730s, the British declared the unpaid debts of any individual to be the obligation of the entire Cherokee town, and traders seized assets from the clans of deceased debtors (Logan 1859, 1: 473), making women responsible for male indebtedness. To prevent transfer of matrilineal clan lands to white traders, Cherokee women were forced to provide more labor to male-dominated tasks and to sacrifice accumulated household assets.

Women avoided indebtedness for nonfood household essentials through their craft production and through exchanges in the informal sector. Prior to the fur trade, women had produced pottery, baskets, carpets, mats, and blankets during the winter months. However, those forms of household output diminished, as women increased their allocation of labor to deerskin processing (Adair 1775, 414, 422–25). Subsistence agricultural cultivation also declined once women spent more of their spring months in skin production (Hudson 1976, 266–72). After European traders began raising their own hogs and chickens, Cherokee women no longer could dispose of their surplus poultry and swine. Villages that once marketed surpluses now purchased British foodstuffs "in the time of light crops, [at] an exorbitant price." In short, subsidization of the male-dominated fur trade locked women into an inescapable circle of deepening dependency on imported commodities (Adair 1775, 240).

Expansion and Devaluation of Women's Work

While their workload may have been inequitable, Cherokee women occupied a pivotal position within their traditional communities. Because they produced most of a town's subsistence requirements, women's farming and gathering were just as respected by the community as male meat production (McDowell 1958–72, 1: 45, 3: 321–22). As the international fur/slave trade assumed primacy, Cherokee men gradually reflected European sexism in their devaluation of women's contributions. Because Cherokee household production was not part of the export economy, traditional respect for women's contributions declined. In sharp contrast to women's traditional control over village subsistence resources, men now distributed the imports acquired from trade with the British (McDowell 1955, 127). Despite the crucial role that agriculture and exchanges in the informal sector played in village survival, male devaluation of those forms of women's subsistence production is clear in these remarks of Cherokee chief Skiagonota: "My people cannot live independent of the English. The clothes we wear we cannot make ourselves. They are made for us.... Every necessity of life we have from the white people" (Adair 1775, 422–25).

At the same time that women's household subsistence and production for the informal economy were devalued, women's labor contribution to skin exports was not publicly recognized (Corkran 1962, 101). Still the Cherokee woman was intricately controlled by the village's contract to pay its indebtedness for trade goods (Hudson 1976, 22–27). To produce the deerskins needed, she was expected to become an invisible subsidizer of men's work. Even though women contributed more labor-hours than men to deerskin production, it was the male acts of deer killing and trade diplomacy that received acknowledgment from Europeans (Reid 1977, 66). Because female work contributed to the deer trade the economic contributions of Cherokee women were hidden and devalued in ways that their traditional agricultural inputs had not been. While women maintained control over their agricultural crops and their crafts, they had no similar jurisdiction over the deerskins they helped to produce (French and Hornbuckle 1981, 3–16).

Women's Work and Ecological Degradation

Economic disarticulation between women's subsistence activities and the male-dominated export sector generated serious repercussions for Cherokee villages. The fur trade degraded Appalachian ecosystems (Bartram 1792, 284), worsening the lot of village women and deepening Cherokee dependence on European trade commodities. Greater risk of external attack triggered the movement of Cherokee towns to more mountainous sites that were easier to defend (Adair 1775, 94). In rougher terrain that provided little cropland, females abandoned fields that lay at a distance from their towns. Once they shifted to smaller garden plots inside the villages, women no longer had sufficient acreage to produce adequate supplies of subsistence corn (Grant 1933, 27–30).

As women allocated more time and energy to subsidize the labor of males in commercial hunting, the Cherokees encountered more frequent famines. By 1756, deer populations were so diminished by the fur trade that women's hogs were being substituted for venison in the Cherokee diet (McDowell 1958–72, 2: 264, 118–19, 151). Because villages could now depend upon British corn, pork, and beef to overcome shortages, male leaders neglected the public granaries that were once filled with women's surpluses (Williams 1927, 179–81, 67). Women's workloads were exacerbated by the deforestation caused by annual burning of meadows and wooded areas to facilitate deer hunting (Hudson 1976, 308). Traditionally, women had fueled the village fires with underbrush and dead trees. By 1740, nearby ecosystems were so degraded that females were walking many more miles each day to gather firewood and forest resources for craft production (Adair 1775, 407–10, 416). Deforestation also eliminated several nuts, herbs, roots, fruits, and berries that had supplemented the household diet. Once the number of trees declined near villages, women produced less maple syrup (Williams 1928, 477–78, 490–91).

As villages imported European livestock, female subsistence production directly clashed with new alien species. Women readily adapted to swine and chickens because they could be raised in pens (Bartram 1792, 263–64). However, they resisted large free-ranging herds that could "spoil their open corn fields." By the mid-1700s, Cherokee males were importing large numbers of horses that became a threat to female crops (Adair 1775, 240, 263, 138–39, 406). Women surrounded their garden plots with stakes, but the horses often broke through the fencing, "to the great regret of the women." After an initial warning to the male owner, a woman farmer sometimes "struck a tomahawk into the horse" (Williams 1928, 257).

In addition to risks to crops, hooved livestock endangered the wild flora from which the women gathered household supplies (Bartram 1792, 30–50, 185–87). Because they provided natural materials for craft production, river cane and several inedible berries, barks, and roots had traditionally been sustained and protected by women. Within 20 years of their introduction to the Southern Appalachians, hooved livestock had devastated the dense canebrakes upon which women depended for subsistence production (Williams 1928, 478). Along the borders of the towns, the carefully sustained mulberry trees died by

1730, eliminating the bark that females collected to weave blankets, carpets, aprons, and mats (Jacobs 1954, 49). By the end of the colonial period, the international fur trade and the introduction of European flora and fauna species had dramatically altered the mountain ecosystem in ways that would threaten the survival of Cherokee households in the early decades of the nineteenth century.

Political Disempowerment of Cherokee Women

In the late seventeenth century, the Cherokees were an agglomeration of autonomous villages, without any unifying structure for coordination of all the dispersed settlements. Traditionally, each town was populated by members of seven matrilineal clans, and every individual Cherokee derived his or her political alignment from membership in one of the clans. Prior to trade dependency, men were not preeminent; women had a voice in all village councils. In fact, "the females may have even had the upper hand since males had little say regarding clan regulations and sanctions, while females played an important role on the war council where an assemblage of 'war women'...offered counsel" (Foreman 1954, 7). Thus, matrilineal clans played a key role in town politics, and a seven-member advisory council represented all the divergent interests (Corkran 1962, 22). Although women could not hold office, they exercised authority over the clans (French and Hornbuckle 1981, 7). Married women of childbearing age held a council that nominated candidates for chief and subchief of each clan (Strickland 1975, 26–39). Each matrilineal clan chose a "Beloved Woman" as its leader, and these seven women formed the Women's Council. Headed by the *ghighau*, or "War Woman," the most venerated female in the community, the Women's Council nominated the candidate for town chief (Perdue 1980, 20–21).

Even though colonial officials suppressed indigenous female voices during the writing and preservation of historical documents, there are significant clues that European restrictions constrained the political roles played by Cherokee women. In 1725, a head warrior told Euroamericans that he "was born in another world" when all community members could participate in village decisions (Cherokee Documents, IHA, Talk of Head Warrior of Tunissee 1725). Ten years later, a European traveler (Tambory 1910, 119) reported that women were playing fewer overt political roles in Cherokee life than he had observed only a decade earlier. How did the cultural, economic, and political power of females diminish so dramatically? Articulation with the world system necessitated a political structure that permitted the Europeans to negotiate with the Cherokees as a single corporate entity (Weber 1958, 180, 105–13). On the one hand, it was economically more rational and more efficient to collect trade debts, make treaties, engineer war alliances, and seek reparations from one leader, who was the "Mouth of the Nation" and who could enter into agreements that "should be binding upon him and all the Nation" (McDowell 1955, 188). On the other hand, Europeans could more effectively manipulate a political alliance if the indigenous group coalesced into a nation-state similar to the English model (Hopkins and Wallerstein 1987, 763–66). Thus, the British

pressured the loosely knit Cherokee towns toward secularization and central-
ization of their nonstate political processes. Because of the distance between
settlements, political councils were convened at a regional capitol, establishing
a system through which the Europeans could more easily co-opt a small number
of spokesmen (Gearing 1956, 122). Despite intermittent resistance against such
policies, the Cherokees gradually abandoned their ultrademocratic methods to
operate under more centralized policies and sanctions (Corkran 1962, 212).

As the Europeans strengthened nationalistic requirements in their diplomacy
and trade, female political participation eroded. Since clans were no longer
equitably represented at regional council meetings, women had fewer avenues
through which to advocate their concerns to the entire community (Williams
1927, 60, 89–91). When Cherokee settlements diminished in number from 60
towns in 1715 to 39 towns in 1755 (Thornton 1990, 191), women's positions
within their clans shifted. While males retained their war and trade reputations,
females forfeited any status or political clout they may have held in their old
towns and had to assimilate themselves into their new communities. As the role
of clans and towns narrowed, so did female decision making. Once the British
began to select Cherokee leaders through war commissions or through trade
co-optation of elites, the Women's Council no longer selected the candidates
for town chiefs and participated in public meetings (Adair 1775, 198, 152–53).
As instances of warfare multiplied, so did the British demand for Cherokee
warriors. In the minds of Europeans, however, women should have no place in
decision making about war. In the early 1700s, a few male Cherokees defended
the right of women to participate in such councils; still, the regional government
succumbed to European gender customs (Hudson 1976, 186–87; Corkran 1962,
216). Ultimately, the British imposed their sexist prejudices by excluding women
from their deliberations with Cherokee males (Hamer and Rogers 1972, 3:
279–80). Women were even deprived of the right to determine the fate of war
captives, once males began to sell such unfortunates to the British for slave
exports to the Caribbean (Reid 1977, 67–70; Perdue 1980, 30–31).

In the early eighteenth century, she who controlled essential resources garnered power. Because farming and child rearing were primarily their responsibility, matrilineal clans controlled village lands, the basic means of survival.
Therefore, women participated in early treaty meetings that involved the transfer of Cherokee territory to the British (Hudson 1976, 186). Ultimately, women
surrendered control over their means of production, as males unilaterally ceded
territory to Europeans to settle trading debts. By the mid-1700s, Cherokee men
were transferring lands without the input of women (Palmer 1875–93, 1: 291).
Within little more than 50 years, the British extinguished indigenous claims to
43,872,000 acres, more than half their ancestral lands (DeVorsey 1961, 162–
63). Moreover, the Cherokees relinquished more than half of that territory for
the payment of male luxury debts (e.g., rum) to European traders (Royce 1884,
117–34).

Despite the persistence of matrilineal clans, the political rights of women
were severely curtailed by 1800. Perhaps the most profound evidence of female

disenfranchisement lies in the diminished role of the war woman in the political affairs of Cherokee towns. By the late eighteenth century, Nancy Ward was one of the most influential women in the Cherokee Nation. Unlike previous females who had attained that status through a long history of community service and sacrifices for the public good, Ward achieved this position because she was a member of a wealthy ethnically mixed household. The offspring of a Scottish trader, she was tied by lineage to Attakullaculla, one of the six Cherokee chiefs who had been part of the 1730 entourage taken to England to execute a treaty with King George. As a member of the acculturated mestizo elite, Ward pressured the Cherokees to accept Euroamerican government customs, trade laws, technology, livestock, and imports.[1] Her value lay in her ability to speak English and to interact with Euroamericans in ways that traditional Cherokees could not (Woodward 1963, 81). However, she was not an effective cultural broker in the opposite direction. On the one hand, Ward engaged in treasonous acts that cost Cherokee lives and destroyed villages. According to Mooney (1900, 203–4, 490), "she distinguished herself by her constant friendship" with white settlers, to whom she "frequently g[a]v[e] timely warning of projected Indian raids." After receiving her advance intelligence, white militias "marched against the Indians, whom they met and defeated with signal loss." When Ward's relatives were captured, the whites treated them "with the consideration due in return for her good offices" (SOW Letters, NA, 25 July 1818). On the other hand, she assumed a subservient tone when dealing with white officials, she adhered to European gender norms that weakened the political role of the war woman, and ultimately she met white demands to disband the Women's Council. Most importantly, she was not able to intervene successfully with whites to prevent land losses.

Two indigenous narratives offer glimpses into the erosion of women's cultural, economic, and political power. Because females were excluded from the negotiations, War Woman Nancy Ward sent a 1781 "written talk" to U.S. treaty commissioners who were seeking Cherokee land cessions. Clearly showing that she recognized her violation of Euroamerican gender norms (Block 1978) through her overt political participation, she apologized by saying, "You know that women are always looked upon as nothing," assuming a deferential tone that would not have characterized the status of previous generations of *ghighau*. Like southern white females, Ward appealed to the centrality of reproductive and household roles when she reminded Cherokee male negotiators, "we are your mothers; you are our sons" (CIAT Reports, NA, July 1781, 2 May 1817). There is nothing in her tone or her words that recalls female leadership of clans or women's traditional right to speak in public meetings. Thirty-six years later, the war woman authored another document in which she emphasized elements of white separate spheres conventions that did not accurately

---

[1] Rather than use the racist terms *full-blood* and *half-blood* that typify far too much research about Indians, I will employ the terms *mestizo* (to refer to part-white Cherokees) and *traditional* (to refer to those who sought to preserve Cherokee culture and political organizations).

describe the economic roles of Cherokee females. Showing her acquiescence to male control over work and farmlands that had once been the women's sphere, she instructed the men to "enlarge [thei]r farms and cultivate and raise corn and cotton" while females would "make clothing" for their families using the spinning wheels and looms offered by the U.S. government. In addition to losing their agricultural predominance, matrilineal clans relinquished authority over communal lands. "Take pity and listen to the talks of your sisters," the war woman pleaded. In sharp contrast to the worldview of her female ancestors, she stated a colonial myth in the fashion of an unwelcome *subaltern*. "Never before," she erroneously stated, had wives and mothers "thought it [thei]r duty to interfere" in decision making about Cherokee lands (SOW Letters, NA, 6 May 1817).

Racial Conflict on Postrevolutionary Cherokee Frontiers

By the end of the eighteenth century, the global demand for deerskins had plummeted (Wallerstein 1989, 76–78). As a result, the Cherokees "c[ould] not dispose of their furs and skins to advantage" (Weeks 1916, 360). Moreover, Cherokee towns were devastated by the Revolutionary War, household wealth was destroyed or confiscated, and villages had been depopulated by high mortality from warfare, famine, and a 1783 smallpox epidemic (CIAT Reports, NA, 7 Dec. 1801, 21 June 1811, 17 Feb. 1816). The international fur trade and the establishment of Euroamerican farms and settlements had altered the mountain ecosystem, and Cherokee villages were in deep debt. Free-ranging hooved livestock, deforestation, and the introduction of alien species had extinguished the canebrakes from which women gathered resources for household subsistence. Worse, the forests near indigenous settlements were "almost depopulated" of deer and other game, leaving only "heaps of white gnawed bones" (Bartram 1792, 263–64, 185–87, 283). In the face of a shifting world economy and a degraded ecosystem, "their hunting [wa]s fast failing them" (Adair 1775, 388, 424).

The Declaration of Independence defined the only legitimate inhabitants of U.S. frontiers to be white Euroamericans who must be protected from the "merciless Indian savages" (Morris 1976, 565). Given that racist foundation, it is not surprising that white encroachment on Cherokee territory was the major point of friction on the Southern Appalachian frontiers after the Revolutionary War (see Map 8). Indians engaged in the futile strategy of trying to instill so much fear that settlers would stop emigrating. For example, the *Knoxville Gazette* (15 June 1794) reported 71 killed and scalped, 1 wounded, and 16 missing, presumed captured," after Indian raids in east Tennessee. Still in 1796, Indian agent Benjamin Hawkins recorded that Cherokees understood that "the encroachment[s] of the whites were constantly going against them, notwithstanding their treaties" (Weeks 1916, 24). Old Tassel complained to the Tennessee governor, "Your people from Nollichucky are daily pushing us

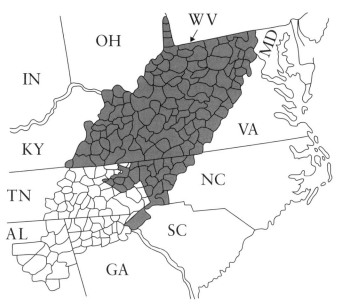

MAP 8. The Southern Appalachian Settler Frontier in 1790. Indians had ceded gray areas to white settlers. The Cherokees still controlled Appalachian land area in white. *Source:* Thorndale and Dollarhide (1987, 11, 79, 122, 152, 245, 297, 314, 349, 367). 1860 Appalachian county boundaries are shown.

out of our lands. We have no place to hunt on. Your people have built houses within one day's walk of our towns.... Our older brother promised to have the line run between us agreeable to the first treaty, and all that should be found over the line should be moved off. But [this] is not done yet" (Richter 2001, 271).

Between 1790 and 1838, emigrants consistently ignored treaty boundary lines. Many of the settlers were the desperately poor, such as 16 northern Alabama squatter households who lived in "small huts, some so recently made as not to have any cleared lands about them." In northern Georgia, "upwards of 50 families settled over the lines," and between Tellico and Knoxville the Indian agents "passed five small settlements" (Weeks 1916, 148–54, 287, 294). In the Coosa Valley, five white families built cabins and fences and planted crops. Obviously aware that it was the state's political intent to deal lightly with such squatters, the Georgia Indian agent queried the governor whether he should "drive them of[f] or take Rent or Let them Stay till they gither their Crops." In a long-running dispute, George Waters contended that for more than five years white squatters cleared and cultivated sections of his Cherokee land and foraged cattle that damaged his crops. Ultimately, the Georgia legislature ruled that Waters must permit the squatters to rent (Cuyler Papers, UGA, 25 June 1833, 23 Jan. 1832, 31 Jan. 1832). Given the laxity of state policies and the sympathy of troops for whites, such intrusions occurred repeatedly. Moreover, the growing squatter populations became the rationale employed by national and state governments to demand more land cessions from the "threatening" Indians (Richter 2001, 226).

Emigrants were openly hostile to federal treaties with the Cherokees, and they aggressively ignored the legal boundary lines to establish farms and plantations on Indian lands. When future French king Louis-Philippe visited east Tennessee in 1797, he reported that tensions were high because of impending military eviction of squatters. For example, Judge Campbell held a North Carolina deed for Indian lands outside Knoxville upon which he had established a sizable plantation. However, "the state's interpretation of the border treaty differed from the federal government's current version." At the time of this visit, "the colonists [we]re about to be expelled," but they were counting on a massive war that would result in annihilation or removal of the Indians. The emigrants thought their status as trespassers was "only a temporary hardship, and that after the first Indian war their property w[ould] be restored." The Campbell farm was not unusual, for well-to-do squatters were sure enough that they would not be permanently evicted that they had established "seven or eight very fine plantations and one mill" along the Tennessee River. As Louis-Philippe traveled farther south, he learned from Cherokees that "the last treaty ha[d] aroused serious discontent among the whites, who would like a war with Indians so a new treaty c[ould] strip them of the coveted lands" (Becker 1977, 99).

Absentee planters established illegal farms and mills by moving slaves and white tenants onto Indian lands. In southeast Tennessee and northern Alabama, for instance, three such slaveholding families had moved onto Indian land "and brought thirteen tenants with them." Settlers also frequently encroached on Indian territory to hunt, to fish, and to forage livestock. In 1797, Cherokee territory along the Little Tennessee River in the Smoky Mountains was "thickly settled" by white squatters raising vast herds of cattle. Five years later, the Indian agent reported again that the military had not removed whites who were illegally keeping "a great quantity of cattle on Little River." When their livestock disappeared, squatters blamed the Cherokees for "stealing" them and sent raiding parties to retaliate against Indian settlements. When they went searching for stray animals, it was not unusual for whites to shoot the first Indians they encountered (Weeks 1916, 459–60, 314). One Indian chief complained about such violence, telling the Indian agent that whites "cannot be restrained well; they do not understand stipulations" (Cuyler Papers, UGA, 13 May 1832).

As settler greed for land intensified after 1790, newspaper and fictional accounts became overtly racist and bloodthirsty. Even though only a tiny number of women were physically assaulted or captured, rumors of rape were common. An examination of all 1790s issues of eight newspapers in North Carolina, Georgia, Tennessee, and South Carolina uncovered only one account of contact between Indians and white women, and the outcome belied the racial

FIGURE 6. A member of Louis-Philippe's entourage painted this Cherokee village of 8 or 10 houses located near the Tellico Block House in 1797. The circular structure was the thatched town house, which was covered with reeds and corn husks. According to Louis-Philippe (Becker 1977, 83), Indian dwellings looked "very much like all the houses of the poor" in the area. *Source:* Library of Congress.

demonizing that typified settler attitudes at the time.[2] The *Knoxville Gazette* (19 Nov. 1791) reported that "a company going thro' the wilderness to Cumberland, was met on the road by a party of Indians. Upon first sight, the men (being seven in number) rode off with utmost precipitation, and left the women (four in number) who were so terrified they were unable to proceed. The Indians came up, shook hands, and told them they should not be hurt, made a fire for them." Between 1790 and 1800, most of the so-called Cherokee depredations amounted to no more than white claims about stolen property or to vague language describing emigrants as having felt "threatened." After "two Indians came in and stole two hoarses," western North Carolina settlers began "an advancing Campaign against the Cherokee Nation." When the thieves returned the stolen livestock, the owners "put the Indians to death and scalpt them." Subsequently, the Indians "kil'd and Skilp'd two men for satisfaction." Immediately, "the inhabetints of Buncome County ... apply'd to [the Governor] for the Priviledge to drive them out of the state" (Newsome 1934, 311). Old Tassel

[2] At the Library of Congress, I reviewed all 1790s issues of the *Knoxville Gazette*, the *Tennessee Gazette*, the *State Gazette of North Carolina*, the *North Carolina Minerva and Raleigh Advertiser*, the *North Carolina Gazette*, the *South Carolina Gazette*, the *Augusta Herald*, and the *Georgia State Gazette*.

captured the impossible position in which Cherokees found themselves when he told the Indian agent that whites "kill our game; but it is [treated by whites as] very criminal in our young men if they chance to kill a cow or a hog for their sustenance when they happen to be in your lands" (Brown 1938, 166–67).

Even if there were some sympathetic whites on the frontier, racial hatred and demonization of the Cherokees predominated. Contemporaries thought there was a significant disparity in racial attitudes among settlers in different sections of the Appalachian frontier, animosities running highest among whites in Alabama and Georgia, where Cherokees still held the most territory (Scott 1864, 1: 318). Between 1790 and 1820, the number of Cherokee deaths from interethnic conflict far exceeded the number of white deaths (Thornton 1990, 77–81). Thus, there is more documentation of white mistreatment of Cherokee women than can be found to verify rumors about Indian assaults on white women. In 1777, the Georgia legislature began to offer land grants to whites who would illegally settle near Cherokee territory in the northern part of the state. One newspaper advertisement offered settlers the safety of "two battalions of minutemen" and "500 acres for every head of a family and 50 acres for every white person or Negro (up to 10) belonging to that head" (Bacot 1923, 687–88). One Cherokee woman described the tensions and assaults that followed the influx of whites. She was poor, she said, "not from want of industry," but because her town had been attacked several times by whites (Weeks 1916, 18).

Settlers were preoccupied with fears of Indian raids, and they made no distinctions when they retaliated. In 1788, the North Carolina governor addressed a strong warning "to the people living on Nolechucky, French-Broad and Holstein," protesting their murders of peaceful Indians, including women and children (*Knoxville Gazette*, 24 Nov. 1777, 15 June 1793). Settlers also attacked friendly parties of Indians on the roads, and the victims were disproportionately women. In August 1801, for instance, there was "a most wicked and barbarous murder, perpetrated on Stock Creek, in Knox County, on the body of an Indian woman who was with her young child and part of her family on her way to Knoxville seeking a market for the products of her industry" (Weeks 1916, 366). States relied on unregulated and poorly trained militias that acted more like lynch mobs than peacekeepers. Convinced that "the people of the frontiers...[would] never find a man guilty of murder for killing an Indian," a local militia that called itself the "Augusta Boys" killed a group of traveling Cherokees near Staunton, Virginia (Hamilton 1921–62, 5: 737). While Cherokee males were away in 1814 to help the U.S. Army put down a Creek rebellion, local militias plundered Cherokee villages. The commander of the federal Hiwassee Garrison complained to the secretary of war that Tennessee militias had engaged in "wanton marauding & depredations" through Cherokee settlements because so many whites "would rejoice to have some pretext to drive them off their lands" (Allen Papers, UTK, 5 May 1814).

Tensions were exacerbated by three types of opportunistic white males. Some settled illegally near Indian settlements in order to trade, and their price gouging triggered racial conflict. Benjamin Hawkins described ruthless northern Georgia whites who took advantage of shortages in villages that had not recovered from the Revolutionary War. Cherokee women were charged two of their scarce chickens for "2½ yards of binding worth 2 cents, a bushel of corn for a quart of salt and sometimes a pint." One woman exchanged "a bushel and a half of chestnuts" for "a used petticoat" (Weeks 1916, 35–36). Because white transients trafficked in liquor, the Cherokee National Council attempted to regulate the sale of alcohol (*Laws* 1852, 6–7). In 1803, the Georgia commissioners to the Cherokees expressed concern that "there are Numbers of white people in the Nation who . . . Carry on a Triffling Commerce with them and are averse to any further, or better understanding between whites and Indians" (Georgia Commissioners, GSA, Jan. 1803). Hawkins blamed most of the livestock disappearances in Cherokee territory on unscrupulous white males who had "reduced the stealing of horses to a system." This practice was "so deep-rooted," he reported, "that it would require much exertion and some severity to put an end to it" (Weeks 1916, 366). On the one hand, whites benefited from stealing and exporting Indian livestock. On the other hand, Indian settlements were repeatedly destroyed by militiamen who accused Cherokees of rustling settler cattle and horses (Lowrie and Clarke 1832, 1: 655).

Cherokee Resistance against White Cultural Domination, 1820–1838

The intent of the federal civilization program was to acculturate Cherokees "to the habits and manners of civilized life" by replacing their cultural traditions with gender-bifurcated work and family patterns. "The best informed and more intelligent" mestizos may have been "very favorably disposed" toward the schools, as the missionaries claimed. However, most Cherokee women were "extremely jealous of their customs" (Brainerd Journal, HUL, 29 May 1822, 15 Mar. 1830). They resisted white and mestizo pressures for cultural change, and they mounted aggressive and continuous opposition to missionaries (CIAT Reports, NA, 6 June 1806). Even though student enrollments doubled between 1809 and 1828, no more than 3.2 percent of Cherokee children ever attended mission boarding schools in 1828 (McLoughlin 1986, 378–79). One student drew a sharp distinction between Cherokee families. A few who had "large plantations and a great number of cattle" accepted Christianity and enrolled their children in schools. However, most "live[d] miserably" and "d[id]n't send their children to school" (Payne Papers, NLC, 8: 58). Because mothers and children resented the denigration of their indigenous dialect, missionaries were successful at teaching English to only about one-third of their students (BFMB Papers, ABH, 27 Mar. 1827, 4 Feb. 1828). Little wonder that only a small minority of the Nation's population was literate in English (McLoughlin and Conser 1977, 693–94), but many could read and write in the Cherokee dialect. By 1825, Sequoyah's new Cherokee syllabary was "spreading through the nation like fire among the leaves." Missionary Samuel A. Worcester observed that Cherokees "have but to learn their alphabet, and they can read at once" (ABCFM Papers,

ABH, 8 Aug. 1824). Through "only a few hours of instruction," women taught children, young adults, and elderly people to read and write Cherokee so that, by 1828, "one-half of all the Cherokees c[ould] read in the new character" (Chamberlain Journal, HUL 25 Jan. 1825). Between 1810 and 1827, women's resistance was heightened by the enactment of 97 national laws that eroded the traditional rights of matrilineal clans and of wives. Women blamed missionaries for influencing mestizo leaders to implement such regulations, and their antimission sentiment fueled a second cultural revitalization movement. After 1820, Cherokee women grew increasingly alarmed about land allocations for white churches and schools (McLoughlin 1984b, 109–23, 180–212), so they circulated "false tales of almost every description . . . against missionary operations" (Brainerd Journal, HUL, 11 Feb. 1823, 2 Aug. 1821). Because of public antagonism, the National Council more closely regulated mission expansions and required missionaries to obtain approval before adding new personnel (ABCFM Papers, HUL, 3 Jan. 1822, 9 May 1822, 11 June 1823, 22 Jan. 1823, 11 Aug. 1824, 6 Nov. 1824).

After 1822, missionaries prioritized "evangelical labors," so they expanded their itinerant preaching circuits into more sections of the Nation. In their camp meetings and church services, the missionaries intensified their public assaults on conjuring and annual dances. White preachers contended that communion wine should replace "the black physic," a ceremonial drink that had been traditionally brewed by females. In the tradition of Cherokee "hospitality," one was expected to provide food and shelter to any stranger or traveler who approached one's home (Adair 1775, 107). While Cherokees viewed such resource sharing as a necessary human courtesy, Euroamericans considered this custom to be unwanted begging by trespassers. Consequently, missions began to refuse food to women and children who came to their doors and to preach against this Cherokee ethic (ABCFM Papers, HUL, 11 June 1823, 11 Dec. 1827, 26 May 1824, 13 Sept. 1826, 5 June 1828, 11 Dec. 1827, 26 April 1824, 20 June 1824, 20 Aug. 1824, 18 Sept. 1824, 24 Oct. 1824, 25 Apr. 1825). Because missionaries threatened these traditional customs that were pivotal to women's lives, females organized public expressions of defiance. The missionaries reported frequent incidents in which women and teenagers "on the outskirts of the congregation were inclined to make disturbances." As a nonviolent demonstration, a crowd of women and boys "assembled in plain sight of the Mission House"; the young males "stripped themselves entirely naked, and for a time played Ball" (CM Papers, MA, 5 June 1827). When the Brainerd Mission determined in 1824 to stop feeding strangers, "all their members except 4 persons," two-thirds of whom were women, "turned to the Methodists" (Butrick Journal, HUL, 5 May 1825).

However, it may have been the missionary attacks on conjuring that generated the most intense female animosity and the most frequent organized resistance. By the 1820s, half or more of the conjurers were women, and this professional skill provided them income, influence, and standing in their communities. At Willstown, a missionary encountered a woman convert who "had been in the habit of doctoring in the Cherokee manner." The preacher probably did not comprehend the woman's confusion and disdain when he "told her it was very good for her to administer medicine to the sick, but it was not good to use the art of conjuring" (ABCFM Papers, HUL, 28 Nov. 1828). One 90-year-old woman, who "had for years been a conjuress," presented herself for baptism, only to be rejected by the missionary because "she expressed unwillingness to renounce conjuring" (Chamberlain Journal, HUL, 29 June 1822). In one five-year period, two-fifths of the converts near the town of Etowah were "excluded from membership" for returning to Cherokee traditions like the Green Corn Ceremony and reliance on conjurors to treat illnesses (CM Papers, MA, 26 May 1824; Butrick Journal, HUL, 3 Aug. 1829).

The missionaries viewed Cherokee conjuring as "purely heathen," and their sermons on the topic generated more popular protest than any other "heathen evil" they addressed. Most Cherokees, including converts, "in all their wants applied only to their conjurors." Perhaps that was why preachers began to seek out conjurors for public confrontations about religion, the origins of the earth, rainmaking, and healing. Conjurors engaged in direct debates, one traveling "50 miles to urge the people to hold on in their old ways" (ABCFM Papers, HUL, 19 Nov. 1818, 28 July 1827, 6 May 1828, 8 Sept. 1830, 11 Dec. 1827, 31 Aug. 1821, 3 Sept. 1824, 8 Nov. 1824, 13 Sept. 1826). Women and their teenage children heckled meetings where preachers condemned conjuring and rainmaking (BFMB Papers, ABH, 11 Dec. 1830, 1 Apr. 1828). Reverend Daniel Butrick reported that females "were very much dissatisfied on account of the sermons [he] preached on conjuring, rain-making, etc." His assaults on "idleness, sabbath-breaking, and especially conjuring, and [his] determined public opposition to them, ha[d] excited" intense antagonism. During his sermons, women began to taunt him with remarks about his ignorance of the healing arts. When Butrick decided "publicly to reprove and instruct" conjurors and members who consulted them, "the whole church" (three-quarters of them women) "forsook" him (Butrick Journal, HUL, 8 Sept. 1830, 6 May 1828, 28 Nov. 1828, 8 Sept. 1830, 28 July 1827). Because of their animosity toward missionary ethnocentrism, women conjurors kept Cherokee cultural resistance simmering (CM Papers, MA, 16 May 1827).

Ethnic Cleansing and Depopulation of Indigenous Appalachians

Even though Indian agents claimed that their aim was to "better the condition of the tawny and oppressed daughters of the woods," their true intent was to emasculate and to tame male hunter-warriors in order to speed land cessions to whites. As Indian agent Benjamin Hawkins traveled through northern Georgia and northern Alabama in the late 1790s, he repeatedly criticized the absence of Cherokee males from their families. Because of ecological degradation and game scarcity near their villages, the men spent several months hunting along the Duck River in middle Tennessee and as far west as the Mississippi Valley, often "gone into the woods and not expected to return till from the first of March to the beginning of September." Hawkins was alarmed to find some families in which teenage girls were tending children because mothers had accompanied their husbands on these long-distance hunts. While "the men were all in the woods hunting," women and children were left alone to face white assaults and to produce items to fulfill household survival needs (Weeks 1916, 19–20, 23, 31, 241). Because Cherokee men were still following such hunting practices a decade later, Indian agents were growing increasingly impatient. Jonathan Meigs thought the government should immediately claim Cherokee territory along the Duck River because males were using this area for hunting and other "Savage habits" that "opporate[d] against civilization" (CIAT Reports, NA,13 Feb. 1805).

There were two elements to federal policy that were meant to expedite Cherokee land cessions between 1798 and 1820. Even though the civilization program aimed to acculturate males away from hunting, the U.S. government established "fur factors" at Tellico and Hiwassee (Harmon 1932, 138–45). In 1800, the secretary of war explained the rationale for a strategy that contradicted "civilizing" goals. "Were the Indians to become indebted for goods furnished by the trading houses," he informed Congress, "the United States must sooner or later be reimbursed therefore by a cession of land equivalent to the debt" (Henri 1986, 112). In 1803, President Thomas Jefferson reiterated this hidden agenda when he wrote, "I would be glad to see the good and influential individuals among [the Indians] run into debt, because we would observe that when these debts get beyond what the individual can pay, they become willing to lop them off by a cession of lands" (Sheehan 1973, 171). The second element of federal policy was meant to emasculate males by acculturating their women into agrarian capitalist activities that were more profitable than male hunting. In 1798 Benjamin Hawkins was convinced that a few years would "transmogrify" hunters into farmers. "When the females are able to cloathe themselves by their own industry," he wrote, "it will render them independent of the hunter, who in turn will be obliged to handle the ax & the plough, and assist the women in the laborious tasks of the field, or have no wife." In a rare interview with a northern journalist, Hawkins delineated the gender dynamics of his approach. Underlying his plan was the racist stereotype that it was nearly impossible to "overcom[e] the aversion of the men to labor. Inured alternately to hunting, indolence and war, they threw all the toil of domestic affairs, the carrying of burthens and the drudgery of life upon their females." To speed male acculturation, he advised females "to refuse favors to their sweethearts" and to "repel the caresses of their husbands," until the men agreed to "assist them in their daily labors" (Mitchill 1818, 360). Drawing a direct connection between future land acquisition and these civilization policies, Hawkins claimed to the secretary of war, "We believe that a few years perseverance in the beneficent plan . . . will prepare them to accommodate their white neighbors with lands on reasonable terms" (Weeks 1916, 383–85, 478). In 1806, Cherokees did, indeed, "accommodate their white neighbors." In two transactions negotiated by only a handful of males, the Indians ceded 9.6 million acres of hunting grounds for a federal payment of $10,000 (Mitchell and Groves 1987, 164). The two sales never benefited the majority of Cherokees, for the proceeds were mostly consumed to pay trader debts (McLoughlin 1984a, 17–18, 58–60).

Depopulation of Appalachia's indigenous people occurred through the spread of European diseases, warfare, enslavement, and the impacts of ecological degradation. By 1761, Cherokees numbered only one-tenth of the size of their village populations in 1685 (Thornton 1990, 21, 29–30). As white settlers populated surrounding areas, Cherokee women and children were enslaved in several ways. Quite often, surviving Cherokees were enslaved after frontier skirmishes with whites. For instance, Milton Starr's Cherokee mother was taken in an Indian raid in Tennessee and sold into slavery. Chaney Mack's mother "wuz a pureblood Indian" who had been born near Lookout Mountain in southeast Tennessee. "De white people wuz trying to drive dem out and in an uprising wid de whites, all [her] mother's folks wuz killed but her." So the army officers took the young girl and "give her" to a local white slaveholder. After 1793 "depredations by Indians" in Wear's Cove, white militiamen discovered several trails in the mountains "which at last terminated in one plain, beaten path, leading to Tallassee," a Cherokee village. Along that trail the whites overtook and killed a party of Indians, except for "4 squaws," who were subsequently advertized for sale as slaves (*North Carolina Gazette*, 14 Sept. 1793). Near Lookout Mountain, Tennessee, in 1797, "the whites assassinated two Indians (one a chief called Red Bird), hoping that the provocation would lead to reprisals [from the Cherokees] and trigger a war." After her family was killed, one of the children, Sarah Red Bird, "a pureblood Indian," was sold to a Mississippi slaveholder (Rawick 1977, 9: 1419–20).

Adjacent Indian groups sometimes sold Cherokee war captives to white slaveholders, and poor whites dabbled in the human export business by kidnapping free persons. Such violent slave trafficking occurred frequently enough that regional newspapers coined the term "blackbirding" to refer to such cases. Lottie Beck's Cherokee father was stolen "when he was about eight or nine year old from his folks in Georgia." Cherokees of mixed-Negro heritage were also captured for profiteering, as was the case with one extended family that was kidnapped from their western Carolina village and sold into slavery in Mississippi. In 1808, the Cherokee Council ordered Evans Austill, a nearby white farmer, to release "a woman and her children which you have in your Possession which appears to be one of our own people . . . she is freeborn as any White women – although you have paid for her as a Slave." The third method was the enslavement of Indian offspring of white or ethnically mixed mothers. Even though Maggie Broyles was the daughter of an indentured Irishman and "a full-blood Indian" mother, she was still enslaved. Because she was the part-Cherokee child of a white woman, Katie Harrison was "sold on the block" in Tennessee "as a slave." Because Harriet Miller's father was Cherokee, her white mother sold her to a white slaveholder when she was three years old. After her "half Spanish and half Indian" mother died, a Bradley County, Tennessee, female was raised as a slave by the mistress of the plantation on which

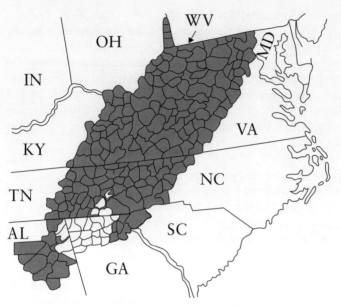

MAP 9. The Southern Appalachian Settler Frontier in 1820. Indians had ceded gray areas to white settlers. The Cherokees still controlled Appalachian land area in white. *Source:* Thorndale and Dollarhide (1987, 13, 82, 125, 153, 248, 299, 317, 352, 370). 1860 Appalachian county boundaries are shown.

her parent had worked (Rawick 1977, 12: 293, 64, 145, 359; Rawick 1979, 1: 68; "Unwritten History," FUA, 199).

After the Revolutionary War, invading white settlers threatened the survival of Cherokee communities, as federal and state governments repeatedly pressured indigenous Appalachians for land cessions. By 1790, Cherokee territory had dwindled to only about one-third of its original size (Foreman 1953, 87–113), and the indigenous group accounted for only 4 percent of the total regional population (see Table 1, Web site). In 1820, Cherokees controlled only a tiny portion of their ancestral lands, and they were surrounded by a rapidly growing Euroamerican population (see Map 9). At that point, fewer than 1 of every 50 Southern Appalachians was indigenous to the region. After the discovery of gold on Cherokee lands in northern Georgia, federal and state pressures for land cessions increased, and vast numbers of whites moved illegally onto Cherokee lands to begin prospecting (Yeates, McCallie, and Kind 1896, 17).

In 1832, the U.S. Army was still only half-heartedly trying to stem the influx of prospectors (Cuyler Papers, UGA, 13 May 1832). The rapid repopulation of areas around and within the Cherokee Nation culminated in the ethnic cleansing from the region of the vast majority of the indigenous population in 1838. The Cherokees were depopulated from 35,000 in 1685 to only a few hundred in

1860. By this point, there were 52 times more African-Americans and 280 times more whites than there were indigenous Appalachians. By the time of the Civil War, an eastern Cherokee could expect to encounter a member of her or his own ethnic group about once in every 67 contacts with western Carolinians, only once in every 333 contacts with east Tennesseans, and only about once in every 500 interactions with Appalachians in Alabama or Georgia (see Table 1, Web site).

White Appalachian prejudices toward Cherokees did not end after the 1838 military removal of a majority of the population. Federal documents reported that most local whites viewed them "as a colored population . . . in a middle position between the negro and the white man" (Pudup et al. 1995, 34–36). Several facets of the small indigenous communities attracted white suspicion. Few Cherokees could speak English, and they retained many traditional clan ties and rituals. Clerics thought it barbaric that Cherokees still relied on conjurors and that there were few Indian weddings "in the white fashion" (Lowrie and Clarke 1832, 2: 274–75) The *New York Times* (15 Mar. 1863) described eastern Cherokees as a "wretched, ignorant, half-civilized offscouring of humanity." Their reported evidence of barbarism was that they were "long-haired, greasy-looking savages who could not even speak a word of English." Community knowledge about past white massacres caused some Cherokee children to be "excessively alarmed" by encounters with Euroamericans, so much so that they would scream and run away to hide. Some Cherokees were kidnapped by whites and sold into slavery (Dunaway 2003b, 151). In reaction to local requests, the federal government attempted to remove eastern Cherokees in 1841, 1844, and the mid-1850s. Macon and Haywood County whites petitioned the North Carolina legislature to remove the remaining small indigenous population, one petition stating that "the removal of the Cherokees West . . . would give Satisfaction Generally." In reaction to such petitions, the Joint Select Committee recommended to the North Carolina Legislature in 1843 that the rest of the Cherokees be forcibly removed, justifying such action with the warning that "the mixing of these people with our white population must have a demoralizing influence which ought to be resisted by all the means within our power" (Pudup et al. 1995, 47n41).

Conclusion

It is important to focus sharply on the bloody and greedy conflict for Cherokee lands that made it possible for Euroamericans to claim this territory by 1838. To justify that land grab, invading settlers otherized Cherokees into the "frontier enemies" who needed to be obliterated. The settler view of the indigenous people who stood in the way of their "progress" was grounded in ethnocentrism, racism, and sexism – not in any desire to share resources in an equitable manner. In such a context, everyday life for women was transformed into repeated cycles of slave trading, warfare, back-breaking work to prepare skins for export, high death rates from European diseases, rapidly degrading ecosystems, relocation of towns, and a struggle to grow and to gather enough food to feed unstable villages. Between 1700 and 1838, Cherokee women faced almost constant racial conflict with white settlers and dramatic change in every arena of their lives. Integration into the colonial fur trade generated trade dependency and debts, transforming women into invisible laborers to process male-controlled fur exports. Introduction of new species and European farming threatened the natural resources upon which women depended for household survival, and frequent slave trading and warfare made women and children more vulnerable than males. Over this period, women gradually lost political rights and were disenfranchised. Stereotyped as sexually promiscuous and as "public women" because of their economic autonomy and their control over households and children, Cherokee women were viewed by whites as unchristian and barbaric. Colonial and postrevolutionary policies were intended to "civilize" them away from traditional family constructs toward separate gendered spheres bounded by patriarchal privileges.

Over this period, Cherokees lost their lands, and this fundamental rupture struck at the very heart of women's roles. On the one hand, matriarchal clans that had traditionally controlled lands were weakened by male cessions to whites. On the other hand, American civilizational policy called for noncommunal land use patterns in which families were pressured to move out of towns onto small, scattered farms. These disruptions threatened both the work base and the political rights of women. Over this period, women's pivotal roles in agriculture were challenged, as external change agents put increasing pressure on them to leave the fields and turn over farming to males. Despite the pressures toward separate spheres, Cherokee women retained their control of agriculture, and most of them continued to head their households. They resisted missionary efforts to eliminate matrifocal families, clans, and numerous customs that traditionally kept women visible and recognized in their communities.

Cherokee women seemed to have little in common with either Euroamerican or black women, with whom they rarely had contact. Except for a few black and poor white females who worked alongside them, the two settler races of females thought of these indigenous women as "dangerous savages" who were very much unlike them. On the one hand, there was no shared sisterhood across these racial divides, especially since white women directly benefited from the oppression and removal of Cherokees. On the other hand, Cherokee women mobilized to resist the imposition of patriarchal family constructs, cultural mores, and work patterns to a degree that was not evidenced by white or black Appalachian women. As we shall see in subsequent chapters, however, Cherokee women's work and the patriarchal pressures on their family lives were comparable to the everyday life realities faced by poor white and black women. Indigenous, black, and poor white females exhibited similar patterns of poverty, housing, sexual autonomy, and public men's work that caused affluent

Appalachians to stigmatize them all as "racial degenerates" who were incapable of "civilized motherhood." Even though they experienced parallel sexist treatment within a legally and socially constructed patriarchal system, these three groups of women never crossed racial boundaries to coalesce around gendered subordination.

3

Not a Shared Sisterhood of Subordination

Racism, Slavery, and Resistance by Black Appalachian Females

> Slaveholding white women rarely perceived or acknowledged ... the humanity of
> their black sisters. Most of these white women saw black women as a color, as
> servants, as children, as adjuncts, as sexual competition, as dark sides of their
> own sexual selves – as black Other. They beat black women, nurtured them,
> sentimentalized them, despised them – but they seldom saw them as individuals
> with selves commensurate to their own.
>
> (Minrose Gwin 1985, 5)

From the opening of regional frontiers to Euroamerican settlers, African-
Americans played a key role in the political economy of Southern Appalachia. In
1810, enslaved blacks composed 17 percent of the region's population. Judging from early county tax lists, nearly one of every five Appalachian households owned slaves, but enslavement was entrenched in an uneven pattern.
Slaves were owned by nearly one of every three of the households located
in Appalachian counties of Virginia. About one of every five Appalachian
households in Kentucky, Maryland, and South Carolina held slaves, but only
about one-tenth of the Appalachian households in Tennessee and West Virginia
reported slaves. Between 1790 and 1810, the number of slaves increased in all
sections of Appalachia so that the proportion of slaves in the 1810 population was 1.6 times greater than it had been in 1790. We get the best sense of
the economic significance of slaves by examining the ratio of slaves to white
male adults. By 1810, there was nearly one slave to every white adult male
in the region. In the Appalachian counties of South Carolina and Virginia,
there was more than one slave to every adult male, followed closely by western
Maryland, where there was three-quarters of a slave to every adult male. In
the Appalachian counties of Kentucky, North Carolina, Tennessee, and West
Virginia, there were two white adult males to every slave.[1]

---

[1] Derived from analysis of Appalachian county totals in U.S. Census Office (1791, 1801, 1821).

Nationally throughout the antebellum period, there were fewer females in the white population than there should have been. Consequently, we should expect to see demographic parallels among slave populations. However, females accounted for more than half of the Appalachian slave population in 1820.[2] Since the proportion of enslaved males was far lower than we would expect it to have been, it is evident that Appalachian slaveholders were engaging in structural patterns that caused the gender imbalance among their slaves. The gender composition of the region's slave population diverged from national trends for three reasons. First, females were overrepresented in the Appalachian slave population because owners valued women's reproductive capacities. Second, Appalachian plantations probably built their early slave labor forces by investing in greater numbers of females, who would be disproportionately assigned to field labor. Third, Appalachian slaveholders had begun to export surplus slaves by 1820, and they exported more males than females (Dunaway 2003a).

In 1860, nearly 3 of every 10 adults in the region's labor force were enslaved, and African-Americans were about 15 percent of the population. However, slaves were not the only unfree laborers in Southern Appalachia, for laws regulated free blacks in ways that kept them structurally and economically subordinate. By implementing discriminatory laws, Southern Appalachian employers could, by the midnineteenth century, exploit free blacks as oppressively as they did slaves (Dunaway 2003b, 17–20). To lay groundwork for analysis of women's work in Part II, I will first describe the historical and social context of race relations between enslaved and poor white Appalachians. Following that is analysis of three patterns of racial repression that constrained the lives of black Appalachians. In the final sections, I explore gendered patterns of slave resistance.

Accommodation and Conflict between Enslaved and Poor White Appalachians

Appalachian employers routinely utilized ethnically mixed labor forces. On middle-class and richer farms, poor whites worked the fields alongside slaves, free blacks, and sometimes Indians, and the work gangs were often gender-integrated, especially during harvests. The manuscript records of Appalachian slaveholders document regular hiring of white men and women who worked at the same tasks as slaves, sometimes supervised by black drivers or foremen (Bell Papers, DU, 13 Nov. 1861, 5 Mar. 1862; Greenlee Diary, UNC 1849–50). On small plantations, "a few whites [we]re usually working near slaves, in the same field" (Olmsted 1860, 208). The labor forces at industrial and commercial sites were almost always ethnically mixed (Starobin 1970, 138). Appalachian gold mining drew much newspaper attention because of the frequent commingling of black and white workers, including women (Green 1935, 210). A northern Georgia editor (*Auraria Western Herald*, 30 Apr. 1833) penned a ditty about

---

[2] Derived from analysis of Appalachian county totals in U.S. Census Office (1821).

the Appalachian gold frontier: "Where whites and blacks are all the same" and "Where no respect is paid to rank." Buckingham (1842, 2: 112) was shocked to find blacks and whites working "indiscriminately together" at a Charlottesville textiles factory, "the white girls working in the same room and at the same loom with the black girls; and boys of each colour, as well as men and women, working."

Such close workplace connections were the context for some ethnic mixing and accommodation between these groups. In spite of legal strictures, Appalachian slaves frequented the grog shops, restaurants, cobble shops, clothing stores, and other small enterprises operated by poor whites. In towns, blacks rented rooms in boarding houses run by poor whites, and they occasionally purchased the services of white prostitutes (Wood 1995, 71–79). Illicit trading networks between blacks and poor whites were routine. Traveling peddlers and hucksters regularly traded goods to slaves, and poor whites often purchased items from slaves (Takagi 1999, 31, 69, 136). At agricultural, industrial, and commercial sites, Appalachian slaves worked alongside free blacks and whites, establishing the connections for contacts outside the workplace. Poor whites were the nearest neighbors of most Appalachian slaves because the typical regional master "hired a lot of help" (*Janney's Virginia* 1978, 67). Julius Jones "never seed the like of the poor white folks that lived" around his middle Tennessee plantation, and Fleming Clark "remember[ed] plenty poor white chillun" working for his Botetourt County owner. Similarly, "dere was plenty of po white neighbors" near Jerry Eubanks's northern Georgia farm, and the slaves termed the ones they trusted "home-raised folks." Of 159 newspaper advertisements for Appalachian runaways, nearly 4 percent reported aid from poor whites.[3] According to Banks County and Lumpkin County ex-slaves, poor whites "would help" slaves hide out or run away "fur there wuz some white people who didn't believe in slavery." Twenty-year-old Beck Parker escaped from her Appalachian owner with the help of "a white waggoner" (*Alexandria Gazette*, 23 Apr. 1815). By "pass[ing] for the master," an indentured white teenager eluded patrols that were searching for him and his missing black friend (*Raleigh Star*, 23 Sept. 1814). One Wilkes County slaveholder advertised in the *North Carolina Mercury* (27 June 1799) that he expected his "arch, cunning" runaway to "attempt to pass as a freeman" because he was aided by a literate poor white (Rawick 1972, 12: 200, 16: 23, 14: 333, 13: 270; Rawick 1977, 8: 1221, 7: 690, 3: 102).

Perhaps the most powerful interactions among Appalachian slaves and poor whites were cultural. On the one hand, poor whites imparted two significant customs to the daily lives of black Appalachians. In the vast majority of Appalachian slave weddings, the bride and groom "jumped the broom" (Dunaway 2003a, 52–60, 117–20), a tradition that was most likely adapted from old Anglo-Saxon customs. Through cultural blending, Appalachian slave children

---

[3] Calculated using 297 newspaper advertisements for runaway Appalachian slaves in Meaders (1997) and Parker (1994).

were fed in a troughlike container, a holdover from a similar custom among poor and working-class Irish and British households (Gutman 1976, 275–83, 596–98n). However, cultural fusion probably moved more frequently in the other direction. Many of the social gatherings common among slaves were also prevalent among poor whites. Corn huskings were often ethnically mixed affairs, with poor white tenants and farm laborers working alongside slaves and free blacks (Faulkner and Buckles 1978, 34–42; Love Papers, UNC, "Recollections," 29–30; Chenault 1937, 42; Abrahams 1992, 287–93). Poor whites quickly absorbed foodways from slaves, including their consumption of many foods that had been taken to the Americas by Africans, such as okra and sweet potatoes (Gomez 1998, 138–40). The root cellar that was unique to Appalachian slaves was absorbed into the small cabins of poor whites, and black "root doctoring" cures permeated poor white households that had no better access to medical care than slaves (Singleton 1995). Since they socialized with enslaved females in textiles-producing work parties, some poor white women integrated African color patterns into their quilting (Malson 1990, 11). There was little difference between the religious practices of Appalachian slaves and poor whites, particularly among those who attended Baptist or Methodist churches or camp meetings. Genovese (1974, 239) and Du Bois (1969, 142) argue that poor whites copied from slaves' religious gatherings, rather than the other way around. Shut out of elite churches by class divisions and pew expenses, poor whites fell back upon customs like brush arbors and camp revivals that were common among slaves (Rawick 1979, 9: 3873–74; Holtzberg-Call 1989, 15–17). However, the most striking cultural fusion lies in the region's musical traditions. Black music and dance were not only subversive because they were tools of resistance. They were also "hidden transcripts of the powerless" (Scott 1985, 330) in the sense that these artistic forms had a long-lasting influence on the culture of poor and working-class whites. Because slaves used the context of interracial work parties to preserve and to transmit their unique forms of music and dancing, these artistic styles were gradually accepted by whites (Cantwell 1984, 254–74; Conway 1995, 89–133). These patterns of cross-racial proximity created the context for elite whites to fear frequent sexual interaction among poor white females and black males.

Maintaining racial distance between groups was crucial to the slaveholder's managerial control of an ethnically mixed labor force, so Appalachian masters structured an environment in which blacks and poor whites were pitted against one another. State and local laws imposed high fines and jail time on whites who assisted slaves to learn to read, to gamble, to consume liquor, or to escape. Hanging was the punishment for any white who aided a slave rebellion. Laws required written permission from owners before merchants could legally buy and sell to slaves, and legal actions were often taken against poor whites who violated such ordinances (Takagi 1999, 67–68). According to one North Carolina slave: "One reason for the prejudice which the plantation owners had against the poor white people . . . was that these poor white people naturally sympathized" with the slaves (Singleton 1922, 6). Thus, owners were convinced that poor whites "might teach [slaves] to read or might give [them] some [dangerous] information." According to Nan Stewart, "the poor white neighbahs warn't 'lowed to live very close" to her small West Virginia plantation because her master "wanted de culured slave chilluns to be raised in propah mannah." Similarly, another middle Tennessee ex-slave recalled that black children were not allowed "to even look at the po' white children" (Rawick 1972, 16: 7, 88). Because poor whites traveled in "old covered wagons pulled by oxen," the slave children on one small east Kentucky plantation were "whipped to keep [them] away from the road for fear [itinerant whites] would steal [them]" (Rawick 1972, 14: 403). In addition to owner concerns about corrupting influences and kidnapping, many Appalachian masters distrusted strange whites as inciters of rebellion. Consequently, "slaves were never allowed to talk with white people other than their own masters or someone their masters knew, as they were afraid the white man might help the slave run away" ("Unwritten History," FUA, 21).

The visibility of ethnically mixed work crews caused travelers and journalists to underestimate underlying racial conflicts. Black and white wagoners slept overnight at the same Appalachian taverns, but they were assigned to segregated quarters, and "a separate table was invariably provided for the colored wagoners" (Searight 1894, 109). On steamboats, slaves "were kept at work separately from the white hands; and they were also messed separately" from the Irish immigrant workers (Olmsted 1856, 564). At railroad construction sites, slaves "worked separately and at a distance from any white laborers who [were] employed in the same line of work" (Flanders 1933, 198). When the Virginia and Tennessee Railroad was being constructed, Irish immigrants resisted working alongside slaves (Noe 1994, 82–83). Similarly, some puddlers at iron manufactories refused to work with blacks (Starobin 1970, 142). A Welsh immigrant verbalized the antagonism of western Maryland coal miners against slaves. An ethnically mixed workplace did "not agree with [his] views" because "the Creator never intended them to be equal to a white man" (Conway 1961, 182–83). One major source of that conflict derived from wage inequities. In the late antebellum period, employers typically paid $120 a year to poor white laborers, but $140 annually for a hired slave assigned to the same tasks (Olmsted 1860, 275). At western North Carolina gold mines, poor whites worked alongside black laborers, but the whites were paid a lower wage than the owners of hired slaves (Verplanck 1832, 89). In 1849, a Rome, Georgia, carpenter complained that "because of Negro competition he couldn't get as much as two dollars a day for his work" (Flanders 1933, 205).

Employers offered justifications for devaluing and distrusting white laborers. First, they had a greater degree of legal and day-to-day control over enslaved workers. Second, they believed that poor whites were less skilled and that they could more easily locate artisans and skilled foremen among the slaves. Third, hiring slaves offered the added benefit of employing a crew of laborers who had prior experience working as a team. The James River and Kanawha Canal provides a good example of this pattern of *split labor markets*. In the early

1830s, the Canal Company sent agents to Europe to contract immigrant laborers who would constitute two-thirds of its work force. By the later 1830s, Irish and Scottish workers vocalized growing hostility toward the higher wage scale for annual slave contracts. Following an 1837 strike by white workers, the company became frustrated with what it called "the inaptitude of the still preponderating mass of foreign laborers." At that point, the company's board of directors decided to redesign a "more manageable and stable" workforce. Subsequently, two-thirds of the canal laborers were hired slaves because the company was convinced that hiring whites meant paying "wages for those of inferior grade" to people "who war against our institutions and refuse to work with our slaves" (JRKC Papers, VHS, 1836 Annual Report, 93; 1837 Annual Report, 246; 1838 Annual Report, 331–32; 1839 Annual Report, 508; 1846 Annual Report, Pt. 4; 1850 Annual Report, Appendix).

White Patroller and Overseer Violence toward Black Appalachians

No doubt, the social perceptions of masters molded the attitudes of blacks, for Appalachian slaves disparaged the lowly station of laboring poor whites. One Bluegrass Kentucky ex-slave expressed the racial and class stereotype that "dere was no po' white trash in our [com]munity; dey was kep' back in de mountains." Mollie Moss personally felt that she "ain got no time for po white trash" because "dey warn't teached manners an' behavior" like she was. Another enslaved artisan clearly saw himself as having higher status than poor whites, for he was convinced that slaves "who would associate with the po' white trash were practically outcasts and held in very great contempt." Sam Stewart "didn't think much of the poor white man. He was down on us. He was driven to it, by the rich slave owner." One Chattanooga slave identified poor whites as the Irish, and he verbalized the same prejudices that were typical of Appalachian masters. In his view, "the Irish man come to this country, and then crossed in with the Caucasian and he is half a Mongo" (Rawick 1972, 6: 164, 12: 143, 14: 403, 16: 55; Rawick 1979, 3: 669, 10: 4723; Anderson 1927, 29; "Unwritten History," FUA, 152).

Maugan Sheppard expressed a widespread sentiment when she described her overseer as being so "po' white and mean" that the slaves "wouldn't Mister him." Silas Jackson added that hired poor whites drove slaves "at top speed and whipped at the snap of a finger." Slave mobility was constrained even more intensely by patrollers, against whom Appalachian ex-slaves expressed great hostility. "Dey was de devil turned a-loose," recalled Callie Elder. According to Jim Threat, "one of the things dat the [slaves] dreaded most was a patroller." The structural linkage between overseers and patrols caused a great deal of racial animosity among poor whites and black Appalachians. On William Irving's plantation, "de overseer lived between de cabins," in order to monitor slave movements closely. Overseers could be dismissed if slaves complained to their owners about abusive treatment, so they often shifted the risky disciplining to the patrollers. If any of Irving's peers "didn't work," the overseer "had de patty-rollers" provide the whipping, thereby avoiding any disfavor with his employer. In such an arrangement between overseer and patrollers, Zek Brown's uncle was whipped "so hard dat him am layed up fo' a week." Enraged "'bout dat whuppin'," Brown's owner "tried to find out who 'twas dat whupped uncle but never could." Henry Freeman reported the overseer practice of paying patrollers to paddle selected slaves when they were spotted on the roads. When slaves were absent without leave or ran away, patrollers were contracted by owners and overseers to "git after them and bring them in with the hounds" (Rawick 1972, 12: 311, 4: 273, 16: 32, 10: 42; Rawick 1977, 12: 325; Rawick 1979, 5: 1864, 3: 501, 4: 1433; "Unwritten History," FUA, 132–33).

As a defiant expression of opprobrium, slaves applied the term "paddy-rollers" to these policing agents. By fusing the popular anti-Irish slur *paddy* with *patroller*, black Appalachians were expressing deep racial antagonism toward landless Irish immigrants. An antebellum journalist captured the cause of the interracial hostility when he observed that "the Irish population, with very few exceptions, are the devoted supporters of Southern slavery. They have acquired the reputation of being the most merciless of negro task-masters" (McKivigan 1996, 141). It is also clear in the regional slave narratives that most black Appalachians identified patrollers as a class of people far beneath the status and the morality of their owners. Rachel Cruze thought that "paddyrollers were poor white trash" because "nobody who amounted to anything would go about the country...like dogs hunting rabbits" (Rawick 1977, 5: 299). In this way, slaveholders were highly successful at structuring circumstances so that they shifted hostility away from themselves. On the one hand, the owner could deny any responsibility for the "uncontrollable" brutality or harassment of poor white patrollers. On the other hand, this form of policing was legally forced upon impoverished nonslaveholders by county courts and state legislatures that were politically shaped by the slaveholder agenda (Rawick 1972, 16: 25, 31–32, 12: 311, 4: 273, 10: 42; Rawick 1977, 1: 361, 12: 325, 5: 299; Rawick 1979, 5: 1864, 3: 501, 4: 1433; "Unwritten History," FUA, 132–33).

Slave Trading and Black Family Disruptions

In the judgment of black Appalachian women, slave trading was a far more harmful form of repression than patroller violence. Regional slave trading disrupted a high proportion of slave families, caused a gender imbalance among black Appalachians, and generated matrifocal households from which family members were almost always missing (see detailed discussion in Chapter 7). In the United States, the European demand for cotton triggered the largest domestic slave trade in the history of the world. Between 1790 and 1860, U.S. enslavement underwent a major transformation such that two-thirds of the country's slaves were reconcentrated in the region producing the most profitable staple for the world economy. Over this 70-year period, the Lower South slave population nearly quadrupled because the Upper South exported two-fifths of its African-Americans, the vast majority sold through interstate transactions, about 15 percent removed in relocations with owners (Fogel 1989, 63–70). Census returns and personal narratives of African-Americans provide conclusive evidence that white Appalachians contributed significantly to the interstate traffic in slaves. Between 1840 and 1860, black Appalachians were the victims of nearly one-fifth of all the interstate sales that occurred in the United States. To put it another way, Appalachia was home for one of every eight of the slaves involved in the interregional black diaspora between 1840 and 1860. Appalachian slaveholders routinely commodified black laborers in two ways. One of every three Upper South slaves was sold annually, most through the interstate slave trade, but fewer than one-third of all Appalachian slave sales were transacted locally. Instead, two of every five Appalachian owners sold slaves to traders engaged in interstate trafficking, many of whom made regular annual or biannual circuits throughout the Upper South. In addition to itinerant traders, some Appalachian entrepreneurs engaged in the practice of buying up local slaves for export. In reality, about 1 of every 154 Appalachian households acquired part of its income from slave trading activities. Much more often than selling, Appalachian masters engaged in commercial trading by hiring out their slaves on a profitable basis. Since one-fifth of the Appalachian narratives record instances of slave hiring, it is evident that Appalachian masters leased out slaves more frequently than other southern slaveholders (Dunaway 2003a, 18–41).

Appalachian slaves were marketed publicly, quite often by sheriffs, from auction blocks erected in county courthouse squares (e.g., Holland Papers, UVA, 1846 bill of sale; Warrenton's *Palladium of Liberty*, 15 Jan. 1819; *Winchester Republican*, 23 June and 18 Aug. 1826; *Chattanooga Advertiser*, 8 Jan. 1857; *Rome Southerner and Advertiser*, 26 Aug. 1860). Winchester, Warrenton, Cumberland, and Fredericktown were hubs of intense slave trading, and their slave auctions were advertised in distant newspapers (*Alexandria Gazette and Virginia Advertiser*, 6 and 10 Jan. 1858; *National Intelligencer*, 2 July 1833). Weekly slave auctions were held in Charleston, West Virginia; Knoxville and Chattanooga, Tennessee; and Rome, Georgia. At Rome, slaves were kept in a house "built just like cow's stalls" until they were "sold on a high block." At the tiny town of Christiansburg, "dey kept de slaves in de jail, an' dey would bring 'em out one at a time to be sold. Dere was a huge tree dat had been . . . shaped into a big block 'bout six feet tall." In Talladega County, Alabama, commission firms or the sheriff would "cry slaves off to the highest bidder" on the first Tuesday of every month. Jim Threat recalled that each slave would "turn slowly round" on the Talladega auction block "while the buyers inspected them. They'd even look at their teeth" (*Weevils* 1976, 60; Rose 1976, 341; Rawick 1977, 7: 688, 12: 335–36).

The slave trade was structurally integrated into Appalachian community and town life. Even when their own slave populations were small, Appalachian towns provided the locus for the congregation of buyers and sellers; the pens, jails, and depots; the exchanges and auction blocks that supported the slave trade. For instance, an east Tennessee slaveholder advertised in local newspapers that he was "offering for sale 5 Negro slaves in pursuance of the Circuit Court...sitting at Tazewell," a tiny rural village (*East Tennessean,* 7 Mar. 1840). Despite the low black population density in that area, ex-slaves described auction blocks sprinkled all over east Kentucky, including sites in the counties of Laurel, Clay, Floyd, Knox, and Bell (*Kentucky Gazette,* 27 Sept. 1788). In addition to sales at courthouses or specialized businesses, auction blocks were a routine component of river wharves (Rawick 1979, 9: 3880). Even many of the region's smaller crossroads villages operated regular slave auctions that were handled by the local sheriff. Off the beaten path in the Virginia Blue Ridge, the small hamlet of Luray sold slaves on an auction block that measured five feet high and only 17 inches across. Despite their very small slave populations, east Tennessee villages at Rogersville, Andersonville, Robertsville, and Crab Orchard were gathering points for public sales on court days (Lambert 1989, 64; Hoskins 1979, 37; Seals 1974, 58). In McDowell County, North Carolina, four slaves were "exposed to Public Sale at the Court House door" in the little town of Marion (Walton Papers, UNC, 9 Nov. 1848). As a result of such widespread marketing of humans, the 1860 black Appalachian population was only about half what it should have been if the interstate slave trade had never occurred.

White Religious Repression of Slaves

In addition to patroller violence and slave trading, black Appalachians endured religious repression. Because slaveholders knew they did not have hegemonic control over the culture and ideology of slaves, they implemented coercive constraints. After 1830, public ordinances prohibited black religious services without white supervision (Drake 1950, 18). More then three-quarters of Appalachian masters required enslaved families to participate in white religious instruction, and the vast majority of Appalachian slaves attended weekly services at the white churches where their masters were members.[4] Antebellum church records document the routine attendance and membership of blacks in the white congregations attended by slaveholders. Legally, a slave "eider b'long to de chu'ch he master b'long to or none 'tall." Thomas Cole recalled that slaves on his farm were required to "walk bout five miles" in order to "allus goes ter church mos every Sunday." Similarly, Henry Johnson described "a great string of slaves in de road on Sunday," surrounded by "buggies wid de white folks" in front. At most churches, slaves were segregated in rows along the side, at the rear, or in the balcony. At small churches, slaves "had ter stay outside," sometimes forced to sit "on a log in de broiling sun." Occasionally, the two audiences were "separated by a partition." Civil War veterans recalled slaves' "sitting in the back seats" at east Tennessee churches like Good Hope in

---

[4] I analyzed slave narratives and church records to assess slave attendance at white churches. I perused manuscript minutes and records for 34 churches listed in the Bibliography under GSA, HPL, NCDAH, UNC, UVA, VHS, VSL, and WVU.

Meigs County, the Cumberland Presbyterian in White County, or First Presbyterian in Hawkins County. In the Cherokee Nation, Springplace missionaries assigned blacks "special seats at communion" and passed them the cup "last of all" (Hamilton 1971, 47). In other situations, white churches held segregated services for slaves. In Appalachian counties where there were few organized churches, slaves attended only irregular community meetings held by circuit preachers (Rawick 1972, 11: 207–8, 6: 279, 12: 195, 197, 349, 13: 128, 16: 3, 12: 195, 197; Rawick 1977, 7: 692; Rawick 1979, 3: 672, 802, 4: 110, 1433, 5: 1559; Dyer and Moore 1985, 197, 550, 597–98, 914). Despite the social stigma, one female slaveholder organized prayer meetings and traveled around southwest Virginia evangelizing slaves (Wheat Diary, UNC).

Seeking to deprive blacks of any collective faith that might oppose their own version of Christianity, many Appalachian masters personally provided religious instruction to their slaves. Penny Thompson's owner distributed "two fingahs" of peach brandy with prayers "ever' mo'nin' an' night" (Rawick 1979, 9: 3871–72). When there were no formalized Sunday services, several white slaveholding women led prayer and singing "out of the doors, in the yard" (Rawick 1972, 7: 26). Appalachian slaves were indoctrinated in specially designed plantation catechisms (e.g., Jones 1837), which emphasized faithful service, honesty, and loyalty to the master. Published guides listed interrogatives that the owner should pose, followed by the responses to be memorized by slaves. For instance, one script in the 1855 *Southern Presbyterian Review* (8: 1–17) read: "The fifth commandment is: Honor thy father and thy mother." The master was then instructed to read the question: "What does this commandment require you to do?" Slaves were expected to respond that God required them "to respect and to obey my father and mother, my master and mistress, and everybody else that has authority over me."

Because he believed them to be "in a degraded and dependent condition," one western Carolina minister read his slaves the prescribed Presbyterian catechism, instructed them at length, then "asked them Questions" to test their comprehension of "the right way." Like other Appalachian masters, he was convinced that "suitable" religious instruction would "make better servants" (Greenlee Diary, UNC, 30 Jan. 1847, 15 Sept. 1850). Appalachian ex-slaves consistently recalled the white clerical emphases upon obeying the slave laws and upon "serving the Lord" by behaving in ways that pleased masters. One middle Tennessee ex-slave reported that very few white clerics taught slaves "about religion." Instead the "biggest thing" they preached about was "'Servants, obey your mistress and master." At a Chattanooga church, the minister taught slaves that "Sampson slayed the Abolitioners, not Philistines." A northern South Carolina ex-slave recalled clerical preoccupation with the tenet "The better you be to your master the better he treat you." Even though most of them were illiterate, Appalachian slaves comprehended the contradictions in the religious interpretations of white clerics. Henry Buttler recalled that neighborhood slaves were required to attend a weekly sermon preached by a white minister who "was inconsiderate in the treatment of his own slaves." Thus, "his brotherly talk was not taken seriously." When a listener "laughed at the minister's remarks" during a discourse on kindness, the cleric "administered twenty-five lashes to the unfortunate negro" (Rawick 1972, 10: 82, 11: 207–8, 11: 231; "Unwritten History," FUA, 98, 148; Rawick 1979, 3: 555–56).

Offended by the lively antics and singing of blacks, many white congregations created segregated services, with black class leaders, catechists, watchmen, and exhorters. Slave preachers earned credibility and trust through their roles in white-supervised activities. Black ministers sometimes traveled the circuits with Baptist and Methodist clergymen and helped them conduct services for blacks and whites, and a few slaves served as assistants to the clergymen who owned them (Blassingame 1972, 91–92). There are numerous accounts of white-sponsored churches for blacks, especially among the Baptists and Methodists. In Talladega County, for instance, the Baptists were eager for blacks to "have churches of their own with black preachers to lead them in a language of their understanding." So they constructed a small brick meetinghouse, started the African Cottonfort Church, and trained a local slave who ministered to 130 blacks (*Southwestern Baptist*, 24 July 1856). Similar white-sponsored services were created throughout the region. While the Charlottesville African Church was led by a white minister, the Methodists trained eight black preachers and nine exhorters in Frederick County (Jordan 1995, 113). The Roanoke Baptist Association (Records, VSL, 17 Mar. 1851) purchased a slave and trained him to "preach the Gospel." At Lexington, Virginia, the black Baptist church was "a poor log house," hidden from view outside town. On Sundays, two whites supervised a service in which a black male "gave out" the hymns to an illiterate audience (Reed and Matheson 1835, 1: 217–22). There were even a few free black ministers, like West Virginian John Chavis (Ruffner Papers, VSL, Chavis Folder). However, the predominant pattern was the establishment of informal plantation chapels, with black preachers or exhorters leading services. During these official services, "there was always some white people around." The typical plantation church was no more than "an old shed with seats made out of old slabs and fence rails." On Andrew Goodman's plantation, a neighbor's slave "used to git a pass Sunday mornin' and come preach," and he "baptized in a little mudhole down back of [the] place." At an Alleghany County, Virginia, plantation, slaves would gather on Sundays at a large cabin "with one of the overseers present," and the illiterate coachman would hold church. "When communion was given the overseer was paid . . . with half of the collection," as much as 25 cents (Rawick 1972, 4: 75–76, 274, 13: 84–85, 16: 89, 111, 32; Rawick 1977, 3: 272; "Unwritten History," FUA, 217, 239, 54, 214; Rawick 1979, 5: 1791).

Gendered Patterns of Religious Resistance

Even though masters designed their white-supervised religious instruction to extend their ideological dominance, slaves resisted their cultural hegemony in several ways. Even though a majority of Appalachian masters required slave participation in white church services, less than 10 percent ever joined those churches. Major southern denominations boasted in 1860 that one-quarter of all adult slaves were church members, as were one-third of adult whites. According to these clerics, one million slaves were under the regular tutelage of white churches (Bruner 1933, 58–60). Such inflated claims are certainly not an accurate description of the white church membership of Appalachian slaves. Using manuscript records of the major denominations that operated in antebellum Southern Appalachia, it is possible to track a close count of black church membership. The Virginia Baptist Association reported 8,207 black members, representing only a small percentage of the total African-American population. In east Tennessee, blacks constituted less than 8 percent of the entire membership roll of the Holston Conference of the Methodists. The Holston Conference was even less successful in southwest Virginia, where only 2 percent of their members were black. In northern Georgia, only about 10 percent of Baptist Church members were black. Those 13,348 blacks who had joined Methodist and Baptist churches accounted for only about 7 percent of all the African-Americans in the Appalachian counties of Tennessee, Virginia, and Georgia. With very few of their churches situated in Appalachian counties, Episcopalians and Presbyterians attracted a high percentage of slaveholders, but those churches enrolled far less than 1 percent of the entire black population of the states of Alabama, North Carolina, South Carolina, and Virginia.[5] Appalachian slaves recognized the hypocrisy of their owners' Christianity, and that awareness accounted for their reluctance to join white congregations. "How can Jesus be just," one Appalachian slave queried a white cleric, "if He will allow such oppression and wrong? Don't the slaveholders justify their conduct by the Bible itself, and say that it tells them to do so?" (Jordan 1995, 106)?

The Role of the Black Male Preacher

Despite legal restrictions and close surveillance, black Appalachians participated to a greater extent in their own underground religion than in white services, and they coined the phrase "stealin' the meetin'" to describe that illicit activity. After "Nat Turner's insurrection broke out," reported one Blue Ridge Virginia preacher, "the colored people were forbidden to hold meetings among themselves.... Notwithstanding our difficulties, we used to steal away to some of the quarters to have our meetings." In addition to their meetings in the quarters, Appalachian slaves constructed "brush arbor" churches or held night services in the woods. The brush arbor provided space to accommodate visiting slaves, who sometimes walked six to eight miles to attend secret night gatherings (Rawick 1972, 16: 31; Rawick 1977, 7: 692, 8: 914; "Unwritten History," FUA, 106; *Weevils* 1976, 157; Rawick 1979, 4: 1433). Perhaps the most feared agent of social change among Appalachian slaves was the black preacher. In 1831, Governor John Floyd, an Appalachian planter, called for laws that prohibited

---

[5] Church statistics were derived from Blassingame (1972, 346–60). Appalachian estimates were derived from U.S. Census Office (1863).

the unsupervised activities of black preachers. Floyd contended in his annual message to the Virginia Legislature that "the most active incendiaries among us, stirring up the spirit of revolt, have been the negro preachers" (Ambler 1918, 159).

White Appalachians disparagingly referred to slave ministers as "chairback-ers," to signify their movement from one plantation to another to conduct services, that mobility being a major source of white apprehension about them (Harris 1985, 51). Black preachers were often included among the newspaper advertisements for runaway slaves. A Yancey County, North Carolina, slave-holder offered a reward for David, a young preacher who had taken two others with him when he escaped. The owner warned readers of the *Carolina Centinel* (10 May 1828) that this "greatest rogue" would "cloak his villainy" by "pretend[ing] to be religious...singing and psalms." An ad in the *Alexandria Daily Advertiser* (10 July 1813) called attention to the noticeable religious traits of a truant 22-year-old West Virginia slave, who "professed to be a baptist, prays very well." Masters feared not only the connection between runaways and black preachers but also their role in educating slaves. Illicit religious meetings were the settings in which nearly half the tiny minority of literate Appalachian slaves learned to read and write. Some preachers also taught women how to keep their own records of family births, deaths, and sales in a Bible they hid in their root cellars (e.g., Rawick 1972, 16: 111; Rawick 1979, 3: 801).

Black preachers were also a threat because they were better educated, quite often better dressed, than the poor white Appalachians who worked the road patrols. Seeking to cement their power through cultural terrorism, Appalachian masters targeted black preachers for punishment. According to one black Appalachian, "patrollers wuz mostly after de preacher 'cause he wuz de leader of de meetin' an' if dey caught 'im, he knowed dar wuz a beatin' fer 'im." An Appalachian runaway named Clem had "a lump on his back, occasioned by a whipping he received for being a clerk to a negro preacher" (*Alexandria Daily Advertiser*, 31 Dec. 1805). The Pickens County, South Carolina, court found a slave "guilty of seditious language" and sentenced him to 300 lashes, after he was overheard telling a group of blacks "that God was working for their deliverance" (*Abbeville Banner*, 22 June 1850, 7 July 1850, 16 Aug. 1850, 14 Sept. 1850). Some preachers were aggressive in designing strategies to protect themselves and their congregations. In Garland Monroe's community, night services were held at the foot of Hardware Mountain. When patrollers rode "down de mountain side," they were knocked off their horses by slaves hidden above the meeting site. If patrollers invaded his thicket service, Alfred Williams "would sit there with his gun on his lap to keep them from whipping him." An *oppositional discourse* emerged in the illicit meetings of Appalachian slaves because "the heaviest emphasis in the slaves' religion was on change in their earthly situation and divine retribution for the cruelty of their masters." Nan Stewart described how black preachers selected Bible passages from which they could construct a coded message of future liberation. A preacher who regularly visited her Charleston, West Virginia, plantation liked to read Michah 4:4 because it held the promise that slaves "would soon be undah [their] own vine an' fig tree and hab no feah of bein' sold down de riber to a mean Marse." Thus, many black Appalachian preachers caused great apprehension among owners because they used their secret underground religion to foment dissatisfaction with subjugation. As one Appalachian slave noted, "The idea of revolution in the conditions of whites and blacks [wa]s the cornerstone of the religion of the latter." Slaves may have disguised their religious rhetoric at official services, but they transformed Christianity into a *liberation theology* that framed the certainty of future deliverance and retribution (*Weevils* 1976, 210; "Unwritten History," FUA, 4; Hughes 1897, 54; Blassingame 1972, 133; Rawick 1972, 17: 142, 16: 89).

Because they seemed loyal during white-sponsored services, slave preachers maintained the privilege of movement between plantations. That mobility made it possible for them to emerge as the charismatic leaders of the underground slave religion. Julia Daniels described her uncle, Joe, who served his owner by holding Sunday "meetin' in front de [big] house." During such official services, the black preacher "had to be careful what he said 'cause the white folks were there and listening to him, so that he couldn't have anything to say to cause uprising of slaves." Out of the sight of the master at night, however, Uncle Joe and another nearby preacher would "make it 'tween 'em" to hold secret meetings." According to one western Carolina woman, "colored folks jes kinder raised 'em up a colored preacher" who was held in high regard in the slave quarters. As a young child, Thomas Cole idolized his uncle, Dan, who "would read de Bible ter de rest of [them] and tell de meanin' of it." James Pennington's western Maryland community treated an illiterate slave with equal respect. After their master "sternly resisted" efforts by the Methodists "to evangelize the slaves," illicit services were organized by an exhorter who "could not read . . . but he knew a number of spiritual songs by heart, of these he would give two lines at a time very exact, set and lead the tune himself" ("Unwritten History," FUA, 100; Rawick 1972, 4: 274; Rawick 1977, 8: 914; Rawick 1979, 3: 801; Pennington 1849, 66–68).

Women's Religious Resistance

Despite the important role of males, women lay at the center of slave liberation theology. Black males may have been highly visible in African-American religious practices, but black women organized and conducted far more services. In comparison to white females, black women far more frequently led prayer meetings and were much more likely to be respected in their communities for their religious leadership roles. With respect to black Christianity, whites institutionalized a double standard that paralleled the patriarchal structure of white churches. Because white-trained male preachers were considered to be semilegitimate leaders of Christian services for blacks, slaveholders endowed them with the privilege of neighborhood mobility. In contrast, slave women were routinely punished for conducting nighttime singings and prayer meetings – imposing on black females sexist constraints that paralleled the discrimination confronted

FIGURE 7. Like this Rabun County, Georgia, gathering, Appalachian slaves participated illegally in nighttime religious services. Because they were assigned textiles production at night, women combined that regular labor with unauthorized prayer meetings and singings. Thus, black females were punished for such resistance more often than males. *Source: Scribner's* 1874.

by white females in their churches. Even though whites passed legislation to regulate the male preacher, females were far more frequently punished for religious activism. Indeed, women were whipped nearly three times more often than men for their participation in unauthorized religious services or nighttime singing. Women engaged in prayer meetings or singings while they completed their evening textiles production; thus, females were more likely to be caught at such forbidden activities. Women "would get the cloth spun during the time they were having prayer meeting," and the older female textiles driver was quite often the individual who "organized secret prayer meetings." On one middle Tennessee plantation, the owner "would hit [women] fifty lashes for praying" at night ("Unwritten History," FUA, 4, 106).

Alongside their Christian beliefs, U.S. slave women kept alive African *conjuring* customs. Even though most black Appalachians participated in Christian services and held black male preachers in high repute, most of them held in equally high esteem the conjuring women in their communities. More than three-fifths of the Appalachian slave narratives offer descriptions of conjuring and herbalists, and almost all these experts were females. According to

Raboteau (1980, 288), "Conjure could, without contradiction, exist side by side with Christianity . . . because, for the slaves, conjure answered purposes which Christianity did not and Christianity answered purposes which conjure did not." Even though Sallah White regularly attended her owner's Hardshell Baptist church and slave prayer meetings, she was also a conjurer. She bragged, "I kin do er lot o' doctorin', but I woan tell nobuddy what I use kaze dat is my and God's secret." Even after their Christian conversions, Nancy Gardner and Byrl Anderson relied on help from conjurers. Ellis Jefferson was a devout Christian, but he "believe[d] some people can put a 'spell' on other people." Similarly, Nan Stewart thought she needed both Christianity and conjuring to help her through life's troubles. Reverend Charles Williams admonished slaves to reject charms and magic as evil, but he never denied the skills of conjurers (Rawick 1972, 7: 109–10, 9: 37, 16: 90; *Weevils* 1976, 9; Rawick 1977, 5: 462, 471).

Little wonder, then, that women blended Christianity with elements of conjuring in the illicit prayer meetings they organized. While drums and tin pan beatings were common in some communities (Rawick 1979, 6: 2281), the African vestige most often evidenced was the practice of using "the pot" during secret religious meetings (Raboteau 1980, 215–16). West Africans used iron pots in religious rituals to symbolize divine protection. Convinced that the pot provided them a supernatural defense, New World slaves "had the courage to gather at night for prayer meetings to assert and develop their community, even though such meetings were prohibited" (Rawick 1973, 39–45). Pot rituals varied slightly from one community to another, sometimes used to prevent noise, other times to signal the location for a secret meeting. Females most frequently described the practice of turning the pot down outside the door of the woman's cabin where the secret meeting occurred. While they completed their nighttime spinning or weaving, women would either "stick [thei]r heads in a big iron pot to keep de noise away from de big house," or they would carry the pot inside the cabin "and raise one side up a little from the ground" ("Unwritten History," FUA, 45, 118, 12, 53, 98, 117–18, 148–49; Rawick 1972, 1: 55–56, 16: 38, 67: Rawick 1977, 1: 432–33).

A conjurer possessed an accumulated intergenerational knowledge of magical tradition and herbal medicine that was widespread among U.S. slaves. Even after their original meanings had been lost, bits of African faith and religious practice persisted in slave folk beliefs and customs (Raboteau 1980, 80–81, 288). These derivative practices from voodoo were countercultural in two ways. On the one hand, Christian church manuals admonished slaveholders to punish blacks who engaged in such "heathenish"practices because they were a threat to the advance of Christianity (Jones 1837). On the other hand, slaveholders feared voodoo as a system of practices that emboldened blacks to resist. Believing that charms made them invincible to white control, slaves might engage in rebellions. In conjurer tales, "ghosts, witches and conjurers redressed the wrongs which the slaves could not" (Raboteau 1980, 283–84). For these reasons, southern black codes outlawed remnants of voodoo, such as drums, amulets, and charms, and mandated death penalties for slaves who used conjuring to kill whites (Morris 1996). In addition, Appalachian ex-slaves reported that their owners whipped them for wearing amulets or charms and for expressing religious belief in conjurers.

Two conjuring systems were reported in slave narratives: (a) use of magic for evil purposes and (b) applications of antidotes to sorcery and witchcraft.[6] For good luck, Appalachian slaves frequently wore amulets or charms or carried rag packets called "tobies" or "jacks." In addition, children and adults wore asafetida bags "round deir necks to keep off ailments." Conjurers dispensed silver dime amulets or blue and white beads "to keep off evil spirits," red flannel wrist bands "to keep from loosin' de nerve," rabbit feet "to keep chills and fever off," or talismans "to keep the spells off." In addition to these protective devices, some conjurers were rumored to "bad mouth" or "put the evil eye" on people through spells and hidden charms. Aunt Clussey described a conjuring spell that caused a woman to eat nothing but tree bark until ants "come out de pores of her skin." After he refused to dance with her, Ben Chambers was convinced that an "ol' lady named Liza" used rattlesnake dust to cause swelling under his arm. Melinda Ruffner thought her husband's sudden death was caused by a conjuring spell purchased by another male, who wanted his job. If one "got conjured," Julius Jones explained, "the only way for you to get cured or have the spell lifted" was to seek help from another conjurer "who knows more bout it than the one who conjured you." For example, Jim Threat believed that a "conjure woman" sent a chicken to his house to carry a curse, so he consulted another conjurer to learn how "to break her charm" (Rawick 1972, 12: 351, 16:24, 12: 312, 16: 35; Rawick 1977, 11: 20, 7: 697, 8: 1220, 1: 20, 8: 1220, 12: 332–33; Rawick 1979, 3: 673, 4: 1103, 3: 674; *Weevils* 1976, 244).

The reputations of conjurers reached legendary proportions in many Appalachian slave communities. According to Simon Hare, whites "couldn' rule" Aunt Harriet, "a powerful woman" who "wasn' sca'ed of nobody." On Chaney Mack's plantation, "nobody fooled wid" the conjurer Big Sarah because whites and blacks "wuz afraid of her." Fleming Clark's mother was a conjurer who was highly respected by whites and blacks because her herbal concoctions cured and prevented diseases. Ellis Jefferson recalled a conjurer who was renowned for her ability to forewarn slaves and whites of future crises. Jim Threat described a conjurer who could mix a "dried roots" potion that would help slaves escape from jails, and he knew a conjurer who could make a toby strong enough to "keep de marster from whippin you." However, slaves held in highest esteem those females who had the power to "hoodoo masters." Julius Jones described such a conjurer, who could put lizards in the closet of a white and cause the death of that person. The same woman was reputed to call forth the ghosts of badly treated slaves to haunt their owners' houses. Tom

[6] These two systems of voodoo were widespread in the Caribbean (Raboteau 1980, 33–34). As a result of the removal of Caribbean slaves, these customs became vulgarized over time in the United States.

Neal explained that the most talented conjurers "took on other forms" that were small enough to enter through key holes into their owners' locked homes or buildings. Jordon Smith agreed, claiming that a conjurer on his plantation often assumed "different forms and shapes, sometimes like a dog or cat, or even like a man." Dilah Walker described a conjurer who put such a potent spell on the white mistress that "millions of black wings" came out of her dead body. Oliver Bell recalled a "Jack-mer-Lant'en" that "stirred up" a male's mind so he could not recognize where he was. In this way, the conjurer could attract a master or overseer to his death ("Unwritten History," FUA, 100; Rawick 1972, 9: 37, 16:24, 10: 182, 6: 402, 1: 58; Rawick 1977, 9: 1420, 12: 334, 8: 1220–21; Rawick 1979, 8: 918, 3: 674, 9: 39).

In addition to their magical practices, Appalachian conjurers possessed significant medical knowledge, especially about the creation of herbal healing remedies.[7] Because "there wasn't any doctors seeing after colored folks" (Rawick 1972, 10: 182), female conjurers played crucial roles in community health care. Self-treatment was the primary medical strategy of the vast majority of Appalachian slaves, for only a few owners relied on paid physicians for anything except the most serious cases (Dunaway 2003a, 131, 150–51). Ex-slaves repeatedly recalled the scenario in which an elderly conjurer "got her hoe and sack and went gathering herbs to make medicines," and then the sick person "would be all right." Elderly "root doctors" routinely dispensed herbal cures and preventatives, treated wounds and injuries, provided prenatal advice, delivered babies, and tended postpartum mothers. In addition, they experimented with herbal birth control methods that were inserted into the vaginal tract to prevent pregnancies or to trigger miscarriages. Combining African and Native American knowledge about indigenous plants, black Appalachian healers used a variety of teas, poultices, salves, ointments, and mixes that were made from herbs, roots, berries, barks, and animal bones. Conjurers also commonly grew several medicinal herbs in their garden parcels (Rawick 1977, 6: 2282; Rawick 1979, 3: 550, 8: 914, 6: 2284; Rawick 1972, 16: 47; "Unwritten History," FUA, 100; *Janney's Virginia* 1978, 47–48). Many of the herbal remedies documented in the slave narratives have been identified in modern scientific studies as effective medicinal plants that grow wild in the Appalachian Mountains (Krochmal, Walters, and Doughty 1969).

Gender Differences in Other Resistance Patterns

In addition to female religious resistance, women-headed slave families were the pivotal units in which resistance was taught, planned, and executed. The struggle of Appalachian slaves was not revolutionary in the sense that they attempted to overthrow the system of oppression that trapped them. Rather, their everyday resistance was focused upon the amelioration of conditions of life for households and upon the protection of their families. Indeed, there

---

[7] A majority of U.S. slave conjurers were also herbal healers (Raboteau 1980, 279).

was a noticeable connection between kinship and socially prohibited behaviors. *Illicit information networks* and an *ethos of sanctuary for runaways* lay at the heart of their subculture of resistance, and those strategies had to be taught and orchestrated by women. For example, children were trained in the arts of reconnaissance and espionage. As girls worked in their owners' houses or tended white children, they overheard conversations, stole papers or books, and dropped misleading information to their owners. Nearly half the whippings were punishment for acts of defiance by enslaved women who were trying to protect family members. About half the incidents of spying on whites or illicit communication involved the transmittal of information by adult slave women about pending punishment, sales, or hires of family members. Impending sales or distant hires of family members triggered more than two-fifths of the successful escapes of Appalachian slaves to the North. Furthermore, two-thirds of the incidents of *truancy* (absence from home plantation without a pass) were not escape attempts. Instead, most of the miscreants were traveling to visit families, with every intent to return to their assigned workplaces.[8] Indeed, males utilized truancy and *laying out* more often than any other nonviolent resistance strategies. Even in the face of patrollers, whippings, or worse punishment, some slaves repeatedly left their plantations without the required passes. To avoid removal – the most serious risk for their families – resistant men hid out for extended periods. Nearly one-fifth of the slave narratives described caves, underground pits, and isolated spots in rough terrain that were used to conceal truants from detection while they remained near families. Sanctuary for such truants was part of the resistant ethic of Appalachian slaves, for laying out required the complicity of women who slipped them survival essentials.

Because more than half of Appalachian slave households were headed by females (Dunaway 2003a, 53), those women stood alone to protect children against whites and to prevent their own sexual exploitation. Because of the absence of males, there was a striking gender differentiation in patterns of resistance and punishment.[9] Men and women were physically punished at comparable levels of frequency; however, males and females committed different infractions. Consistently, women were more likely than men to be punished for behaviors that were aimed at family protection or maintenance. Nearly

[8] An abroad family resulted when slave spouses had different owners. This marital relationship is discussed in Chapter 7.

[9] Punishment trends were derived from analysis of 383 incidents in which adult slaves were whipped or received severe physical punishment that were recorded in regional slave narratives and slaveholder manuscripts. Of the whippings, 31.9 percent were administered because of work deficiency, property destruction, or food stealing; 68.1 percent involved social infractions. Of the victims 189 were females; 194 were males. Of the incidents, 19.7 percent involved work deficiencies, 7.4 percent stealing, 4.8 percent property destruction. The social infractions included verbal violations 22.7 percent, physical assaults on others 20.9 percent, absent without passes 13.3 percent, illicit communication or spying on whites 5.5 percent, unauthorized religious services 3.3 percent, attempts to become literate or possession of written materials 0.7 percent, attempts at permanent escape 0.5 percent, socializing with free blacks or untrustworthy whites 0.2 percent.

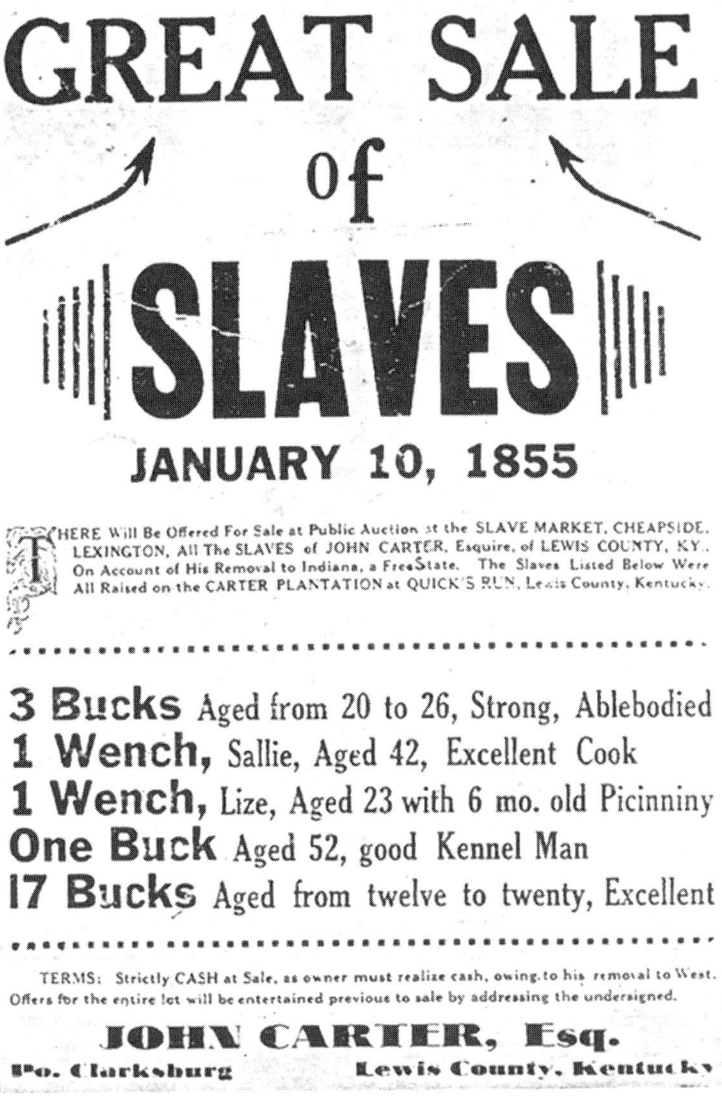

GREAT SALE

of

SLAVES

JANUARY 10, 1855

THERE Will Be Offered For Sale at Public Auction at the SLAVE MARKET, CHEAPSIDE, LEXINGTON, All The SLAVES of JOHN CARTER, Esquire, of LEWIS COUNTY, KY., On Account of His Removal to Indiana, a FreeState. The Slaves Listed Below Were All Raised on the CARTER PLANTATION at QUICK'S RUN, Lewis County, Kentucky.

● ●

3 Bucks Aged from 20 to 26, Strong, Ablebodied
1 Wench, Sallie, Aged 42, Excellent Cook
1 Wench, Lize, Aged 23 with 6 mo. old Picinniny
One Buck Aged 52, good Kennel Man
17 Bucks Aged from twelve to twenty, Excellent

● ●

TERMS: Strictly CASH at Sale, as owner must realize cash, owing to his removal to West. Offers for the entire lot will be entertained previous to sale by addressing the undersigned.

JOHN CARTER, Esq.

Po. Clarksburg   Lewis County, Kentucky

FIGURE 8. The export of black laborers and permanent disruption of slave families were the most extreme acts of racism in which Appalachians engaged. This east Kentucky slaveholder was migrating westward, so he sold 23 slaves at public auction in Lexington. As was the case at most slave sales, families were not sold as complete units, and children younger than 20 were removed from their parents. *Source:* Coleman Papers, University of Kentucky.

two-fifths of the women were punished for verbal offenses, usually triggered by white threats toward children or extended kin. Consequently, women engaged in sassing and oral insubordination 1.3 times more frequently than males. Because of their high employment as nurses and caretakers for white children, women and girls were more frequently punished for spying on whites. Women were more frequently punished for illicit communication with other plantations, the only method they had to warn abroad spouses about family crises.

There were striking gender differences in other patterns of resistance. More than one-third of the men were whipped for absences without passes. Males ran away nine times more often than females, reflecting the much higher probability that husbands, fathers, and sons would be removed from their families through forced labor migrations. Because they were more frequently hired out to distant employers, men tried to escape permanently five times more often than women. As a result of their greater employment in skilled occupations that permitted chances to learn to read and write, males were slightly more likely than females to be involved in attempts at literacy. Men and women also had different motivations for their violent resistance against whites. Surprisingly, women engaged in physical attacks on whites a little more often than males. While males more frequently defended themselves against white physical abuse or torture, women most often assaulted whites in order to protect family members or to resist sexual exploitation.

Conclusion

There was a deep schism between white and black Appalachian women. Whether rich, middle-class, or poor, white Appalachian women enjoyed a structurally privileged racial position, so they certainly did not share a *sisterhood of subordination* with African-American females. As Mary Anglin (2000, 72) has observed, "White Appalachian women – both slaveholding and nonslaveholding – benefited from black oppression and racial discrimination. Even though white women were oppressed by a patriarchal system that proffered advantages on males and even though poor white women were especially damaged by that system, we still cannot equate their plight with the brutal dehumanization experienced by African-Americans."

The daily lives of black women set them apart from most elite and middle-class women. Violent acts by patrollers, overseers, and other white males were continuing tensions in black women's lives, but these were stresses that white women did not face. Black women routinely worked alongside white males in interracial work, and that proximity to Caucasian men made them vulnerable in two ways. On the one hand, such racially mixed workplaces exposed many black women to a greater likelihood of sexual assaults. On the other hand, such cross-racial interaction generated public scrutiny of free black females, especially if they cohabited with white males or bore mulatto children (discussed in Chapters 7 and 8). Slave trading and hiring generated households from which males were absent, leaving women alone to care for children and to confront violence and sexual exploitation from whites. However, black women were not just victims of oppression, for they frequently engaged in and trained household members in patterns of resistance. While male black preachers were held in high esteem among slaves, women organized and were punished more frequently for illicit religious services. Black women resisted white patriarchal religious conventions by assuming far more leadership roles than were open to white women. Like indigenous Appalachian women, black females kept alive their ancient arts of conjuring. While Cherokee women rejected Christianity in order to preserve their culture, black women merged Christianity with African conjuring. In the process, they fostered a liberation theology that felt very threatening to white owners.

4

Not Even Sisters among Their Own Kind

The Centrality of Class Divisions among
Appalachian Women

> Class differences among females have received far too little attention in Southern
> women's history production.
>
> (Wilma A. Dunaway)

Despite a few recent attempts to encourage "a different view of Southern history" (Scott 1993, 1) a number of class-blind mistakes still predominate in studies of southern women. Even though three-quarters of white, Indian, and free black females lived outside slaveholding households, most writers still insist that the histories and identities of antebellum southern women were "predominantly shaped by slavery" (Fox-Genovese 1983, 216). Overwhelmingly, southern women have been portrayed as elites, as evidenced by their sheltered domesticity and by their relationships to the slaves they owned. Because researchers have been preoccupied with slaveholding women (e.g., Clinton 1982, 164–79; Weiner 1998, 53–71), they have fostered the misperception that all southern women shared the same structural position with respect to enslaved women and men. Consequently, poor and middle-class southern women are still grossly underrepresented in the literature (Sharpless 1993). Assumptions like these reduce women and households within the same racial group to a homogeneous category, thereby implying that there were far greater economic equality and cultural uniformity than actually existed. As a result, the economic polarization and social distance among nineteenth-century women are ignored. This study offers a sharp break with analyses that ignore the class differences among women. Antebellum Appalachian women were not only separated by racial chasms and antagonisms. They were also deeply divided by class within their own racial groups. In the sections that follow, I will examine

- Cherokee women's class struggle against cultural change;
- gendered class divisions among slaves;
- color, class, and gender divisions among free blacks; and
- class conflict among white Appalachian women.

Cherokee Women's Class Struggle against the White Civilizational Agenda

In the communal Cherokee way of life, she who controlled essential resources garnered power.[1] Because farming and child rearing were primarily their responsibility, precapitalist women controlled households and village lands. However, agrarian capitalism necessitated a major restructuring of labor mechanisms and of ownership of the means of production. Thus, Cherokee leaders committed themselves to elimination of the outward trappings of matrifocal families and matrilineal land control. After the Revolutionary War, the U.S. civilizational agenda polarized indigenous Appalachians by gender, race, class, and culture. Power, wealth, and land were concentrated in the hands of a small ethnically mixed group of merchant-traders, planters, and entrepreneurs who formed the nucleus of the nationalist leadership. In sharp contrast, nearly 80 percent of the families were poor small farmer-hunters who barely produced enough to survive (McLoughlin and Conser 1977, 681).

Agrarian capitalism left little place for the historical role of the wife's clan as her ultimate source of security (Perdue 1980, 20–21). Between 1808 and 1825, elite leaders attempted to institutionalize male dominance, patrilineal descent, and the cult of domesticity (McLoughlin 1986, 330–34). After 1800, Cherokee women were not only stigmatized and demonized on the basis of their inferior racial status in relation to whites. In addition to their gendered subordination, the vast majority of them were also differentiated by a nonwhite racial status lower than that of affluent ethnically mixed males, by their lower socioeconomic standing, and by a cultural traditionalism viewed as "savage" and "backward" (OIA Letters, NA, 12 Mar. 1825). However, a majority of Cherokee women did not acquiesce to the separate spheres ideologies that the ethnically mixed male elites sought to make culturally hegemonic. Between 1800 and 1835, Cherokee women engaged in class-based resistance against land cessions, against female disenfranchisement, and against culturicide (Fenelon 1998, 17–38).[2]

Women's Resistance against Land Cessions, 1800–1838

Between 1808 and 1825, the National Council instituted a series of laws that eroded matrilineal control over Cherokee lands (*Laws* 1852, 3–5, 45–46, 57, 119). On the one hand, the male leadership intended the shift toward patrilineage to symbolize to whites that Cherokee women were progressing toward

[1] Parts of this section first appeared in *American Indian Culture and Research Journal*, vol. 21, no. 1. The material is reprinted by permission of the American Indian Studies Center, UCLA.

[2] While Perdue (1985) and Taylor-Colbert (1997) argue that Cherokee women acculturated rapidly to elite white gender ideals, those writers derived their generalizations from analysis of the lifestyles of that small portion of the population who were affluent ethnically mixed males and their wives. As a result of such methodological blunders, they silenced the majority of indigenous women, whose rebellious presences haunt the uneasy pages written by racist missionaries, Indian agents, and regional newspapers. Subsequently, Perdue (1998, 229n64) changed her view about the degree to which Cherokee women absorbed the cult of domesticity. Because she drew her generalizations from documents that only reflect the lifestyle of an elite male and his wife, Taylor-Colbert (1997) ignored the resistance and the poverty of a majority of Cherokee women.

the cult of domesticity ideals of the U.S. civilizational program (Brainerd Journal, HUL, 12 Oct. 1817 and 13 Feb. 1817). On the other hand, the struggle to end communal land control by matrilineal clans derived from demands for individual property ownership to facilitate economic growth and wealth accumulation. As political decision making was centralized in the hands of elite males, women's public sphere of influence contracted. Consequently, women's voices had effectively disappeared from deliberations about land cessions to the U.S. government by the late eighteenth century (McLoughlin 1986, 330–34). Still, missionaries acknowledged that each of the seven matrilineal clans "ha[d] its separate portion of land, which [wa]s held in common" (ABCFM Papers, HUL, 10 Oct. 1828). Consequently, Georgia women circulated a petition in 1817 to lodge their protest "against an exchange of country." They urged the men to "keep [thei]r hands off of paper talks" and "not to part with any more of [Cherokee] lands." During that same year, the women were instrumental in organizing town opposition to National Council negotiations with the U.S. government. Fifty-four towns and villages convened outside the sanction of the National Council "to deliberate and consider the situation of our nation, in the disposition of our common property of lands" (SOW Letters, NA, 6 May 1817).

Women continued their resistance against elite transfer of Cherokee lands to whites by presenting a second petition to the Ustanali council the next year. That males dominated such matters is clear from the apologetic tone of the women. "Your mothers and your sisters ask and beg of you not to part with any more of our lands," they pleaded (SOW Letters, NA, 25 July 1818). Although the elite leadership continued to dominate land diplomacy with the U.S. government and to shift Cherokee territory away from matrilineal control, the National Council enacted a provision in 1820 that was intended to appease female disquietude. White husbands were no longer permitted to sell the lands of their Cherokee wives, and it would be an act of treason for any such individual to transfer ownership of Cherokee lands without approval of the National Council (Evans 1981, 73).

Women's Resistance against Disenfranchisement, 1800–1838
In addition to concentrating land into the hands of a few mestizo elites and interracial households, agrarian capitalism triggered public policies that disempowered women. Between 1800 and 1838, elite males constructed a centralized government based on dispersed farming and patrilineal families (McLoughlin 1986, 91–97). Missionaries fostered the view that "so long as the Indians lived together in towns, they always would remain lazy, careless, miserable, and poor folk" (Brainerd Journal, HUL, 29 Dec. 1818). The U.S. government pressured Cherokees to "disperse from their large towns, buil[d] convenient houses, clear and fence farms" (Hamilton 1971, 32–33). In an attempt to demonstrate widespread indigenous progress toward this civilizational goal, Cherokee elites claimed incorrectly in official records and letters that traditional villages "ha[d]

disappeared" by 1826 and that town governance had been replaced by eight district councils and a 13-member national committee (Sturtevant 1981, 81). In addition to weakening women's control over family and land, the National Council severely narrowed the public presence that women had exhibited in precapitalist villages. There is little evidence that women continued their traditional political participation in postrevolutionary centralized governance, for matrilineal clans were no longer equitably represented in national affairs. Under the guidance of elite ethnically mixed War Woman Nancy Ward, the Women's Council was disbanded in 1818 (SOW Letters, NA, 25 July 1818), eliminating the legitimate structure through which female voices were integrated into community decision making.[3]

Like politically silenced Euroamerican females, Cherokee women could no longer vote or hold office in the new "democratic" national structure (*Laws* 1852, 20–21, 14–18, 31–32). For females in interracial marriages, communal life, the clan system, and the extended family had faded by the early 1820s. Those households were moving steadily toward the nuclear family, toward adaptation of the cult of domesticity, and toward patriarchal gender norms (Strickland 1975, 97). However, the majority of Cherokee women resided in traditional households and were exhibiting few signs of acculturation. Though dispersed throughout the countryside, many women continued to live in small extended-family clusters that protected their rights within matrilineal clans.[4] While they may have been excluded from national decision making, women kept clans and towns alive as origination points for grassroots resistance, thereby diminishing the control of the National Council over the majority of families. In 1822, one-third or more of the population "continue[d] to live in towns" (Evans 1981, 62). During the five years following the creation of the National Council, missionaries documented their attendance at several town council meetings in which resistant Cherokees conducted community business in secret. In a northwest Georgia town, "the council hall was partly underground." Trusted visitors were conducted "through a dark labyrinth with sepulchral surroundings into the August presence of the chiefs, who sat in solemn silence, and arrayed in costume" (Brainerd Journal, HUL, 17 Oct. 1817, 2 Nov. 1818, 22 Jan. 1822, and 20 Nov. 1817).

After 1820, the mestizo National Council passed several laws that were designed to diminish the authority of local leaders who were elected by matrilineal clans to manage town affairs (*Laws* 1852, 4–20). Despite those national regulations, local communities preserved elements of the traditional political

---

[3] Two women accompanied the official delegation to the president in 1808, and women presented two petitions about land disposal to the National Council in 1817–18. Other than these three examples, women do not appear in the official records of governance (McLoughlin 1986, 224–36, 326–30, 398).

[4] In northern Georgia, for instance, there were still a "great many Indian camps" along the Coosa River in 1837. Each "camp" consisted of several small cabins, surrounded by "some few acres cleared" and planted with women's corn, beans, and squash (Greenlee Diary, UNC, 1: 3).

participation of women, as the details of one 1822 town meeting demonstrate. When two Brainerd missionaries sought permission to open a school and to hold Christian services, the Turkeytown chief told them he "would lay the subject" before the town's council of seven clan heads. The missionaries accompanied the chief to the council house, where they "found perhaps a hundred sons and daughters of the forest." As custom demanded, the chief spoke briefly, asking the group to listen to the talk of the missionaries. After their speech, the visitors were expected "in token of friendship, to shake hands with all the people," who then passed before them in order of their status in the town. Finally, the chief "exhort[ed] all to attend to what they had heard," and the meeting closed without any vote in the presence of the white outsiders (Brainerd Journal, HUL, 19–21 Jan. 1822, 31 July 1837, 11 Feb. 1823, 20 Nov. 1823). One year before removal, missionaries were still reporting such meetings in numerous town council houses. Throughout the 1820s, traditional Cherokees identified missionaries as threats to town authority (CM Papers, MA, 26 May 1824; *Cherokee Phoenix*, 22 Oct. 1828). Because the centralized government made decisions about missions, towns could not legally restrict their activities. In 1823, Pathkiller "spoke with approbation of the laws, which the young chiefs [we]re introducing, so differently from their former customs." When the National Council refused to remove missionaries from their region in 1824, the Etowah Cherokees boycotted the school because the missionaries were "trying to doe away" with their "common custom of meeting" in their townhouse. In 1825, missionaries labeled the town council house at Taloney "the Devil's meetinghouse," inflaming a convert and his friends to burn the building. The missionary reported that "the wicked [we]re very much enraged and threaten[ing] to harm [thei]r School House" in retaliation (ABCFM Papers, HUL, 16 July 1825, 20 Aug. 1825, 22 Aug. 1825, 21 Nov. 1825).

Cherokee women laid the political and cultural groundwork for a widespread popular call for a return to traditional town decision making. According to missionary accounts, "the majority of people [we]re dissatisfied" with the barrage of laws that had been implemented during the 1820s. Women's cultural resistance, especially that of female conjurors (CM Papers, MA, 16 May 1827) and their followers, fueled "assertion of [cultural] pride against white arrogance," and opposition to constitutional government culminated in White Path's Rebellion of 1827–28. The goal of the revitalization movement "was to achieve tolerance toward and self-respect for the majority who still adhered to the religion and traditions of their culture" (McLoughlin 1984b, 213–38). One worried missionary reported that "there is now existing in this nation a most fearful division among the Cherokee. The full Cherokees have risen up against the laws of the Nation and appear to desire their old form of government" (ABCFM Papers, HUL, 29 Mar. 1827 and 10 May 1827). Subsequently, the National Council banned the kind of dissident town meetings that had spurred the resistance. One hundred lashes would be the punishment for instigators of "unlawful meetings with intent to create factions... or to encourage rebellion" (*Laws* 1852, 117).

Women's Resistance against Culturicide, 1811–1828

A majority of Cherokee females certainly did not succumb passively to the white patriarchal system. Quite the contrary, women were pivotal activists in two major resistance movements aimed at cultural revitalization: the 1811–13 religious revival and the antimission movement of the 1820s. Widespread participation in the cultural revitalization movement of 1811–13 began with a vision calling for a return to the production of corn by women's traditional methods, and prophets emphasized the need to revitalize two practices. First, Cherokees should return to the use of Indian maize instead of the "corn of the white people." Second, men should "do away with mills," so women could "pound" the corn in the old way. "This change was essential because 'the Mother of the Nation ha[d] forsaken [the people] because all her bones [we]re being broken through the grinding'" (Springplace Diary, GHC, 11 Feb. 1811).

Missionaries and the Indian agent expressed racist alarm that cultural traditionalists were "calling them back to a simpler form of agricultural life" in which women engaged in communal farming to produce most of the food essential to village survival. Cultural activists admonished Cherokees to return to subsistence farming and swine herding, economic activities in which women specialized (Perdue 1980, 27–30). The movement also advocated resurgence of (a) conjuring of illnesses with traditional herbs and rituals and (b) the annual observance of the Green Corn Ceremony, public activities in which women participated equitably with men. The revitalization vision did not call for a return to the male-dominated fur trade or for reclamation of lost male-dominated hunting grounds. Rather, the dissidents warned Cherokees to recover from whites the land where their sacred "mother towns" lay. Thus, the appeal was for a return to the cultural and political traditions that characterized life in towns where matrilineal clans and women had played active roles in community decision making (McLoughlin 1984b, 86–89). Women played central roles in this resistance against elite-dominated nationalism and missionary-driven culturicide, and female conjurors frequently presented visions and predictions of disasters or crises. Two of the three people who received and spread the first vision were women. A young woman made a trip to the Indian Agency to warn Jonathan Meigs that the Cherokees "ought to throw away the habits of white people and return to the ancient manners." After an old woman named Laughing Molly accurately predicted earthquakes that rocked the Nation, women accosted and warned more acculturated females to return to traditional dress. As a result, the Indian agent reported that "some of the females [we]re mutilating fine muslin dresses" (CIAT Reports, NA, 19 Mar. 1812). Women also objected to Cherokee adoption of white dances and music at traditional feasts and entertainment, so they would appear at the homes of "disrespectful" families to tell them "they must discontinue dancing reels and country dances which ha[d] become common amongst the young people" (Springplace Diary, GHC, 17 Feb. 1812, 11 Feb. and 1 Mar. 1811).

After 1825, the lifestyle of the mestizo national leadership became increasingly polarized from the majority of Cherokees (Perdue 1985, 51). By 1828, more than one-fifth of the National Council were Christians, but only 8 percent of all Cherokee adults had converted (Payne Papers, NLC, 8: 110–11, 23). Missionaries recognized that there was "a very great difference" between the small acculturated "highest class" and the "lowest class" majority (CM Papers, MA, 21 Aug. 1809). Only a tiny minority of Cherokees were commercial farmers, but that acculturated gentry applied to a majority of their neighbors the same class-based animosities that prosperous southerners used to marginalize poor whites. Cherokee agrarian capitalists frequently used the bilingual *Cherokee Phoenix* (2 July 1828) to demean and to try to stimulate a public outcry against "the backward lower class," who were "holding back the nation's progress." Paralleling race and class hostilities of elite whites, affluent Cherokees claimed that the "unenlightened parts" of the Nation needed to be "cured from their idleness," which was "deeply engrained in their nature" (Lowrie and Clarke 1832, 2: 651–52).

Over the objections of the majority of women and of the population, about 50 highly acculturated pro-slavery elites ceded southeastern Cherokee lands to the U.S. government in 1835. To justify such a nondemocratic intervention, the *Cherokee Phoenix* editor contended that the ruling mestizo elite could "see strong reasons to justify the action of a minority of fifty persons – to do what the majority *would do* if they understood their condition" (Perdue 1983, 162). Their self-interested land cession would culminate in the 1838 military removal of Cherokees to Oklahoma. Eastern Cherokee class differences between dark-skinned and mestizo, between traditionalists and progressives, and between slaveholders and nonslaveholders would become even more pronounced among females in the western Cherokee Nation. The *Cherokee Advocate* (4 Feb. 1851) proclaimed that "those who cling with death-like tenacity to our old rites and ceremonies do not consider that a moral change is taking place in the Cherokee world." In the 1850s, dark-skinned girls complained about discrimination and scapegoating at the Female Seminary where lighter skin coloring and hair were idealized in the school paper (Ruiz and DuBois 2000, 183–96). Class and ethnic cleavages are clear in the public stance of the ethnically mixed superintendent of the Female Seminary. "It is the white blood that has made us what we are," she proclaimed. The solution to the "backwardness" of the majority of Cherokee females, therefore, lay in "encourag[ing] intermarriages with whites" (*Cherokee Rose Buds*, 2 Aug. 1854). While graduates of the Female Seminary represented the most acculturated and affluent families of the Cherokee Nation, a majority of girls either were never enrolled in school or were assigned to trade schools where they worked to cover the costs of board and tuition (*Kansas City Times*, 29 July 1889). In other words, there are few signs that most Cherokee females had acculturated toward the "cult of true womanhood" as late as 1860.

Gendered Class Divisions among Appalachian Slaves

Revisionist women's historians have challenged the myth that there were sharp class differences among slaves, arguing that most black women worked in the fields rather than their owners' homes (Fraser, Saunders, and Wakelyn 1985, 15). Similarly, there was no sharp status disjuncture on most Appalachian plantations because very few female slaves were assigned to occupations other than field labor. Indeed, only about 13 percent of all adult female Appalachian slaves worked full-time at nonfield labor assignments, so very few were employed at tasks for which they were provided atypical privileges (see Table 7, Web site). On small plantations, the occupational structure was bifurcated by gender, resulting in the assignment of higher status to males, who were either artisans or skilled workers hired out on profitable annual contracts. By 1820, staple crop production had generated a gender-bifurcated division of labor. Females were increasingly assigned to unskilled manual field labor, and the work of slave women was less varied than that of men. No matter the staple crop or the scale of operation throughout the New World, females were disproportionately assigned to field labor, freeing males to work at more profitable occupations. Thus, females experienced fewer alternatives to field labor than male slaves. Almost universally, skilled labor was men's work; and enslaved females were concentrated in the fields. The upper echelon of the occupational hierarchy (about 20 percent of the slave labor force) was heavily dominated by male slaves, who were drivers, blacksmiths, carpenters, millwrights, wheelwrights, mechanics, coopers, tanners, shoemakers, and skilled livestock experts (Fogel 1989, 46–51). Enslaved Appalachian males were employed as drivers, skilled artisans, and manufacturing or commercial laborers 14 times more often than females. When women were employed in industry or commerce, they were 50 times more likely than males to be utilized as unskilled laborers. While Appalachian slave women were most often hired near home as lower-valued domestic servants, hotel maids, or field laborers, males were more likely to be hired out to distant industrial or commercial employers (see Table 15, Web site).

Elite occupations were those that released slaves from field labor and diminished the degree of white supervision. In addition, elite occupations were those skills associated with the master's accumulation of profit. While all slaves were assigned some nonagricultural tasks, a sizable minority were highly skilled and specialized. In the United States, about one-third of all male slaves and about one-quarter of all female slaves were employed in occupations other than field labor. Among male slaves, 3.2 percent were drivers, 3 percent were domestics, and another 26 percent were skilled and semiskilled artisans and livestock specialists. On average in the United States, slave women had fewer opportunities for acquiring skills, so 18.4 percent were domestics, and 8 percent were textile artisans or semiskilled specialists (Fogel and Engerman 1974, 1: 43). However, Appalachian plantations structured opportunities for the emergence of male artisan occupations more often than these national trends. Appalachian slaves were skilled industrial artisans and commercial laborers 1.3 times more often than other U.S. slaves, and they were three times more likely than other southern slaves to rise to *driver*, the top management position to which a slave could aspire. More than one-quarter of male slaves were employed full-time as skilled artisans or as hireouts to commercial and industrial employers, but females were not assigned to such elite occupations. While Appalachian slaves were allocated to full-time domestic occupations 1.3 times more frequently than other U.S. slaves (see Tables 15, 16, Web site), most of these female assignments were low-paying hireouts to distant employers rather than positions of visible privilege in owners' households.

On Appalachian plantations, slave women worked alongside men at most productive economic tasks, including fieldwork, meat production, tobacco manufacturing, milling, cotton ginning, and leather tanning. Despite this gender blurring, women did the dirtiest, least-skilled, most back-breaking tasks. Even when slave women assisted with skilled crafts, their contributions remained hidden and unrewarded. One example was the regimen necessary to support the male-dominated shoemaking process. Women did most of the labor to gather tanning bark, keep fires fueled, and prepare and cure the hides (Wiggington 1975, 75–78, 163n). At one western Carolina farm, women hauled bark from the forest while a male operated a mill to grind the wood into the powder needed to produce tannic acid. Women cleaned, stretched, and dried the hides; in the evenings they also kneaded and rolled them to make them more pliable and soft. Women also made small animal skins into shoe strings and prepared a mixture of tallow and beeswax to soften and waterproof shoes. Women carried wood and maintained fires under the vats while a male stirred hides in the tannic acid solution. After the skins were initially tanned, women stretched, dried, and softened them again. In fact, women probably contributed several weeks' labor in the tanning process to every hour that males spent finishing the leather into shoes. Despite their greater labor inputs, however, female contributions were unacknowledged, and women added these tasks to their regular fieldwork and nighttime textiles production. In contrast, the male shoemaker was rewarded with field release time, cash-earning opportunities, and the diminished white supervision that accompanied higher work status (Greenlee Diary, UNC, 16 Jan. 1851, 10 Feb. 1851, 15 May 1851).

Slave women clothed the entire labor force, and sometimes the owner's household, thereby minimizing the cash outlay of their masters for manufactured goods (see Chapter 6). Why, then, were female textile artisans less rewarded than male shoemakers or blacksmiths? Clearly, the explanation does not lie in the complexity or the physical demands of the gender-segregated tasks. First, it is inaccurate to presume that most male elite jobs required greater strength or skill than women's crafts. When selecting artisans, masters utilized height, skin color, and loyal deference as much more important criteria than brute strength or intellectual prowess (Fogel and Engerman 1992, 176–77). If women were assigned less often to crafts because they were not as physically strong as men, why did females predominate in the field labor force? Because they were assigned a quota of nightly textiles output year-round, women worked longer hours than males each day. In addition, they utilized textiles equipment that required greater dexterity, stamina, and physical strength than the equipment of the male shoemaker, cooper, tanner, or livestock specialist. In many ways, textiles production required much more accumulated knowledge, manual skill, and physical persistence than any of the elite male crafts. Still, these important crafts did not generate the cash-earning opportunities or release time for women that elite occupations did for males. Moreover, female textiles producers were frequently supervised by their white mistresses while white masters typically permitted male artisans to work independently, even to travel in the neighborhood to market their manufactured commodities or services.

Obviously, the work of male artisans was not ranked at the top of the occupational hierarchy because it required greater skill or stamina. Neither were males at the top of the occupational hierarchy because slaveholders were reluctant to assign females to work under male overseers. While men supervised most of the field tasks done by Appalachian slave women, most male artisans worked without close supervision. Indeed, elite occupations were those that were linked directly to the profitmaking enterprises of the master, and they generated significant cash returns. The economic value of "women's work" was unrecognized because it was more clearly tied to the subsistence needs of the master's family and to the production of black household survival needs. In short, owners devalued the household production of enslaved women in the same manner they rendered invisible the economic contributions of their wives and daughters. Even in the assignment of slave laborers, the dominant gender conventions of Appalachian slaveholders reflected the values, aspirations, and anxieties of the dominant southern class. Outside the kitchen, masters rarely placed women in command of men, and they assigned women to the least profitable enterprises. Through these labor management strategies, Appalachian slave women were disadvantaged by the redefinition of their labors as "housewifely" tasks that did not have the market value of the work of male artisans or hireouts. The transformation that impacted Appalachian slave women was capitalism's "steady devaluation of the work of women...and a corresponding emphasis on the value of the adult male's work" (Wallerstein 1983, 25). In order to relieve men for hireouts at higher profit rates, Appalachian masters reacted to the gender-bifurcated slave trading market by assigning males to nonfield occupations. A skilled male artisan was priced 150 percent higher than an unskilled male of the same age, but complex craft skills, such as weaving, rarely increased the sales value of female slaves (Fogel and Engerman 1992, 31–53).

Color, Class, and Gender Divisions among Free Black Appalachians

Unlike enslaved Appalachians, free blacks were differentiated by color-class differences. Using county registers of free blacks, we can examine the complexities of class, race, color, and gender among free black Appalachians. The registers of free blacks exhibit a clear pattern of marriages along color lines, for a black/mulatto marriage almost never appears in these documents. In addition, a majority of mulatto females did not marry, even when there were children in their households. While 14 percent of the free black families were composed of members of more than one color, the majority of these households were either black women living with mulatto children or extended families composed of kin who were of various skin colors (see Table 45, Web site). However, we should not assume from these limited records that a majority of free blacks were making choices along color lines, as opposed to working within constraints imposed upon them by local elites and officials. Very few of the unmarried mulatto mothers bore black or dark children or lived with light-skinned males. Consequently, we should suspect that these women continued to be trapped in exploitative linkages with white male sponsors. The registers document stays of two or more decades for mulatto families. However, mixed-color families averaged stays of only eight years, and black or brown families remained in the county less than four years. Between 1831 and 1842, the Knox County, Tennessee, court heard 14 petitions from free blacks; the judge permitted 12 mulattoes with strong white ties to remain, ordering 2 darker blacks with insufficient local "white guardianship" to leave (Howington 1986, 162–63).

The registers indirectly make clear another aspect of the complex interaction of class with racial discrimination and privilege. While the laws regulating free blacks were rigid in rhetoric, the registers do not demonstrate that those laws were implemented stringently. Only a fraction of all the free blacks enumerated in the censuses and tax lists were actually registered by county court clerks.[5] Indeed, the registers primarily document mulatto families who persisted in the counties over several generations. Often, the recorded language of the court clerk is highly informal, noting that freedom is proved by the unspoken white familial past of a specific emancipated mulatto. By leaving history unstated for this progenitor, the clerk is indicating that "everyone" in the community knows this person and the historical ties to local elites. In contrast, a majority of free blacks were historically silenced and trapped in a vulnerable legal context. In reality, most free blacks were *undocumented illegal aliens*, and they could be arrested or detained by sheriffs or patrols, prosecuted by the courts, and sentenced to long-term indenturement or sale into slavery. In effect, then, the county court's failure to document proof of freedom made it easier for local elites to reenslave free black laborers. The registers of free blacks are no more than a historical chronology of a small number of families who were born in the county, had ties to local slaveholders, and had never engaged in behaviors that caused whites to view them as threats. In other words, the registers legitimated a few mulatto or color-mixed families whose ties to white patriarchal families were known, but kept publicly silent.

When they failed to meet ancestry, color, and class criteria that were not formally entrenched into written laws, individuals or families could expect either to be expelled or to be marginalized as a "dangerous class" of "unsavory poor blacks" who threatened community security. To be among the favored few, the free black must have been born in the county, be mulatto in skin color, be tied to local elites, and have no history of unacceptable behaviors or associates.

---

[5] Bodenhorn (2002) found low registration of blacks throughout Virginia.

However, favored mulattoes were also constrained from helping their nonresident kin to migrate. Staunton mulatto Robert Campbell was first registered in Augusta County in 1814, and his subsequent kin were enumerated continuously through 1864. By the 1850s, his family consisted of 11 adult children, and he had accumulated far more wealth than was typical of free blacks in the county. Still, the court was not friendly toward his request to relocate his adult daughter from Petersburg. When Margaret Smith was finally registered, the county court extended to the father and one of her brothers a privilege usually reserved only to whites. While the clerk permitted Robert Campbell and his adult son to stand as "her securities," the court also required that the family pay a "bond in the sum of five hundred dollars" (Bushman 1989, 108, 113, 114, 124, 126, 128, 138, 139, 140, 142).

Primary documents show a sharp class-based contradiction among residents about the degree to which free blacks should be regulated. When the North Carolina legislature moved to restrict voting rights, Surry, Wilkes, Burke, and McDowell Counties advocated limited suffrage for black landowners. During the same period, however, Buncombe County citizens petitioned the state legislature for high taxes on free blacks to deter "the constant influx of free negroes of every character & description into the western part of the state." Similarly, 3 Appalachians were among the 14 senators who voted against a North Carolina law to ban free black migration into the state (Franklin 1943, 118–20, 43). In the same year, citizens of Loudoun and Hampshire Counties forwarded contradictory petitions to the Virginia legislature. One called free blacks a "degraded population" who "elude the officers of justice by flying from county to county." The second attacked "the law requiring the removal" of emancipated slaves from the state. Because free blacks were a "valuable labor supply," several Loudoun County, Virginia, merchants and shop owners petitioned for relief from the law requiring emancipated slaves to leave the state. Even though they also submitted several petitions demanding permanent removal of free blacks, Fauquier and Frederick Counties refused to indict free blacks for remaining in the state. Hundreds of petitions were filed by Appalachian citizens requesting the legal right for specific free blacks to remain in their counties.

What accounts for this lack of white Appalachian racial solidarity? A majority of the petitions to county courts or state legislatures were interventions made in behalf of a small group of racially mixed African-Americans who possessed "white social capital," reflected in their social ties to influential elites and their higher incidence of "gentility," literacy, and occupational skills. These stereotypes about free blacks were a reflection of slaveholder preference for lighter-skinned domestic servants and skilled artisans. In addition, ethnically mixed female slaves were more often targeted for sexual liaisons, establishing the motivation for owners to liberate women who bore their racially mixed offspring. Thus, affluent whites considered "industrious, deferential, loyal" mulattoes to be stronger assets to their communities than most landless whites. Sharp color-class distinctions were drawn between "undesirable" impoverished free blacks and those few who had acquired property (like Arthur Lee of Alleghany County) or those who had close ties to local slaveholders (like Edmund Kean of Winchester). For instance, several Pocahontas County landed whites signed the petition of Robert Trout, a free man of property, attesting that he was "not In Clined to Stir up mischief with those that air slaves in this Neighborhood" (Legislative Papers, VSL, 1812–49 petitions).[6]

In contrast, a majority of the petitions for removal or greater legal constraints originated from small groups of middle-class and working-class nonslaveholders who resented paying taxes to fund local patrols and to operate poor houses for "lazy blacks." Even though some elite and middle-class slaveholders intervened in behalf of a select few free blacks, there is no evidence among legislative petitions or primary accounts that poor whites joined with elites in support of efforts to keep selected free blacks in Appalachian counties. Slaveholders attempted to convince the general public that the free mulattoes they protected were "a better class" because they offered services or labor skills that were in demand in the community. For example, a large number of Warrenton whites attested to the suitability of African-American barber Daniel Warner. Winchester townspeople defended the continued stay of Randle Evans, who operated a confectionery that was "a source of great convenience and utility." In addition, white Appalachians resisted the deportation of ordinary laborers who were closely connected to local elites. To warrant such concern, free blacks had to be defined as "generally useful and industrious," as "honest," as "marked with correct deportment," and as laborers who had exhibited "fidelity & devotion" to past owners. Since Sam Digges was married to an enslaved woman owned by one of their peers, 38 Fauquier County elites sought to protect him, even though he had "for some time been a waiter," serving liquor illegally in "the Tavern at Fauqr. Ct. House." Nearly 100 Leesburg whites (including 7 justices, 16 merchants, 6 lawyers, and the postmaster) championed the cause of Harriet Cook, a washerwoman – an occupation that typically stigmatized a female head of household (Russell 1913, 84–88, 159). In one instance, Giles County slaveholders endorsed the unusual petition of three blacks for the legal right to carry firearms on the grounds that these livestock drovers needed rifles to protect their employers' cattle and hogs "from wild beasts in the mountainous countryside."

It is important to add a qualification to these trends. First, free black registers are not representative of the entire African-American population, so we do not know whether marriages across color lines occurred routinely among the majority of free black Appalachians who were undocumented. Indeed, the frequency of color mixing represented in Reconstruction photographs and the degree to which Appalachian ex-slaves described light-skinned spouses should cause us to question how deeply color-class lines were embedded in local black

[6] Between 1812 and 1849, there were petitions from the counties of Albemarle, Allegany, Augusta, Berkeley, Cumberland, Fauquier, Frederick, Hampshire, Jefferson, Lee, Loudoun, Monongalia, Pocahontas, and Wythe.

TABLE 3. *Wealth and Class Divisions among White Southern Appalachian Households, 1860*

Appalachian Counties of	Poor Households		Low Income & Working Class		Middle Class		Wealthy Elites	
	%	$ Avg. Wealth	%	$ Avg. Wealth	%	$ Avg. Wealth	%	$ Avg. Wealth
Alabama	40.9	122	10.8	454	41.9	2,136	6.4	38,105
Georgia	38.3	93	7.2	450	39.6	2,666	14.9	20,788
Kentucky	40.0	115	9.6	452	48.8	1,845	1.6	14,339
Maryland	43.7	61	8.2	473	36.2	2,155	11.9	28,106
North Carolina	46.0	82	9.2	447	36.4	2,130	8.4	19,787
South Carolina	45.6	110	5.9	431	32.4	2,408	16.1	20,731
Tennessee	40.8	111	7.0	448	42.6	2,394	9.6	18,595
Virginia	54.4	67	5.0	459	26.6	2,507	14.0	27,639
West Virginia	45.8	92	6.9	451	37.8	2,331	9.5	26,276
Region	41.7	95	7.5	402	38.1	2,286	12.7	23,906

Sources and notes: Derived from analysis of a systematic probability sample of 3,056 households drawn from the 1860 Census of Population enumerator manuscripts. By national standards, an impoverished household held less than $350 in total assets, low income/working class = $350 to $599, middle class = $600 to $7,499; wealthy elites = $7,500 and up; see Soltow (1975). The % column indicates the percentage of all households that fall within each class grouping.

communities in which females so outnumbered males. What we can generalize, however, from registers of free blacks, from the frequency of elite petitions for a favored few, and from other primary sources is that elite and middle-class whites drew sharp class-color distinctions among free blacks, most often privileging mulatto descendants of prestigious local white families (Legislative Papers, VSL, Giles County Petitions, 9 Dec. 1824, 18 Dec. 1841).

Class Conflict among White Appalachian Women

White Appalachians were sharply polarized between more affluent households and those who were impoverished. Composing about 13 percent of the region's households, the wealthiest families monopolized nearly three-quarters of total regional wealth (see Table 5, Web site). They were well educated, and their material consumption reflected their average household wealth of nearly $24,000 – an economic level that was more than 200 times the household assets of nearly half the population and 10 times greater than the holdings of the typical middle-class household. About 38 percent of the region's white households were "respectable" middle-class farm owners, government officials, and clergy, who averaged about $2,300 in assets (see Table 3). In 1860, families with less than $300 in assets earned $100 yearly or less, and they were impoverished by national standards (Soltow 1975, 63–65). About half the white Appalachian population fell among the country's poor. About 8 percent of these households owned small farms, but the majority of these families were landless laborers who either sharecropped parcels, worked as unstably employed day laborers, or earned wages at nonagricultural occupations. In the sections that follow, I will examine

- class junctures among elite and middle-class Appalachians,
- cultural biases against poor white Appalachians,
- class struggle about the dignity of work, and
- elite biases against working women.

Class Junctures among Elite and Middle-Class Appalachians

While middle-class Civil War veterans sometimes reflected cultural biases parallel to those of elites, there was much that separated them from the region's wealthiest families. In addition to running small plantations, Appalachian middle-class households cut across a wide urban/rural spectrum of nonslaveholding merchants, industrialists, travel capitalists, professionals, farmers, and extractive capitalists. Moreover, many families among the minority religious sects, especially the Quakers, fell among the middle class in their communities. While there were a few abolitionist schools (e.g., Tennessee's Maryville College and Kentucky's Berea College) and a few middle-class antislavery proponents, such as Elihu Embree (1820) and Ezekiel Birdseye (Dunn 1997), I have found no primary sources to document widespread white Appalachian opposition to slavery. Indeed, middle-class whites benefited from the slavery system and many aspired to achieve the levels of wealth and power held by the richest slaveholding elites in their communities and states. While the political roles of middle-class males expanded, the nonslaveholding poor remained unrepresented. In West Virginia, for example, the proportion of judges from the wealthiest decile declined to less than half by 1800, making room for local middle-class lawyers in the courts (Smith 1973). A Civil War veteran whose family owned 40 slaves and nonagricultural investments in mountainous Bledsoe County, Tennessee, pinpointed one of the major ways in which middle-class nonslaveholders were invested in maintaining "the peculiar institution." Because many middle-class Appalachians "did not regard manual labor as respectable for a gentleman," they "usually were employed" as attorneys, holders of local political offices, teachers, or doctors who provided public services to slaveholders. To support their professional lifestyles, they frequently hired slaves (Dyer and Moore 1985, 317).

Still, there was a great deal of variation in the wealth levels of these middle sectors, and they were less visibly affluent in their dwellings and household goods and far less fashion-conscious than southern elites or northern urban middle classes. Even though her family was much more prosperous than half the population of her community, it was not unusual for the wife of a middle-class farmer, merchant, or industrialist to reside in a large log cabin or wood frame house. While traveling in the southwest Virginia countryside, a

young slaveholding elite female identified two subtle traits that caused a household to be recognized as that of a middle-class nonslaveholder: "striped paper
curtains in the parlor" and young ladies wearing cotton "sacques" rather than
the imported attire popular among rich females (Buni 1969, 98). Compared to
the northern middle class (Porter 1996) and to southern elites (Fox-Genovese
1988), Appalachian middle-class individuals were more likely to be illiterate
or to be poorly educated (see Table 13, Web site). Indeed, middle-class females
were more likely to be illiterate than males. In one Appalachian Quaker family, for instance, neither grandmother could read or write, and the son reported
that his mother and all his aunts "could do either but poorly" (*Janney's Virginia*
1978, 112).

The recorded experiences of Mary Campbell provide a rare glimpse into the
impassable chasm between middle-class and elite slaveholding women. Even
though her father was one of the most politically powerful and economically
influential men of east Tennessee, Mary had little formal education. After their
marriage and relocation to Abingdon, Virginia, her husband was a lawyer who
operated a small plantation, but his family connections made him influential
enough to be elected to the governorship. Despite their abilities to interact with
elites within the contexts of economic and political matters, she and her husband recognized the social distance between them and the richest families. By
1830 in Appalachian communities, the wealthiest elites segregated themselves
in tiny Episcopalian or Presbyterian congregations while a majority of their
middle-income and poor neighbors concentrated themselves in Methodist or
Baptist congregations. Slaveholding elites did not just accumulate wealth; they
also shaped the ideals of "cultured" womanhood, and they inequitably possessed limited social capital, including education, training in social etiquette,
clothing fashions, travel, and sociopolitical networks. Mary recognized her
class distance from the "arrogant aristocracy" because she was untrained in
the cultural and gender norms of elite slaveholding society. Consequently, she
described her years of social obligations in the Richmond Governor's Mansion
as "misirey and unhappiness." Sorely aware of the inadequacies of her social
capital and her lack of knowledge of the fine points of etiquette that could only
be learned at a finishing school, she cautioned her adopted daughter about how
crucial the appropriate education was for a southern woman. Of her attempt
to overcome the barriers between her own Appalachian middle-class past and
the lifestyle of Virginia's wealthiest slaveholding elites, Mary wrote: "I have
moved through the great wourld [of the Richmond Governor's Mansion] with
humbled and painfully blited feelings, for fear I could not acquit myself in the
established rules of the present order of society. O the heartrending and dis-
tressing feelings that have passed over me" (Appleton and Boswell 2003, 85,
99–100).

Cultural Biases against Poor White Appalachians

Despite these gradations of social distance, elite and middle-class households
were far less polarized from one another than they were from more than half the

FIGURE 9. This poor white woman is peddling cakes and beer to tourists at Natural Bridge in southwestern Virginia. Sharp class cleavages are made obvious in three ways: differences in dress, the poor woman's need to do public work outside her home, and the financial capacity of elite and middle-class women to afford leisure time and travel. The artist captured a look of pity or disdain on the face of the female tourist in the rear. *Source: Harper's Monthly* (August 1855).

white population who were poor. Because of land and wealth concentration, Southern Appalachia was one of the poorest geographical sections of the United States, and its white households were nearly twice as likely to be poor as families in the country as a whole (see Tables 8, 9, 10, 11, Web site). Half the population owned less than 3 percent of all regional wealth, averaged less than $200 in assets, and had less than $67 annual income. Land provided the economic basis for the structuring of polarized communities in which the richest families amassed a majority of the acreage while more than half the white households remained landless. The concentration of regional land resources into a few hands also meant that Appalachian farm operators were 1.7 times more likely to be tenants or sharecroppers than other Americans. By 1860, nearly two-fifths of the farms in Southern Appalachia were cultivated by operators who did not own the land. These landless farm laborers lived a precarious existence, and they were constantly on the move in search of employment.

The chances that a nineteenth-century white Appalachian could rise from the bottom of the social ladder were empirically delimited by several harsh realities. Land was heavily concentrated (Dunaway 1996), wage rates collapsed in the 1840s (Clark 1990, 306–7), and economic wealth did not trickle down to poor households (Soltow 1975). To improve their lot, working-class people needed to acquire a professional or specialized skill. In Southern Appalachia, however, education was accessible only to those who could afford to pay subscription fees or to send their children to distant academies. As a result, more than one-quarter of the whites older than 20 could not read or write, and probably another third were functionally illiterate (Hamer 1933, 1: 356–57). Slaveholding elites "held themselves a little aloof as they were as a class better educated," thought Samuel Miles of the tiny town of Kingston, Tennessee. With respect to schooling, affluent landowners "had the advantidg and used it," reported David Moss of Cherokee, North Carolina.[7]

Another barrier to upward mobility was caused by the lack of employment and entrepreneurial opportunities in the region. To complicate matters further, wages for agricultural labor were seasonal and low. In contrast to the elite myth of an easy rise to prosperity, nearly nine-tenths of the impoverished white Appalachian veterans were convinced that "the poor man had no chanc" to accumulate enough wealth to buy land. Averaging 23.4 years of age at the beginning of the Civil War, these young men on the lower rungs of the social scale had few jobs available to them, except unstable agricultural labor at wages averaging $6.00 per month. For these households, "money was mighty scarce," and "money jobs were hard to be had." Indeed landless rural whites "was vary pore men" who relocated almost yearly. At best, the antebellum economy promised the laborer a living, but little more. Thus, poorer households barely earned enough to meet subsistence needs, so there were no assets left over to accumulate toward the future (see Table 14, Web site). Because "it took all that a family could make to live," Appalachian veterans with limited means experienced work histories in which there was little possibility of acquiring land. In their estimation, it took considerable "time and toil for a young man to save enough to buy a farm for some of them had to take trade for their labor." Consequently, very few of the poorer veterans ever "saved enough to buy a farm." In some counties, even the opportunities to become a tenant farmer were seriously limited because affluent landholders would rather "allow their lands to grow up in sprouts" than rent parcels to poor men (Dyer and Moore 1985, 1, 22, 45–46, 94, 699, 801, 878, 940, 1063, 1235, 1946, 2165).

---

[7] More than half the veterans were from poor landless or small farm owner families, and almost all the respondents reported limited free public schooling (e.g., Dyer and Moore 1985, 5, 9, 13, 20, 897, 1080, 1229, 1360, 1922, 2013, 2086).

Landless and holding zero wealth, Washington Dawson, John Dinsmore, and Anderson Roach were convinced that "the poer class had a bad chance" because working-class people "was kep down as much as pasable." Joel Acuff emphasized that elite and middle-class farm owners "didn't want to elevate the poor boy very much." An Overton County veteran was even more direct in defining the nature of the class conflict between poor whites and elites. This landless husband could provide only a one-room cabin for his family because he could not find any way to earn income other than raising small numbers of livestock. "If they had not owned slaves," he angrily averred, "a man working as I was could have secured better wages" (Dyer and Moore 1985, 1, 45, 87, 88, 97, 107, 655). There is a great deal of scattered manuscript evidence to support the veteran's defiant assessment. For example, the Gwyn family paid white laborers 35 cents daily, but they preferred to hire slaves at 45 cents per day (Gwyn Papers, UNC, 29 Dec. 1845). In addition, railroads, canals, mines, and steamboats paid higher annual contract fees to slave owners than the wages offered to whites (Starobin 1970, 52).

In fact, more than a third of Appalachian households remained landless most of their productive years. Typical of this pattern was east Tennessean Isaac Brown, who reported at the age of 80 that he had farmed all his life "mostly on rented land." Walter Davenport recalled that poor white men and women worked on the farms of others "until they were so old they could not perform manual labor." Because of his family's near-starvation conditions on sharecropping parcels in Scott County, Virginia, Noah Garrett said, "I was a slave myself." A long-term analysis of landholding in mountainous Blount County, Tennessee, offers enlightening insight into the longevity of this pattern. Less than one-quarter of the Appalachian surname groups that were landless in 1801 had acquired land by 1860. More than three-quarters of these 1801 landless surname groups were either still unpropertied in 1860 or gone from the county. In addition, 16 percent of the 1801 landowning surname groups lost their holdings by 1860. A similar pattern occurred in Greene and Johnson Counties, Tennessee, where three-fifths of the landless households tracked over a 20-year period failed to acquire land, and 15 percent of the landowners lost their property (McKenzie 1988, 120). Typical of this pattern of intergenerational landlessness are the work histories of 59 laborers on the Lenoir Plantations of western North Carolina. Several of these agricultural households initiated sharecropping arrangements before the 1820s, yet none of them experienced this form of land tenure as a transitory step toward ownership. In fact, it was not unusual for the Lenoir tenants to renew their annual contracts for 20 to 30 years or longer. Josiah Anderson, for example, leased from 1828 until 1858. Daniel Henson, who began sharecropping in 1820, saw two of his sons become tenants in 1826 and 1833; in 1837 all three were still landless Lenoir laborers (Reid 1976, 71–73). Most poor white wage laborers were engaged by middle-class and wealthy farmers to complete specific short-term tasks or to assist with planting and harvest. The low, unstable wages of day laborers amounted to no more than food and shelter. In some Appalachian counties, one-quarter or more of laboring men were "out of honest work." For instance, Marion County, Tennessee, was "full of pore men," who "had to wourk hard on farming to raise their family." A Hall County, Georgia, veteran reported that landless young men like him "could not get a job" (Dyer and Moore 1985, 64, 1932, 1057, 243, 395, 780, 801, 940, 1387, 1435, 1670, 1858, 1404).[8]

The cultural and economic antithesis of the lifestyle of the "respectable" classes were the precarious living conditions endured by the landless two-fifths of the region's white households, who averaged less than $100 in accumulated wealth (see Tables 5, 12, Web site). These families were seven times more likely than landed Appalachians to be lacking in the "cultural capital" that was reflected in literacy and education. Popular intellectuals like Herbert Spencer (1851) argued that *biological determinism* – not societal inequalities – explained such human differences. Consequently, most elite and educated middle-class Americans were convinced that the poor failed to exhibit "social and cultural capital" (i.e., education, attire, speech, social connections, and pursuit of materialist goals) because they were handicapped by inherited weaknesses, gender predispositions, and racial inferiorities (Hofstadter 1944, 31–50). According to one Civil War veteran, there was a cultural "contempt on the part of prosperous nonslaveowners and thrifty slave-owners for the thriftless known as 'poor white trash'" (Dyer and Moore 1985, 801, 1235). Thus, the white Appalachian laborer was often culturally demeaned "as being no better than a slave" (Dyer and Moore 1985, 107). While his workers sat in earshot, "coarse, dirty, silent, embarrassed," one middle-class southwest Virginia slaveholder quipped to Frederick Olmsted (1860, 275–6) that white laborers "were very stupid at work, almost as much so as the negroes, and could not be set to do anything that required the least exercise of judgement." In sharp contrast to such stereotypes, poor white Appalachians struggled at any work they could find, often in life-threatening circumstances. One northern Georgia slaveholding mistress claimed that poor whites were "hardly protected from the weather by the rude shelters they frame[d] for themselves" (Kemble 1984, 110). Much like the region's rough one-room slave cabins, the average house of a poor white Appalachian was a single floorless room, with a large fireplace that was vented through a stick and mud chimney (Olmsted 1860, 200–201, 205). The census manuscripts provide strong evidence that a majority of these landless poor whites were malnourished and suffered high mortality rates (see Table 12, Web site). According to east Tennessee slave Rachel Cruze, "The pore white folks mostly had a harder time than the colored folks" (Rawick 1977, 5: 320–21).

---

[8] In a systematic probability sample of 3,056 households drawn from the 1860 Census of Population manuscripts, NA, 47 percent of the landless heads of household were younger than 34 while 56 percent were older than 35, one-third of them older than 47. Blount County's 1801 tax list and 1860 census manuscripts were computerized and alphabetized to permit longitudinal tracking. Households were grouped by surname and each surname group was tracked in both sets of records. To check for inheritance, 1801 landless heads of household with the same surname as landholders were tracked again in the 1860 Census. Data about unemployment of day laborers were also derived from analysis of this sample; see Web site for methods.

Class Struggle about the Dignity of Work

As a result of the class inequalities associated with wealth, land, and slaveholding, antebellum Southern Appalachia was characterized by a sharp cultural
division of labor between the region's white elite and middle-class households
and the poor and working-class majority. Hamilton County, Tennessee, veteran John Allen referred to a community schism between "the Two Classes
of People," a phrase that divided those who had to do manual labor from
those who had servants. Since wealth, land, and political power were heavily
concentrated in their hands, affluent Appalachians could utilize their local positions to sustain within their communities an exploitative division of labor and
to foster a cultural sphere predominantly divided along class lines. Elite and
middle-class Appalachians reflected antipoor stereotypes that were widespread
in the United States, and they set criteria for "respectability, thrift, and cultural
refinement" that were beyond the reach of three-fifths of the Caucasian population. Analysis of the Civil War veteran questionnaires (Dyer and Moore 1985)
shows that most middle-class farmers and merchants – both slaveholding and
nonslaveholding – tended to agree with elite value judgments about the poor.
Appalachian elites "were in separate and distinct classes," according to the
son of a Meigs, Tennessee, large slaveholder. Still those "Southern gentlemen
always recognized *worth* and *merit* and *respectability*." While respectability
might hinge on wealth earned from work, the standards of worth and merit
were assigned only to those individuals who possessed the appropriate personal social capital. That is, the lower-status person could not achieve these
heights because she needed to be "of equal intelligence, refinement and education," ideological camouflage that eliminated a majority of the population. The
son of a middle-class Watauga County, North Carolina, slaveholder, Stephen
Brown, remembered that his close circle of friends assumed that people were
poor because they "wouldn't work." So they "rather looked down" on the poor
because they "were not respectable." John Fain Anderson, owner of 15 slaves
in the small town of Loudon, Tennessee, worked eight white hands long hours,
but he still claimed they "did not work" because they were "trifling, worse than
a mean negro" (Dyer and Moore 1985, 4, 197, 402, 698–99).[9] Middle-class
slaveholder John Horry Dent (Farm Journal, TROY, 22 Mar. 1869) of Floyd
County, Georgia, stereotyped free laborers as inefficient, lazy, and too stupid
to be taught skills.

Middle-class whites often reflected the cultural biases of elites in their prejudices toward the poor. One nonslaveholding furniture manufacturer was just
as antagonistic toward white workers as upper-class slaveholders. The only
poor individual, he claimed, "was the lazy fellow whose habits were not above
those of the negro." In scathing stereotypes, one middle-class east Kentucky

---

[9] I cannot report whether white religious minority groups agreed with the class prejudices described
in this chapter since I could not locate primary sources for the Quakers, Mennonites, or Moravians.

commentator described the poor as "very similar in their habits and manner to the aborigines, only perhaps more prodigal and more careless of life" (Thwaites 1904–7, 4: 107). One Civil War veteran described the propertied poor as "a third class of white people," who lay outside the social boundaries of the elites and middle classes. The most prosperous of this group were small farm owners and shopkeepers who were less literate than and had acquired only about one-fifth of the wealth of a middle-class farm owner. Having accumulated only about $400 in assets, about 8 percent of white Appalachians were "marginally respectable" small nonslaveholding farm owners and skilled wage workers, such as millwrights (see Table 5, Web site). Appalachian veterans described the vast social distance between small farm owners and the more affluent families of their communities. Alexander Cantrell recalled that both middle-class farm owners and richer slaveholders "were unfriendly" and "did not associate" with these struggling households. William Harrad could not remember any poor small farm owner who had "ever received any encouragement" from upper- or middle-class neighbors. David Moss was hostile toward both elite and middle-class landowners of Cherokee, North Carolina, because they "would not let" a small farm owner like his father "eat at their table." John Bishop was convinced that more prosperous landowners would "never grade themselves" equal to small farm owners. Surry Countian William Dickson said that both middle-class farmers and elite slaveholders "felt biggety" in comparison to small farm owners like his parents (Dyer and Moore 1985, 388, 44, 64, 97, 321, 443, 2016).

Examination of the responses of Appalachian Civil War veterans provides a unique look at social perceptions of antebellum class mobility. Since a majority of these veterans had been Confederate soldiers, their attitudes cannot be dismissed as reflections of pro-Union leanings. Three-fifths of the surveyed veterans thought that economic opportunities were very limited because upper-class landholders "kept the poor man down" (see Table 6, Web site). More than 80 percent of the veterans whose parents were landless laborers or poor small farm owners were convinced that the impoverished Appalachian had little possibility for upward mobility because economic resources were so concentrated in a few hands. In sharp contrast, three-quarters of the landed Appalachians were convinced that ordinary laborers experienced few difficulties in buying a farm or business. Southern Appalachia's elite and middle-class families culturally affirmed the notion that anyone could be economically mobile – even from the worst of circumstances – simply "by applying himself." In their ideological and cultural denials of any class distinction except that between "hard-working people" and the "shiftless poor," the Appalachian petty bourgeoisie embraced the dominant American class myth (Glickstein 1991, 32–52) that laborers could rise from poverty with relative ease and frequency.[10] By using the culturally

---

[10] Social mobility discussion derived from analysis of 474 Appalachian respondents in Dyer and Moore (1985).

coded affirmation that they helped only those who were "deserving," elites and petty capitalists supported their ideology that poverty was "proof of great indolence or intemperance" and that no "respectable" individual existed in this condition (Tucker 1824, 13).

Idealization of prosperity, ideological camouflage of the extent to which capitalism caused poverty, and derogation of "working for a living" served as cultural legitimations of the inequitable divisions of wealth, land, labor, and quality of life. Culturally, the working classes were stigmatized because "the larger land and slave-owners did not regard manual labor as respectable for a gentleman" (Hundley 1860, 58). "To work with our hands is contrary to the pride of this life and to the customs," one middle-class Charleston, West Virginia, minister averred. Similarly, a middle-class Frederick County, Virginia, wife lamented that "it almost broke [her] heart" to see her sons "work as hired labourers for other people." Working-class veterans were painfully aware of the structural distance between them and more affluent families. "There was no neighboring with the poor man and rich man," one Civil War veteran stated emphatically. William Babb thought farm owners who could afford slaves or servants "moved in a circle to themselves, thinking themselves on a hier plane than the laboring man." In Anderson Roach's small town of Rutledge, Tennessee, upper- and middle-class farm owners and merchants "did not mingle freely with" and "seem[ed] to feel themselves better than" people who did manual labor. Moreover, a landless laborer who hired his time to either rich or middle-class landowners "was principally looked down on as being no better than a slave and was treated so" (Dyer and Moore 1985, 8, 107, 1058).

When 1837 and 1838 issues of *Farmers Register* (5: 474, 6: 458) declared that the poor white laborer was "a far greater pest" than a black worker because he "charged too much, took offense at trifles, and incited unrest in slaves," the periodical was reflecting the biases of most affluent Appalachian employers. Slaveholders of Frederick, Fauquier, and Loudoun Counties reported that they "found white labor unsatisfactory" (*Richmond Whig*, 25 Jan. 1853). Similarly, a middle-class western Carolina farm owner was convinced that "the white men here who will labor, are not a bit better than negroes. [Y]ou have got to stand right over them all the time, just the same." One northern Alabama slaveholder stereotyped poor whites as "common, no account people," who were thieving, landless vagabonds that "make a heap of trouble." After he discharged a white laborer who "had often been seen lounging in the field," the middleclass farmer generalized that blacks "would come somewhere between white folks and such as he" (Olmsted 1860, 228, 210–11, 219, 207). Ethnic prejudices and class biases toward Irish immigrants were particularly rancorous. Railroad companies and extractive industries attracted large numbers into western Maryland and Blue Ridge Virginia through indenturement contracts with workers who were recruited in Europe and transported at the expense of the employer.[11]

---

[11] For information about indentured servitude prior to 1820, see "Indentured Servitude on Appalachian Frontiers," Web site.

One Appalachian iron manufacturer was convinced that the Irish "do well at first ... but after they've been here a year or two, they get to feel so independent or keerless-like, you can't get along with 'em" (McKivigan 1996, 196–97). Another Blue Ridge Virginian was even more explicit in his stereotypes when he wrote, "The Irish, when they come to this country, get above themselves – they think they are free, and do just as they have a mind to! Then, again, they are very much given to drink, and they're very saucy when they're in liquor" (Ruffin 1847, 20). Clearly, Appalachian elites assigned lower economic value to their poor white laborers than to their slaves. Compare this owner's treatment of these two types of workers. A western Maryland master wrote in his journal: "Isaac Widows [a white cropper] called and begged for 2 Bushel corn says the family has no bread." Two weeks later, he added: "Isaac Widow called wants meat Bread and money. gave him none. negro George came gave hime $1 to purchase a hat" (*Ferry Hill* 1975, 13, 19). Several times during the antebellum period, wage rifts between free laborers and slaveholders were reported in Appalachian newspapers. Slaveholder control over local politics generated intense class conflict when landowners called for public regulation of wage rates (e.g., Martin 1836, 210). Using a militia of 40 men, a faction of northern Georgia slaveholders controlled local elections to ensure that poor whites could not vote against the pro-slavery policies of the governor and the Georgia Legislature (*Georgia Messenger*, 25 Aug. 1837). One West Virginia slaveholder believed that "a death struggle must come between the two classes, on which one or the other w[ould] be extinguished forever" (McKivigan 1996, 99).

Such class struggle provides evidence that there was class struggle against elite ideology about the stigmatization of manual labor. The families of many middle- and lower-class Appalachian Civil War veterans constructed a countercultural ethic in which idleness of the rich was ridiculed. Overton Gore was highly critical of "that class of people who thought they was too good to work and regarded labor as [a] low calling to be done by someone else." According to a middle-class nonslaveholding Rhea County schoolteacher, "all the better class" hired their work done. Alfred Hocher described slaveholders as "idle people" who "did no work." Because they were the only households in his community that "lived lives of idleness," slaveholders were "in a class to themselves," contended George Crawford. Exhibiting pride in the manual labor that separated his family from those affluent enough to have servants, A. J. Childers asserted that "the common class did work." There were some "that didn't work," he added with disdain, only because they owned or hired men and women. All the work was done "by the laboring class of people," commented William Babb. By claiming that "honorable" men and women undertook whatever efforts were necessary to support their families, Babb attacked elite notions of "worth" and countered the stereotype that those who shunned manual labor were "elevated above the laboring class of people." Alford Dale bragged that poor white laborers "were the bone of the country" and that "a good [white] worker was as popular as the slave"(Dyer and Moore 1985, 8, 61, 72, 405, 503, 585, 619).

Despite the economic dominance of the upper class, their gender ideologies were *not* culturally hegemonic. While the "cult of true womanhood" idealized leisure and domesticity as the appropriate status symbols to demarcate elite "ladies," middle-class periodicals advocated very different ideals for farm women (Hagler 1993). Manual labor to run a household or to be the husband's helpmate on the farm was often praised in agricultural periodicals (e.g., *Farmer and Planter* 8: 47–48, *Southern Agriculturist* 9: 502). "All young females should possess some employment," the *Carolina Watchman* (16 May 1850) admonished, "by which they might obtain a livelihood in case they should be reduced to the necessity of supporting themselves." Magazines like the *Southern Cultivator* (2: 33, 14: 270) suggested ways that women could earn household income outside the sphere of domesticity, advocated the expansion of manufacturing jobs for women and children, and touted women's "civic duty" to engage in manual work on the farm and income-producing activities outside the home. The phrase "eat the bread of idleness" was frequently applied to white women who disparaged manual labor. Rather than acquiesce to separate spheres constraints, one middle-class western North Carolina woman placed greater moral value on income earning outside the household. "Choosing not to eat the bread of idleness" and "to let [economic] independence be [her] aim," she undertook manual labor and business endeavors that elites viewed as occupations reserved to the male public sphere (Montgomery 1924, 3).

Elite Biases against Working Women

Elites ranked manual labor as "the limit" that "separate[d] virtue from vice" for women. In their view, the less affluent woman who violated that limit "fell far below even the slave" (DeBow 1853, 2: 207). The most visible class distinction between affluent and working-class whites was the workload of women. "Respectable" females did not engage in manual labor of the types assigned to working-class males or to nonwhites. As we will see in Chapters 5 and 6, most Appalachian females routinely worked the fields, and they regularly earned income through an array of publicly visible nonagricultural activities. Because of their lack of education and their demeaned public work, more than half of white Appalachian women lacked the material and cultural symbols of status that elites associated with respectability. More affluent whites stereotyped poor white females as dirty and uncivilized and considered them unsuitable to be hired as domestic servants in their homes (Olmsted 1856, 84). Even though recent Irish and German immigrant women could be hired "cheaper than slaves," many western Maryland landowners still preferred hiring blacks because they could "order slaves about" (McKivigan 1996, 196–97). Melvin Proffitt (Transcript, ALC) described the sharp class barriers to courtship and marriage between the offspring of east Kentucky middle-class landowners and the children of poor whites. Similarly, George French of Wise County, Virginia, thought elite and middle-class women "were inclined to be aristocratic" and were opposed to "matrimony between the two classes" (Dyer and Moore 1985, 860). Poor white women were culturally stigmatized as "a distinct and rather despicable class," with whom prosperous females "wanted to have as little

FIGURE 10. A northern journalist depicted these three class distinctions while traveling in western North Carolina. He distinguished between "the ugly duck" of the poor household (left); the "thriving, polite" daughters of the middle-class family (center); and "Civilization" (right). *Source: Harper's Monthly* (May 1858).

to do as possible." One cleric expressed a common class stereotype when he described females who worked in the fields as "nasty, beastly, and not fit to be imployed" in domestic duties (Force 1963, 3: 12).

Two antebellum manuscripts provide insight into the sharp gendered class distinctions that elite and middle-class commentators made. As northern land speculator John Brown traveled throughout western North Carolina at the end of the eighteenth century, he described two categories of females in the homes where he stayed overnight. He repeated many times the image of the impoverished, stooped, drudge inhabiting a "hovel unfit for decent folk." Only rarely did he compliment a housewife with the phrase "a Well Bred Lady" (Newsome 1934, 309). A second closeup of such class-based stereotyping appeared in an 1858 travel account in *Harper's Monthly* (92: 175–76). A middle-class northern journalist was accompanied by local slaveholders into the rural area around Bakersville, North Carolina. The party first visited a middle-class justice of the peace, where the journalist commented upon the signs of prosperity inside the home, drew sketches of the daughters, and described the wife as "a comely young matron, whose maiden beauty had not yet entirely succumbed to the hard trials of wedded life." The next household to be visited was that of a poor family, who "gristed corn on shares for neighbors." Upon arrival, the entourage met the young daughter, Dorkey, who was dressed in patched homespun and "running barefoot in the frost." By carefully contrasting sketches of poor Dorkey with the more affluent local children and with "civilization" as represented by an elite female dressed in an imported ball gown (see Figure 10), the journalist provided a visual record of the material bases for class distinctions.

Even his reactions to social etiquette were linked to the presence or absence of accumulated wealth. When females in two different classes engaged in the same breach of gender-segregated discourse as prescribed by the cult of domesticity, the writer demeaned only the woman of lower status. In contrast to his positive descriptions of "the greatest interest and curiosity"of the more affluent mother who eagerly exchanged quips with the sketch artist, the writer described the poor housewife as "uncouth" because she joined enthusiastically in a male-dominated conversation. Let me make clear that this journalist was *not* stereotyping Dorkey because she was "Appalachian," else he would also have disparaged the local middle-class family. Moreover, we learn directly from the published report that the local slaveholders and justice of the peace agreed with his assessment of the backwardness and lack of social capital of the young poor child and her mother. As they sat by the fireside in the middle-class home, they projected a gloomy, short-lived future for Dorkey. In their estimation, there was no potential for social mobility or the acquisition of wealth or social capital, for Dorkey would remain uneducated and be required to do the kinds of back-breaking work that set her apart from "respectable" and "worthy" females. Nor would she ever be able to dream of the kind of "gentility" that they associated with a truly "civilized" woman. She would find her husband among the impoverished landless males alongside whom she worked at manual labor. They imagined that the courtship would "be nourished by presents of bird-eggs and squirrels" and that the young couple would move together into a tiny cabin far worse than that of their parents. "I cannot help thinking," the writer summarized, "what a superb figure that child might make one day, if perchance, she were taken and educated in all the graces of civilization." Drawing a metaphorical comparison between a wild animal and the young girl running in the snow to help her father, he concluded: "I suppose I must abandon the idea of taming my little gazelle.... [I]f her life here is less brilliant, it will be more natural and poetic."

There are other similar glimpses of the class chasm between poor and more affluent women. While teaching in a northern Georgia subscription school, Emily Burke (1850, 25, 27) was disheartened by "the neglect and scornful treatment" two poor girls received from middle-class females. Adult poor women were just as stigmatized, according to Burke, and "they [we]re not treated with half the respect by the rich people that the slaves [we]re." Household slaves often observed firsthand the vast gulf between their mistresses and poor white women. As a mulatto offspring of an enslaved female and the owner's teenaged son, Rachel Cruze was raised by her mistress. Rachel was very perceptive about the class distance between a seamstress and her middle-class white grandmother. When neighboring Fanny Oldsley came to sew, the mistress instructed Rachel not to play with her daughter, claiming that she was dirty and had lice (Rawick 1977, 5: 31–32). Such Appalachian mistresses were members of a self-consciously upwardly mobile class in which poor white women had no place. Even when they attended the same churches, elite and middle-class women rarely socialized with poor white females (Dyer and Moore 1985, 987). Lewis Guller (Transcript, EHU) recalled that "the majority" of Scott County, Virginia, landowners "felt themselves better than an honorable poor man," so more affluent and impoverished women "didn't assoate with one another."

Conclusion

This chapter offers empirical evidence of the complex intersections of race, gender, and class. Among the Cherokees, traditional females were marginalized as less progressive and as less civilized than the wives of mestizo males. Class struggle occurred between the majority of impoverished women and the affluent men who legislated patriarchal families and disenfranchised females. Among slaves, the predominant class division was gendered, for males in high-status occupations were set apart from the majority of black women, who did the back-breaking fieldwork and did not enjoy the privileges that these males were allocated by their white owners. Among free blacks, class was determined more by color, by elite white connections, and by "worthy" and "respectable" behavior than by degree of poverty.

Despite their veneer of racial solidarity, there were sharp gradations of class among white females. What is clear from these accounts is that women simultaneously occupied racial and ethnic positions that were complicated by class definitions that were measured by whites in terms of "respectability" and "worth." The accounts in this chapter make clear the degree to which a woman's class or racial status was socially constructed by those who were more affluent or powerful. As we shall see in subsequent chapters, poor white women were often "racialized" as barbaric throwbacks because their work and family patterns were too similar to those of nonwhite females in the minds of affluent Appalachians. In the terms of biological determinism theses so popular with affluent Americans before the Civil War, "whiteness" was evidenced by superior living conditions, character, sexual behaviors, and work patterns (Vogt 1864). Whites reflected similar complex class distinctions among nonwhite Appalachians. Cherokees who were of "mixed blood" through commingling with whites were viewed as more progressive and acceptable, so long as they stayed within the norms of separate spheres ideals. Among free blacks, those with white heritage who behaved "like respectable whites" were deemed more respectable and of a higher class than the majority of African-Americans. In short, the race/class position of poor white and nonwhite women was both legally structured and socially constructed by affluent whites. Dialectically, however, these women were not constrained by separate spheres conventions. In their own subcultures, they experienced acclamations of worthiness and respectability for the diverse portfolios of work described in Chapters 5 and 6.

PART II

STRUCTURAL AND SOCIAL CONTRADICTIONS BETWEEN WOMEN'S PRODUCTIVE AND REPRODUCTIVE LABORS

She looketh well to the ways of her household, and eatheth not the bread of idleness.

(William Duance 1887, 158)

Reproductive politics refers to struggles which decide whether, when, and which women can reproduce legitimately and also to struggles over which women have the right to be mothers of the children they bear.

(Rickie Solinger 2005, 38)

By documenting women's diverse work portfolios and by focusing upon the degree to which race, ethnicity, and class determined the nature and scope of women's work, I question the validity of separate spheres notions in Chapters 5 and 6. Elite gender conventions did not constrain the labor decisions of a majority of women. Most women superimposed several types of income-generating labor upon their domestic responsibilities, and they often produced market commodities or rendered services in their homes. In the poor white and nonwhite families that constituted a majority of households, there was no clear gender division of labor that bifurcated work into "women's production for subsistence" and "male-dominated production for exchange" (Matthaei 1982, 114–19). Even though females were subordinate to men legally, politically, and economically, there was no clear *male public sphere* when it came to the female labors that were essential to family survival. On the one hand, households were arenas for both reproductive work and productive income-earning labors. On the other hand, women did not isolate themselves inside their households; nor did they leave the public economic sphere to males. In reality, more than two-fifths of antebellum U.S. white women worked outside their homes, most white and nonwhite females earned income through informal sector activities, and it was not unusual for wives of all classes and racial groups to accumulate cash through home-based occupations. Even though class and race determined the likelihood that a woman would engage in hard manual labor, most females wove together a creative tapestry of labors in order to accumulate a consumption fund adequate to sustain their households.

Such publicly visible labor was not without costs. Chapters 7 and 8 explore the ways in which women's economically productive work conflicted with their socially expected reproductive roles and caused them to be publicly demeaned as unworthy mothers. According to McClintock (1995, 42, 56, 112–17), "Women who transgressed the Victorian boundary between private and public, labor and leisure, paid work and unpaid work became increasingly stigmatized." Drawing from those popular biological determinists who linked the highest evolution of females to domesticity (Spencer 1851), separate spheres advocates claimed that women who worked outside their homes had inherited such "base" propensities through a racially inferior bloodline. Women's public manual work was decried as "a species of labor that forms one of the few remaining links by which our present civilization is united to a barbaric past." Only the female who kept herself within the constraints of a household controlled by her husband was exhibiting evidence of racial superiority. Moreover, variations from the nuclear, two-parent, patriarchal family were considered "domestic barbarism" that was "a marker" of racial inferiority. In short, Caucasian females who broke the ideological taboos about appropriate women's work were "figured as having fallen . . . from the perfect type of white," for involvement in manual labors that were in the male sphere were reserved for women of color (Vogt 1864, 81).

Because such gender ideals were aimed at protecting the interests of fathers, husbands, and sons in affluent Caucasian families, domesticity conventions respected the boundaries of womanhood and family only for those southerners who possessed the economic means for males and females to function in distinct gendered spheres. In reality, then, the *institutionalized* cult of domesticity discriminated against marginalized classes of women through publicly mandated standards that differentiated between "moral" and "undeserving" wives and mothers. Alternative household constructs were economic threats to the social and legal privileges of the patriarchal nuclear family, most especially patrilineal control of offspring and property inheritance through the father's lineage. Moreover, female sexual autonomy was a direct affront to legal sanctions that placed marriages and families fully under the authority of males. Consequently, southern elite and middle-class males employed cultural and religious standards about marriage and family to justify the public sanctions they legislated to protect slave ownership, to shield themselves from legal responsibility for sexual liaisons outside formalized marriages, and to institutionalize patriarchal family structure. As we shall see, a woman's race and class determined the degree to which her family was treated by Appalachian communities as the inviolable institution that the cult of domesticity idealized motherhood to be.

5

The Myth of Male Farming and Women's Agricultural Labor

> The commitment to a life grounded in the land and its elements brought rural women an unexpected boon. While women may have known about the standards of ladylikeness and Victorian decorum, the realities . . . demanded something quite different. The exigencies of farming, the presence of large animals, the requirements for survival drove women into an intense relationship with the outdoors. Almost without their realization, farm women emerged as a new physical type within the sphere of femininity. Accomplished, toughened, and confident, women accepted any physical task.
>
> (Anne Butler and Ona Siporin 1996, 111–12)

While a majority of all Appalachian women worked at field labor and outdoor farm tasks to some degree, class and race determined the extent to which a woman worked regularly at heavy manual labor. Even though the cultural ideal may have been that "southern ladies, by definition, did no fieldwork," the vast majority of Appalachian women undertook agricultural labors in order to ensure the survival of their households. More than one-third of white adult females, half of free black females, 95 percent of Cherokee females, and two-thirds of enslaved females worked in agriculture (see Table 4). In the sections that follow, I will examine

- women's outdoor farm tasks that were defined by separate spheres advocates to be "men's work,"
- why women did fieldwork, and
- other economically significant farmwork done by females.

Cherokee Women's Agricultural Work, 1790–1838

After the Revolutionary War, the U.S. government implemented its "civilization program," which aimed to reorient the "natives of the forest" toward agrarian capitalism (Brainerd Journal, HUL, 28 Dec. 1821). The "plan for their

TABLE 4. *Occupations of Appalachian Women, 1860*

Occupation	% All Adult Women			
	White	Black	Cherokee	Enslaved
Homemaker listed as only occupation	49.6	4.4		
Agricultural Occupations	33.6	49.8	95.0	65.1
Farm owner	17.9		3.3	
Farm laborer	15.7	49.8	91.7	65.1
Nonagricultural Occupations	7.5	32.6		18.6
Merchants or shop proprietors	2.5			
Professionals	0.5			
Artisans	0.7	6.8		1.3
Industrial laborers	1.1	10.7		5.0
Commercial laborers	1.0	7.1		5.0
Domestic servants	1.7	8.0		7.3
Nonwaged Informal Sector	43.0	64.2	80.0	12.0
Boarding house operator	3.4	0.3		
Boarders in home	35.0	15.0		
Washwomen	4.6	9.8		
Food/candy preparation	3.8	0.8		
Prostitution	1.5	11.7		
Peddling agricultural produce	0.7	1.2	25.0	
Nonwaged Protoindustrialization				
Textiles output in home	85.8	90.0	80.0	100.0
Craft production other than textiles	80.0	80.0	80.0	45.0

Sources and notes: Totals more than 100 percent because some women had two or more occupations. The occupations of white wives were scrutinized in a systematic probability sample of 3,056 households drawn from the 1860 Census of Population manuscripts, NA. The occupations of white female heads of household were derived from analysis of a systematic probability sample of 2,795 female heads of household drawn by selecting every tenth female head from the 1860 Census of Population manuscripts, NA. Free black estimates derived from a systematic probability sample of 1,200 free black households drawn from the 1860 Census of Population manuscripts, NA. Cherokee estimates from analysis of the 1835 Census of Cherokees, NA, and primary narrative sources. Enslaved estimates derived from analysis of Appalachian slave narratives. White estimates for textiles and craft production derived from analysis of Appalachian oral histories.

civilization" called for men to develop "a desire for individual property" and "to acquire it, by attention to stock, to farming and to manufactures." Cherokee women were expected to cease the publicly visible "men's work" they did outside their homes, so they could assume "domestic duties" that were characteristic of elite white women. According to Richter (2001, 226), the civilization program "sought to teach Indian people to abandon their traditional gendered economy of male hunting, female agriculture, and communal landholding in favor of male plow agriculture and animal husbandry, female domesticity, and, especially private property." In the late 1790s, Benjamin Hawkins traveled through northern Georgia, southeastern Tennessee, and northern Alabama to assess the degree to which Cherokees were making "progress." The Indian agent visited numerous women's groups, and he was disappointed that they clung to traditional skills. In southeastern Tennessee and northern Alabama, he saw women "gathering hickory nuts" and "picking up red oak acorns for the purpose of making oil" (Weeks 1916, 19–20, 23, 31, 241). The women were far from enthusiastic about Hawkins's admonitions that they should cultivate more cash crops. One northern Georgia group questioned whether they should increase their output of surpluses when they "never could sell" the extra corn they produced. Probably a little testily, they informed him "that they were willing to labor" in the manner he was recommending "if they could be directed how to profit by it." It seems clear that the women were insulted by his culturally biased presumptions that they were not working hard enough. In order to deride the "laziness" and irresponsibility of males, Hawkins emphasized that females "performed almost all the [agricultural] labor, the men assisted but little and that in the corn." In addition, they raised great numbers of hogs and poultry and grew cotton for textiles production. Even after delivering babies, the women told him, "most of them turn out the next day [to] pursue their ordinary occupations" (Weeks 1916, 21–22).

When he documented the tasks that Cherokee women performed "away from their own hearths," his class-biased ethnocentrism caused him to define as "men's work" the activities in which they were engaged. Chagrined that they were not becoming "housewives" who did the kinds of domestic arts that were considered "respectable" by elite and middle-class women, Hawkins recorded that Cherokee women "turned out" in early spring "to clear up their ground & prepare for planting," as was their traditional custom. Because he was looking for evidence to support the myth of the "indolent Cherokee male," the Indian agent detailed several households in which "civilized gender norms" were breached. In northern Alabama, a farm owner told Hawkins that he "f[ou]nd no difficulty in hiring the Indian women" to pick cotton at the rate of half a pint of salt, one-quarter pint of molasses, or "3 stran[d]s of mock wampum beads" per bushel. Even though her husband was prosperous enough to own 200 cattle, 120 horses, 150 hogs, seven slaves, and 20 bee hives, one Indian wife engaged in outdoor tasks not typical of white slaveholding women. She "show[ed] much attention to the [live]stock about the plantation" and "govern[ed]" the field slaves. She also "attended the pack horses to market, swam rivers to facilitate the transportation of their goods." While the Indian agent was impressed that the wife was "civilized" enough to preside over a "neat and well supplied" table, he did not understand why "she d[id] much" of the cooking "with her own hands," rather than assigning these tasks to slave women (Weeks 1916, 30, 40–41, 47).

While traveling through Cherokee country in the late eighteenth century, future French king Louis-Philippe claimed that Indian males "ha[d] all the work done by women. They were assigned not only household tasks; even the corn, pease, beans, and potatoes are planted, tended, and preserved by the women" (Becker 1977, 73). In 1818, Anne Royall (1830, 112–14) observed clan groups of Cherokee women at work in their household tasks. While Royall was correct in her judgment that the most noticeable indicator of acculturation was their attire, Cherokee women were still collecting in traditional clan work parties, contrary to goals of the civilization program. Obviously, Indian females were not rapidly acculturating toward white separate spheres conventions.

The Postrevolutionary Cherokee Economy and Internal Polarization

By 1820, the Cherokee Nation occupied a small segment of the Southern Appalachians (see Map 9), but it had opened 300 miles of roads to connect to trade hubs at Charleston, Augusta, Nashville, and Muscle Shoals, facilitating river transport to New Orleans (Evans 1981, 79–80). In 1828, the Cherokees exported to Lower South plantations nearly one-fifth of their hogs and 40 percent of their cattle.[1] Large numbers of horses and cattle were marketed in Georgia, South Carolina, and Virginia, and Cherokee farmers sold large herds to the annual drives of Tennessee speculators (Bays 1991). In 1835, the Cherokees sent to distant markets 260,975 bushels of corn, 14,114 cattle, 9,573 hogs, and 1,747 sheep – amounting to the sale of 46 percent of their corn, two-thirds of their cattle, one-quarter of their hogs, and three-fifths of their sheep. In 1830, a missionary lamented that "little progress ha[d] been made in manufactures" since "agriculture [wa]s the principal employment and support of the people" (Brainerd Journal, HUL, 15 Mar. 1830). What this biased clergyman did not report was that the Indians were very similar, in this regard, to nearby white settlers. More than three-quarters of emigrant families were employed in agriculture (Dunaway 1996, 218–21), compared to little more than 70 percent of Cherokee households. Also like nearby Euroamericans, the Cherokees dramatically increased their livestock production and their milling between 1809 and 1828 (CIAT Reports, NA, 1 Dec. 1809; *Cherokee Phoenix*, 23 Oct. 1820, 27 Aug. 1831). By 1835, Cherokee farms were generating corn and livestock at a level that surpassed southern and white Appalachian outputs in 1840. Thus, the Cherokees were producing per capita 1.5 times more corn, 1.7 times more hogs, and 1.7 times more cattle than 1840 farms throughout the United States. Only in their cultivation of wheat did Cherokee farms lag behind white farms.[2]

However, those economic outputs were not as evenly distributed as these averages suggest. While power, wealth, and land were concentrated in the hands of a small group of ethnically mixed merchant-traders and planters, nearly 80 percent of the families produced little surplus on parcels of less than 15 acres (McLoughlin and Conser 1977, 681). For example, Lidda Millar owned

---

[1] Grain and livestock production derived from the *Cherokee Phoenix* (1 June 1828) and Cherokee Census Roll, 1835, NA.

[2] Cherokee averages from analysis of Cherokee Census Roll, 1835, NA. U.S. output averages calculated from farm and crop data in U.S. Census Office (1864).

"1 Cabbin 16 by 16" and farmed 10 acres while Elizabeth Duncan's family lived in a "dwelling house 16 by 18" and grew crops on 6 acres. Coo es Ter had only "3 acres of best up land" and "3 apple trees, 3 peach trees," while Sally Cooper had only a "turnip patch" and "2 acres of ground well cleard" valued at $26 (Valuations, UTK, 2, 17, 27, 212). In addition to the material split, Cherokees were stratified around degree of racial mixing and geographical location.[3] Three-quarters of the Cherokees were poorer traditionalists who spoke no English, and these households were concentrated in the mountainous sections of east Tennessee and western North Carolina. In 1822, Chief Charles Hicks reported that the Cherokees were "in a progressive state of improvement, more particularly those in the middle part of th[e] nation." Significant economic change had occurred, he claimed, except among those Cherokee families "in the mountainous part of th[e] territory, who have not had the same advantages as those have had in the middle and lower parts of th[e] nation" (Evans 1981, 69). While Indian agents and missionaries viewed mestizos as "civilized" and "progressive," a majority of traditional, impoverished Cherokees were stigmatized as "wild, but little on this side of their primordial condition" (Scott 1864, 1: 318).

Throughout the antebellum period, Lower South plantations kept demand for horses and cattle high (Wallerstein 1989, 181–82). Little wonder that Chief Hicks observed in 1822 that "the high prices demanded . . . for live Stock ha[d] primated the interests of farming labor" (Evans 1981, 69). So Cherokee males responded to the vicissitudes of the market by shifting their energies to the production of cattle and horses (Bays 1991, 131–34). Hicks also reported that no household was "without a stock of hogs," a type of livestock production that women nearly doubled between 1809 and 1828. By 1835, the Cherokees were raising more cattle per capita than U.S. farms averaged in 1840 (see Table 56, Web site). However, this economic activity polarized the population. While elite Cherokees utilized "immense tracts of wilderness" to graze large export herds (CIAT Reports, NA, 13 Feb. 1805), the majority of farms combined the cultivation of grains and subsistence vegetables with small-scale swine and chicken production (Bartram 1853, 326). In 1802, the Indian agent reported that only small amounts of cotton were being raised by women (Lowrie and Clarke 1832, 2: 651–52). Once female-dominated subsistence crops became profitable as export commodities, the U.S. government and the mestizo elite pressured males to take charge of those forms of agricultural labor (Perdue 1985, 47). As external prices of corn and cotton rose, however, wealthier male slaveholders gradually expanded their control over cultivation of those two crops. By 1825, the Cherokees were shipping cotton and corn down the Tennessee and Mississippi Rivers to New Orleans. In 1835, Cherokee farms grew enough surplus to

---

[3] Because of its racist connotations, I have chosen not to utilize the term *fullbloods*. Instead, I have employed the terms *traditionalist* and *cultural conservative* to refer to those Cherokees that most scholars usually term *fullblood*. I have applied the term *mestizo* to Cherokees who had intermarried with whites.

sell nearly one-half their corn, but a small minority of the households produced most of those exports.[4]

Cherokee Women's Persistence in Agricultural Labor

By 1820, Cherokee elites presented to whites the image that the population was so "dispersed over the face of the Country on separate farms" that villages and communal farming no longer existed. According to one chief, "Local laws to govern the labour of the citizens who acted in concert in cultivating their patches have disappeared" (Sturtevant 1981, 81). Despite the glowing accounts of Cherokee progress that appeared in print, mestizo elites, missionaries, and the *Cherokee Phoenix* misrepresented the degree of acculturation (Perdue 1977, 211). Indeed, the civilization program was handicapped by a fundamental problem. Cherokee women engaged in five forms of gender-integrated outdoor work that white elites did not consider respectable duties for wives: farming, fishing, hunting, livestock raising, and communal labor gangs. By the 1820s, mestizo elites claimed that "the hardest portion of manual labor" was performed by male farmers; however, women worked in the fields "more by choice & necessity than anything else" (Brainerd Journal, HUL, 15 Mar. 1830). Indeed, one missionary condemned Cherokee males for allocating "the heaviest part of the labor to women" and being too "lazy" to do the types of agricultural labor that well-to-do Euroamericans defined as men's work (Butrick Journal, HUL, 4: 27). Most families supplemented their crops with subsistence hunting and fishing, and women did not abandon their auxiliary roles in those activities (Adair 1775, 403–5). Continued female participation in hunting is evidenced by the passage of an 1824 law that was designed to eliminate time conflicts with women's agricultural roles (*Laws* 1852, 41). Women demanded the regulatory change because spring hunts and skin preparation required heavy labor inputs when they needed to prioritize the preparation of fields and the planting of new crops. Women worked alongside men in communal work gangs that assisted the elderly and infirm. By 1819, women also participated in transformed *gadugi* that functioned as cooperatives of 12 per gang who hired out their services to whites for wages (Speck and Schaeffer 1945).

In the eyes of missionaries and Indian agents, female activities were "not held in any degree of reputable estimation," in comparison to men's accumulation of wealth through livestock exports (CIAT Reports, NA, 13 Feb. 1805). However, it was War Woman Nancy Ward who produced the first large cattle herds in the Nation and who urged Cherokee males to abandon hunting for livestock grazing.[5] Women in traditional households raised a few extra cattle for trade, and several wealthier females raised large herds. In addition, women raised all the chickens and sheep and a sizable segment of the Nation's annual exports of

---

[4] There were 1.5 cattle per person in 1809, and the importance of livestock raising was reflected in the laws (Bays 1991, 113–24). The Cherokee term for *cow* is linguistically Spanish.

[5] Nancy Ward's marriage to a British trader helped her to become one of the wealthiest Cherokee slaveholders and innkeepers (Tucker 1969, 192–200).

hogs (Bays 1991, 166–68, 98–102, 114). Women regularly traded their hand-crafted textiles for cattle, and they engaged in trades and sales of hogs with white merchants (Thomas Papers, DU, Store Account Books 1828–38). As part of annual livestock drives from the Nation, women contracted their surplus chickens or hogs to Cherokee drovers who took them south on commission (Thomas 1839, 20–25). While horses were believed to be male commodities, some women raised "pretty ponies" for export (Rawick 1972, 13: 130).

In the 1820s, the Indian agent expressed concern because women were actively engaging in field labor (Meigs Journal, NA), and Chief Charles Hicks provides an 1822 clue that women were still dominant in agriculture. Cherokee farms "might raise plentiful crops of corn," he admonished, "were they to get into the habit" of removing one or two of the plants from each hill (Evans 1981, 69). Hicks was criticizing women's tradition of planting beans, squash, or gourds in the hills with corn seed (Adair 1775, 406, 409–10). As late as the 1830s, women were actively growing corn and cotton for household textiles production through the traditional cultivation of small patches near their cabins (Payne Papers, NLC, 6: 196). Traveling along the Coosa River in northern Alabama in 1837, James Greenlee (Diary, UNC, Folder 1, 3) spotted several clusters of Cherokee homes of the traditional style, "made with forks and poles fastened on & then d[au]bed with clay." Cabin interiors had frame beds built into two walls, "a cane mat" covering each. Women cooked on the ground inside "a block of Clay round." Indicating long-term female farming, "the Land for several rods around ha[d] been cleared for many years." According to the Brainerd missionaries (Journal, HUL, 15 Mar. 1830), each Cherokee wife had adjacent to her cabin "a small patch of cleared ground with corn and beans."[6]

Integration of Cherokee Males into Fieldwork

In the late eighteenth century, Cherokee villages still farmed communally "in one vast field," and women organized the first stage of agricultural production. In May, Cherokee villages "work[ed] together in one body, in sowing or planting their crops" (Adair 1775, 406–7, 430). By 1800, most Cherokee families had shifted to individual corn parcels (Bartram 1853, 325–26), and men were more fully integrated into fieldwork (Hudson 1976, 268). This postrevolutionary restructuring of gender roles in agriculture impacted more Cherokee households than did any other cultural transformation, for males were making the transition to "women's work." Even within traditional families, "the men labor[ed] in the fields" on a consistent basis throughout the cultivation process (Williams 1928, 261). Since hoes and mattocks improved communal farming, Cherokees adopted those tools quickly (CIAT Reports, NA, 10 Oct. 1802, 25 Feb. 1804, 27 Mar. 1804). Because they represented a move toward individualized labor and

---

[6] An eastern Cherokee cabin photographed in the 1890s is a very close adaptation of the type of Cherokee dwelling depicted in eighteenth-century paintings (Hudson 1976, 482; Sturtevant 1978).

dependence on horses, which few females owned, Cherokees accepted plows much more slowly. By 1828, however, the use of plows, wagons, gristmills, and sawmills had increased dramatically (see Table 57, Web site), showing the widespread entry of males into agriculture. By the 1820s, missionaries claimed that the "ancient custom" of gender-integrated communal farming was "nearly done away" except among traditionalists and "those in the mountains" (Brainerd Journal, HUL, 3 July 1822, 15 Mar. 1830). However, only a few mestizo families were in the vanguard of this social change (McLoughlin and Conser 1977, 681), and most women "cl[u]ng to their old customs as much as possible" (Weeks 1916, 20–21). According to Mollie Sequoyah, "Women did not want men in the fields [because] the growing of maize was a sacred activity involving specialized magical and practical knowledge" possessed only by females (Payne Papers, NLC, 6: 201–2). Obviously, the government and the missionaries were not successful in bringing about the total shift in occupational or gender roles central to their conception of "civilized" existence, for only that small group of Cherokee women who lived in well-to-do households could afford the luxury of house-bound domesticity.

In 1830, the Indian agent observed that among "the great mass" of the traditionalists "the improvement, if progressing at all, [wa]s so slow that it [wa]s scarcely perceptible" (OIA Letters, NA, 4 Mar. 1830). By 1835, fewer than one-quarter of Cherokee families were undergoing or had made the transition to agrarian capitalism, and only a small minority of slaveholding families were engaged in extensive cultivation of cash crops. While three-fifths of the families marketed small amounts of corn, hogs, or cattle, less than 7 percent of the households generated large surpluses for export to distant markets (see Table 58, Web site). These wealthy mestizo slaveholders generated nearly two-fifths of the Nation's entire grain and livestock production on landholdings that were 10 to 20 times larger than the typical Cherokee farm. Three-fifths of the families produced about one-third more than they needed for survival while another one-third produced no surpluses at all. This subsistent third consisted of the most impoverished and the least acculturated households, and there were many more of these families than there were educated, acculturated mestizos. For example, there were 750 "verry Poor" families in northwestern Georgia who cultivated only four to five acres each. "Their principal dependence for Support [wa]s from what Ground They Cultivate[d] in Corn, pumpkins, potatoes & beans" (Scudder, GSA, 17 Sept. 1831). Clearly, the vast majority of Cherokee households had not reorganized around export agriculture to the same degree as adjacent white Appalachians. The typical white farm produced three times more grains and livestock than it needed for survival (Dunaway 1996, 123–56) while most Cherokees were farming at or slightly above subsistence levels. While most white Appalachians consumed less than one-quarter of their annual grain and livestock production, more than 90 percent of Cherokee households absorbed two-thirds or more of their corn, cattle, and hogs.

The Nation's elite agrarian capitalists averaged eight times more corn and nine times more cattle and hogs than nine-tenths of Cherokee households. In those acculturated households, women embraced the cult of domesticity and shaped their lives around household management. However, most Cherokee women lived in more traditional households where it was necessary for them to do outdoor tasks that missionaries and mestizos considered "men's work" (Sturtevant 1978, 81). Contrary to the goals of the civilization program, most Cherokee women kept their households oriented toward the traditional goals of subsistence production, augmented by small surpluses for informal sector exchanges (McLoughlin 1986, 260–61). Even after males were more fully integrated into fieldwork, most wives persisted in traditional female planting and harvest, and they tended family garden patches and raised livestock for household consumption (Brainerd Journal, HUL, 15 Mar. 1830). It is for that reason that the Georgia governor justified Cherokee removal as the only way to reallocate their lands to "moral use of God's resources" by "civilized men" (Lumpkin 1907, 2: 15).

Farm and Field Labor of Post-Removal Cherokee Women

After the 1838 forced removal, Cherokees held an invisible status in southern race relations. They were not recognized as citizens of the states in which they squatted; nor were they permitted the legal right to own land (Pudup et al. 1995, 25–27). In 1860, more than 1,200 Cherokees remained in Haywood, Cherokee, and Macon Counties, North Carolina, with another 845 scattered in northern Georgia, southeastern Tennessee, and northern Alabama (Chapman Roll, NA, 12: 1). Even though federal census takers were instructed not to report Indian households, one 1860 enumerator listed the Cherokee households who resided in Quallatown, North Carolina. Of the 30 households documented, only 9 held deeds to their parcels, and nearly one-third were headed by females. One woman owned a farm and assets valued at $8,500, distinguishing her not only from her Indian peers but also from a majority of her white neighbors. In the Sand Town community, Alee Woodpecker owned a 100-acre farm that included a log cabin with separate kitchen and smokehouse, indicating that her family was doing better economically than most other Cherokees and most poor whites. However, the typical household was landless and lived below the national poverty line. Male and female heads of household averaged about the same levels of accumulated wealth (less than $200). In male headed households, wives were all listed as "farm laborers," reflecting the local recognition that these women customarily still worked in the fields and did outdoor agricultural tasks.[7] Travelers described western North Carolina Cherokee households as "being so nearly like the whites in their manner of living that a stranger could rarely distinguish an Indian's cabin or little cove farm from that of a white man." A majority of these Indian families were living at about the same economic level as adjacent poor white farmers, whose wives and daughters also worked in the

---

[7] Derived from analysis of 30 households enumerated in the 1860 Census of Population manuscripts, NA, of western North Carolina counties.

fields. Indeed, white observers described them as "little, if any, behind their white neighbors" (Mooney 1900, 176, 181).

The 469 Cherokee households in northern Georgia, eastern Tennessee, and northern Alabama were not doing nearly so well as their counterparts in western North Carolina. Most of these Cherokees struggled to survive as migratory laborers or as temporary squatters on white-owned farms. We can get a brief glimpse of their living conditions by examining three crossed-out entries that I discovered among white households in the census manuscripts. The enumerators recorded no names for these households because they could not understand the dialect. In McMinn County, Tennessee, a female head of household and her four children were all listed as "squatting farm laborers." The mother was also listed as a weaver, her tools accounting for the $195 reported as the family's total assets. In Dade County, Georgia, an unnamed male headed a household that consisted of two parents, three children, and an elderly female. Described as "squatting farm laborers," they had total household wealth of only $70 in household goods and farm implements. A household of "squatting farm laborers" in Jackson County, Alabama, was even more destitute, their family of seven owning only $20 worth of farm implements. The 1860 census enumerator noted in the manuscript borders that this family "live[d] on the side of the mountain in a very savage state. They raise[d] a little corn by digging up the ground with a hoe." The living conditions of one east Tennessee squatter household are typical of the circumstances of these itinerant Cherokees during the 1838–60 period. After sharecropping for a number of different landlords, the family moved to a farm where they tended the gristmill.[8] Agnes Lossiah (1984, 90) recalled that her "grand pa used to sleep in a cave up on the hill above the mill." She would "climb mountains hunting cows and would bring them home" for the owners. As a slave in present-day Stephens County, Georgia, Harriet Miller interacted with itinerant Cherokee women who "camped on the river bottoms," where they grew crops and made "de beautifulest baskets" to market to whites (Rawick 1972, 13: 130).

Farm and Field Labor of White Appalachian Women

As antebellum commentators observed, poor white Appalachians lived in rural circumstances not unlike those experienced by Cherokees.[9] Even though an overwhelming majority of white Appalachian households were engaged in farming, only about one-half of them owned land in 1860.[10] Nearly one-third of these landless households were desperately poor by national standards because

[8] Entries from 1860 Census of Population manuscripts, NA, for McMinn County, Tennessee; Dade County, Georgia; and Jackson County, Alabama.

[9] Women's agricultural labors on the Appalachian frontiers were very similar to labor patterns in the later antebellum period; see "Women's Frontier Agricultural Labors," Web site.

[10] With respect to landlessness, Appalachians were not unlike other U.S. citizens. Land was a precious commodity that was not attainable for more than half of all nineteenth-century households (Friedenberg 1992, 22–27).

they owned less than $100 in accumulated assets, earned only about $30 per year, and were unemployed three to five months annually (see Tables 5, 8, 10, 12, 29, 33, Web site). Nearly two of every five Appalachian farm operators were tenant farmers or sharecroppers for landlords who were producing cash crops and livestock herds for export (see Table 27, Web site). These landless farm laborers lived a precarious existence, and they were constantly on the move in search of employment. Because more than four-fifths of these households failed to produce enough food to meet their household consumption needs, the productive inputs of wives were essential to family survival.

Virtually every wife whose tenant or cropper husband worked in close proximity to the home was expected to contribute labor as an assistant to the market-oriented production of her spouse. However, her work was "absorbed into an enterprise identified as exclusively his" (Boydston 1986, 9). Though her labor contribution remained hidden behind that of her husband, the typical land-less Appalachian farm wife was intricately controlled by the husband's land tenure contract. In some instances, the husband was required to work for the landlord, neglecting the family parcel. Because his father only "farmed some at home," Robert Bayless's mother was responsible for cultivating crops on their rented parcel while her husband "worked away from home for the landlord." William McLarrin's mother did "all the work that was required of a poor man" because his sharecropping father was frequently absent to produce shoes and barrels for the landowner (Dyer and Moore 1985, 1460). As part of the process in which labor and resources were transferred within households, the tenant or cropper wife and her children were expected to become "unpaid employees" in the cultivation of the landlord's cash crops. In their northern Georgia cropper household, Sarah Dowdle's mother "worked in the fields same as the house" (Wiggington 1973, 111). When local farmers were short-handed at harvest or spring planting, "all worked alike," so the husband might sell more of his wife's labor time to neighbors, then collect the wages for her work. In one east Tennessee community, slaves, tenants, and white female croppers worked in the same field each day (Rawick 1972, 14: 332). Some women, like Maxie Northrup's (Transcript, ALC, 5) grandmother or the mothers of Isaac Chatman and James Cloyd, managed their rented parcels without any adult male help. From a young age, "all that were able to work did so," and girls were hoeing and weeding by age five, plowing by age eight, much like Appalachian slave children. John Hank's mother worked her own sharecropper parcel because she was "a lone woman with seven children to maintain." E. D. Hendrickson's mother also sharecropped without any adult male help, so all the children "worked hard to earn a living." The woman probably worked hardest of all, for she did "all sorts of housework," in addition to "plowing, howing, teaching singing school" (Dyer and Moore 1985, 293, 493, 521, 542, 595, 641).

In many landless farm households, it was not unusual for the husband to obligate his wife to complete tasks for the landlord beyond her field labor. In an 1828 east Kentucky agreement (Wickliffe-Preston Papers, UKY, 1 Nov. 1828), the husband contracted his wife's time "for her care and attention to the dairy and smokehouse" and for spinning clothes for the owner's slaves. The husband agreed "to purchase all the family's produce and provisions and furniture" through the landlord, who expected the wife's "spinning and milk in exchange for the wheat." In other instances, the landlord brought pressure to bear directly on the landless wife to perform additional tasks or to produce crafts for the owner's household (*Ferry Hill* 1975, 15–17, 19, 22, 25, 33, 41, 65). Landlords were also able to expropriate unpaid labor from the wives by requiring them to contribute additional work in exchange for food allocations (Aldie Memorandum Book, UVA, entries for seamstress Mrs. Foster). Rather than charging provisions against the husband's future crop production, the landlord could mandate a "pay-as-you-go" arrangement in which the woman traded "piecework" tasks for the family's subsistence rations (Dyer and Moore 1985, 1401).

Women's Work in Poor Farm Owner Households
One-fifth of the region's farm owners held less than 100 acres, averaged less than $300 in assets, and were impoverished by national standards. Because most of these farms could not afford to hire hands, women and girls regularly engaged in field labor and outdoor farm tasks. Half the Civil War veterans were born into such households, so their family details give rare voice to the mothers and daughters in such circumstances. Without any demeaning criticism, these men indicated that their female kin worked in the fields, tended livestock, milked cows, cultivated garden patches, and assisted with the annual hog slaughtering and meat processing. Mark Shelton's mother "done any kind of work had to be done" on their 20-acre farm, and Adam Boy's mother and sisters "plowed and hoed and [did] anything that was necessary" on their 80-acre farm. John Cooley's family lived in a three-room log cabin on a 50-acre farm in Meigs County, Tennessee. In addition to housework and textiles manufacturing, the wife and daughters "picked cotton" and did fieldwork. On an 80-acre farm in northern Alabama, John Goins's mother managed a two-room log house, "plowed and hoed all through crop time and spun thread at night to make clothes."

According to William Cox, whose family cultivated a 150-acre farm in upper east Tennessee, "all worked . . . in order to live." On John Haston's middle Tennessee farm, his father worked as a part-time carpenter, but the family was still poor. So "men and women had to worke at farm work to live." In similar fashion, John Neel commented that "all worked together and thought it was the thing to do." Samuel Moulock's family lived in a one-room cabin and cultivated 82 acres in Hawkins County, Tennessee. In sharp contrast to the "cult of domesticity," the son specified that "the duties of my mother was composed of in door and out door work." James Nicely's mother "went and helped the men folkes in the field." In S. F. Paine's Burke County, North Carolina, community, "women went to the field, to plant corn, hoe corn, and some plowed." In short, veterans who grew up in small farm owner households did not think there was anything unusual about female fieldwork, and they certainly did not assign their mothers, wives, or sisters to a "separate sphere" of domestic labors (Dyer and Moore 1985, 84, 111, 362, 553, 580, 915, 1044, 1604, 1630, 1640, 1682).

Poor White Women as Agricultural Waged Laborers

In addition to females in households that operated farms, another 15 percent of white Appalachian women were identified in census manuscripts as waged farm laborers (see Table 4). These women lived in some of the most desperately poor households in the region, and their families moved repeatedly in search of new employment. Most of these women would have worked in day laborer households in which "wages" often amounted to no more than subsistence. Civil War veterans indicated that it was not unusual for day laborers to be paid "in trade," rather than in "money wages" (Dyer and Moore 1985, 243, 395, 780, 801, 940, 1387, 1435, 1670, 1858, 1404). The Ferry Hill Plantation sometimes hired 30 or more such laborers at a time, some exchanging their work for firewood or for housing in the planter's town properties (*Ferry Hill* 1975, xiv–xvi, 46, 55, 58–59). East Tennessean John Sevier ("Journal" 1919, 246) remunerated his farm laborers with provisions, such as "an order to Millers store for half bushel salt." A larger West Virginia farmer (Wilson-Lewis Papers, WVU, 1846 diary) paid wages only in meat rations. For instance, one woman "had worked four days and a quarter got a shoulder fifteen pound." Only the wealthiest farmers paid money wages, leaving housing and meals to the workers. On the Barbour Plantation, for instance, day laborers earned "one dollar a day," the worker "finding himself."[11] South Carolina's governor estimated in 1850 that at least one-quarter of these day laborers could "not gain a decent living" (Wallace 1961, 498–99). According to one middle-class western North Carolina farm owner, day laborers earned about 50 cents per day, but they were unemployed five to six months of the year (Olmsted 1860, 260).

It was common for the females in these poor white households to work the fields alongside white or black males. Faced with the crisis of "half-starved" children, one white mother picked cotton alongside slaves on a nearby plantation. She "kept at it two days, and took her pay in corn" (Rawick 1972, 14: 332). In 1848, Nancy Burgess, the wife of a western North Carolina laborer, "worked for wages for a landless farmer," earning "more than $7 for performing a variety of jobs: weaving, washing, scouring, and binding wheat and oats" (Bolton 1994, 38). At western Maryland's Ferry Hill Plantation (1975, xiv–xvi, 72), one slave squad gathered and hauled wheat while a crew of white women loaded the grain into the barn. "Bad planned and poorly managed Negroe dictation," the slaveholder commented in his journal at the end of the workday – indicating that the white females had been supervised by a black male slave driver. As he traveled southward through the Appalachian counties of Virginia, Tennessee, North Carolina, and Alabama, Olmsted (1860, 219–20) claimed

---

[11] Advances of food charged against wages in Johnson Account Book, UVA, and Barbour Memorandum Book, UVA.

that in a single month he had "seen more white native American women at work in the hottest sunshine" than he had encountered in any other part of the country.[12] Poor white women also worked alongside slaves at community work parties, like corn huskings or log rollings (Dunaway 2003b, 145–47).

Women's Work on Middle-Class Farms

About one of every three Appalachian wives resided in a household that owned or hired slaves, and about one-quarter of the large nonslaveholding farm owners hired servants for their wives (see Tables 11, 26, Web site). These females never engaged in field labor, heavy manual tasks, or waged labor to supplement family income. For instance, William Alexander's northern Alabama father was a wealthy planter who operated a cotton gin, traded in livestock and real estate, and had accumulated more than $100,000 in assets. The family lived in a 10-room frame house, and the wife "devoted her time to caring for her 7 daughters & 5 sons" because the "household work was done by the servants." Similarly, the women in John Crawford's Rhea County, Tennessee, family did little of the work that was typical of a majority of Appalachian wives. While slaves and hired white hands did the housework and the fieldwork, the Crawford women "worked only as [they] wanted to," primarily doing "knitting, sewing, and fancy quilt work." While her husband served as postmaster and clerk of the Knoxville Chancery Court, Mrs. Deaderick managed their 140-acre farm by relying on an overseer and seven slaves. According to the son, his "mother's duties were like those of the old time ladies" since "she had several excellent servants" (Dyer and Moore 1985, 193, 587, 661).

In comparison to elite wives, women did more housework in middle-class slaveholding households, but they still did far less manual labor than poorer females. The women in one middle-class Quaker farm household worked close to the house, except on those occasions when they "would take to the harvest field a liberal lunch" for the men (*Janney's Virginia* 1978, 67). Josiah Bewley's mother and sisters never did outdoor farmwork, and they only "assisted" slaves and hired white girls in housework. Veterans made it clear that a majority of women in prosperous households had the luxury of doing only "work belonging to the home." For example, Isaac Broyles's mother "superintended all the work done in and about the house." Robert Crouch's mother "only directed her household affairs," while "Negroes did the labor." Using six slaves, Edwin Cunningham's father managed a cabinet making and carpentry shop and a tavern while the wife "did all kinds of woman work" (Dyer and Moore 1985, 13, 134, 202, 271, 405).

William Allen's mother was among that 25 percent of nonslaveholding middle-class wives who combined heavy housework with some outdoor work. While the husband, seven sons, and hired whites worked the 211-acre farm, the mother and daughter did the housework, tended a garden patch, and spun

---

[12] Note that Olmsted is using the term "native" to refer to females of Euroamerican heritage who were not recent immigrants.

and wove the family's clothing. Because there were no household servants, the boys were assigned nighttime spinning duties. In some middle-class households, daughters did some fieldwork while wives did housework. In Thomas Barnett's family, his oldest sister "did most of the hoeing" because her father was busy at his cooper trade. Without any servants, the wife "did the housework," which included manufacturing textiles, milking cows, and tending the family garden. Except for the sons of slaveholders, the Civil War veterans almost never employed the phrase "women's work" or any other term that segregated females into a sphere separate from "men's work." In fact, a majority of Appalachian veterans included within the scope of "housework" many outdoor farm tasks that the cult of domesticity reserved for males (Dyer and Moore 1985, 601, 610).

Like their counterparts in other sections of the country, some antebellum Appalachian women acquired their own agricultural land. Fewer than 8 percent of the region's farm owners were females, and nearly one-fifth of the white female heads of household owned their own farms (see Table 4). Three-quarters of them were middle-income or better in economic status, and they fared slightly better than their male counterparts. Female farm owners averaged 374 acres while males averaged only 335 acres; moreover, female owners averaged nearly $2,000 more in total wealth than male owners. In these households, the female owners hired laborers or held slaves, but they still did not fit the idealized image of the "cult of domesticity" because they engaged in farm management that was typically considered men's work. For example, John Anderson's mother "managed the property" with 15 slaves and white hired help. She assigned daily household tasks and outdoor chores to female servants, and every morning she laid out to the overseer the field-worker quotas. In the evening, she entertained "at table considerable company." Lee Billingsley's family resided in a 12-room brick house in mountainous Bledsoe County, Tennessee, where his mother used two overseers and 40 slaves to "manage the property." Nonslaveholding middle-class women, like Nicholas Frazier's mother, managed farms without overseers, directing male field laborers, occasionally supervising the planting or harvests along the rows in the same manner their husbands once did (Dyer and Moore 1985, 4, 317, 850). Obviously, these women did not fit the cultural ideal of house-bound domesticity because they were active in farm management, they supervised male workers, they were knowledgeable of prices and marketing methods, and they controlled household finances.

White slaveholding women on small plantations had fewer domestic servants than their counterparts whose households owned more slaves, so they engaged in several forms of labor that were culturally stigmatized as "unladylike." About 1 of every 10 of these women were widows who managed their own farms, often going to the fields to lay out the daily work assignments, sometimes even punishing slaves for low output or mistreatment of livestock. These mistresses typically worked their own household gardens with the help of their children and young slaves. To cut costs, wives often raised sorghum cane to substitute for costly imported sugar, so they managed cane cutting, boiling, and syrup storage every fall. Small plantation wives and daughters also managed dairy production, which included milking, storage, and supervision of slave children who moved the cows from pastures to barns. Butter and cheese preparation were the only steps completed indoors. Many of these wives also raised their own poultry and eggs and were responsible for supervising annual sheep shearing and wool preparation. With the help of slave children, these wives also gathered fruit and organized wild berry pickings. Finally, these women almost always participated in annual slaughtering and meat production, hard manual labor that certainly did not fit the constraints of the cult of domesticity. Consider Carrick W. Heiskell's affluent east Tennessee household. His father, editor of the *Knoxville Register*, owned a 1,000-acre farm and 25 slaves. Even though this family lived in town and would have been in the public eye, the wife supervised farm tasks that were typically handled by males on large plantations. Heiskell's mother "attended to her house, as every other gentlewoman of her time, over-looking the spinning, weaving, cooking, of the slaves, looking after the education of her children and wellfare of slaves. Some of the work of slaves she overlooked were curing of meat, rendering lard, making shoes, etc." (Dyer and Moore 1985, 1069). In short, only the women on the most affluent plantations fit the idealized image of the cult of domesticity, for middle-class farm women were engaging in many forms of labor that separate spheres advocates described as men's work.

Farm and Field Labor of Free Black and Enslaved Appalachian Females

Nearly one-half of all free black household heads were engaged in agriculture, and two-thirds of them were day laborers. Less than 10 percent of free black Appalachian families operated farms, and less than 0.1 percent of the region's farm owners were African-Americans. Less than 2 percent of the region's tenant and sharecropper households were headed by emancipated African-Americans, and these households rarely produced sufficient food and were perpetually indebted to slaveholders.[13] Most of them were engaged to complete specific short-term tasks or to assist with planting and harvest. In Cumberland County, Virginia, for example, the Hubard family (Papers, UVA, 1827 diary entries) hired free black women to construct irrigation ditches. Beulah Perry described the role of girls in fieldwork on her family's sharecropping parcel. "When we got to be ten or twelve years old, we could go to the fields. After I got big enough, I worked right along with the boys. We usually had to do about everything we could do; I don't think we had any choice" (Wiggington 1975, 409).

The vast majority of enslaved females worked in the fields full time, and a sizable segment of domestic servants were reassigned periodically to field

---

[13] Derived from analysis of a systematic probability sample of 1,200 free black households drawn from the 1860 Census of Population manuscripts, NA.

chores, especially during harvests (see Table 24, Web site). For instance, Henry Williams's mother "cooked, ironed, and worked in the field in time of push." One Warren County, Tennessee, mother "worked everywhere, out in the field and in the house." On small plantations, "all the women worked in the fields," except one or two house servants. In the summers, Sarah Gudger "had t' wok outdoo's," but her Asheville, North Carolina, master shifted her to house duties and wood cutting during the winter. Sarah did all kinds of "men's work," including field tasks, chopping wood, and hoeing, "till sometime [she] feels lak [her] back sholy break." On larger Appalachian plantations, assigned tasks were gender-specific, and field women worked primarily in the company of other women. Typically, men plowed and women hoed, supervised by a woman leader. The diary of James Hervey Greenlee (UNC, 21 May 1849) provides a detailed look at the inconsistent patterns with which Appalachian owners segregated workers by gender. On his Burke and McDowell County, North Carolina, plantations, this middle-class slaveholder organized slave women into crews to cut briars, plant pumpkin seed, pull flax, gather clover seed, dig sweet potatoes, prepare new ground for planting, and hoe corn. Women harvested corn and fodder and stacked it at the ends of rows while males hauled it from the fields. Later women shucked and shelled the corn and packed the fodder into the barn. Men cut firewood and timber while women carried it to the road and stacked it. While men tanned leather, women collected the tree bark used to brew tannic acid. Delia Garlic "was a reg'lar fiel' han'" on a large plantation; her duties included "plowin' and' hoein' an' choppin' cotton." During planting and harvest on midsize and large plantations, women frequently worked alongside men. On two western North Carolina plantations, males usually plowed, the women following behind to lay out hills for corn, potatoes, or tobacco. Males plowed wheat fields and sowed the seed; women brushed soil over the sown wheat. Males plowed, followed by women "plastering." Since they did not employ huge labor forces, few Appalachian masters maintained a finely honed gender division of labor. On such farms, 3 percent of the slave women acted as drivers. On one White County, Tennessee, farm, "the women would plow, hoe corn, just like the men would." A Dunbar, West Virginia, master "worked men or women slaves just alike, and women done all kinds of work, such as hoe tobacco, pull and dry it, then [they] cut rails for fences." The smaller the plantation, the more varied and gender-integrated was fieldwork. When tasks required great numbers of laborers, even large Appalachian plantations dropped gender conventions ("Unwritten History," FUA, 156, 51, 217; Rawick 1972, 11: 168, 229, 14: 353, 10: 254. 20; Rawick 1977, 1: 151, 18, 432; Rawick 1979, 5: 1554, 6: 2273, 2276, 2240).

In the United States, slave girls entered the fields at a younger age than boys because owners thought they were better physically coordinated and exhibited higher crop picking rates than boys (Fogel 1989, 55). When Ann Ladly was seven, her master "load[ed] up a barrel full of water" and assigned her to distribute drinks throughout the rows. To increase children's efficiency at dropping seed corn during planting, they "made a cross" to allow them "to put the corn right." One Warren County, Tennessee, slave girl was assigned this task before she was physically mature enough to drop the seeds into the hills. She recalled that she "got a whipping" for being clumsy until she "learned to drap" the corn correctly. Children "would have to drap it fast" because adults "would be behind [them] to cover it up." Fanney Sellers recalled that children "never had no time to play." Every field hand was assigned a daily quota of rows to pick into a large bag fastened by straps around the neck. To learn to harvest crops, children worked alongside adults, putting their "pickin's in some growed slave's basket." As soon as northern Alabama children "got big enough ter pick and puts de cotton in baskets," they joined the fall harvest crews. Children either worked with their parents or alongside another hand. Sally Brown "wuz put to work in the fields when [she] wuz five years ole, pickin' cotton," adding it to the bag of the older woman who was teaching her (Rawick 1979, 6: 2257, 9: 3638; Rawick 1977, 5: 216, 9: 1525, 11: 166, 206, 14: 354).

Why Were Women Doing Fieldwork?

Out of necessity and by personal choice, there were four reasons women engaged in back-breaking field labor. As we will see in the next chapter, there simply were not enough nonagricultural jobs for Appalachian females. Commercial and industrial enterprises preferred to utilize cheaper immigrant and enslaved males, limiting the employment of white and free black females. Second, these women did field labor without any recognition they were stepping across gender boundaries into "men's work." Their households operated as inequitable *resource pooling units* (Dunaway 2001) in which every member was expected to contribute labor and resources to ensure the survival of their families. Perhaps Caney Hall (Transcript, ALC, 8) best expressed the idea that the household members knew they had to function together as a survival unit when he said: "People lived hard. Didn't believe we couldn't work. All of them – not just one." Caney's oral history does not include a single comment that indicates any recognition that there should be a separate sphere for females. In the Farrell household, the wife routinely helped her husband in the fields "when the crop got behind" (Dyer and Moore 1985, 797). East Kentuckian Lula Cook (Transcript, ALC, 3) understood clearly that "times were very hard" for her antebellum grandmother's sharecropping household and that mother and daughters "had to work in the fields." We should not just view these women as unidimensional females whom we should pity because they were victims of menial toil assigned to them by patriarchal husbands and fathers. Some women actually preferred outdoor farmwork to domestic duties. Neely Adams's (Transcript, ALC, 7) grandmother left her preteen daughters in the house to prepare meals and clean while she did the fieldwork and outdoor tasks. Cynthia Corvin "hated to be tied to the house," so she "delighted in" outdoor tasks and "was a master hand for field work" (Goodrich 1931, 71).

Poor white women's narratives reflect a certain pride in their contributions to household survival or in their abilities to accomplish work that was typically credited to males. There certainly was no sense of stigmatization when Bertha Frazier (Transcript, ALC, 8–9) told the interviewer that her antebellum grandmother "raised big gardens and big corn fields and big potato patches. Dig them and hoe them and have plenty of potatoes to do all winter. Just rig up the old mule and hook it to a plow and plow the corn." During harvest, she would also "cut up the corn and make big fodder shocks . . . haul it into the crib, raised maybe as high as three hundred bushel of corn to feed the winter to the mules." Delphia Ramey drew attention to the centrality of women's work. When the family "needed anything done," she said, "women did it, such as taking care of the [live]stock, hoeing corn, plowing, and making a garden" (Shackelford and Weinberg 1977, 126). Lee Greer (Transcript, ALC, 4) described his Wise County, Virginia, mother as always making "somethin' out of nothin'" in the fields. In the estimation of her daughter, Dorie Cope "was so capable [that she] could outthink and out do most of the men she knew" (Bush 1992, 6, 24–25, 73). According to Estie McDaniel, her mother "had little choice in life. . . . Life was hard, but [she] faced it with great courage" (Thompson 1976, 141). June Ehle (Transcript, ALC, 6) and Julie Price (Transcript, ASU, 8) summarized their mothers' philosophies about a "woman's place in life," that sphere being "work at anything to get food for her family."

Many enslaved women preferred fieldwork to domestic service. Assignment to the master's household increased the likelihood that females would be sexually exploited by white males. In their productivity levels, some of the enslaved women competed with males. Aunt Clussey of Etowah County, Alabama, "could plow as well" as any male field hand. Liza Tanner's mother "was a fast hand in the field," and she could still outwork her husband when "she was getting old." On her small mountain plantation, Anna Lee's daily plowing quotas matched those of males. Lula Walker "hadda work powerful hard," just "like a man." She "hoed, plowed, ditched, split rails an' anything else dat needed to be did" (Rawick 1972, 10: 255; Rawick 1977, 1: 19, 432; Rawick 1979, 6: 2276).

The third reason they did field labor was that husbands and fathers became ill or died. In fact, nearly 10 percent of the Civil War veterans described mothers who took charge of farms in such circumstances. Wiley Christain's father only did farmwork "when well enough." Because the family was poor and had no assets, Wiley's mother was "a busy Christian woman." Reversing gender roles, the husband carded wool on a putting-out arrangement while the wife and children "had to work" at farming "in order to make ends meet." James Anderson's father "wasant able to work" on their small farm, but he tried to "boss" wife and children and "show [them] how to work." After their husbands died, the mothers of Bertha Frazier (Transcript, ALC, 2) and John Moore took over all the farmwork. After their fathers' deaths, the mothers of Isaac Gore and E. D. Hendrickson cultivated their small farms and accumulated enough surplus to pay off their husbands' debts. After her father's death, Alice Slone's (Transcript, ALC) mother "never stopped. She was up at four o'clock in the morning, all day long [doing] something." James Cloyd's mother cultivated

rented land and "occasionally taught school." When the father died in their
sharecropping household, John Doyle's mother "worked on the farm, Cooked,
Washed, Spun, Wove." When his sharecropping father died suddenly, Richard
Rigsby's mother took over the parcel and bound out the 13-year-old son to
a shoemaker. Slaveholding women were much better prepared to handle the
loss of their husbands. With the help of one slave, William Lusk's mother took
charge of their 675-acre farm and "raised 8 children." With slaves and overseers
to assist her, Lee Billingsley's mother supervised both farm and household of
their $85,000 estate (Dyer and Moore 1985, 36, 94, 207, 317, 521, 718, 927,
1073, 1403, 1845).

The fourth explanation for female field labor derived from the need to free
males for nonagricultural work. Enslaved women were assigned to field labor
to release males for occupations that would earn their owners greater profits. While skilled male artisans brought higher market prices, women were in
demand in the Lower South for field labor (Fogel and Engerman 1992, 31–53).
Similarly, nearly one-fifth of the Civil War veterans described poor or middle-
class white mothers who took charge of farmwork in order to free their fathers
to undertake nonagricultural occupations. More than half of those women were
in nonslaveholding households that had no servants or hired hands. The fathers
of one of every eight of the veterans left farm management to their wives while
they pursued commercial enterprises, professions, or artisan trades that kept
them away from home for long periods. For instance, circuit riders traveled continually, leaving farming to their wives and children. According to Finke and
Stark (1992, 81, 175–76), "The Baptists typically paid their preachers nothing
at all," while Methodist circuit riders earned only about $100 annually. Because
husbands were absent from their families to engage in occupations that paid
them very little, the burden of household survival shifted to the women and
children. One southwest Virginia wife sharecropped 30 acres while the Baptist preacher-husband earned an annual salary of only $13.20. The family was
so poor the children "had to work part time for a neighbor in exchange for
the use of a horse to till a field." Russell Brown's father was "away a lot" to
preach, so his mother cultivated their 200-acre farm, doing well enough to hire
someone to take over her textiles manufacturing duties. Ozias Denton's family
did not do as well. Because his father "just preached," the wife took charge of
their 282-acre farm, on which the family held only one cow and one horse. The
son recalled that his mother was always "cooking, spinning, weaving, washing,
scrubbing, and growing crops." The Anthony household lived in a one-room
cabin on about 100 acres of rough terrain. According to the son, "The land was
practically all in woods and had to be cleared.... My father being a minister
had often as many as 15 churches under his charge and preached every day in
the week and so of course was at home less than 1/3 of his time." While her
husband was absent, the wife "had charge of her six sons," who helped her
with the fieldwork and livestock. In addition to the farmwork, she "did all the
housework, carded and spun and wove and would cut and make the clothes
for her family" (Dyer and Moore 1985, 216, 400–402, 673–74).

Male teachers were also preoccupied with professional duties, so they treated farming as an activity that received only their tertiary attention. Isaac Broyles's father taught school and served as justice of the peace in Rhea County, Tennessee, while his wife "superintended all the work done" by hired white workers on their 178-acre farm. In the struggling middle-class Lowry household, the husband taught school while the mother did "anything essential to the up build an accumulation of a living and support" on their 160-acre nonslaveholding farm. Peter Boring's father had a large medical practice, so he "devoted his time to his profession." With "hired help," Mrs. Boring managed their 130-acre farm, did all the housework, and manufactured textiles. Largely as a result of her economic outputs, the Borings achieved middle-class status, lived in a six-room frame house, and had accumulated $3,500 in wealth. Thomas Arnold's mother had fewer assets and far less help. While her husband "pracktist medison" and spent most of his time traveling to treat his far-flung patients, the wife managed their 600-acre farm without household servants or slaves. The families of slaveholding professionals fared better. "Being a preacher," Thomas Coffey's father "dident work regular on the farm." However, the household held two slaves and could afford hired laborers to assist the wife in running the farm. While Henry Doak's father taught at Washington College Academy and preached, his wife relied on three slaves and hired whites to "superintend" their 300-acre farm. The father of Nathaniel Harris was a slaveholding doctor who "was rarely at home." With advice from her nearby brother-in-law, Mrs. Harris managed the farm with five slaves and "hired white hands." While she did not work in the fields herself, this middle-class woman ignored the gender ideals of the cult of domesticity. In the absence of her husband, the wife "looked after the household affairs, spinning, weaving and making clothes for the children, directing the cooking and getting the hands to work." Slaveholding merchants, like the father of James Coffin, quite often left farm management to wives, who had "immediate supervision" of overseers. Robert Crouch's mother managed eight slaves, who "did the labor" on the 450-acre farm while she "directed her household." W. A. Dickinson's father "staid in the store" while his wife employed 10 slaves to cultivate their 400-acre farm. While F. F. Fisher's mother and siblings produced household crops on a 10-acre farm, his father operated a store, a steam gristmill, and a cabinetry/carpentry shop and worked as a millwright. In addition to supervising a slave field hand, Mrs. Fisher "with the help of a slave woman did the housework" and "sewed sacks" in which her husband exported his flour and meal (Dyer and Moore 1985, 84, 231–32, 346–47, 405–6, 531, 532, 600–601, 684–86, 698, 818, 1021–24).

Some nonslaveholding artisans left the farming to wives and children while they ran town shops or traveled to work at distant sites. William Roberts's father worked as a blacksmith while his wife "did all kinds of farm work" and bound out her son. So that John Bray's father could work as a miller and millwright, his wife worked in the fields alongside her sons, "looked after the cows the sheep chickens carded spun." Samuel Brown's father spent most of his time managing a tannery and mill while his wife supervised white laborers to cultivate their 600-acre farm. Wives and children cultivated small mountainous farms because the fathers of John Holbachs and Samuel Shrader traveled to complete long-term carpentry contracts. John Barnett's wife and children did "all kinds of farm work," so he could earn a living as a cooper. Because Federick Jones's father "Wagon Hauled wheat . . . Hauled goods from Nashville, Hauld Salt from K.Y.," the wife managed their 150-acre farm, helped only by young children (Dyer and Moore 1985, 10, 20, 24, 71, 74, 109, 115–17).

Some women, like the grandmothers of Bertha Frazier (Transcript, ALC, 8) and Bevin Childers (Transcript, ALC, 3), farmed in order to free their husbands to seek wage-paying jobs that were not available to females. While her husband worked "long hours at the sawmill," Dorie Cope "planted the garden and took care of the livestock. All summer she worked toward making the long winter a comfortable one. She preserved all the food, milked, churned the butter, spun and wove material for clothing, and then hand-sewed all they wore" (Bush 1992, 10). Arie Meaders described a complex variety of outdoor farmwork and household duties left to her grandmother, whose husband "hauled lumber for the sawmill" (Wiggington 1983, 101–2). In Lee County, Virginia, the Furrys were sharecroppers who lived in a two-room log cabin and had accumulated no assets. The husband "worked at [a] small iron furnace hammering out pig iron" while the wife "attended to the house duties and looked after farming." In the Royston household of Sullivan County, Tennessee, the mother and children farmed while the husband was employed as a foreman at the iron furnace. In Coffee County, Tennessee, Harrison Farrell's father earned good wages as a railroad construction worker, but he was gone months at a time, leaving his wife to manage their 200-acre farm with hired laborers. In addition to her farm duties and her "work to keep the house in order," Mrs. Farrell produced and sold men's pants and coats, "pleted bossom Sunday shirts and other fine needlework." Mrs. Woody sharecropped the family parcel while her husband worked for wages in a Burke County, North Carolina, gold mine (Dyer and Moore 1985, 796, 869, 1887, 2240).

Other Economically Significant Work

In addition to their field labor, women engaged in several other labors that were viewed by separate spheres advocates to be men's work. During annual slaughtering and meat processing, the entire white family participated, and there was no clear gender segregation in tasks (Adams Transcript, ALC, 16–17; Frazier Transcript, ALC, 15–16). On middle-class farms and small plantations, one of the most unladylike roles of wives entailed their participation in and supervision of the slaughtering and meat processing. On middling to large plantations, however, most of the work was done by slaves, and every female "had a job" to do alongside her male counterparts (Rawick 1979, 3: 78).[14] Appalachian

[14] For photographs and details about poor white women, see Wiggington (1972, 189–207). For details about slaves, see "Slaves in Livestock Production," http://scholar.lib.vt.edu/vtpubs/mountain_slavery/index.htm.

women also contributed economically to their households through their outputs of poultry, maple sugar, dairy and orchard products, garden produce, ginseng, and herbs. In 1840, Appalachian women produced 11 percent of the country's poultry, nearly 10 percent of its orchard products, more than 10 percent of home manufactures, and nearly 15 percent of the ginseng and herbs. Even though they constituted only 5 percent of the country's 1840 population, Appalachian women generated more than 8 percent of women's household outputs of these items nationally. Per capita, Appalachian farm women accounted for more than 5 dollars in these outputs while the typical American farm woman brought in only about 3 dollars to her household through these activities (see Tables 55, 61, and 62, Web site). Homemade sugar was one of the most essential items that Cherokee, white, and African-American women produced. Mamie Shull (Transcript, ASU, 6) and others described women's "sugar orchards." After the grandmothers of Marie Martin (Transcript, ALC, 11) and Bertha Frazier (Transcript, ALC, 16) planted, tended, and gathered the sorghum, the entire family milled the cane and boiled the syrup that would be made into sugar. Nettie Combs (Transcript, ALC, 14) was convinced that growing sorghum and boiling molasses were much less labor intensive than the production of tree sugar because "it took so much sap to make such a little amount of sugar." James Campbell described "maple sugar makin' time" among West Virginia slaves, a gender-integrated process "mostly dun at night by lime stone burnin'" (Rawick 1972, 16: 19).

One-half the wives of farm owners and two-thirds of the women in landless farm households marketed whatever produce or crafted items they could spare (see Table 4). In more than half of the poor farm owner households, both men and women produced grain and livestock surpluses for exchange, and women in three-fourths of them reported to census enumerators that they had sold market produce. Sales of butter "provided a significant addition to the income of farm families" (Jensen 1980, 17). Farm women also generated household cash through their production of cheese, beeswax, orchard products, home manufactures, market produce, poultry, and ginseng. Women's production of surpluses and marketing of these items were so common that census enumerators valued them in monetary terms. For example, the 1850 census for Tazewell County, Virginia (U.S. Census Office 1854), valued at $51,000 women's outputs of maple sugar, beeswax, honey, butter, cheese, wool, flax seeds, and textiles. In fact, white females generated $1.00 in household products for every $3.46 in male-dominated agricultural crops (see Table 38, Web site). On average in 1860, the region's white farm women generated nearly $63.00 worth of items to trade in the informal sector, a level of output that was 1.3 times the national average. Valued at more than $9 million by census enumerators, women's farm outputs made significant contributions to their local economies. In the Appalachian counties of the Carolinas, women's farm outputs had greater economic value than did manufactured or extractive commodities, and industrial outputs were not far ahead of women's outputs in the Appalachian counties of Alabama, Georgia, and Kentucky. In West Virginia, males were producing only $1.63 in agricultural commodities to every $1.00 accumulated by women. In small farm

FIGURE 11. Women's maple sugar was an important household resource and such a significant source of family income that this activity was reported in the 1840 Census of Manufacturing. This drawing depicts an antebellum tree sugar camp operated by women in Tazewell County, Virginia. *Source:* Bickley (1852, 65).

owner households, women averaged more than $100 worth of commodities, accounting for nearly one-fifth of family income (see Table 5). Even a middle-class farm owner's wife produced more than 2 percent of the total household income. However, wives in tenant or sharecropper households generated as much as three-quarters of the cash income acquired by the households.

Conclusion

The experiences of a majority of Appalachian women call into question separate spheres assumptions. It is simply not methodologically reliable for researchers to purport that the class-biased and racist ideologies of elite and middle-class writers accurately represented the everyday lives of a majority of women anywhere in the United States in this historical period. First, such applications of womanhood ideals ignore indigenous women. Second, most poor and a few middle-class white females and a majority of Cherokee and free black women worked in the fields, at back-breaking outdoor tasks, and at other farm tasks that generated household income. Thus, it was not just race that circumscribed the location and the degree of manual labor that southern women did, for there was a class and income hierarchy in the nature of "women's work." Strikingly,

TABLE 5. *Farm Women's Outputs as a Percentage of Household Income, 1860*

Farm Tenure	% All Households	Average Household Income	Women's Outputs	
			Avg. $ Value	% Household Income
Tenants/sharecroppers	26.1	$57	42.80	75.1
Small farm owner	38.2	$563	104.09	18.5
Middling farm owner	28.2	$1,761	38.20	2.2
Large farm owner	7.5	$4,350	13.05	0.3

Source and notes: Average value of women's outputs derived from analysis of a systematic probability sample of 3,474 farm households drawn from the enumerator manuscripts of the 1860 Census of Agriculture. For methods, see Web site. Small farm owners held less than 100 acres and no slaves.

a majority of Cherokee, poor white, free black, and enslaved women worked at the same agricultural tasks (often side by side). Moreover, the contrast between the work of poor and affluent white women was no less sharp than the distinction between the work of affluent white women and slaves. In addition to enslavement, poverty or distance from it determined the degree to which women's work fit the idealized model of feminine domesticity that could only be accomplished in households with servants. While the lifestyles of some white middle-class and wealthy women met the ideals of separate gender spheres, a majority of frontier Appalachian women engaged in forms of agricultural and nonagricultural labor that pinpointed them as "plain women, not ladies." On the one hand, we certainly cannot generalize to all Appalachian females from the vantage point of the minority of affluent women who were polarized from the daily lives of the ethnically diverse majority of impoverished Appalachian women. As Kierner (1998, 34) admits in passing, a cultural ideal of womanhood "that stressed domesticity and the cultivation of feminine sensibility" was attainable only for "literate and leisured" women with servants in landowning, affluent households. Consequently, a majority of women were not isolated in a domestic sphere that protected them from dangerous manual labor or from the public spheres of waged labor and the market.

While a majority of all Appalachian women worked at field labor and outdoor farm tasks to some degree, class and race determined the extent to which a woman engaged regularly in heavy manual labor or work away from home (see Table 6). While Cherokee, African-American, and poor white women labored in ethnically mixed field crews alongside males, middle-class females predominantly worked only with fathers, husbands, and sons on a short-term basis. The more affluent the household, the greater the likelihood that females would be relieved of field labor and outdoor farm tasks by servants or slaves. White women worked in the fields because household survival required it, because farm prosperity depended on the use of family laborers rather than hired help, because husbands were ill or dead, or because there were no alternative

TABLE 6. *Nineteenth-Century Agricultural Labors of Southern Appalachian Women*

Labor Arena by Racial Group	Unpaid Labors	Paid Labors			
		Nonwaged	Waged	Contract	Enterprise Owner
Farm or plantation: white or free black	Household maintenance and reproduction Fieldwork and outdoor farm tasks on family farm Production of dairy products, eggs, feathers, small livestock, and garden produce for household subsistence	Marketing of dairy products, eggs, feathers, small livestock, and garden surpluses Laborer on tenant or sharecropping parcel	Farm laborer	Operator of tenant or share-cropping parcel	Farm or plantation owner
Farm: Cherokee	Household maintenance and reproduction Fieldwork and outdoor farm tasks on family farm	Marketing of small livestock, garden surpluses, and cash crops Laborer on tenant or sharecropping parcel	Farm laborer	Operator of tenant or share-cropping parcel	Farm owner
Plantation: enslaved	Household maintenance and reproduction Fieldwork and outdoor tasks as assigned by owner	Marketing or trading of chickens or garden surpluses	Owner hireout or self-hire as farm laborer	Annual contract laborer	None

nonagricultural waged jobs. In addition to those general trends, some surprises emerge from women's narratives.

- More frequently than has been thought, Cherokee females and middle-class and elite white women managed farms and landless white women cultivated tenant or sharecropping parcels.
- Nearly half of all free black women, about 15 percent of white women, and many poor Cherokee females were waged farm laborers. Similarly, owners hired out enslaved females as field laborers more often than males.
- Mistresses on small plantations did outdoor farm tasks much more frequently than elite slaveholding women, and middle-class white women worked in the field more frequently than many historians have assumed. However, these women contributed labor as assistants to the market-oriented production of their spouses, and their work was "absorbed into an enterprise identified as exclusively his" (Boydston 1986, 9). Consequently, much of their outdoor farm labor was rendered socially and economically invisible by class peers who judged them against the cult of domesticity to a greater degree than they applied separate spheres ideals to nonwhite or poor white women.
- Most Cherokee and enslaved females and some white women actually preferred manual farm labor to indoor household chores.

Rather than equalizing gender differences, as some scholars have claimed, antebellum U.S. farms mirrored the gender contradictions that resulted from the emergence of capitalism.[15] According to Faragher (1981, 550), "Men were free to pursue the work of the public world precisely because the inequitable division of labor at home made them beneficiaries of women's and children's labor." Consequently, some women worked at field labor in order to free males to earn wages or income at nonagricultural occupations or professions. While the farm labors of wives and children permitted males to migrate to search out greater income off the farm or to work in towns, women were not released from the labors of farm and home. In this sense, nongendered flexibility in the allocation of farm labor effectively created overwork for women. As Shaunna Scott (1990, 111) has observed, "Trading work across gender boundaries functioned primarily in one direction: that is, women were routinely deployed in 'men's' field activities, but men rarely did housework." Thus, the demarcation between farm and house was not nearly as constraining as some investigators have assumed, especially not for nonwhite women, who experienced no cultural assignment to limited house-bound work. Many white women absorbed outdoor farm tasks into their household regimen, never making any "separate spheres" distinction between these forms of labor. Just as their unpaid household labor was

---

[15] For an author who argues that family farms created gender equality, see Osterud (1991). For authors who argue that antebellum farms were gender inequitable, see Folbre (1991) and Faragher (1981).

rendered socially invisible and viewed as having little economic value, much of the farmwork of white wives disappeared from public view in a society that credited males for farm success and assigned husbands the legal right to negotiate in "the marketplace as the 'possessors' of their wives' labor" (Boydston 1986, 22).

6

The Myth of Separate Spheres and Women's Nonagricultural Labor

From our birth to our death, we women are the slaves of prejudice and of circumstance. My ambition was not that of being idle.... There was one thing I felt sure of, and that was a living, if no more; that was by hard work at the straw millinery.... Work, constant, honest, well directed work: that is the only road to permanent distinction, lasting success.

(Emily Austin 1882, 222, 245)

The cult of domesticity assigned income-producing efforts to the male domain and household activities with little or no market value to the female arena. Jeffersonian agrarianism was grounded in the notion that "the citizen farmer would be supported and enabled through the services of a woman who tended to the home and did not venture into his domain" (Fink 1992, 24). Women were assumed to be outside the male-dominated marketplace (Sigourney 1838, 232; Ellett 1857, 18). Matthaei (1982, 51, 106, 110) argued that capitalism structured a sexual division of labor in which family life was assigned specifically to women while income-earning activities were removed from the home and developed "into a distinct masculine sphere." The "absence of white homemakers of all classes from the labor force" occurred because domesticity was "self-consciously chosen" by a majority of Caucasian females. In contrast, nonwhite women did not embrace the cult of domesticity and were far more likely to engage in labor outside their homes. The everyday lives of a majority of Appalachian women were a stark contrast to this mythology, and their nonagricultural labors were in evidence from the frontier years throughout the antebellum period. In reality, a majority of women earned income through nonagricultural activities inside and outside their households. In the sections that follow, I will explore women's income-earning activities that occurred in both home and public spheres.

Women's Textiles Production

After the Revolutionary War, one of the most hidden market activities was female participation as "disguised industrial proletarians" (Mies 1986, 118) in textiles production. By the late eighteenth century, Southern Appalachia's countryside was exhibiting patterns of labor organization that were typical of *protoindustrialization*, characterized by the coexistence of agriculture, household-based craft work, and centralized factory production. Also referred to as *cottage industries* by some writers, these rural handicraft industries occurred in regions where there was a surplus class of underemployed rural laborers who had few occupational options (Kriedte, Medick, and Schlumbohm 1981, 117, 219), as was indeed the case in antebellum Southern Appalachia. Because household survival could not be ensured through agriculture alone, many adults became involved in "the part-time or full-time transition from land-intensive agrarian production to labor-intensive craft production" (Medick 1976, 297). From the frontier years until the Civil War, Cherokee, white, and black females engaged in home-based textiles production. By 1840, women dominated the textiles manufacturing labor force.

Textiles Production on Appalachian Frontiers

Since the Indian agent believed that "the work of civilizing" the Cherokees was "to teach them agriculture and domestic manufacturing," Indian progress toward "civilization" was measured by the degree to which men had accepted plows and women had taken up white domestic arts. The Indian agent did not believe that men were becoming farmers fast enough, but he was pleased that women acquired easily the skills of spinning and weaving (Weeks 1916, 338, 20). Because women increased their textiles production, cotton was "universally raised for domestic consumption" while sheep raising tripled between 1809 and 1828 to supply needed wool. In 1817, the Indian agent described "the pursuits of the females" as "raising Cotton, Indigo, spinning, dyeing yarn & weaving & taking care of family household affairs" (CIAT Reports, NA 30 Jan. and 2 May 1817). A decade later, missionaries praised Cherokee women for manufacturing "a great quantity of cloth" (ABCFM Papers, HUL, 10 Oct. 1828). There were 2,495 households when the *Cherokee Phoenix* (20 Mar. 1828, 1 June 1828) reported 2,792 plows, 2,428 spinning wheels, and 769 looms. By that account, there were nearly as many spinning wheels as horses. These statistics make it appear that every household had a spinning wheel and that one-third of the families had acquired looms. By 1835, the numbers had grown to 2,484 weavers and 3,129 spinners, seemingly indicating that nearly three-quarters of the 4,328 adult women could spin while more than half could weave (McLoughlin and Conser 1977, 695). Like their white counterparts, Cherokee slaveholding women like Mary Dougherty and Maria Coody established "Loom Houses" in which enslaved and hired women produced textiles (Valuations, UTK, 101–2, 117). Even isolated poor women accepted the spinning wheel. For example, Brainerd missionaries recorded that they "slept in a solitary hut" in southeast Tennessee where "a neat old woman, of 70 or 80 years of age, [was] very busily engaged in spinning" (Brainerd Journal, HUL, 2 June 1820).

However, missionaries and government officials overstated the extent to which women had acquiesced to the civilization program, for females in mestizo households received most of the very scarce textiles technology. According to McLoughlin (1984a, 18–19), mestizos "got the lion's share" of government funds and equipment. Only 6 percent of the annual operational budget of the Cherokee Indian Agency was spent on equipment for textiles manufacturing. Much of the limited funding (Disbursement by Meigs, UTK) was shifted away from Cherokee households to provide looms, spinning wheels, and cards to missionary schools that taught only a few mestizo girls "to spin, weave & sew." Despite shortages of equipment, Benjamin Hawkins claimed that, by 1801, "the wheel, the loom and plough" were "in pretty general use." He omitted telling Washington officials that his methods of distributing tools had polarized the women. Cherokees in western North Carolina were disgruntled that they had received less equipment and training than settlements in northern Georgia and northern Alabama. Representing those more "progressive"communities who had benefited from textiles demonstrations and a greater supply of agricultural equipment, John Watts, Weele, and Doublehead reported, "There is a division now among ourselves" because the chiefs east of Chilhowee Mountain "say we have had more [spinning] wheels and cards than our share, and in consequence are more advanced in making our own clothing" (Lowrie and Clarke 1832, 1: 647, 39).

Even though traditional Cherokee women were accustomed to textiles production in clan kinship units, Hawkins employed immigrant male weavers to teach them, and he stationed those instructors in mestizo households. In 1797, he "sent a weaver" to a mestizo home in which "cotton was raised and spun" by two females. The weaver "fixed up a loom and wove it," and "he was much visited during the time he was weaving, by the women...who expressed a determination to attend to the raising of cotton." Absent from those visiting women, however, were a majority of the poorer women, who would not have been welcome in the home of a more prosperous family (Weeks 1916, 137, 293, 228, 232, 362). By the later antebellum period, Cherokee women engaged in textiles production just as frequently as poor white females. For example, Flora Youngblood recalled that her mother grew and spun cotton from which she sewed dresses and men's suits "for other people." In addition, she traded cotton for wool, in order to knit "boys' wool socks and babies booties" to sell to merchants (Wiggington and Bennett 1985, 21–22).

On Appalachian frontiers, the most significant nonagricultural labor in which white women engaged was household textiles manufacturing. After the Revolutionary War, U.S. textiles production displaced the heavy imports that had characterized the colonial period, and women accounted for most of that output in their homes (Innes 1988, 44). In 1810, only 7.4 percent of U.S. cloth was produced by factory machinery. Because the country was heavily dependent upon household textiles production, the early national censuses acknowledged the economic value of this type of women's work. Since the census distinguished household looms and the cloth "made in families" from factory textiles and equipment, it is clear that women were weaving 13.4 yards in their homes to every 1 yard of cotton or wool cloth produced by factory equipment. There were cloth mills in only four Appalachian counties, so households wove nearly 7.5 million yards of cloth valued at more than $3.6 million. More than half the white adult females owned looms, and they averaged nearly 207 yards of cloth annually, valued at more than $100. Per capita, Southern Appalachian weavers created 2.6 times more yards of cloth than other U.S. females. Unfortunately, we cannot use those census reports to determine what proportion of that textiles production was actually done by slaves within elite or middle-class households.[1]

In 1810, the United States had only 1,776 carding machines and 1,682 fulling mills to process cotton, flax, and wool into thread or yarn. Fewer than 2 million pounds of cotton and wool were spun in mills while households spun more than 26 million pounds. Before women could weave cloth, they had to complete the tedious preparation of raw materials into thread or yarn. Despite the significance of this stage of textiles manufacture, census enumerators did not collect reliable counts of women's tools or their spinning output. In North Carolina, the only state that made a reliable count, two of every five of its adult white females owned spinning wheels. In the Appalachian counties of North Carolina, women's spinning was even more extensive. The census enumerated 1.7 wheels for every adult white western North Carolina female, indicating that a majority of households had both the small wheel for flax and the large wheel for wool and cotton. In addition, more than half the households reported flax brakes, indicating a heavy output of linen and linsey-woolsey.[2]

Other primary sources also describe the household textiles production of women in every section of Southern Appalachia. Recognizing the significance of these household manufactures, the Virginia General Assembly passed an early law mandating that county courts "provide and sett up a loome and weaver, in each of the respective counties." Any county failing to do so was fined 2,000 pounds of tobacco. In frontier southwest Virginia, settler women mixed a wild nettle with buffalo hair to produce yarnlike threads that were "woven into substantial cloth, in which the men and women were clothed." They also wove cotton into a strong cloth for household use and for marketing in Williamsburg (Bickley 1852, 145). In West Virginia, "almost every house contained a loom, and almost every woman was a weaver." In one household, "weaving proved serviceable to the family" because a woven belt could be paid to a farm laborer for a day's work (Peyton 1894, 48). Unlike their counterparts of the later antebellum period, frontier middle-class women spun and wove.

[1] Derived from analysis of national and Appalachian county totals in U.S. Census Office (1814).
[2] Derived from analysis of national and Appalachian county totals in U.S. Census Office (1814, 5–7). Analysis of census enumerator manuscripts for the western North Carolina counties.

In one Pocohontas County, West Virginia, household, the wife had a separate "Loom-house" where hired whites and slaves manufactured textiles. In general, according to one traveler, the women of this area made their households "self-sustaining" through their spinning and weaving. "The big wheel and the little wheel [we]re birring in every hut," he claimed, "and throwing off woolen and linen yard to be worked up" (Doddridge 1824, 113–15). In Berkeley County, West Virginia, Sarah Nourse (Diary, UVA) did not spin or weave, for these duties were assigned to slaves in her affluent household. Yet she spent 65 to 77 days a year sewing, knitting, and mending clothes. One eighteenth-century traveler claimed that western North Carolina settler girls were "bred to the Needle and Spinning" (Salley 1911, 32). William Byrd (1929, 66, 68, 304, 306) praised southwestern Virginia and western North Carolina women who "cloathe the Whole Family" because poor and middle-class females "all Spin, weave and knit." In Appalachian South Carolina, white settlers and black slaves "in the various settlements would meet alternately at each other's house to pick the seed out of the cotton and prepare it for the wheel." One traveler reported soon after the Revolutionary War that white women in the western Carolinas "now manufacture most of their linens (such as cost in England from 12 to 18 d. a yard), Linsey-Woolsey, and even coarse cloths" (Bacot 1923, 684).

In their textiles manufacturing, Appalachian women were not unlike other U.S. women of this era. An 1859 issue of *DeBow's Review* (27: 211) observed, "The high and low, the rich and poor, were alike attired in home-spun, made by the industrious and ingenious hand of the busy housewife." However, there is much evidence of marketing, trading, and income earning from textiles production. In east Kentucky, "the weaver [wa]s paid either in toll from the cloth or in corn." Women who did the weaving "for a certain proportion of the manufactured article" received "two yards out of three fore their trouble." According to Toulmin (1794, 80, 97), east Kentucky "manufactures of WOOL, and mixtures thereof with cotton and flax . . . [we]re a much superior quality to those imported from Europe. Besides the coarse woolen cloths they manu-facture linsey-woolsey, Negro cloth, coverlets, counterpanes, and stockings." In western North Carolina, most settler women did their own spinning, but some women "took in weaving from neighbors." Not all the fabric was coarse, for some of it was intended for trading or selling (Lewis 1991, 215). Anna Baker ran a small commercial spinning and weaving business in her Surry County, North Carolina, home (Smith and Wilson 1999, 47). Sarah Graham recalled the importance of her mother's cloth production to their east Kentucky household. She wove surplus cloth from which she traded "seven yards of cot-ton for one sow shoat" and "with nine yards she got some salt" (Rohrbough 1987, 36).

Frontier newspapers also attest to the economic significance of women's cloth. To attract female customers, frontier stores advertised that they would accept in trade "good linen" and other homespun fabrics. Advertisements fre-quently offered "a generous price for country manufactured flax," the source of the linsey that was so widely used all over frontier Appalachia. In the 1790s, east

Tennessee merchants valued "good flax linen ten hundred" at "three shillings and six pence per yard." In 1791, a Knoxville store advertised the sale of "well chosen goods from the markets of Philadelphia and Boston." In exchange, "the highest price w[ould] be allowed for good linsey, seven hundred linen." Another store accepted "good linen" in trade for all kinds of imported goods. Like stores in Knoxville, Jonesboro, and Greeneville, Tennessee, a Rogersville merchant advertised "superfine, second, and coarse" fabrics and "fine handkerchiefs, shawls, scarlet cloaks, Irish linen," which he had accepted in trades with local women. Stephen Duncan and Company accepted "cash, furs, skins, corn, pork, or beef" in exchange for locally produced fabrics and clothing. A farmer near Abingdon offered "stud services" to the public, for which he would accept payment in cash or "good trade," including cloth. The Washington County, Virginia, Salt Works listed three exchange rates, the lowest price offered to those trading good-quality local cloth. The *Knoxville Gazette* was induced by the "scarcity of cash" on the frontier to accept subscription payments in the form of linen and linsey.

Though they represented less than 8 percent of U.S. population, adult Southern Appalachian females produced nearly one-third of the country's cloth in 1810. Not all the fabric traded by women stayed in their resident counties, as is evidenced by distant businesses that advertised in Appalachian newspapers. One Richmond commission merchant was "set up more particularly with a view of doing a Western Country business." In southwest Virginia and east Tennessee newspapers, he offered to trade all sorts of European imports for "western produce," most especially good-quality cotton, linen, and woolen cloth. For export to West Indies plantations, an eastern North Carolina commission merchant sought to purchase cloth produced in western North Carolina. Boothe and Dews, an auction and commission house at Knoxville, offered to market on consignment "every description of dry goods," including "cotton yarn" and fabrics that could be exported to the Lower South.[3]

Textiles Production in the Later Antebellum Period
According to Dublin (1979, 4), women maintained these frontier patterns of home-based production and accounted for the vast majority of the country's clothing until the latter part of the antebellum era. Early factories "did not so much replace household manufacture as complement it. By mechanizing the slowest, most laborious steps in the production process, the carding and fulling mills actually contributed to increasing production of cloth in the home." In similar fashion, a majority of post-1820 Appalachian textiles production occurred in homes, and antebellum historians commented on the economic significance of this form of women's work. In Tazewell County, Virginia, for example, "linsey, jeans, tow-linen, flax-thread, hose, and carpets [we]re the principal home manufactures" (Bickley 1852, 111). While small factories carded

[3] Derived from analysis of U.S. Census Office (1814, 2–7); *Knoxville Gazette*, 10 Mar. 1818, 15 Aug. 1787, 21 Jan. 1840.

wool, most of the spinning and weaving was done in homes. In fact, there was only 43 cents worth of clothing finished in factories or artisan shops to every $2.65 worth of textiles home manufactures (U.S. Census 1865). For example, the 1840 per capita value of western North Carolina household manufactures was more than twice the per capita value of the outputs of all U.S. households. By 1850, the households in this Appalachian subregion were averaging nine times the outputs of other American families.[4] Textiles home manufacturing declined in this period only in the Appalachian counties of Maryland, Tennessee, Virginia, and West Virginia, where the greatest number of clothing factories had emerged (see Table 36, Web site). As Medick (1976, 297, 299, 301, 303–4, 312) has observed, "The logic of family economic production became effective all because of the inclination of the poor, landless producers to fall back on 'self-exploitation' in the production of craft goods, if this was necessary to ensure customary family subsistence and economic self-sufficiency." Assisted by their children, women were the laboring vanguard in protoindustrialization. In the sections that follow, I will examine

- production by poor white and free black women organized around extended kin work units
- and nighttime production by slaves on small plantations.

In 1860, only 16 percent of U.S. white wives and female heads of household were identified by census enumerators as seamstresses, spinners, or weavers (Matthaei 1982). However, the vast majority of women described in Appalachian oral histories engaged in these occupations. More than 90 percent of the mothers described by Civil War veterans either produced their own textiles or supervised servants or slaves in the spinning, weaving, and sewing processes. Half of all western North Carolina households owned spinning wheels, and three-quarters held linen and flax equipment (Smith and Wilson 1999, 311n11). Because of the economic significance of spinning and weaving equipment, state laws designated it the property of wives, therefore exempt from their husbands' debts or estate settlements. Census data and other primary sources indicate that a majority of the women who thought of themselves as skilled textiles artisans were poor, nonwaged workers in their own cottage industries. Women's household textiles were

- marketed to stores, shops, or public town markets,
- sold or traded to more well-to-do women who wanted to be relieved of the most onerous labor involved in textiles production, or
- produced as part of *putting-out systems* operated by factories, clothing artisan shops, or stores.

Household-based textiles protoindustrialization was a multiprocess labor system that required a variety of tasks ranging from menial labor to highly skilled artisanry (Mendels 1972, 249–50), but few women were skilled enough

---

[4] NC trends were calculated using Table 7.1 in Anglin (1995, 197).

to do all the tasks. On the low-skill end of the process, the vast majority of white women carded wool, while only two-fifths completed the tedious steps to process flax. While most spun, knitted, sewed, and quilted, only about two-fifths had acquired the complex weaving skills and equipment (see Table 37, Web site). Poor women's textiles protoindustrialization continued for three reasons. In the region's small towns, there were very few commercial enterprises that produced finished clothing. In the entire vast geographical area, there were only 40 artisan shops reported as manufacturers of clothing, gloves, mittens, hats, and caps, and there were only 72 clothing factories, which were located in less than one-third of the region's counties.[5] Second, more prosperous women employed textiles workers to do most of the manual labor or to supervise their slaves. For example, John O'Neal's mother supervised a helper who did "weaving and spinning to clothe 13 children." Russell Brown's mother carded and spun but hired a white girl to weave the cloth. The Sims family of White County, Tennessee, "hired Some poor white girl to do the weaving" while Samuel Reynolds's mother "sode [sewed] for the Rich Peeple." The Osbornes "had a white seamstress" who supervised slaves in the textiles manufacturing process (Dyer and Moore 1985, 24, 942, 1019, 1972).

Third, there was a market for finished goods among more affluent households. Most middle-class women did not undertake the most back-breaking, time-consuming initial steps to process wool, flax, or cotton. Even though they utilized the finished thread, yarn, and cloth to engage in knitting, sewing, and quilting, middle-class farm women were rarely spinners, weavers, or seamstresses. Instead, they "hired the wool spun on shares," then they utilized the finished yarn to knit (Roberts Transcript, ALC, 2). One western Carolina woman carded, spun, and wove "on shares" for her more well-to-do neighbors and for the store in town, never seeing any cash for her work. The wife of a northern Georgia physician hired a woman to "stay with them through the winter months.... She'd sew, quilt, card wool, spin, and weave" (Wiggington and Bennett 1985, 76–77). Neely Adams's (Transcript, ALC, 3) east Kentucky mother "wove for people," who "furnished everything." A. H. Gross's mother "took in sewing" in her home, but western North Carolina farm women often peddled their cloth in towns (Goodrich 1931, 4, 75). James Harris's mother was a seamstress who "made suits of clothing for both men and women" and "did spining, weaving, of cotton raised on the farm and picked out by hand." The mothers of Jacob Sliger and Samuel Brown "wove cloth for the rich people" (Dyer and Moore 1985, 270, 400, 797, 1655, 1670, 1826, 1961). One western Carolina woman had to work long hours at her craft because it was "hard to make a livin' out of plain weaving" (Montgomery 1924, 51).

Some women participated in the textiles putting-out system organized by factories, stores, or artisan shops. Many retail stores advanced raw materials and equipment, paying women one-third in cash and two-thirds in yarn or

[5] Derived from analysis of Appalachian county data in U.S. Census Office (1865).

supplies.[6] During the 1830s and 1840s, for example, one east Kentucky merchant credited the yearly accounts of several local women for their labor at wool carding, clothing production, and spinning (Forsythe Papers, UKY, Store Accounts). In some towns of western Maryland, Blue Ridge Virginia, and West Virginia, artisan shops consigned work to household-based women, who were either paid wages or allocated a small share of the output. In heavily industrialized Wheeling, West Virginia, 119 women labored in their homes for milliners, dressmakers, and merchant tailors, who advanced them the wool, cotton, or cloth to card, spin, weave, or sew finished goods. In that town, the vast majority of needleworkers were seamstresses who did contract piecework for eight merchant tailors (Delfino and Gillespie 2002, 145n55). In 1842, an east Tennessee woman requested government intervention to deter the flow of factory goods that were displacing home-based textiles. She informed her state legislature that local households sold surplus textiles "to the merchants to procure other necessaries for [thei]r families." Once stores began to import textiles, local women were told that northern and eastern manufactures could be sold "at so low a price" that household cloth and clothing could not "bear a competition with them" (*Raleigh Register*, 1 Feb. 1842).

Civil War veterans described mothers who subsidized household income through putting-out arrangements. Federick Jones's mother "was a taylor by trad[e]," who spun and made her own cloth, and it was not unusual for western North Carolina Moravian females to be employed as tailor shop assistants or as milliners. In their landless poor household, George Payne's mother was an excellent "coatmaker," who sewed winter clothing for the slaves of neighboring plantations. Because "the pore had to work," observed Louis Segle, his mother was a washwoman who sewed coats, pants, men's weskits, and children's clothing for more well-to-do neighbors. In Abingdon, Virginia, John Jones's mother farmed 30 acres and "made a specialty of making men's suits." John Tallant's mother was probably the poorest woman described by veterans. Without any adult male in the household, she did the farmwork on her nine acres and made extra money for her children by "weaving, spining and tailoring"(Dyer and Moore 1985, 74, 860, 1257, 1519, 1711, 1931, 2024).[7] Women's textile production was so important during the Civil War that equipment scarcities were reported. Because Transylvania County, North Carolina, women were making soldier uniforms, "cotton and wool cards c[ould] scarcely be had at all, the old ones being about worn out" (Smith and Wilson 1999, 64–65, 129). When Mrs. E. M. Beasley was denied an army contract to produce military apparel, she

---

[6] For example, women's account credits were found in these manuscript collections: Samuel D. Thorn Ledger, Garrison Records, 1836–60 Guseman Records, WVU; 1800–1820 entries, Graham Account Book, UKY; Sherrill Account Book, Foster Papers, Account Books, 1845–47, 1827–67, Rhodes Memorandum Book, Pennybacker Daybook, Orr Papers, Mercantile Accounts, 1854–55, DU.

[7] Represented in the recollections of Civil War veterans there are only two middle-class women and no wealthy females who earned a living producing finished textiles.

FIGURE 12. In 1840, spinning wheels were owned by a higher percentage of Appalachian households than was typical of the rest of the country. To provide household essentials and to earn cash, poor white, free black, and Cherokee women routinely spun. The top view is an ex-slave who had treasured the handmade wheel used by women in her family for many generations. The bottom view is a poor white woman with a wheel of the sort typically used by free Appalachian females in the nineteenth century. *Source:* Library of Congress.

complained to Confederate officials, "I did not expect to get a refusal, merely because I am a woman" (*Raleigh Standard*, 18 Nov. 1862).

In white households, women organized the production process by pooling the skilled laborers from a close circle of relatives, forming an extended kin production unit. Because their cabins were small, Neely Adams's (Adams Transcript, ALC, 2) mother and aunts stored the various pieces of equipment at their different homes, each one keeping the tools that were essential to the part of the process she would complete. For less skilled work such as preparing flax or wool or quilting, women pooled their labor from relatives and neighbors by organizing work parties. Marie Martin (Transcript, ALC, 11) recalled that groups of women and girls would quilt on "frames that hung from the ceiling."

Textiles protoindustrialization was a form of *superexploitation* of women, who juggled their time among agriculture, household chores, child rearing, crafts, informal sector marketing, and sometimes waged labor (Mendels 1972, 254). Many poor women did most of their textiles production and quilting in the fall and winter months "because there wasn't enough time while the crops were being tended" (Thompson 1976, 140). Arie Meaders's grandmother raised and stored all the household crops, tended livestock, sheared sheep, slaughtered hogs, processed meat, and "kept rodents and birds out of her crops." In addition to the usual array of indoor household chores, she carded wool, spun thread, and wove cloth. As Arie put it: "She had all that t' do. She was raised up to it and she had it t' do" (Wigginigton 1983, 101–2). Other females worked late into the night, after a day of farm and household work. "Many an' many a night I've been workin' when two o'clock come in th' mornin – cardin' n' spinnin' 'n' sewin'," one wife recalled (Wiggington 1972, 30).

In addition to requiring female overwork, textiles production required early work socialization of girls. Frances Goodrich (1931, 51) observed that most Appalachian girls were "experts" at preparing the wool for their mothers to spin, "the cards having been put into their hands as soon as they were old enough to hold them." Girls did all kinds of unskilled tasks and menial labor to assist more skilled spinners and weavers, and they began to spin and knit during the preteen years. Sophia Roberts (Transcript, ALC, 5) was the necessary "second pair of hands" to help her grandmother put "about a hundred yards" on her large outdoor warping frame. The young girl "helped her carry that thread back an' forth" until it seemed as if she had "walked miles an' miles." According to Medick (1976, 299), protoindustrialization organized the household labor around the need to accumulate the needed resources for survival. As a result, the varied labors required of women led to "the disappearance of the traditional separation of labor between the sexes." For example, more than one-fifth of the poor women sheared their own sheep, a process thought of as "men's work" by many middle-class females (*Janney's Virginia* 1978, 80, 102). On middle-class farms, cultivating and outdoor preparation of flax were men's work, but more than half of poor white women did that manual labor (see Table 37, Web site). Even though textiles production was essentially "women's work," there was no gender distinction between boys and girls by poor mothers who produced fabric or clothing. Until they were teenagers, boys, like J. W. Andes and Jeptha Fuston, helped their mothers and sisters with textiles tasks. Edward Gannaway "done everything from turning the spinning wheel and handing threads to older sisters in the loom to weave clothing for the family" (Dyer and Moore 1985, 202, 212, 871, 877).

Textiles protoindustrialization was not generally accompanied by sustained increases in the standard of living of the workers or their families (Mendels 1972, 252). There was a vast economic divide between the small shop owners and the women who worked in cottage industries. In 1860, the typical woman who owned a textiles shop earned about $632 annually and had accumulated nearly $2,000 in household wealth. In contrast, females who worked in their homes as seamstress, spinner, or weaver averaged about $61 annually, placing their families well below the national poverty line. Those wives who did textiles production in addition to their farm labor averaged only about $49 in cash annually.[8] In addition to these income inequalities, the working conditions posed health risks. According to one physician, there was no occupation that was "more unhealthy or which yield[ed] ... a higher death return than the several classes of sewing women – dress makers, milliners, and those engaged in and for the several large tailoring establishments" (Reeves 1870, 26–27). Many oral histories include comments about the harmful effects on eyes, hands, shoulders, and backs, and much of the hard physical labor would have endangered the health of pregnant women and their fetuses. Carding was one of the simplest tasks, but it was "a wearisome job and hard on the shoulders" (Goodrich 1931, 51). Charles Broyles's mother "worked by tallow candle light" in the evenings (Dyer and Moore 1985, 27) while Dorie Cope kept her small flax loom near the only window where she could hope to get some sunlight on overcast days (Bush 1992, 26). Because of lack of space, women often completed much of their preparation for weaving and spinning in the cold outdoors (Wiggington 1983, 101–2).

Textiles production with primitive tools was an endless, tedious, backbreaking process, but it was also an art that allowed women to express creativity and love for their families. Civil War veterans marveled at the skill and tenacity of their mothers, who "worked from sunup to sundown." After a day's fieldwork, Charles Broyles's mother "made the clothing by weaving, spinning, and sewing often working until 9 to 10 o'clock at night." In addition to her work in the house and on the farm, Harvey Chase's mother "could weave 3 or 4 yards of cloth per day." In their Burke County, North Carolina, home, S. F. Paine "never seen [his] mother sit down and be idle and do nothing. Always had [textiles] work in her hands" (Dyer and Moore 1985, 27, 489, 562, 1682).

The third form of home-based textiles protoindustrialization was group production by slaves on small plantations. The smaller the plantation, the

---

[8] Derived from analysis of a systematic probability sample of 2,795 female heads of household drawn from the 1860 Census of Population manuscripts, NA. For the antebellum national poverty line, see Soltow (1975).

FIGURE 13. Household-based textiles production was widespread among nineteenth-century poor white, Cherokee, and African-American women, who produced fabrics and clothing for household use and for marketing. The top view shows a poor white woman weaving in the barn because the loom was too large for a typical small cabin. The bottom view shows an enslaved woman weaving at night while tending her children. *Sources:* Library of Congress and Love (1907, 10).

more likely it was to depend almost exclusively on slave production of fabrics, bedding, and clothing (Dunaway 2003a, 169). In fact, enslaved Appalachian women were assigned to produce cloth 11 times more frequently than other U.S. slaves (see Table 23, Web site).[9] Enslaved females clothed the entire labor force, minimized the cash outlay of their masters for manufactured goods, and supplied their owners with surpluses to sell. Burning pine torches, candles, or rag lamps, women worked late into the nights to produce assigned quotas of textiles. Except to supervise, very few white slaveholding women participated in textile manufacturing (Dyer and Moore 1985, 317, 413, 541, 601, 621, 625, 814, 865, 912, 1074, 1447; "Unwritten History," FUA, 56; Rawick 1979, 3: 671; Rawick 1972, 16: 11–16). On the few occasions when Gentry McGee saw his slaveholding mother "on the loom bench," she was "only instructing the servant" (Dyer and Moore 1985, 1439). The vast majority of enslaved Appalachian women were assigned daily quotas of spinning that were to be done "after the slaves would do their day's work." The women "had to work in the field and spin four cuts before they went to bed," each cut consisting of 300 yards. They wanted to finish their evening work before dark "'cause it mighty hard handlin' dat thread by fire-light" ("Unwritten History," FUA, 91, 149). Robert Falls's mother worked until 10 o'clock every night "because her part was to spin so many cuts a day" (Rawick 1972, 16: 13). After a day's work in the field and the master's house, Sarah Gudger "had t' ceard an' spin till ten o'clock" (Rawick 1972, 14: 353).

By combining their varied skills, slave women completed a manufacturing process that required significant labor input every day, all year round. In the first stage, women spent many hours preparing the raw materials. A few large plantations sent their wool to nearby mills for carding into yarn, but most slaves completed the entire process by hand. On small plantations, wool preparation was a time-consuming process that began with washing and cleaning. Women used two sets of metal cards, one to separate fibers, one to comb wool into rolls for spinning. After ginning, raw cotton was cleaned of stems, seeds, and debris before it could be carded.[10] In the second stage, women spent many hours spinning the raw fibers into threads or yarns. In the third stage of textile production, threads or yarns were treated to prevent shrinkage, to whiten them, or to add colors. At the top of the hierarchy of artisans were the weavers, who specialized in the fourth and most complex stage of textiles production. Weaving "was a thing the women prided in doing," and the loom "was kept going all the year." Typically, loomers "didn't do nothing but weave," after other women had prepared the thread. Before weaving could begin, however, the woman spent 8 to 10 hours filling the loom with threads. The typical daily quota for a weaver was six to seven yards of cloth (Rawick 1972, 13: 267,

---

[9] Less than 6 percent of U.S. slave women produced cloth (Fogel and Engerman 1992, 139) while more than half of Appalachian slave women were employed at textiles production.

[10] For descriptions of wool and cotton preparation, see Rawick (1977, 5: 297–98, 7: 689, 11: 131, 3: 478) and Rawick (1979, 10: 4273).

FIGURE 14. This Greenbrier County, West Virginia, milliner made pheasant-tail hats for elite and middle-class women who visited the prestigious mineral spa at White Sulphur Springs. Summer tourists at White Sulphur were sharply polarized from the majority of local Appalachian women, who could not afford such luxurious travel or living conditions. *Source: Harper's Monthly* (August 1855).

6: 155, 12: 308; Rawick 1977, 5: 297). Except on the smallest slaveholdings, only a few women transformed the fabric into the final items of clothing. In the final stage, seamstresses and tailors collected and sized patterns, then cut and sewed garments. Although not as respected by slave women as the weaver, the seamstress or tailor was also highly skilled. "They'd be sewin' for weeks and months." Almost all the women "learned to knit and made stockings" for slave use. Individually at night, women cut scraps from old clothing to piece quilt tops in front of the fireplace. Because there were not enough slaves on many Appalachian plantations to complete all the needed textiles specialties, women organized communal work parties. The neighborhood's most reputable artisan supervised the work, assigned tasks, and set quotas, whether it was spinning, dyeing, weaving, rugmaking, or sewing. If they were quilting during the winter, they would "just go from one house to another" in the community until everyone's bedding was completed (Rawick 1977, 7: 689; Rawick 1972, 8: 46).

Females in Textiles Manufacturing

Because of their extensive home-based skills, women were employed more frequently in factory textiles production than in any other industrial sector. Females composed two-thirds of the labor force in textiles manufacturing (Dunaway 1996, 148). In 1860, women represented more than 70 percent of the workers milling cotton and making finished clothing. Ironically, women dominated household weaving, but males moved into this occupation as waged jobs expanded. Even though women outnumbered males, there was a gender bias in the wage scale. While males monopolized the higher-paying weaving looms, women did carding and spinning, and young girls quilled looms, did piecing, and acted as gophers for adults (Sumner 1910, 52, 55, 58). In the Appalachian cotton mills of Alabama, Georgia, North Carolina, and Tennessee, women made up more than three-quarters of the labor force. Half to two-thirds of the workers in West Virginia and western Maryland clothing factories were females. Women also represented more than one-third of the workers at wool manufactories, an industrial sector that was male-dominated nationally.[11] An 1859 issue of *DeBow's Review* (27: 695) claimed that the women and girls who worked in northern South Carolina mills "f[oun]d their condition very much bettered by the change from their . . . employments upon farms and rented lands." However, those manufactories paid men $139 annually while women averaged only $89 (Lander 1953, 167, 170). West Virginia men earned two to three times more per month than women at the Virginius Island cotton factory (Johnson 1995, 14) and at Wheeling's woolen mills (Delfino and Gillespie 2002, 126). Similarly, western Carolina and northern Georgia mills set the female wage cap at only about half the level assigned to men (Buckingham 1842, 2: 113). No doubt the employers were exploiting the poverty of these women and girls, who were described in the *Augusta Evening Dispatch* (4 Mar. 1859) as "generally of a class who formerly suffered for want of even the common necessaries of life." In addition to employment in textiles factories, a few women operated their own enterprises. In fact, two-thirds of the region's textile manufacturers were small artisan shops that sold finished clothing, mittens, gloves, hats, and caps. About 1.5 percent of all white wives and female heads of household identified themselves to census enumerators as owners of such shops (see Table 4). In east Kentucky, for instance, a female tailor merchant earned more than $4,000 annually and was one of the wealthiest heads of households in her county.

---

[11] Derived from analysis of Appalachian county data in U.S. Census Office (1865).

Female Employment in Nonagricultural Occupations

By 1820, women and children represented nearly 12 percent of the region's manufacturing labor force, and they were already highly visible in those occupations in which they would be concentrated in the later antebellum period. In western Maryland, one of every four industrial laborers was a female or a child while nearly one-third of western North Carolina's manufacturing workers were females and children. One of every five of the industrial laborers in the Appalachian counties of Virginia was either a woman or a child, as was 1 of every 10 of these workers in east Kentucky. Females were concentrated in certain types of industries, such as commercial textiles manufactories. In east Kentucky, western Maryland, east Tennessee, West Virginia, and the Appalachian counties of Virginia and South Carolina, women and girls accounted for one-third to three-quarters of the waged laborers employed in cloth mills. Females were one-third of the laborers at paper mills in western Maryland while three-fifths of the workers at east Tennessee paper mills were females. In West Virginia, five of every six flour mill workers were women. Females were also employed in heavy manual labor at extractive industries. More than half the salt manufacturing laborers in Lewis County, Kentucky, were women and girls. One of every 10 laborers at iron manufactories in east Tennessee was a female, while women and children represented 41 percent of the labor force at the iron enterprises in Shenandoah County, Virginia. One of every four of the saltpeter miners in Pendleton County, West Virginia, was a woman. In Kanawha County, West Virginia, there were nearly as many females as men engaged in iron production. As part of the salt industry in that county, women were also employed to make flatboats and barrels.[12]

By 1860, more than half of all Appalachian women engaged in nonagricultural labor and income-generating activities outside their homes (see Table 4). They were employed in every nonagricultural economic sector, and the vast majority of them were employed in occupations that have been culturally ascribed by many scholars to be the kinds of "men's work" that were closed to females. In 1860, almost one-third of the white wives of landless farm operators and nearly one-fifth of the white wives of poor and middle-class farm owners reported wage-paying nonagricultural occupations to census enumerators. Nearly 7 percent of the white women, one-fifth of the free black women, and nearly 15 percent of the enslaved women were employed in town commerce, professional services, domestic service, hotels and inns, travel enterprises, and transportation systems. In addition, three-quarters of all women earned cash or acquired household resources through informal sector trading.

We must be careful, however, not to overstate the degree to which women were finding income-earning opportunities outside agriculture. By 1860, nearly three-fifths of all American adult laborers were employed outside agriculture, primarily in industrial occupations (Matthaei 1982, 114–19). In contrast, little

---

[12] Derived from analysis of Appalachian county totals in U.S. Census Office (1823).

more than two-fifths of Appalachian adult laborers were employed outside agriculture, predominantly in occupations typified by frequent unemployment and low wages. To complicate matters, most of the region's 23,357 industrial wage laborers were men (Dunaway 1996, 127, 161–64, 315). According to the 1860 Census of Manufacturing (U.S. Census Office 1865), less than 1 percent of the region's white adult females were earning wages at manufactories or extractive enterprises. One has only to compare these statistics with those for New England or a large southern city to put them in perspective. By 1850, there were 40 mills employing 10,100 workers in Lowell, Massachusetts – more than 10 times more workers than all the women employed in industry in the vast Appalachian region (Dublin 1979, 137–39). In Savannah, Georgia, one-third of the white women and three-quarters of the free black women earned wages in nonagricultural occupations (Delfino and Gillespie 2002, 104). In Appalachia, however, only about 1 of every 10 white females and about one-third of free black women identified themselves to census enumerators as wage earners outside agriculture. Despite their poverty, two factors slowed the movement of women from the fields. First, commercial and industrial development occurred unevenly throughout the region. Large commercial and industrial enterprises were concentrated in only about one-fifth of the counties. Most of the region's towns remained small, and manufacturing and extractive firms employed small labor forces. Second, antebellum southern industries – including those in Appalachia – relied much more heavily on male slaves than on free laborers (Starobin 1970, 9–21). Thus, waged opportunities were diminished for white and nonwhite females. In the sections that follow, I will examine women's income earning work in

- manufacturing and extractive industry;
- town commerce, professions, and domestic service;
- transportation industries and travel capitalism; and
- the nonwaged informal sector.

Women in Manufacturing and Extractive Industry

By the 1830s, Appalachian women were earning income in nearly every industrial sector. Thus, slightly more than 14 percent of the manufacturing and industrial labor force were females in 1840 (see Table 35, Web site). In the Appalachian counties of Maryland, Tennessee, Virginia, and West Virginia, 8 to 10 percent of the industrial labor force was female. In the Appalachian counties of Alabama and Georgia, 5 to 8 percent of the industrial workers were women while east Kentucky females constituted less than 3 percent of the industrial labor force. Western North Carolina stood out as an anomaly because more than 15 percent of its industrial labor force were women.

Even though the work was dangerous and back-breaking, women were employed in all types of mining and timbering. Free and enslaved females accounted for 15 percent of the workers in extractive industries. Women composed nearly 2 percent of those employed to smelt copper ore and 6 percent of the salt manufacturing workers.[13] In 1851, for example, 12 male and female Cherokees built the road to the copper mines in Polk County, Tennessee, and later worked at copper smelting (Thompson 1982, 108). Nearly 7 percent of the region's coal mining work force were females. At Coal Creek Mining Company in Anderson County, Tennessee, a father and daughter hauled coal in the 1840s (Delfino and Gillespie 2002, 301). One northern Alabama woman worked "as hard as the men" to fulfill her husband's sharecropping quota at a farm owner's coal pit (Olmsted 1860, 208–9). Women also were employed in the mica industry (Pudup et al. 1995, 185–86), and Moravian females of western North Carolina produced potash (Smith and Wilson 1999, 64–65). However, women had the most significant presence in the region's iron manufacturing and gold mining.

Some of the largest extractive complexes in antebellum Southern Appalachia were engaged in iron production. Established in 84 of the Appalachian counties, bloomeries, furnaces, forges, and rolling mills produced nearly one-fifth of the country's total iron in 1840. Employing 6,216 slave and free laborers, the region's 250 iron manufacturers turned out pig iron, blooms, castings, bar iron, and railroad iron. Large factories by national standards, these firms averaged 25 workers, many of them females (Dunaway 1996, 170–71). At the Oxford Iron Works, for example, more than two-fifths of the laborers were women. Seven of 32 workers in the "coaling ground" and "ore bank" were females. Eleven of 31 furnace and forge laborers were women, and 15 of the 25 field laborers were females (Bolling Papers, DU, List). The elite among the iron slaves were the refiners, molders, and blacksmiths, but the most menial tasks were reserved for females. Women fed ore into crushers and furnaces, and girls worked as "leaf rakers" in the charcoal pits. At Buffalo Forge (1843–53, UVA), women hauled cinders, repaired roads, made fence rails, and chopped wood; they also disproportionately supplied the labor to cultivate large crops of corn and wheat. Women also produced clothing and assisted with shoe production.

The Empire State Iron and Coal Mining Company of Dade County, Georgia, advertised "to hire or buy 100 able-bodied hands" (*Richmond Times*, 15 Jan. 1851), and they were desperate enough to accept women (Bruce 1980, 463). In the 1840s, male and female Cherokees dug iron ore and worked as wage laborers at the Tellico, Tennessee, iron furnace (Van Benthuysen 1951, 12). Western Maryland iron facilities shifted to cheap immigrant labor in the 1830s, at least one-third of whom were females (Harvey 1969, 8–15). East Kentucky iron producers commingled white immigrants and enslaved workers in industrial enclaves averaging populations of 386. In east Kentucky's Hanging Rock iron district, laborers were housed in one-room cabins with rear appendages in which women raised chickens and cows. In addition to raising gardens and livestock for household consumption, women worked for menial wages in the iron production process (Smith 1982, 231, 235, 245). Women represented

---

[13] Derived from analysis of Appalachian county data in U.S. Census Office (1865).

households in company store exchanges just about as frequently as men (e.g., Davis Co. Papers, UVA, 5 Jan. 1856; Tredegar Letter Book, VSL, 25 Dec. 1860).

Early in the nineteenth century, the nation's first gold rush erupted in Southern Appalachia, and a mix of free and enslaved women accounted for about one-third of all gold mining laborers (Dunaway 1996, 169–70). In western North Carolina, Avery and Company (Records, UNC, 4 Nov. 1844) hired male and female slaves to mine gold. Until the 1850s, William F. McKesson employed 45 of his own slaves, half of them women (Phifer 1977, 214). In 1851, an Albemarle County, Virginia, planter sent his son to western North Carolina to explore the feasibility of shifting the family's slaves from agriculture to gold mining. The son advised his family to arrange annual labor contracts with area mining companies, who were hiring slaves "at $100 for men – $60 to $70 for women – $40 to $50 for boys from 12 to 15 yrs" (Barbour Diary, UVA). In addition to several white male and female workers at the Capps mine, there were "38 negroes, 10 were women" (*Western Carolinian*, 24 Aug. 1838). James Scott (Papers, NCDAH, 12 Nov. 1833) advertised for "one or two half grown boys & one or two stout young women at 30 or 40 dollars a piece according to quality." Some small farm owners prospected in the off seasons, and wives and daughters worked alongside the males (Featherstonhough 1844, 2: 353–54; Dyer and Moore 1985, 2239–40). Free blacks Dan and Lucinda Riley panned for gold on shares with Cherokee County, Georgia, land holders (*Auraria Western Herald*, 9 Apr. 1833). In Amherst, Fauquier, Greene, Franklin, and Madison Counties, Virginia, white and black females worked small gold deposits alongside males (Silliman 1837, 117, 127–28). According to an 1855 issue of *DeBow's Review* (18: 241–42), enslaved women were frequently assigned to some of the most back-breaking gold mining tasks.

Even though males continued to hold most manufacturing positions, women had entered every economic sector by 1860. Black women were much more likely to be employed in industrial jobs than were white females. Nearly one-quarter of all free blacks worked in manufactories, mills, and extractive industries, and more than 1 of every 10 free black women and 1 of every 20 enslaved females were employed in such industrial jobs (see Table 41, Web site). Even though they represented a small minority of the total manufacturing labor force, women had a significant presence in several sectors. Females accounted for only 1 of every 10 workers who produced flour, meal, leather, or liquor. However, meatpacking and tobacco manufacturing were much more gender-integrated. Females constituted half the labor force at the region's large meatpacking plants while free and enslaved women represented nearly one-fifth of the labor force of the region's 85 tobacco manufacturing firms. For example, a mixed labor force of enslaved and poor white women composed 79 percent of the laborers who manufactured tobacco in western North Carolina. West Virginia cigar and tobacco plug manufacturers relied more heavily on white immigrant females, who represented nearly two-fifths of the total labor force. Western North Carolina Moravian women were employed as tanners, coopersmiths, and barrel dyers (Smith and Wilson 1999, 64–65). Females represented one-quarter to

FIGURE 15. Rather than being isolated in a feminine sphere within their homes, poor white and nonwhite females worked at many forms of nonagricultural labor that elite and middle-class commentators considered to indicate weaknesses of character. To the left, two barefooted white women are rocking cradles to separate gold ore from rocks at a western North Carolina gold mine. A third female worker is at the right. *Source: Harper's Monthly* (April 1857).

one-third of the labor force in paper manufacturing and printing. Even though they accounted for only about 12 percent of the workers who produced house-hold goods, women supplied most of the labor to manufacture baskets, brooms, carpets, pottery, mattresses, and soap and candles. Women also processed most of the commercial foods, primarily bread and confections. Shoes and boots were the only households goods in which male labor remained dominant (see Table 35, Web site).

Women in Town Commerce, Professions, and Domestic Service

In addition to their roles in industry and textiles production, women worked at income-earning activities in towns (see Table 4). About 4 percent of white women owned shops and stores or were professionals and artisans, and another 1 percent identified themselves as commercial laborers. Elizabeth Blackwell was a rare female professional, who taught at Asheville's Presbyterian School and later became the country's first female physician. Western North Carolina Moravian women worked as midwives, taught school, and even served as town bell ringers (Smith and Wilson 1999, 27, 43). Because they were concentrated in the region's towns, free black women were four times more likely to be visible in urban commerce than were white females. Moreover, one of every three free blacks bound out by the region's poor houses was indentured to a town dweller who was engaged in some commercial pursuit (Dunaway 2003b, 21, 52). Free

FIGURE 16. About one-fifth of all Appalachian slaves were employed in nonagricultural occupations, like this chambermaid in an Abingdon, Virginia, hotel. Such hireouts increased the likelihood that enslaved females would be sexually exploited by white males and separated from their children most of the time. *Source: Harper's Monthly* (May 1857).

black women supplied labor for public works, for retail enterprises, for inns and hotels, and for artisan shops. Even though free blacks were seven times less likely to own land than their white counterparts, a lucky few females owned their own shops, and about 5 percent of them operated boarding houses or were traders (see Table 41, Web site). Along two narrow alleys in Winchester, Virginia, 19 free black men and women operated shops, including a baker, a druggist, four blacksmiths, three coopers, two potters, five shoemakers, and three wagon makers (Ebert 1986, 50). In 1860 western North Carolina, women constituted two-thirds of the 40 free black artisans, who included blacksmiths, shoemakers, carpenters, bakers, harness makers, tailors, barbers, mattress makers, hatters, saddlers, and stonemasons.[14]

Enslaved females were nearly twice as likely to be engaged in commercial jobs as white women (see Table 23, Web site). Male and female slaves provided most of the labor to construct courthouses in McDowell, Cherokee, Watauga, Macon, and Henderson Counties and university buildings in Blue Ridge Virginia. The towns of Roanoke and Charlottesville in Virginia and McMinnville and Knoxville in Tennessee hired female slaves for all kinds of menial public services. Knoxville hired female slaves at $10 monthly to collect garbage and manage waterworks deliveries (Dunaway 2003b, 77–78). Slaves were also employed in retail stores and shops. Isaac McNeel (Papers, WVU 1850–60) used female slaves in the family store at Mill Point, West Virginia. Calvin Cowles (Papers, UNC, 11 Feb. 1861), a western North Carolina merchant, paid enslaved women $8 monthly to pack roots and herbs for export to the U.S. Northeast and to England. Cowles also hired and purchased women, then sublet them to other commercial or industrial enterprises. At his Murphy, North Carolina, store, William Holland Thomas (Papers, DU, 5 Jan. 1860) utilized slave women to organize and shelve merchandise and to pack commodities for shipment.

Self-hiring was the most frequent method through which slaves earned wages in towns. Some were permitted to "hire their own time," by giving "their master a certain sum per month" (Jackson 1942, 180–81). One western Carolina owner permitted a female to hire herself out "during her life at 50$ pr year" (Olmsted 1861, 48). By paying her owner $30 annually, Bethany Veney (1890, 131–32) could live on her own so she could take in washing, clean houses, and work in the fields, "getting a job wherever [she] could find it." A western Maryland slaveholder gave one woman permission "to work for herself provided she gave him one half." As a sideline to her job as cook in the village tavern, she prepared and sold pies and pastries. Her business increased to the point that "it became necessary that she should buy a horse and wagon to convey her goods." Later, she began "running a second hand clothing store on a small scale and made quite a respectable living" (Gwyn Papers, UNC, 4 July 1859).

Only about 2 percent of white women worked as domestic servants (see Table 4). Most of these white servants were younger than 21 and unmarried, or they had fallen on hard times after the loss of a spouse. Abandoned by her husband, a western North Carolina woman "promptly went to work at the home of a prosperous free black artisan whose wife was 'sick & unable to work.'" For the next several years, she "live[d] at different places upon wages"

---

[14] Enumerated in 1860 Census of Population manuscripts, NA, for western North Carolina counties.

FIGURE 17. This free black woman operated a small inn that served rafts and boats on the Tennessee River outside Chattanooga. Such "men's work" attracted the attention of Appalachian sheriffs and courts to such "dangerous class" female household heads. *Source: Harper's Monthly* (July 1858).

(Bolton 1994, 39). Similarly, the grandmother and mother of Georgette Pettis (Transcript, ALC, 7) spent most of their lives as domestic servants, frequently living apart from their families for extended periods. Another northern Georgia female got her "first job" at age seven in a boarding house, where she "cleaned rooms, made beds, done the dusting, and waited the tables" (Wiggington 1979, 72). Similarly, Dorie Cope could not find any work before marriage except the most onerous forms of domestic service. At age 13, she was paid in food or cloth to tend newborns, to nurse the ill or dying, and "to prepare bodies for burial" (Bush 1992, 6).

Only two of the white mothers described by Civil War veterans worked as domestic servants. After John Moore's father died, his mother worked a small farm on shares, did part-time teaching, and was employed as a "special good cook" in a middle-class household. While Peter Collman's father traveled to do carpentry work, his impoverished mother worked as "a hired servant" (Dyer and Moore 1985, 39, 94).[15] Black females were much more likely than whites to work as domestic servants. About 8 percent of free black women and about 7 percent of the region's enslaved women worked as domestic servants (see Table 4). Rural masters frequently hired surplus female slaves to work in towns, where middle-class families employed nurses for infants and young children (Dunaway 2003b, 78). Slaves could be hired for domestic service at monthly courthouse auctions. On "hiring day" in January 1858, for example, "at least 500 servants were for hire" at the Warrenton courthouse (*Alexandria Gazette and Virginia Advertiser*, 6 Jan. 1858).

---

[15] In contrast to those in Appalachia, the vast majority of Upper South cooks and house servants were black, but white females constituted nearly half the children's nurses (Delfino and Gillespie 2002, 76).

Women in Transportation Industries and Travel Capitalism

A majority of the workers for transportation companies were African-Americans. Even though white females were rarely hired to work on railroads, canals, or roads or at mineral spas, a few immigrant women were used for the least skilled jobs. More than 8 percent of slaves and about 6 percent of free blacks, about one-third of them women, were employed by transportation companies (see Tables 24, 41, Web site). Eighteen wealthy Cherokees utilized slaves to operate boats and make repairs at their 23 ferries, including females who repaired barges and worked in the supply depots and warehouses (Shadburn 1989, 62). In the 1830s, the Muscle Shoals canal paid $15 monthly for male slave hires, $10 for females (*Huntsville Democrat*, 5 Sept. 1833). The James River and Kanawha Canal purchased and hired slaves, about one-third of them women (VBPW, VSL, 1854: 388–89). John Jordan and John Irvine contracted to construct the canal extension from Lynchburg to Buchanan, relying on 48 owned and 600 hired slaves, nearly half of them women ditchers (JRKC Papers, VHS, March 1865 minutes). A Rockbridge County contractor used female slaves to repair locks and to do regular maintenance (Gilliam 1982, 117). In 1855, *DeBow's Review* (18: 350–51) claimed that "in ditching, particularly in canals," a female slave could "do nearly as much work as a man."

Enslaved women were disproportionately represented among the laborers hired by towns to maintain roads and turnpikes (Starobin 1970). For example, hired female slaves are listed in the census manuscripts for the villages of Jacksonville, West Virginia, and Athens, Tennessee. The Massie Family (Papers, UVA, 10 Dec. 1853, 8 Jan. 1849) regularly hired surplus women and girls to maintain roads and bridges in Bath and Alleghany Counties. Private companies owned and hired male and female slaves to construct and repair several turnpikes in Virginia and West Virginia, including Junction Valley, Swift Run Gap, Rocky Mount, Martinsburg and Potomac, Sinking Creek, and Craig's Creek (VBPW, VSL, 1854: 128–54,133–34, 187; 1858: 297–310). The Western Plank Road Company of North Carolina hired female slaves at cheaper monthly rates than the rates paid for annual male contracts (Starling 1939, 16–17). The James River and Kanawha Turnpike Company (Lambert Papers, WVU, 16 Sept. 1851) and the Giles, Fayette and Kanawha Turnpike (Watson Papers, UVA, 6 July 1857) used female slaves for road construction and repairs. The Guyandotte Turnpike, the Beverly-Fairmont Turnpike, and the Frederick and Valley Turnpike Companies employed mixed labor forces of white males and female slaves to construct and repair roads (Monroe County Archives, WVU, 12 Sept. 1832, 19 Apr. 1844, 3 July 1858). Female slaves were used to build and repair the Rockbridge County bridge across North River, but a male was assigned the elite job of collecting tolls (Gilliam 1982, 115).

Southern railroad construction surpassed national averages after 1845, and railroad development had occurred in 53 Appalachian counties by 1855 (Dunaway 1996, 215–17, 293).[16] Since railroad construction companies solicited

---

[16] For a detailed map of all antebellum Southern railroads, see Phillips (1908).

laborers at $150 annually, Appalachian masters contracted one-fifth of their annual slave hires to these transportation companies, one-third of them women. The Blue Ridge Railroad relied on a labor force of male and female Irish immigrants and slaves. Working eight-hour shifts for the Virginia Central Railroad, 60 male and female slaves dug from each end of the Blue Ridge Tunnel (BRR Accounts, UVA). Between 1854 and 1862, the Baltimore and Ohio Railroad Company hired and purchased male and female slaves from western Maryland and West Virginia to work in construction gangs and to provide services to passengers (Bassel Papers, WVU, 1854–62 letters). After 1850, railroad advertisements to purchase and to hire slaves for construction projects appeared regularly in Virginia newspapers, and railroad developers were often eager to employ cheaper female laborers (*Richmond Daily Dispatch*, 18 and 31 Dec. 1853, 22 Dec. 1856, 1 Jan. 1857; *Alexandria Gazette*, 4 Jan. 1859). In the 1840s, the Randolph family (Papers, UVA, 1847–48 letters) hired female slaves to work in construction gangs on the Louisa Railroad. A railroad agent assured one western Carolina master that he could hire his male and female slaves "to advantage" prior to his harvest (Clark Papers, NCDAH, 12 May 1862). Northern Alabama masters hired their female slaves to railroad construction projects in central and southern Alabama at $20 monthly (*Huntsville Confederate*, 28 Jan. 1863). Male slave gangs dug track beds and laid rails while female slaves cooked and washed for the construction crews. In Talladega County, Alabama (1860 Manuscript Slave Schedules, NA), 35 slaves were "hired railroad laborers," 28 of them males, 7 of them females.

The Southern Appalachians were dotted with 134 mineral spas that were annually patronized by 10,000 to 15,000 tourists (Dunaway 1996, 305–7). All the larger spas owned male and female slaves and advertised to lease slaves during their busy seasons. Male slaves were employed for the most visible occupations, such as valets, waiters, musicians, coachmen, hustlers, and guides, while even larger numbers of women supplied the hidden domestic labor. Appalachian slaveholders hired out surplus female laborers to service baths, clean, wash clothes, and cook (Russell 1913, 150n). In 1853, one newspaper advertised "Fifty servants wanted for the Springs, viz. Dining Room Servants, Chambermaids" (Jackson 1942, 80). West Virginia's White Sulphur Springs, the queen of the Appalachian resorts, boasted $100,000 worth of real estate and $56,000 in slaves, more than three-quarters of them women (1860 census manuscripts, NA, Greenbrier County, West Virginia).[17]

In addition to spa tourism, more than one-third of the Appalachian counties supplied grain sales and inns for itinerant livestock drives. In the 1850s, drovers moved nearly 2.5 million hogs, nearly 600,000 cattle, and almost 200,000 horses and mules annually through Appalachian counties. At one-day intervals along the network of livestock trails, commercial "livestock stands" provided stables, pens, pastures, and feed for the herds and lodging for the drovers. Between east Tennessee and Asheville, herds were fed by male and female slaves

[17] For a detailed list of mineral spas, see Dunaway (1994a, 1103–5).

at 15 livestock stands, which provisioned 30 to 100 drives per year, feeding 3,000 to 10,000 livestock (Dunaway 1996, 237–38). Moravian females worked regularly in such taverns (Smith and Wilson 1999, 64–65), and several western Carolina masters utilized female and male slaves at the livestock stands they operated to feed Blue Ridge Virginia mule drives and the horse and hog drives moving from east Tennessee and east Kentucky into South Carolina (Burnett 1946, 99).

On the Appalachian frontier, the most visible businesswoman was the inn or hotel operator. Sarah Flynn advertised in the *Maryland Gazette* (16 Aug. 1759) that she offered "genteel Entertainment and good usage" at her western Maryland tavern near Sassafras Ferry. An 84-year-old "backwoods hostess" in northern South Carolina waited on travelers, prepared meals, and managed horses in the stable (Attmore 1917, 32). In southwest Virginia, a well-to-do traveler was shocked by "Mrs. Davis who ke[pt] Tavern Down the mountain" because he thought her to be too forward with male customers to be a "decent lady" ("Memorandum" 1899–1900, 524). "Mrs. Lindsay's Hotel" in Knoxville was one of only four such facilities in that town (*Knoxville Argus and Commercial Appeal*, 2 June 1839). Mrs. Campbell ran an advertisement to alert east Tennessee travelers "that the House of Entertainment formerly at THE SIGN OF THE BUCK kept by her late husband w[ould] be continued by her." One British traveler thought the female-operated "inns in the back country" of western Virginia were "preferable to the inns in many of the most inhabited parts of New England" (Morrison 1922, 122).[18]

By the early 1800s, the Cherokees were operating "stock stands" and taverns to cater to the itinerant livestock droves headed south. Cherokee slaveholder Joseph Vann hired females to operate his large livestock stand on the Federal Road through northern Georgia (*Cherokee Phoenix*, 2 July 1828). Several Cherokee women operated highly profitable travel way stations, livestock stands, and ferries. Nancy Ward operated a nationally known inn and ferry at Womankiller Ford (Tucker 1969, 197), and two young women ran small inns on the road between Nashville and Augusta (1835 Cherokee Census, NA). Sally Robason operated a "ferry boat and landing" and livestock stand and inn on Ooltever Creek in Hamilton County, Tennessee. Near "Nickajack Old Town," Eliza Campbell ran a ferry, livestock stand, and small gristmill. Though illiterate, a woman named Oo-dah-less operated a mill and owned a small company of wagons that hauled goods throughout the Nation. She also sold grain to itinerant droves at her livestock stand. As a result, she "accumulated a very handsome property," including slaves (Valuations, UTK, 29, 193).

Even though women were heavily represented as laborers at the region's inns, hotels, restaurants, and mineral spas, few women owned such businesses.

---

[18] In 1820, less than 14 percent of heads of household were employed outside agriculture (U.S. Census Office 1823). Female-operated inns are also documented in western North Carolina, east Tennessee, and east Kentucky; see Battle (1905, 16, 18, 53, 58, 59), "General Slade's Journal" (1906, 48, 48, 54), Blair (1905), and Newsome (1934, 287–88).

While Henry McKenzie's father worked as a merchant-farmer, his "mother ran a hotel," using slaves and hired white females. With the help of her daughters and three servants, Calvin Crook's mother ran a tavern, where she "took care of the traveling public" and "cook[ed] for the public" (Dyer and Moore 1985, 595, 1447). Travel enterprises relied heavily upon enslaved females. "The business" of an Asheville inn was "left mostly to the black servants" (Buckingham 1842, 1: 193). In Sevier County, Tennessee, John McMahan owned five females to staff his hotel at the foot of the Great Smoky Mountains. Similarly, G. G. Mitchell owned 10 female slaves to service his McMinnville hotel (1860 census manuscripts, Sevier and Warren Counties, TN, NA). Even in tiny villages, stage way stations – like the Netherland Inn in upper east Tennessee – relied on enslaved women (Day and Dickinson 1988). Plantations that offered public accommodations, like Traveler's Rest, assigned female slaves to staff their inns (Bouwman 1980, 164).

Women in the Nonwaged Informal Sector

Despite their entry into waged occupations and business ownership, a majority of women acquired far more income through informal sector activities than from any other occupation. A much higher proportion of antebellum women participated in the informal sector than the combined total for those who owned farms or shops or worked in waged occupations (Hoyman 1987, 70). On Appalachian frontiers, many white Appalachian women traded and sold agricultural produce and craft items. Included in store advertisements for commodities accepted in trade were female-produced flax, wool, linen, linsey, butter, lard, feathers, tallow, beeswax, honey, and maple sugar. It was not unusual for stores to advertise that "for the article of gensang the highest price will be given" or that "the highest price will be allowed for good linsey, 700 linen." Women's "country linen or linsey" was accepted in exchange for "bar iron and castings" and salt.[19] Another store promised "a generous price" for "country manufactured sugar" (Bickley 1852, 109). Women also bartered or sold feathers, beeswax, tallow, butter, and wool. Stephen Duncan and Company sold men's clothing and fabrics that had been produced by local women through a putting-out system (Toulmin 1794, 64–66). In western Maryland, the local militias paid local females for "sundries, hunting shirts, Caps, blankets, rugs, Waggon Cloths, Medicines, and boarding" for their members ("Proceedings" 1918). Women also traded or sold strawberries, watermelons, garden vegetables, apples, and peaches (Thwaites 1904–7, 2: 339). A Scottish "lady of quality" condescendingly described one western North Carolina middle-class woman as

---

[19] *Knoxville Gazette* (17 Dec. 1791, 28 July 1792, 14 Dec. 1792, 6 Apr. 1793, 18 May 1793, 5 and 14 Oct. 1801, 25 July 1803, 16 June 1818).

a pattern of industry. She has (it seems) a garden, from which she supplies the town with what vegetables they use, also with melons and other fruits. She even descends to make minced pies, cheesecakes, tarts and little biskits, which she sends down to the town once or twice a day, besides her eggs, poultry and butter, and she is the only one who continues to have Milk. (Schaw 1923, 178–79)

In the later antebellum period, more than two-fifths of white Appalachian women, two-thirds of free black women, and a majority of Cherokee and enslaved women engaged in nonwaged informal sector outputs in an attempt to earn cash or to trade for household resources (see Table 4). Appalachian women engaged in three forms of *nonwaged* forms of production that generated income or resources through selling or trading in the marketplace:

- *direct subsistence production* meant to generate household survival resources,
- *petty commodity production and exchange* based on labor contributed by household members, and
- *backward capitalist production* or putting-out systems in which laborers complete work on consignment in the household on a piecework basis (Portes 1983, 160–61).

All over the world and in every historical era, women have been overrepresented in the informal sector. Because there were barriers to their equitable participation in waged occupations and because the wages for domestic service were so low, the informal economy was "thrust upon women as a last resort" in the nineteenth century (Hoyman 1987, 76).

Cherokee Women's Marketing Activities

After the Revolutionary War, Cherokee women peddled baskets, chickens, pottery, chestnuts, and wild berries to adjacent whites. Women also produced and traded buckeye wood dough trays, stone pipe bowls, rhododendron hominy ladles, indigo, and oil from butternuts and walnuts. Women gathered, cured, and shipped to Charleston large quantities of ginseng and other herbs for reexport to European cities. During the winter, women sold "brown sugar cakes" to nearby whites (Adair 1775, 388, 424). Cherokee cabins were surrounded by large numbers of peach, apple, and "chickasaw plum" trees, from which women marketed fruits (Valuations, UTK, 9, 17, 35, 101, 194, 211, 239). Some Cherokee women bartered lidded, double-weave cane baskets to white households (Hill 1996, 129–30). In the summers of the 1840s and 1850s, Agnes Lossiah's (1984, 92) grandmother walked the long Great Smoky Mountain road between east Tennessee and western North Carolina communities to "go peddlen" her baskets to tourists at Montvale Springs near Maryville, Tennessee. Judging from the 1828–38 store records of William Holland Thomas (Papers, DU), Cherokee women transacted trades of crafts and produce more frequently than white or black females. At Thomas's western North Carolina store, Cherokee women marketed "finely cut pipes" and "well-made baskets," in addition to ginseng, medicinal plants, dried fruits, and honey. The 1860 census enumerator (Jackson County, AL, census manuscripts, NA) noted information about a family of very poor Cherokee squatters working a small parcel on a secluded mountainside in Jackson County, Alabama. One of his comments in the margins was that the woman and daughter would sometimes "come down into the county and work by the day and bring corn to sell."

Informal Sector Activities of White Women
A majority of the mothers described by Civil War veterans earned income through informal sector exchanges of their butter, cheese, farm outputs, and home manufactures (see Table 4). These exchanges were economically significant to households and to communities. In 1840, white Appalachian women exchanged through informal sector activities $1.00 in household outputs to every $1.70 generated through the formal trade in manufactured commodities (see Table 7). In Washington County, Tennessee, T. H. Howard's mother traded at stores and sold to neighbors "molasses, honey, chicken eggs by the bushel." To earn cash for her sharecropping household, Julius Martin's mother "pedled crockery ware" (Dyer and Moore 1985, 1158, 1497). Women were a common sight at public markets, often traveling great distances. The east side of Knoxville's market square "was filled by the farm women who came in with fresh vegetables and berries in season, plucked fowl, eggs, and butter" (Bush 1992, 51). Frederick Olmsted (1861, 232) described a northern Georgia white woman who used a homemade cart pulled by a bull to make her weekly trips into town to sell "fowls, eggs, potatoes, or herbs." At one northern Georgia town market, groups of poor women "tie[d] their mules, kindle[d] up little fires in the street, cook[ed] suppers, then camp[ed] down upon the cold damp brick" (Burke 1850, 208). When rich Juliana Conner (Diary, UNC, 13 June 1827) encountered a poor white east Tennessee woman headed to the town market with "a large bundle on her head," she was shocked "that a woman, alone, unprotected, and with an infant in her arms [would] perform such a journey." For those women without access to urban centers, there was the option of exchanges with peddlers. One Quaker wife regularly traded "things she might sell" to a huckster who "called once in two weeks" (*Janney's Virginia* 1978, 67). Marie Martin's (Transcript, ALC, 18) grandmother made exchanges with walking peddlers who passed through "just every now and then." Lula Cook (Transcript, ALC, 6–7) recalled her grandmother's oral histories about immigrant women peddlers who "carried their wares tied up in a big bedspread."

Oral histories and other primary sources document all sorts of female informal sector marketing. Becky Hall's (Transcript, ALC, 5) grandmother would "make gingerbread, take it and sell it" in town. Women traded to local merchants their soap, candles, milk, butter, cheese, molasses, eggs, wool, dried fruit, chickens, wool, and tobacco twists. According to Sophie Roberts (Transcript, ALC, 6), "It was hard times continually" for her grandmother, who had nothing except "chickens and eggs to sell to get salt and soda and sugar."

TABLE 7. *Women's Household Outputs Compared to Manufacturing, 1840*

Appalachian Counties of	Total $ Women's Outputs	$ Value Manufactured Commodities	$ per Capita Women's Outputs	$ per Capita Manufacturing Outputs	$1.00 Women's Outputs to Every $ Manufacturing
Alabama	546,194	234,748	6.35	3.36	0.43
Georgia	530,589	361,584	7.52	5.13	0.68
Kentucky	435,749	133,009	4.06	1.39	0.31
Maryland	232,614	3,419,473	2.87	46.75	14.70
North Carolina	767,663	310,237	7.34	3.38	0.41
South Carolina	62,086	43,770	4.33	3.76	0.71
Tennessee	1,100,005	1,316,593	3.95	4.72	1.97
Virginia	2,044,854	4,896,617	5.62	18.59	2.40
West Virginia	1,180,940	951,370	4.76	4.15	0.81
Region	6,800,694	11,567,401	5.02	8.54	1.70
United States	82,012,898	458,180,950	3.05	31.42	5.59

Source: Aggregated from county and national totals in U.S. Census Office (1841).

W. T. Francis's (Transcript, ALC, 10) mother sheared her sheep and picked her geese twice yearly to sell wool and feathers to the local store. For cleaning and packing skins and ginseng prior to export, housewives were remunerated in "due slips" or credits toward family indebtedness. "To get extra money," females gathered and sold blackberries, chestnuts, mayapples, and herbs, such as ginseng, goldenseal, or snakeroot (Dyer and Moore 1985, 316, 1257, 1497, 1912; Tackett and Napier Transcripts, ALC; Shores Transcript, ASU). One of the most unusual items to be collected for trade was "mountain moss," which local stores exported (Wiggington 1983, 102). Effecting exchanges was not always easy. Dexter Ratliff's (Transcript, ALC, 6–7) east Kentucky grandmother would travel great distances to sell her herbs or to trade them for salt across the mountains at Saltville, Virginia.

Informal Sector Activities of African-American Women

Strict public control over the movements of nonwhite Appalachians prevented their open participation in structured trade mechanisms. Denied access to most forms of visible wage labor or commodity production, free blacks were almost totally dependent upon exchanges in the "underbelly" of the market. Tolls for stall space or for inspections put the town market house out of their economic reach. Because of the dominant racist ideology, nonwhite families lived precariously on the fringe, and they could only squeeze into the market economy through a variety of unregulated, illegal, and nonwage activities. Free black women could neither apply for nor afford peddlers' licenses, and towns passed local ordinances ordering the sheriffs to drive out itinerant nonwhites (Stroud 1856, 57–83). As a result, these women engaged in illegal street and door-to-door vending of their wares. Since they were almost never permitted store accounts, they had no means of bartering directly with local merchants. Even though the vast majority of Appalachian slaves engaged in garden cultivation and household production, less than 12 percent of their households ever earned cash or participated in monetary transactions. In fact, other U.S. slaves (Berlin and Morgan 1993, 19) earned cash nearly three times more frequently than Appalachian slaves.[20] In most instances, slave women sold their surplus produce, food items, and crafted items to their own masters. Even though most families had chicken houses, archaeological digs indicate that Appalachian slaves rarely consumed the chickens they raised (Singleton 1995, 124–25). Rather, they sold or traded most of their poultry and eggs to their owners. Enslaved females also marketed items to the stores owned by their masters or employers. At Traveler's Rest in northern Georgia, for example, female slaves exchanged garden produce and poultry for store items (Bouwman 1980, 166–67). At industrial sites, slaves traded food and craft items to the company stores. At Etna Furnace, for instance, female slaves regularly traded sweet potatoes, corn, poultry, pork, bacon, brooms, calves, pottery, and herbs at the commissary. Ann Towles sold large amounts of pork to the company store at Buffalo Forge (Negro Book, 1855, UVA).

In addition to exchanges with owners and employers, some slaves disposed of items in nearby towns. One Amherst County, Virginia, mistress permitted her slave women "to dispose of their wares as they saw fit," so they sold brooms, nails, fruits, vegetables, yarn, woolen cloth, rag carpets, quilts, pigs, chickens, and eggs at the Saturday town markets. Betty Spence hawked two kinds of ginger cakes on weekends. Occasionally, a slave operated a "trading cart" or trapped and dressed small animals or birds. Despite the tendency of towns to drive out itinerant nonwhites, black women engaged in illegal street and door-to-door vending of their wares. Still others aggressively used "street cries" to call attention to their commodities. Common throughout southern towns, black street cries combined the sales pitch for the commodity with religious verbiage and with allusions intended to evoke sympathy from whites. At Jonesboro, Tennessee, an elderly female slave "carrie[d] about a basket of vegetables to people's houses, and solicit[ed] their custom in a tone of distress." In the 1840s, an enslaved woman advertised her garden produce on the streets of Staunton, Virginia, by singing out, "My strawberries are sweet and soun'. I am gwine to glory. . . . Now's de time to get em cheap" (Rawick 1972, 6: 154, 13: 86, 268, 4: 76, 3: 785; Rawick 1979, 10: 4345).

A few masters permitted slave households to cultivate cash crops. When slave women raised cotton or tobacco, the master marketed it with his own exports and then credited the family at the end of the year (e.g., Rawick 1972,

[20] African-American marketing and cash earning patterns were derived from analysis of Appalachian slave narratives.

13: 80; Rawick 1979, 3: 672–73, 5: 1525, 10: 4345). One Coffee County, Tennessee, owner allowed females to cultivate corn and hay on shares ("Unwritten History," FUA, 11). Another western Carolina master permitted women to raise corn on shares (Greenlee Diary, UNC, 12 Feb. 1849, 6 Jan. 1851). One Franklin County, Tennessee, master advanced seed and work stock in exchange for a share of the crops produced. The owner allotted each woman "an acre to work as they would, and he'd loan them the seed for whatever they wanted to raise." While most "raised what they needed for a better table," a few females "planted their entire acre tracts in some kind of money crop. Some raised nothing but cotton, and sold it with [the owner's] crop each year" (Rawick 1979, 10: 4345–46). Slave women also manufactured a wide variety of homemade items, including knitted items, fabrics, clothing, and quilts. At night and on weekends, mothers and children creatively fashioned cornshuck horse collars, brooms, or straw hats (e.g., Rawick 1972, 4: 76; Rawick 1977, 10: 4345; Rawick 1979, 3: 785–91). One western Maryland slave woman earned fees for preparing the bodies for white funerals (*Ferry Hill* 1975, 129). Females wove reed, willow, pine needles, split oak, and vines into baskets that were used for all kinds of household purposes; for fishing and hunting; and for gathering cotton and tobacco (e.g., Rawick 1972, 4: 76, Rawick 1977, 3: 482; Rawick 1979, 5: 1525). A few female slaves engaged in illegal trafficking of stolen items or whiskey, particularly to nearby poor whites (Rawick 1979, 9: 3638).

Provision of Informal Sector Services
Although many scholars emphasize "the centrality of women's sheltered sexuality and domestic identity" (Bernhard et al. 1992, 6), most women did not enjoy the luxury of such a lifestyle. Instead, they marketed as services some of "the same labour processes usually performed as unpaid labour for household maintenance" (Bouquet 1986, 244). Nearly one-third of the wives of farm owners, at least one-third of the households described by Civil War veterans, and more than one-half of the wives of tenant farmers took in boarders and another 3 percent operated boarding houses (see Table 4). For example, Mrs. Inman operated a hotel and boarding house near the railroad depot in Cleveland, Tennessee (McClary and Graf 1959, 110–11). In Virginius Island, West Virginia, Nancy Evans, a poor white woman, ran the boarding house for the Winchester and Potomac Railroad (Johnson 1995, 11). In their six-room house in Grainger County, Tennessee, John Howell's mother "kept travelers before the railroad was built" (Dyer and Moore 1985, 1165). On their small east Kentucky farm, Bertha Frazier's (Transcript, ALC, 12) mother kept boarders, and the daughters "would help cook" for them. As partial payment of household indebtedness, landlords credited tenant or cropper wives for boarding laborers, and town women often took in boarders.[21]

Nearly 5 percent of white women and nearly 10 percent of free black women were identified in 1860 census manuscripts as washwomen (see Table 4). Like

---

[21] Boarders are identified in the entries for households in the census manuscripts, NA.

many other black women, Isom Starnes's mother "made money washing and ironing" (Rawick 1972, 10: 218). Western North Carolina Moravian women often worked as town washwomen (Smith and Wilson 1999, 64–65). A white farmer's wife paid Agnes Lossiah's (1984, 92) Cherokee grandmother in food "to wash for her" and "to split shucks for to put in bed ticks." Women also earned income or household resources for their health care services. Burt Crisp's (Transcript, ALC, 4) free black grandmother and the white grandmothers of Ada Drushall (Transcript, LJC, 7), Lottie Byers and Mary Shelton (Transcripts, ASU), and Grace Dunn, Nettie Combs, and Fronie Johnson (Transcripts, ALC) were midwives who were almost always paid in cloth, food, or agricultural produce. Like many other females, the grandmothers of Polly Tackett and Susie Adkins (Transcripts, ALC) and Hattie Greene (Transcript, ASU) prepared and dispensed herbal medical remedies.

Conclusion

This research pinpoints several historical fallacies in separate spheres mythology. Because this dichotomy fails to encompass all the work of husbands and wives, adequate explanations are not provided by the view that household labor is divided between males' wage labor and women's family-based subsistence work. In fact, most antebellum U.S. women engaged in diverse portfolios of nonagricultural labors aimed at the marketplace, and they completed that work both inside and outside their households (see Table 8). Moreover, there was not a clear division between household labors and market commodity production, as separate spheres advocates have claimed. Women undertook many cash-earning nonagricultural labors within their households, and some of those labors overlapped with work done for household survival and maintenance. In reality, the household was both a center of *productive* market-related labor and of familial *reproductive* labors.

Because their families' subsistence could not be provided solely by males, most Appalachian women engaged in nonagricultural activities to provide significant household resources. Contrary to the separate spheres thesis:

- There is no primary evidence that a majority of Appalachian women accepted the tenets of the cult of domesticity or desired to be ensconced solely in their homes or families. Appalachian women did not choose to isolate themselves inside their households; nor did they leave the public economic sphere to males.
- Among the European ethnic groups from which American settlers derived, married women routinely participated in the waged labor force (Tilly and Scott 1978, 123–36), increasing the likelihood that white Appalachian females would have little cultural disdain for such forms of work.
- Both married and single women (middle-class and poor white, Cherokee, and African-American) entered the waged labor force when economic opportunities emerged.

TABLE 8. *Nineteenth-Century Nonagricultural Labors of Southern Appalachian Women*

Labor Arena by Racial Group	Unpaid Labors	Paid Labors			
		Nonwaged	Waged	Contract	Enterprise Owner
Nonagricultural: white or free black	Household maintenance and reproduction Labor assistant to husband or father who owned or leased enterprise	Marketing of surplus farm commodities, household-produced crafts, or services in the informal sector	Waged laborer in most nonagricultural sectors	Putting out: home-based contracts to produce crafts for merchants or industries	A few female business owners
Nonagricultural: Cherokee	Household maintenance and reproduction Labor assistant to husband or father who owned or leased enterprise	Marketing of surplus farm commodities, household-produced crafts, or services in the informal sector	A few waged laborers in extractive industries, road building	None	A few female owners of inns, taverns, livestock stands
Nonagricultural: enslaved	Household maintenance and reproduction Assignment to tasks by owner	Marketing of surplus farm commodities, household-produced crafts, or services in the informal sector	Hireout by owner or self-hire in most non-agricultural sectors	Annual contract hires in most non-agricultural sectors	None
Other public labor: white or free black	Charitable work Church or camp meeting work	Services marketed through the informal sector, such as prostitution	None	A few white professionals, such as teachers, ministers	A few white professionals, such as doctors
Other public labor: Cherokee	Clan duties *Gadugi* Conjuror	Prostitution Conjuring	None	None	None
Other public labor: enslaved	Significant female role in slave religion	Midwife Herb doctor Prostitute	None	Hired or owned slave in brothel	None

- White, free black, and Cherokee females operated both home-based and public businesses, and middle-class white females were entering the professions.
- All commodity production did not occur outside the household in a male-controlled sphere. In fact, most women routinely marketed commodities and services they produced within their homes.
- Women's home-based protoindustrial activities, especially textiles production, provided significant family income and household resources.
- Women did not just engage in "feminine" occupations when they worked outside their homes. All classes and races of Appalachian women were less likely to earn income or to be hired out as domestic servants than they were to work at all other nonagricultural occupations.
- Women's workloads and earnings were not equal to those of males. On the one hand, females earned lower wages than men for the same work. On the other hand, females were responsible for all unpaid household labor, even when they generated significant income through wages, businesses, or the informal sector.
- Neither white nor nonwhite women engaged in waged labor or other economic endeavors temporarily, as evidenced by the wide age range and differential marital status of females engaged in nonagricultural pursuits.

This research calls into question the scholarly notion that elite slaveholding gender conventions were culturally hegemonic in southern society (Fox-Genovese 1988, 195). Because the daily lives of females were more powerfully circumscribed by the class and race positions of their households within their closest identity groups, the constraints of the cult of domesticity were limited. Even though females were subordinate to men legally, politically, and economically, there was no clear male public sphere when it came to the female labors that were essential to household survival.

Class and race determined the likelihood that a woman would engage in waged labor or types of economic pursuits viewed as men's work. Wide class and racial cleavages separated poor white and nonwhite Appalachian women from their more affluent counterparts. Poor antebellum women were a semiproletariat who, over their life spans, derived the bulk of the means of family livelihood from economic activities that occurred outside the wage labor force (Wallerstein 1983, 95–99). That is not to imply, however, that such work was all household-based, for poor and nonwhite women publicly engaged in "men's work" that southern cultural ideals stigmatized as inappropriate pursuits for "respectable ladies." It was not uncommon for middle-class women to operate their own businesses, to accept waged employment, to undertake professions, or to market goods and services in the informal sector. Indeed, most poor and middle-class females wove together a creative tapestry of labor forms in order to accumulate a consumption fund adequate to sustain their households, even when they completed a greater share of the total work or received an inequitable share of the distributed resources.

In short, we simply cannot learn very much about the labors of antebellum southern women if we blind ourselves with the class-biased and racist assumption that most females were dominated by and acquiesced to the gender norms of the small minority of slaveholding elites. Moreover, the thesis of separate labor spheres portrays house-bound females, who simply were not prevalent. Indeed, the typical woman did not exist inside the cocoon described by the cult of domesticity, and we should not confuse her commodity production or sale of services at home with *nonpublic housewifery* or with *noncommoditized subsistence* that occurred outside the public capitalist economy. Most antebellum U.S. women engaged in diverse portfolios of nonagricultural labors aimed at the marketplace, and they completed that work both inside and outside their households.

Moreover, there was not a sharp division between household labors and market commodity production, as separate spheres advocates like Julie Matthaei (1982, 114–19) have claimed. Women undertook many cash-earning nonagricultural labors within their households, and some of those labors overlapped with work done for household survival and maintenance, particularly textiles production. In reality, the household must be conceptualized as both a center of *productive* market-related labor and of familial *reproductive* labors. Because every nineteenth-century Appalachian household was a microcosm of the structural inequities of the capitalist world system, it was this dual function of the household that created the context in which women's overwork was structured. Consequently, women and girls contributed more labor power to household survival than males, even when they received an inequitable share of the total pool of resources.

Antebellum commentators assigned women race and class positions based on the nature of their work and the degree to which they stayed within expected gender conventions (Boatwright 1994, 127). In the eyes of elites, both middle-class and poor women were pushing beyond the bounds of respectability by working outside their homes. The attitude of affluent women was that "occupations tending toward the manual . . . debarr[ed a female] from social standing as *lady*" (Gray 1928, 275). Among the upper classes, "an impoverished woman who produced a wage was set apart from the coveted social order and lived in an arctic gloom of undisguised pity" (Boatwright 1994, 96). As we shall see in Chapters 7 and 8, affluent whites measured a woman's race, ethnicity, or class by the nature of her work and by the degree to which her labors stayed within the confines of separate spheres gender conventions. The "dangerous classes" of women were nonwhites and poor whites who

- did "men's work" in public view, often in racially mixed and gender-integrated groups,
- appeared to be sexually deviant because they violated separate spheres ideals, and
- managed households in which women played pivotal economic roles that conflicted with cultural ideals of motherhood and patriarchal control of families.

7

Family as Privilege

Public Regulation of Nonpatriarchal Households

> If she deliberately steps beyond the hallowed precincts – the hallowed circle – which encompass her with the halo of divinity, she has wantonly forfeited her privilege of immunity as she has irretrievably lost our regard, and the harshness which she may provoke is invited by her own folly and impropriety.
>
> (*Southern Literary Messenger* 1852, 721–22)

As we have previously seen, most women failed to observe the sharp dichotomy idealized by separate spheres advocates between home and the outside economic world. Because of their race, class, and stigmatized work, poor white and nonwhite women did not meet cult of domesticity standards of female moral superiority or of idealized motherhood. For that reason, a majority of Appalachian women – in fact, a majority of all southern women – were in family constructs that were at risk of public intervention or slaveholder disruption. In reality, only affluent white families were as "sacred" as separate spheres advocates claimed. All female-headed poor white and nonwhite households were legally and socially defined as unacceptable aberrations. Consequently, elite and middle-class white males could rationalize – with support from the women of their classes – that public intervention or slaveholder destruction of these households did not represent disruption of "real families." Since their poverty, inappropriate work, and lack of husbands prevented impoverished white female-headed households from being inviolate, only affluent married white women were afforded the "sanctity of home fires" promised by "moral motherhood" ideologies (Winslow and Sanford 1854, 22–50). However, legal control over children was reserved to fathers, offspring assumed their identity through paternal lineage, and property was inherited through the father. In short, only an affluent white male could claim the *inalienable right* to head a family whose boundaries were inviolable. Thus, family was truly a privilege of race, class, gender, and marital status, certainly a legal freedom ensured only to those formally married Caucasian males who possessed "superiority" of race, gender, and class. If elite gender ideologies had remained cultural, transgressing women would have experienced only social ridicule that did not endanger their families' persistence. However, these gender conventions directly affected non-white and impoverished white females when they were formalized into local and state regulations. In the sections that follow, I will examine

- cult of domesticity threats to Cherokee family persistence,
- public regulation of poor white families,
- public regulation of free black families, and
- structural interference into slave families.

Cult of Domesticity Threats to Persistence of the Cherokee Family

Traditionally, Cherokee women led *public* lives that were viewed by European colonizers as base and uncivilized. Even though their voices were officially silenced, there are infrequent female footprints across colonial documents that provide glimpses of indigenous women's violations of Euroamerican separate spheres norms. Trade meetings at Charleston were halted when British males were offended by the presence of Cherokee women among the indigenous entourages (McDowell 1955, 236–37). In the 1750s, British and French officers were shocked by the presence of female fighters among Cherokee warriors (Salley 1930, 219). Traditionally, the work of Cherokee males and females was gender-bifurcated, but their sexual division of labor violated cult of domesticity definitions of appropriate work for both genders. On the one hand, Cherokee women's agricultural production and trading were celebrated in public ceremonies, but the economic contributions of white females were legally and culturally invisible. On the other hand, Cherokee females participated in town and clan decision making while Euroamerican women remained politically disenfranchised. When strangers entered Cherokee villages, the first "diplomats" they encountered were females, who were fulfilling their social obligations to exhibit the community's hospitality ethic (Adair 1775, 107, 123–24, 186–87, 190). As men became more ensnared in the international fur trade, women assumed greater responsibility for traditional male public roles, especially the *gadugi* and conjuring. Cherokee women were frequently in the presence of white male strangers without their husbands or fathers in ways that violated white gender conventions. They routinely traveled with children or in the company of other women to trade foods and crafts at Euroamerican forts and settlements (Mooney 1900, 395, 419, 501, 453). In addition, the ecological degradation that followed deer killing exposed women to white criticism, as they walked greater distances to gather food, firewood, and craft resources (Williams 1927, 93). In short, Cherokee women were far "too public" and, therefore, could only be defined as "morally corrupt" and "sexually promiscuous" by separate spheres standards.

Since Cherokee households were offshoots of matrilineal clans, Europeans did not view them as "real families." Nor in their view were Cherokee wives truly "mothers," who were needed in families in ways that were idealized for

FIGURE 18. Elite and middle-class whites interpreted as evidence of "degraded racial genes" the similar living conditions of Cherokees (top), slaves (middle), and poor whites (bottom). Not only did these groups exhibit similar living conditions and impoverishment, but females also engaged in many of the same household labors, such as corn pounding in the manner of the Cherokee women (top right). *Sources:* Library of Congress, *Scribner's* (May 1874), and *Harper's Monthly* (Jan. 1853).

white females. For that reason, Europeans did not face ideological conflict between their own family ideals and the enslavement practices they instituted. Because of the demands for labor in the West Indies and in the northern colonies, Indian slaves were the first profitable commodity exported by British settlers. By 1681, the selling of indigenous slaves had begun, and the Cherokees' first diplomatic mission to Charleston in 1693 was aimed at seeking relief from slavery raids (Salley 1928–47, 5: 97). By 1710, perhaps as many as 12,000 Indians had been exported from South Carolina to the northern colonies and to the Caribbean, the majority of them females.[1] During the early 1700s, Indians represented one-quarter of the total slave population in South Carolina, and 70 percent of them were women and children, whose removal had destroyed hundreds of indigenous families. In 1724, there were 2,100 Indian slaves in South Carolina, 1,480 of them women and children (Snell 1972, 85n37, 96). Because women engaged in work at a distance from their villages, they were easy targets for slave raiders. In addition, they were more vulnerable than males to capture because they tended corn in outfields and moved into purity huts during menstruation or after childbirth. Enslavement of Cherokee women and their offspring continued to such an extent after the Revolutionary War that one of every eight Appalachian ex-slaves reported Indian family ancestry (Dunaway 2003b, 201–5).

Because indigenous females operated in communities structured around matrilineage, their moral values and customs about sexuality, courtship, marriage, and divorce represented barbaric deviations from the patriarchal nuclear family of white Europeans. In addition to its hidden agenda of engrossing Indian lands as fast as possible, the U.S. postrevolutionary "civilization" program intended to move Cherokees away from their "savage" matrilineal clan structure so that property would be controlled and inherited through patriarchal families. Indeed, the Cherokee females "most visible to white officials were women who did not behave in ways approved" by dominant reproductive standards, for they controlled households that did not have male heads (Bartram 1853, 66). One cleric argued that there was "no Cherokee family" because "the father does not know his child nor consequently the child his father." Moreover, husbands and wives held "scarcely anything in common" because "marriage g[ave] no right to the husband over the property of his wife." To become a real family, then, Cherokees must "begin by instituting marriage as a solemn inviolable contract" ("Reflections" 1818, 51, 43). The close connections drawn between property and family were intentional, for white policymakers intended to destroy the matrilineal clans that stood in the way of land ownership by Euroamerican resettlers, who were already empowered by federal law to be the only *citizens* of the emergent new country.

In sharp contrast to the father-headed nuclear family idealized by the cult of domesticity, the typical Cherokee household was a multigenerational grouping that consisted of an elderly woman, her daughters, their husbands, and their

[1] According to Crane (1929, 85, 127), the British purchased 208 Cherokees in the period 1711–18.

children. Husbands and children lived in buildings owned by the wife's family, and women did not pass ownership of that property to husbands. Married women controlled houses, fields, livestock, and crops, and husbands spent little time in households, where they were routinely outnumbered by adult females. While the white patriarchal family designated the father as the *breadwinner*, the Cherokee wife supplied most of the household sustenance (Payne Papers, NLC, 6: 209). While fathers sporadically provided deer meat, the vast majority of the diet consisted of maize, beans, squash, nuts, and fruits that were cultivated or gathered by females. White visitors were struck by the sparsity of meat in this indigenous diet, and they were convinced that the Cherokees were "more accustom'd to labour and live upon corn, than to procure their sustenance by hunting" (Klinck and Telman 1970, 130). Little wonder, then, that the important annual Green Corn Ceremony centered rituals around agricultural outputs or that Cherokees inquired about the gender of a newborn by asking, "Is it a bow or a [cornmeal] sifter?" (Mooney 1886, 401).

Cherokee marriage was not the lifetime arrangement that characterized white patriarchal regulations. Women faced few restrictions in choosing mates except that they must marry outside their own clans. Offspring typically married into the clan of the grandfather, thereby clashing directly with white notions of patriarchal kinship and incest. Polygamy was common, the husband most often marrying the sister of his first wife. The only males with permanent connections to a household were those who were part of the wife's clan lineage, creating a context in which maternal uncles had more powerful ties to children than did their fathers (Perdue 1998, 41–60). Wives initiated divorce actions, after which the husband returned to the dwelling of his mother or sister. After divorces, "all the Children [went] along with the Mother and none with the Father" (Lawson 1967, 192). Similarly in the event of the mother's death, maternal clan members – not fathers – cared for children. Clan-based women's courts punished males who showed disrespect for the required mourning period, neglected wife and children, or violated taboos about childbirth, menstruation, or sexual intercourse (Longe 1969, 32; Payne Papers, NLC, 4: 227).

In sharp contrast to the offspring of white patriarchal families, indigenous children grounded their identities and their family lineage in the mother's clan. Missionaries demanded family restructuring "in favor of the issue of the father," and they pressured Cherokee leaders to mandate Christian marriages (ABCFM Papers, HUL, 21 Aug. 1824; Springplace Diary, GHC, 19 Oct. 1827; Payne Papers, NLC, 8: 34, 49). Even though women had traditionally benefited in several ways from polygamy (Perdue 1998, 146), the elite-controlled National Council justified its prohibition of the practice as a way to encourage "morality among men, the same among women" (*Cherokee Phoenix*, 18 Feb. 1829). While succumbing to white missionaries on such issues, mestizo leaders recognized the dangers in legislating the same degree of patriarchal control over property that characterized southern state statutes. An 1819 act retained the Cherokee woman's right to property when the husband died and declared that a white husband could not dispose of the property of a Cherokee wife "contrary to her consent." Moreover, an 1828 act established a nonpatriarchal method for handling estate settlements. When the husband died without a will, "nearest relatives" were authorized to recommend administrators to the court, a disguised way to protect the traditional property rights of the wife and her clan. In 1829, the council passed a third act, which mandated that a wife's property could not be seized for her husband's debts (*Laws* 1852, 10, 111, 142–43). This legislation to protect women's property interests was a sharp contradiction of the southern laws, which granted unilateral property control to white husbands. Thus, the Cherokee National Council never legislated landholding restrictions that made women totally subordinate to men. Unlike Caucasian wives, married Cherokee women did not lose all legal rights to land or to other accumulated property. Nor did the council police its polygamy constraints.[2] As late as 1826, one mestizo elite male claimed that "property belonging to the wife is not exclusively at the control & disposal of the husband, and in many respects she has exclusive & distinct control over her own, particularly among the less civilized" (Payne Papers, NLC, 9: 53). In 1835, at least one-third of the property owners were women heads of household (1835 Census Roll, NA). In the 1850s and 1860s, it was still "not uncommon" among traditional Eastern Cherokees for the women to "own most of the [live]stock, generally as much as their husbands" (U.S. Senate 1867, 147). Despite women's continuing control over property, the civilization program urged Cherokees to adopt the Euroamerican model and "scatter from their towns and make individual improvements" (Brainerd Journal, HUL, 7 May 1821). The disaggregation of town populations onto small separate farms was intended to pressure Cherokees toward patriarchal family structure. To encourage the development of nuclear families and individual landholdings, the National Council prohibited the establishment of farms within less than one-quarter mile of one another (*Laws* 1852, 410–11). Cherokee women paid a high price for this transformation. Because farms were distant from clan relatives, who were themselves often dispersed from traditional villages, Cherokee wives now faced the same predicament as poor white wives when husbands died or abandoned them. One female missionary described the trend toward small patriarchal nuclear families and farms as the "source of much sorrow to poor Cherokee women," who were left "deserted, dejected," with few resources or relatives "to provide for" offspring. Previously, matrilineal clans would have taken care of such families, but maternal uncles now were also situated on small farms without adequate space or income to take in or support destitute sisters and their children (Paine Notebooks, HUL, 2: 20 Dec. 1820). For women separated from clans, patrilineage and individual small farms resulted in socioeconomic powerlessness that traditional Cherokee mothers had not suffered.

In order to facilitate the transition to patriarchal families, white cultural interveners and the National Council encouraged certain types of racial

---

[2] According to Perdue (1998, 151–53), the only prosecution for polygamy was brought by a Cherokee woman against a white husband who had a second white wife and children in Missouri.

intermarriage while forbidding other forms. Because he was convinced that "by this measure civilization [would be] farther advanced than in any other way," the Indian agent "encouraged marriages between white men & Cherokee women" (CIAT Reports, NA, 14 Mar. 1808). At the same time, however, the National Council followed white precedents and banned intermarriage with African-Americans (*Laws* 1852, 77). Because such interracial unions were illegal among Euroamericans (Morris 1996, 40–41), Indian agents, missionaries, and the white public reacted strongly against unions between white females and Cherokee or mestizo males (Payne Papers, NLC, 8: 111). Moreover, southern statutes declared *illegitimate* all mixed-race offspring of white females (Morris 1996, 303–4). While white norms derogated racial *half-breeds*, "the children of white men and Indian women [we]re Indians," in the eyes of Cherokees (Becker 1977, 77). Striking a blow to child lineage through the mother's clan in 1825, the National Council legitimated the offspring of white males and Cherokee women, making those offspring "entitled to all the immunities and privileges enjoyed by the citizens descending from the Cherokee race, by the mother's side" (*Laws* 1852, 121). There was a distinct class element to the prejudices about intermarriages of white males and Cherokee females. Missionaries were very direct in teaching girl students that they should educate themselves and become astute in domestic arts in order to equip themselves to attract either a mestizo elite male or a middle-class Caucasian. According to one female mission school teacher, Cherokee girls could "easily be shown that the attending or good opinion of men without education, taste, or judgement is not worth seeking, & to gain the affection or good opinion of the opposite character, their minds must be improved, their manners polished, their persons attended to, in a word they must be qualified for [Christian] usefulness" (ABCFM Papers, HUL, 21 Aug. 1824). In similar fashion, Indian agent Benjamin Hawkins frowned on unions between Cherokee women and poor white males. He was convinced that most such men only intended to gain control over the indigenous women's lands, to exploit the labor of mother and offspring, or to engage in horse stealing or illicit alcohol peddling (Weeks 1916, 35–36, 366).

Another pressure toward patriarchal families resulted from erosion of female sexual autonomy. Women played such overt roles in control of households, marriages, and families that Europeans described Cherokee society as "petticoat government," in which "women rules the roost and wears the breeches" (Longe 1969, 30). For Cherokees, adoption of the cult of domesticity meant an extreme *reproductive powerlessness* for women that had not characterized their traditional societies. White visitors to eighteenth-century villages considered Cherokee marriages unstable and short-lived because females terminated marriages without any interference from communities or from husbands' clans (Longe 1969, 32). Adair (1775, 145, 153) claimed that "their marriages are ill observed, and of short continuance; like the Amazons, they divorce their fighting bed-fellows at their pleasure." While females often divorced adulterous husbands, males were expected by traditional customs to ignore their wives' infidelities (Klinck and Telman 1970, 125–26). In addition, Euroamericans were shocked by the courts conducted by Cherokee females to punish their husbands, brothers, and fathers for violations of marriage regulations or community taboos about reproduction (Mooney 1900, 240).

After the Revolutionary War, missionaries influenced passage of laws that were intended to constrain Cherokee women's sexual and reproductive autonomy, and they aggressively punished female students for traditional behaviors they labeled sexual promiscuity (McLoughlin 1986, 141, 331). In the early nineteenth century, the National Council and the new court system assumed control over divorces and the registration of marriages. Traditionally, women had practiced infanticide and abortion as means to control population or to eliminate any physically handicapped baby that would become a severe resource burden on the community (Williams 1928, 149–50, 485). Reacting to missionary assessments that "infanticide marks the epitome of savage behavior" (*Panoplist*, 22 July 1805), the National Council banned infanticide and abortions in 1826, setting a penalty of 50 lashes for the violating pregnant woman and any females who assisted her (*Laws* 1852, 79).

Public Regulation of the "Third Class" of White Families

Like Cherokee females, poor white women were "too public" in their labors and too independent of male control over households. A Civil War veteran (Dyer and Moore 1985, 2016) identified three classes of white Appalachians: landed nonslaveholders, slaveholders, and the "third class" of landless poor. The living conditions and work routines of the "third class" of poor white adult women placed them at odds with the gender conventions of slaveholders and middle classes. The stereotype of those who adhered to southern cult of domesticity standards was that "the low bred & uneducated class" was "not a whit . . . superior to a negro." Because they were believed to be descendants of racial throwbacks, poor Euroamericans were viewed as having "a civilization of their own," which caused them to prefer "demoralized" living conditions, "base" family arrangements, and "loose sexual mores." Affluent southerners assessed white families who lived in rough, one-room cabins as "lewd" and "near savage." Women who did manual labor alongside men were stigmatized as "sexually promiscuous," and they were considered to be "whores and prostitutes" when nonwhite males were present in their workplaces. Southern separate spheres advocates contended that slavery was essential to protect decent women from "falling" into the state of racial and moral degeneracy visited upon households that had no servants to do the kinds of public labors required of poor Caucasian females (Simms 1852, 228–30). Often unclean and unwashed and attired in patched homespun clothing, they lacked the "gentility and fashion" of respectable whites (Newby 1989, 44). Their dialects, their forms of public conversation and entertainment, and their lack of household luxuries marked them as people who possessed neither the manners nor the Christian breeding needed by women to build the "moral characters" of children (Welter 1966, 160).[3]

In their failure to observe gendered work spheres and their inabilities to exhibit the "purity and moral virtues" essential to "white womanhood" (Gross 1998, 157), poor landless families were structurally and functionally different from affluent Appalachian households. On the one hand, separate spheres advocates condemned women who were visible in male labor spheres. On the other hand, they *emasculated* husbands who failed to provide sufficient material resources to protect their female "dependents" from the moral dangers of work outside their households (Simms 1852, 97–99). These gender conventions posed impossible economic constraints for poor males who were underpaid and frequently unemployed. Because wives could not afford the luxury of staying at home, poor white Appalachian families failed to meet criteria of "respectability" and "civilization." Moreover, their family constructs were sanctioned by policymakers and clerics. First, they were characterized by a high incidence of "common law marriages" in which males and females resided together and retained separate names, even after they bore children (Newby 1989, 75). One western North Carolina ex-slave remembered that "de poor white folks done de same thing" as slaves when they celebrated a wedding (Rawick 1972, 15: 185). Like local slaves, many poor whites celebrated their unions with unrecorded broomstick wedding customs they retained from their English and Celtic heritage.[4] The second aberration that called public attention to poor white families was a higher incidence of female-headed households, a structural condition that resulted from the shorter life span of impoverished adult males and from the low probability that poor widows with children would be able to remarry. In addition, many poor men migrated from families for extended periods because employers frowned upon traveling contract laborers who took their kin to their work sites. When Jonathan Worth (Papers, NCDAH, 19 Jan. 1850) instructed his southwest Virginia manager to recruit a laborer to migrate to western North Carolina, he insisted: "If he is unwilling to come without his family, I don't want him."

Realities of the everyday lives of poor whites caused the females in those households to be criminalized by affluent male policymakers and policing functionaries. County courts established double standards for dealing with males and females who engaged in some of the same behaviors (Brown 1996, 287–89). Little attention was paid to males who ran inns or taverns or to wives who worked alongside husbands in such public facilities, but county courts criminalized female heads of household who operated such enterprises alone.

---

[3] A young poor white western North Carolina female attacked separate spheres ideology through letters to the editor of the *Southern Weekly Post* (13 Dec. 1850, 11 Dec. 1852).

[4] Such broomstick ceremonies have been documented among New England and southern poor whites, and they were common among Welsh and Irish railroad construction workers. Gutman (1976, 275–83, 596n) contends that slave broomstick rituals were probably copied from these poor white ceremonies.

While males might be fined or lightly treated for public disorder, disturbances in female-headed households were viewed as worse threats to "community order" because of the potential for sexual misconduct across racial lines. While female heads of household faced court prosecution when they had no visible source of legal income or when their children were disorderly, absent fathers were rarely held accountable for failure to provide financial support to children or character guidance to their offspring.[5] While female heads of household were criminalized when they abandoned children, most neglectful fathers were invisible to courts and sheriffs. After the husband deserted her, one poor Appalachian wife nearly starved before she left her "newly born male white child" at a business, "hoping it would be taken care of." Offended by her criminal act of "neglecting her sacred maternal duty," county court justices imprisoned her and indentured her infant to age 21 but took no action against the irresponsible father (*Leesburg Washingtonian*, 25 July 1846).

More than 15 percent of white Appalachian households were headed by females, and poor households were four times more likely to be headed by a woman than were affluent families. Four of every five of these female heads were impoverished, even though nearly one-quarter of them owned small farms.[6] That *feminized poverty* and their stigmatization as women without husbands increased the likelihood that they and their offspring would experience public intervention. That minority of poor female heads who owned farms were not so likely to be criminalized as were the landless poor, who frequently searched for employment and engaged in informal sector income-earning outside their households (see Table 4). Feminized poverty was closely regulated by county poor houses, so any unmarried head of household was at risk of court action if she appeared to be unable to support her offspring economically. Consequently, 1 of every 20 of the agricultural laborers on the region's farms was an adult female who had been indentured by the county poor house. Even when she had borne legitimate children by a husband to whom she had been legally married, the poor widow was closely scrutinized by local public and church authorities for engaging in "base" behaviors, such as management of her husband's tavern. However, parallel actions by a wealthier wife were positively esteemed by those same officials. In contrast to impoverished widows, such "respectable" women possessed the social capital, material necessities, servants, and professional male support to avoid social stigmatization for violating separate spheres ideals. While "head of household" status made a poor female suspect in the eyes of local courts and sheriffs, affluent women were considered to be doing what was socially expected of a wife who took over the absent husband's property

[5] Court records indicate that a few Appalachian counties attempted to identity fathers of the children of unmarried women, in order to hold them accountable for child support. However, they met with little success, and most court records show only intermittent prosecution of absent poor fathers.

[6] Derived from analysis of a systematic probability sample of 2,795 female heads of household drawn from the 1860 Census of Population manuscripts, NA.

and child management roles. Indeed, neighbors interpreted their work as property owners and heads of household as labors that confirmed, rather than challenged, their fulfillment of separate spheres ideals of female self-sacrifice and duty.

Drawing upon the thinking of biological determinists like Herbert Spencer (1851), affluent southerners were convinced that failure to "behave white" was evidence that the Caucasian had inherited weaknesses of character from inferior racial bloodlines. In court cases, witnesses and judges often espoused the notion that "blackness could be hidden behind white physical features." However, the most essential "moral qualities would shine through" if the person were purely white. In court cases and in local communities, the appropriate white female character was idealized with positive stereotypes, such as "industrious, careful, prudent, neat of person, sacrificing mother, never seen in the company of non-kin males." Similarly, judges and juries claimed they could always recognize the race of a nonwhite woman because she would always be "idle, reckless, extravagant, fond of dress and display, sexually promiscuous, and an uncaring mother," stereotypes they also applied to poor white women who violated gender conventions (Gross 1998, 154–56, 168). In other words, race was not just judged by ethnic ancestry or by pseudoscientific evaluation of bloodlines. One North Carolina judge ruled that behavior and associational ties were such powerful indicators of racial heritage that any white with common sense "will be able to discover with almost unerring certainty the adulteration of the Caucasian with the negro or Indian blood."[7] According to this ideology, poor women could not be "purely white" if they engaged in public behaviors, family lifestyles, or extra-household work that affluent Caucasians identified as "base nonwhite" character traits. For these marginalized females the structural and cultural contradictions of their class, race, and gender publicly collided in ways that endangered the survival of their families. The daily burdens they bore in their "lower-class" households prevented them from exhibiting "feminine evidence of whiteness." When a woman reached the juncture of public scrutiny, the community might sympathize with the "worthy" wife whose husband had failed to provide her the economic support, discipline, and community respect demanded of "white manhood." On the other hand, the female whose work and social behavior were negative affronts to patriarchal gender conventions was likely to be stigmatized as an irredeemable unmarried deviant whose hidden nonwhite "true nature" was overwhelming any hope of her achieving the essential attributes of "white womanhood" (Gross 1998, 158–76).

Churches played pivotal roles in regulating female adherence to gender proprieties. "Wayward women" could be publicly ridiculed or excommunicated, and churches typically refused to baptize or record the births of children born out of wedlock. Women bore the brunt of policing of sexual behavior while male partners never were charged in cases of adultery, fornication, or illegitimacy. In a survey of the church records of 31 Appalachian churches, the vast

---

[7] *State v. Jacobs*, Case 7915 (1859), NCSC Records, NCDAH.

majority of sexual offenses were leveled at women, and women were nearly twice as likely as males to be permanently expelled from their congregations (see Table 2). While Appalachian churches routinely brought illicit sex charges against females who showed visible indicators of pregnancy, offending males almost never appear in church records.[8] The proof of Martha Cole's adultery was that she "ha[d] a child born within less than six months after marriage." Martha acknowledged "her guilt in tears – lamenting over the wound her conduct ha[d] given the church." While the male church board took no action against her male partner, they suspended Martha until "she exhibit ample evidence of the sincerity of her repentance" (Byrd Church, VSL, 11 Oct. 1829). Rachael Sconeirs was excommunicated from her church after she was "charged with [the] sin of having a bastard child," but there was no condemnation of the father (Bark Camp Church, GSA, 69). Similarly, Eliza Spurlock's congregation expelled her "for disorder – fornication" (Cabin Creek Church, GSA, 6 July 1844). Because she was "too thick with young men," Mary Bivin was excluded from her church, but the misbehavior of her male cohorts was ignored (Mount Olive Church, NCDAH, September 1849). In some instances, churches took actions against women in reaction to rumors. Sally Sartig was excommunicated after a neighbor reported that she saw her "cover her daughter and a young man together on a bed" (Pleasant Grove Church, NCDAH, December 1838). Not only were females singled out for charges that they had committed sexual offenses, but they were also far more likely than males to be expelled from their congregations. While ignoring the duplicity of males in these sexual behaviors, churches tried females for sexual infractions far more frequently than any other type of violation, In sharp contrast, men were most often called before church tribunals for disorderly conduct, such as drinking and profanity. Churches typically excommunicated females about whom they had strong evidence, such as pregnancy, of sexual infractions, allowing their male partners to remain invisble. Even when their infractions were obvious to the community, males were nearly twice as likely as females to receive only warnings or mild public citations. In fact, none of the men who were charged with domestic violence was permanently expelled, demonstrating that these churches weighed female sexual offenses as far more dangerous than male physical violence toward family members. For example, Wheeler's Church (UNC, May 1831, March 1848) and Pleasant Grove Church (NCDAH, March 1846) cited males for domestic violence, but all three males were counseled in prayer meetings.

Even though some women confronted such gender discrimination in their religious institutions, a majority of Appalachian females were unchurched (see Chapter 1). Consequently, local court officials and sheriffs were the primary policing agents who took action against poor white females. The courts primarily placed constraints on the sexual autonomy of women through fornication charges (for sex outside marriage) and through divorce proceedings. State

---

[8] I perused manuscript minutes and records for 34 churches listed in the Bibliography under GSA, HPL, NCDAH, UNC, UVA, VHS, VSL, and WVU.

and local officials established antifornication laws that criminalized sex out-side marriage, but the punishment for violations almost always fell upon poor white and free black women. While affluent white males were never prosecuted for their sexual liaisons with enslaved or poor free females, fornication charges were frequently brought by local courts and churches against women (Rothman 2003, 57–90). Appalachian women most often filed for divorces on the grounds of cruelty (50 percent) and adultery (30 percent), but they were required by the courts to present testimony that was nearly impossible to obtain from male neighbors who had witnessed the actions they described. In contrast, males most often charged wives with abandonment (nearly 60 percent) and adul-tery (40 percent), and it was much easier for them to gain the sympathy of the courts when they claimed that wives were involved with nonwhite males or men of lower status. Consequently, husbands were far more likely to be granted divorces than their wives.[9]

According to Bolton (1994, 61), the antebellum criminal justice system "directed the lion's share of its energies toward disciplining landless whites." Little wonder, then, that a majority of the indictments for petty crimes in Appalachian counties, such as theft, assault and battery, fighting, trading, sell-ing alcohol, or gambling with slaves, were brought against poor whites.[10] Only members of the prosperous landed classes could serve on local grand juries, and this form of discrimination ensured that the anti-poor biases of affluent Appalachians held sway. Little wonder, then, that the illicit sexual behaviors of poor females would be closely monitored by local community leaders. With-out doubt, the most socially dangerous act in which a poor autonomous female might engage was a sexual liaison with a nonwhite, especially when a long-term relationship produced offspring and accumulated property. While most liaisons between nonwhite males and affluent females were kept socially hidden, inter-racial sexual relations between poor white women and nonwhite men were closely regulated by county courts and sheriffs. Southern laws grounded the need for regulation of female sexual autonomy in tenets of biological determin-ism. Popular intellectuals like Herbert Spencer argued that "lower forms" were exposed to base conditions that caused them to acquire behavioral characteris-tics that they transmitted biologically to their offspring (Blakemore 2000). First, poor white women often lived in conditions as "base" as those experienced by nonwhites, so they were stereotyped as more "forgetful of their free condition" than a woman whose father or husband provided her economic needs. Sec-ond, poor white women were believed to be racially inferior to more affluent females, so their sexual libidos were supposed to be closer to those of nonwhite

---

[9] Analysis of 119 Appalachian petitions for divorce in TSSC Reports, TSL; NCSC Records, NCDAH; Ramsey Papers, Legal Documents, DU; and Legislative Papers, VSL. Hodes (1997, 68–95) and Boswell (2001, 134) found similar trends in other parts of the South.

[10] Analysis of 1858–60 Appalachian court cases in TSSC Reports, TSL; NCSC Dockets and NCSC Records, NCDAH; and ASC Records, ADA. Names were cross-checked with 1860 Census of Population Manuscripts, NA, to ascertain the wealth and landownership status of the defen-dants.

women, who were always driven to "the satisfaction of their lascivious and lustful desires" (Brown 1996, 197–99). For example, Maryland statutes aimed to deter "unnatural and inordinate [i.e, disorderly] copulations" that were "to the disgrace of . . . Christian nations" by prohibiting white females from entering "shameful matches" with men of color (*Archives of Maryland* 1883–1972, 1: 533–34, 7: 204, 13: 547, 30: 290).

Southern elites embraced the biological determinist tenet that the "abnormal" sexual behaviors of poor white and nonwhite females were evidence of an "inferior racial blood line" (Vogt 1864), but they constructed a different standard with respect to the cross-racial sexual behaviors of males. Patriarchal family authority, property ownership, and offspring lineage required male privileges grounded in both race and gender. Thus, southern laws limited to white males the right to have reproductive access to white women, thereby striking at "the dual threat of white female sexual autonomy and black male encroachment" (Brown 1996, 198). Legislators recognized that racial boundaries were often complex and blurred by the presence of "free issue" *mulattoes* (racially mixed children of African-American descent) and *griffes* (racially mixed children of Indian heritage). Consequently, the changing body of accumulated laws needed to structure mechanisms for concealing those social violations. While laws were clear in their sanctions against white females who engaged in cross-racial relationships, white males were granted relative legal immunity from prosecution for their sexual liaisons with nonwhite women. Moreover, most states made it impossible for mixed-race offspring (who were by law born out of wedlock) to place claims against the white father's property. Divorce petitions of white women frequently accused their husbands of long-term affairs with free black women, and cohabitation with enslaved women was the second most frequent complaint claimed in divorce actions in North Carolina and Virginia. Despite that trend, courts required less evidence from and placed fewer constraints on husbands than on wives who sought divorces on the grounds their spouses had engaged in cross-racial affairs. In Appalachian divorce cases, husbands were far more likely to be granted a divorce on these grounds.[11]

Furthermore, the wife's cross-racial error did not always have to involve physical contact, for innuendos about sexual impropriety also weighed heavily against her. When Sarah Burnhum filed for divorce from a husband she termed "physically abusive," the east Kentucky court denied her petition because her neighbors described her as a woman who did not pay adequate attention to her home and children. She "rode about a great deal, and was a great hand to visit," they reported, until well after nightfall, leaving her teenaged daughter "at home with the negroes by herself" (Sears 1989, 11). A married woman could bring a slander suit against anyone who termed her a *whore* if she were involved in an extramarital affair with a white male; such liaisons were labeled by law to

---

[11] For sources, see note 10. Hodes (1997, 78–95) and Rothman (2003, 177–81) found similar patterns throughout the South.

be *adultery*. This distinction was intended to identify the white male as a far more appropriate sexual partner than any nonwhite. In contrast, any single or unmarried woman involved sexually with a nonwhite male was typically labeled in these regulations to be a whore (King 1995, 77–78). Because poor women were stereotyped by court officials as the segment of the white population most likely to violate racial boundaries, statutes prohibited racially mixed public assemblies that included poor white women. However, neither poor nor affluent men were prosecuted for their presence at slave auctions, bawdy houses, or taverns where they were in the company of nonwhite females. Unmarried white women who participated in clandestine or rowdy social gatherings with blacks were particularly suspect. In sharp contrast to the legal and social treatment of parallel female liaisons, any white man could engage as often as he wanted in sexual activity with a black or Indian woman with little constraint from neighbors or courts, so long as he did not attempt to endow that female with the privileges of a white wife (Morris 1996, 91).

There was more intermarriage and sexual interaction among Appalachian whites and blacks than we might have suspected, and the records of those illicit relationships appear in census manuscripts, court records, and slave narratives. Moreover, many of those interactions must have involved white females and enslaved males because there were so few free blacks in most Appalachian communities. Still, the coresidence of free black Appalachians and poor white women is easy to spot in the 1860 census manuscripts. In about 3 percent of the free black households, there was a white wife. Moreover, one or more mulatto children were enumerated as members of nearly 11 percent of the poor white Appalachian households headed by females. Appalachian ex-slaves described broomstick marriages between white laborers and slaves who worked on the same farms.[12] On a small mountainous Meigs County, Tennessee, plantation, Maggie Broyles's father was "an indentured Irishman," her mother a slave (Rawick 1972, 8: 324). One Blue Ridge Virginia church recorded member controversy over the baptizing of a slave infant born to the black wife of an indentured white laborer (*Irish Immigrants* 2003, 445–46). A poor Polk County, Georgia, farm owner "fell madly in love" with a light mulatto house servant, purchased her freedom, and identified her to neighbors as his wife. When the husband died two years later, debtors auctioned off their household possessions, then sold the wife "on the slave block with her son" (Rawick 1977, 3: 479–80).

Much of the deeply hidden trail of evidence that points to such cross-racial liaisons appears in court records and divorce petitions. After being married to

---

[12] Trends derived from analysis of all poor female-headed households in a systematic sample of 3,056 households and all poor female heads of household in a sample of 2,795 female-headed households drawn from the 1860 Census of Population manuscripts, NA. To determine the extent of interracial marriages among free blacks, I isolated all the free black households listed in the Census of Population manuscripts for the seven Appalachian counties of Floyd, Georgia; Madison, Kentucky; Rutherford, North Carolina; Frederick, Maryland; Knox, Tennessee; Wythe, Virginia; and Jefferson, West Virginia.

a white male for several years in southwest Virginia, Elizabeth Cook gave birth to "two mulatto children." Subsequently, her husband was granted a divorce because the midwife confirmed the color of the twins. Similarly William Rucker was granted a divorce after his wife gave birth to "a mulatto." Leonard Owen petitioned for a divorce on the grounds that his wife engaged in "a horrible violation of a marriage bed" by interacting with a nonwhite male, the evidence being that she had borne "a black male child." Millwright Isaac Fouch described his wife as "lewd, incontinent" because he had found her in bed twice with a black male. A white servant substantiated his claim, testifying that the two frequently "went up to the loft together," where she had spied and seen them "in the act." Thomas Cain charged his spouse with being a "whore of the most aggravated character" because she had "become the mother of black children."[13]

Unmarried landless white and free black women who headed households were indicted for fornication and adultery twice as often as other women.[14] Community leaders viewed landless white women who headed households and traveled around looking for work as a threat to traditional sexual and family arrangements (Bolton 1994, 62–63). The worst crimes of "the fallen woman" were "indiscretions" in public settings that exposed her to the "base sexual drives of males" (Hodes 1997, 65). Because the actions of poor white women often put them in conflict with legal authorities and churches, elite white southerners considered them to be "especially prone to sexual depravity and dishonor" (Flynt 1989, 49). Court cases document the prosecution of white females who were arrested for living with black males. In Buncombe County, North Carolina, poor white Lucretia Scroggins and free black Marville Scroggins were prosecuted for living together as husband and wife, and the court was even more outraged that they had their mulatto child "removed to Tennessee" to prevent the court from indenturing him to a local slaveholder. In Ashe County, North Carolina, William Watters and Zilphia Thompson were arrested and tried for cohabiting as husband and wife. The court classified William to be "nonwhite," even though he argued he "was descended from Portuguese, not from Negro or Indian ancestors." John Greenlee was found innocent of slander after he gossiped that poor white Mary Watts was a "whore" because she was pregnant by his slave. The Hawkins County, Tennessee, court prosecuted the poor white woman residing with free black James Bloomer. In an 1848 east Tennessee court decision, mulatto Jesse Brady was found innocent, but his white wife, Louisa Scott, was prosecuted. The judge indicated that the state law specified that only the white person was to be tried as the "offending party" in white-black cohabitation complaints. The Rutherford County, North Carolina, court prosecuted free black Alfred Hooper

---

[13] Appalachian divorce cases in Legislative Petitions, Legislative Papers, VSL: John Cook, 12 Dec. 1812; William Rucker, 5 Mar. 1849; Leonard Owen, 11 Dec. 1809; Isaac Fouch, 22 Dec. 1808; Thomas Cain, 9 Jan. 1841.
[14] For sources, see note 10.

and white Elizabeth Suttles, who "lived together and cohabited as man and wife."[15]

In short, we are far more likely to capture glimpses of poor white women in the pages of court records than to find documented there the cross-racial sexual violations of either poor or affluent males. That double legal standard was historically grounded in the perceived public need to protect white fathers from the "base" nature of these females. Moreover, cross-racial sexual liaisons blurred the racial identities of children, placing offspring at the mercy of courts who sought to protect the privileges of white patrilineal inheritance. When women had offspring by both white and nonwhite males, the "whiteness" of their children could be thrown into public doubt. Courts often decided the race of an individual by examining the racial identities of her closest associates (Gross 1998, 150–51). In Burke County, North Carolina, for instance, the court questioned the race of a 23-year-old white male because he had mulatto siblings who were borne by his mother and her long-term black mate. Legal rulings quite often specified that "acceptance in the white community" was necessary to "signify white identity," but a preponderance of "associations with 'colored' people almost certainly meant blackness." Thus, the court denied western North Carolina mulatto Samuel Love's petition for the court to declare his son by a white female "legitimate." The judge would not grant public approval, he insisted, to "licentious intercourse between persons of opposite colors," by permitting the offspring of such a union to inherit property.[16]

Despite the fornication and divorce cases in which poor white women were punished, southern public attitudes toward cross-racial unions were made more complex by the class, respectability, and color of the parties involved. Local authorities did not aggressively search out all violators of miscegenation laws. Such interracial unions attracted the attention of public authorities only when household members engaged in some disturbance of the peace, filed a divorce action against an adulterous spouse, committed a crime, or failed to support and control children.[17] If a white woman in a cross-racial union never had a white husband, was not poor, and was not rearing white children alongside mulatto offspring, she avoided three major social aberrations that attracted court attention. White women residing with mulattoes with close ties to local elites might be tolerated because their racially mixed partners were often viewed by affluent Appalachians and southerners to be of a higher class position than illiterate and unstable poor white males. In my census manuscript sample, about half the white Appalachian females in interracial unions were

[15] NCSC Records, NCDAH: *Marville Scroggins v. Lucretia Scroggins; State v. William P. Watters and Zilphia Thompson; Mary Watts v. John M. Greenlee; State v. Alfred Hooper and Elizabeth Suttles.*

[16] Miscellaneous Petitions, NCDAH, Petition dated 29 Nov. 1820; TSSC Reports, TSL: *James Bloomer v. State of Tennessee, State v. Jesse Brady*; Ramsey Papers, DU, Petition dated 12 Mar. 1845.

[17] According to Bolton (1994, 61), "Landless people who encountered trouble with the law but had good kin connections could generally expect [court] flexibility."

dwelling with mulatto males. Such relationships were far less likely to be prosecuted by local courts because their nonwhite husbands had kinship connections to local elites with whom they shared the same surnames. Moreover, many mulatto husbands embraced cult of domesticity ideals (Horton 1986), sought to build personal reputations of being stably employed in nonagricultural trades, and preferred to have stay-at-home wives. Southerners were convinced they could detect "negro blood" in a white or nearly-white person through social connections and character. Thus, a mulatto-white union might be tolerated when the husband engaged in a "set of moral and civic virtues that could only be performed by white people" and when he seemed to exhibit greater loyalty toward Caucasians than nonwhites (Gross 1998, 112, 126).

In a study of interracial unions in the Appalachian counties of Alabama, Mills (1981, 22–24) found that subtle caste differences came into play in public perceptions of interracial households. An unmarried white woman who bore both white and mulatto offspring was more likely to receive public scrutiny than white/mulatto spouses in extended relationships who bore no children out of wedlock. Moreover, "mulatto descendants of white women were somewhat more prone to erect caste barriers between themselves and the black population." Those mulattoes who held skilled occupations, were literate, and maintained ties to powerful families possessed more of the *social capital* expected of "white manhood" than did many impoverished Caucasian males. Consequently, such mulattoes usually held a higher status in the eyes of local slaveholders and many middle-class nonslaveholders than the poor white man who demonstrated through his lack of prosperity that he was "not white enough."

Clearly, the racial boundaries were not so rigid that all cross-racial unions were legally attacked as threats to the community. Rather, gradations of color, class, and community reputation either exacerbated or ameliorated the white woman's complex, but blurred, status. In this sense, then, an unmarried poor white woman accused of fornication with a slave was at far greater risk than the white wife of an esteemed mulatto. On the one hand, the white wife of a "respectable" mulatto might not be publicly attacked to the degree that sheriffs and courts harassed unmarried poor white females or adulterous white wives who strayed into cross-racial sexual liaisons. On the other hand, she would still be socially marginalized as a Caucasian female who simply was "not white enough." After all, "proving one's whiteness meant performing white womanhood" through sexual behaviors that exhibited racial purity, moral virtue, and family honor – none of which was possible when the female failed to marry inside her own race (Gross 1998, 156).

Public Regulation of Free Black Families

Even though they represented only 1.4 percent of the population, free black Appalachians were viewed by most whites to be a visible and "dangerous class."[18] Frederick County, Virginia, citizens thought that "next to slavery, the partial emancipation of slaves [wa]s the greatest evil among [them]." Because they might incite slaves to run away or to rebel, owners feared free blacks as a "public danger" and "a great and growing evil" (Legislative Papers, VSL, petition dated 6 Dec. 1823). The editor of the *Lexington Gazette* (20 Oct. 1859) warned readers that free blacks "drink and gamble, lounge about in idleness, and corrupt the slave population by their pernicious influences." Repeatedly throughout the antebellum period, Appalachian communities initiated petitions to state legislatures for the permanent removal of all free blacks (e.g., Legislative Papers, VSL, petitions dated 13 Jan. 1836, 10 Dec. 1847). Some communities urged their state governments or Congress to fund the permanent colonization of all free blacks in Africa (Hamilton 1898–1903, 3: 329). Asheville citizens introduced an 1858 plan to the North Carolina legislature that called for the reenslavement of free blacks (Franklin 1943, 118–20).

Since they represented such a small segment of the population, why were free black Appalachians so feared by local whites? The first explanation is that the small numbers of free black Appalachians had a highly threatening presence because a majority of the region's counties exceeded national, southern, or Upper South averages in the ratio of free blacks to slaves.[19] Except for the Appalachian sections of Alabama, Georgia, and South Carolina that were importing slaves to support their expanding cotton production, most of the region's counties exceeded southern averages in the proportion of African-Americans who were not enslaved. Between 1840 and 1860, three-fifths of the enslaved population that should have been in Upper South Appalachian counties had vanished through the interstate slave trade (Dunaway 2003a, 18–36). At the same time, free black populations increased through natural increase and in-migration from non-Appalachian counties. As a result of forced removals of slaves, 13.4 percent of the African-Americans in 1860 Appalachian counties were free. Seventy-five counties had a higher proportion of free blacks than the northern United States, and another 20 exceeded the rest of the Upper South in the proportion of free African-Americans. The second explanation for the visibility of such small numbers is the degree to which they were concentrated in small Appalachian towns. Free blacks represented one-third or more of the small urban populations. To whites who feared free black involvement in abolitionism, crimes, and cross-racial sex with poor whites, their concentrated presence made them seem to be greater in number than they were. For instance, the editor of the *Knoxville Standard* (12 May 1846) complained about the large numbers of "poor, raggedy" blacks who were "seen every day of the week, lounging on the street corners," seeking day labor. When the First Baptist Church of Knoxville opened its doors in 1850, the local newspaper was alarmed that 20 of its 46 members were black (Ash 1991, 8). Because of the frequent presence of free blacks, Appalachian municipalities regulated their

---

[18] Free black population derived from analysis of Appalachian county totals in U.S. Census Office (1864).

[19] Calculated using Appalachian county statistics in U.S. Census Office (1863).

public behavior, their employment, their trading activities, their religious services, and their interactions with slaves and poor whites (Craven and Hay 1994).

Like other parts of the South, Appalachian communities stereotyped free blacks as "vicious, idle, and disorderly, and therefore a deadweight on the body politic" (*North Carolina Standard*, 6 Nov. 1850). After 1835, state and local governments expanded their restrictions on the movement of free blacks. Except Kentucky, every southern state made slave manumission difficult or impossible. Alabama, Georgia, and South Carolina passed laws to prevent emancipation. North Carolina mandated removal of freed blacks within 90 days of manumission while Tennessee required removal within six months. Maryland and Virginia were slightly more liberal, allowing them a full year's stay (Morris 1996, 371–99). The will of an east Tennessean clarifies the legal difficulties of the emancipation process. After his death, John Brabson freed an elderly slave woman, adding the qualification "if any person will go her security to keep her from becoming a county charge and the county court will allow" (Brabson 1975, 37). Any free black who could not present freedom papers or who overstayed county time limits could be apprehended and sold by the overseers of the poor. Although they could not hold office, sit on juries, or testify against whites, free blacks paid higher poll taxes (in those few states in which they retained the legal right to vote). State and local ordinances made it illegal for free blacks to possess firearms, to operate taverns or sell whiskey, or to market commodities without a written permit from a white landholder. Restrictions were placed on their property rights, and free blacks were denied the right of trial by jury except for crimes punishable by death. Teaching any black to read or write was a criminal offense, and free black churches were forbidden to hold services without white supervision. Appalachian towns passed ordinances making it unlawful for free blacks to ride in hacks or to stay on sidewalks as whites passed. In many communities, whites could peddle without licenses while free blacks were required to pay annual fees and to seek the sponsorship of county justices. Violators of such ordinances were publicly whipped, and local patrollers were empowered to punish free blacks in the same manner they disciplined slaves. When they were convicted of crimes, free blacks were bound out for long periods or sold into slavery (Stroud 1856).

It was in this inimical context that small numbers of free black families attempted to survive in Appalachian counties. Half of free black households resided in the region's small towns and villages, two-thirds of them headed by women who were only slightly better off economically than their counterparts in the countryside. One-fifth of free black females were involved in nonagricultural jobs in towns, about half of them employed in manufacturing or extractive industries. While they did not earn wages equal to those of males alongside whom they worked, free black women were represented in nonagricultural jobs to a greater extent than poor white women. The other half of the free African-Americans lived in the countryside, the vast majority of them residing near slaveholders. Two-thirds of these rural free black households were headed by women who were identified as "farm laborers." These families averaged 5.2 members but typically held less than $30 in 1860 assets and were dependent upon their employers for their subsistence. Since two-thirds of these rural households resided near white slaveholders who bore the same last name, these women heads were either married to enslaved males, staying near enslaved kin, or descendants of emancipated slaves who continued to work for and seek the sponsorship of their former masters.[20] For instance, Nancy Young and her adult sister composed a nonnuclear family in which they were raising six mulatto youngsters. She reported only $5 in accumulated assets, she owned neither farm implements nor work animals, and her household produced only about 44 percent of the food needed for its survival. Since she lived adjacent to a white slaveholder of the same last name, Nancy was probably receiving aid from the owner who freed her, and he or his male kin may have fathered the mulatto Young offspring.[21] The vast majority of free black Appalachian households lived in precarious conditions that mirrored those of the Young household. Most of these families were still extremely poor and had accumulated only about $55 in assets.

Affluent southerners considered unmarried free black women "naturally lascivious and amoral by virtue of their race." Like poor white mothers, free black women could expect county poor house intervention if they did not demonstrate their capacity to provide for and control their offspring. In fact, two-thirds of the adults listed in Appalachian county registers of free blacks are described as having been indentured while they were children. Like poor white women, they were dramatically overrepresented in records of fornication and bastardy cases. Moreover, the composition of their families placed them at odds with separate spheres conventions. The vast majority of free black households enumerated in census manuscripts were mothers and children, and less than 15 percent of free black households had both spouses present. In Appalachian registers of free blacks, the typical household was one in which an elderly mother acted as a matriarch over a family that consisted of two to four generations of her adult children, their spouses and offspring, plus other adult extended kin. Whether female-headed or extended arrangements predominated, these families did not meet the standards of the cult of domesticity. Even when they were connected to free black males, females did not often marry formally. To complicate matters, some of these females were involved in undocumented marriages to slaves or were engaged in illicit relationships with white males. The women in these households defined an ideal womanhood different from the norms preferred by affluent whites. They showed their sense of communal identity by being bound to extended families. For them, virtue lay in their willingness to work hard to provide homes and basic survival needs for their children. Like poor white

---

[20] Findings reported for free blacks are derived from analysis of a systematic probability sample of 1,200 free black Appalachian households drawn from the 1860 Census of Population manuscripts, NA. See Tables 18, 21, 41, Web site.
[21] Young household enumerated in 1860 Census of Population and Agriculture manuscripts, NA, Green County, TN.

female household heads, they challenged the patriarchal nuclear family ideal because they were not economically dependent on husbands.

Some scholars (e.g., Lebsock 1982, 282) have celebrated this outcome as positive agency on the part of women who chose to remain single in order to accumulate greater economic benefits for themselves and their offspring. However, far more sinister structural barriers were at work to prevent free black Appalachian women from formalizing unions. On the one hand, a registered marriage required fee payments to ministers and court clerks, sometimes the posting of a bond with the county court. On the other hand, there was a structured gender imbalance in Appalachian counties that made it unlikely that free black females could locate suitable mates. As Map 10 shows, a majority of Upper South Appalachian counties averaged 104 to 120 adult free black females to every 100 adult free black males while 24 counties were characterized by 1.5 or more to every free black male. Moreover, the median age of males was 7 to 10 years younger than that of females. In addition to the gender imbalance and laws banning marriages with whites or slaves, there was a color bias that made it hard for a darker-skinned woman to marry. Two-thirds or more of free black Appalachians were identified in census manuscripts as "mulattoes" of varying degrees of light skin color. Regional county registers of free blacks provide details that shed light on the inability of free black women to marry. When the registers are computerized and alphabetized to permit reconstruction of kinship over time, two patterns emerge. First, free males of dark or brown skin color rarely renewed their registrations. When I cross-checked the names of dark-skinned men against county tax lists, I found that the vast majority of them disappeared from the county within a year. Moreover, fewer than one-third of the register entries were for individuals who were not connected to families. Unaffiliated individuals rarely renewed their permits to stay, and adult males were overrepresented among this group of isolates.[22]

Obviously, white Appalachians were not uniformly hostile toward all free blacks, and they operated out of a complex racial etiquette that intertwined many factors other than color, race, and gender. It is highly likely, however, that local officials and elites made it very difficult for darker families to persist over time. This ideological disparity created legal loopholes in which a few free black families persisted over time to a degree that most African-American families could not. Using Appalachian county registers of free blacks, we can examine how the complexities of class, race, color, and gender converged to create small degrees of "racial privilege" for a tiny minority of mulatto families. While a majority of Augusta County free blacks lost numerous family members who were undocumented and vulnerable to destructive legal actions, a handful of very light-skinned mulatto families remained intact over several generations. Three-quarters of the 706 register entries identified members of only 41 mulatto

---

[22] Examination of family patterns in Registers of Free Blacks for Kanawha and Washington Counties, VSL, and Augusta County (Bushman 1989). I have been unable to locate county registers of free blacks for Appalachian counties outside Virginia and West Virginia.

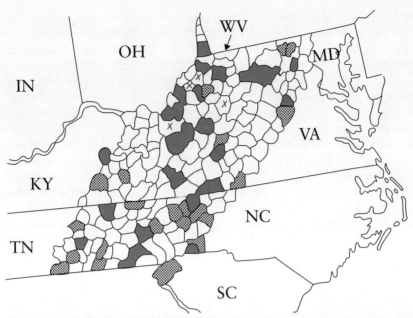

MAP 10. The Gender Imbalance among Adult Free Black Appalachians, 1860

☐ 104 to 120 females per 100 males

▨ 122 to 144 females per 100 males

■ 150 or more females per 100 males

☒ No free blacks in this county

Source: Calculated using Appalachian county statistics in U.S. Census Office (1863).
The Appalachian counties of Alabama and Georgia do not appear because their free
black populations were minuscule.

and color-mixed families. Nineteen mulatto families monopolized one-third of
the entries so that their kinship ties and legal rights to stay in the county were
formally acknowledged over several generations. These few mulatto families
averaged 12 adult members in 1860 and an extended kinship network that
represented three to five generations back to the late 1700s or early 1800s
when their family lineage was initiated through the liberation of a mulatto
slave.[23] Unlike the majority of black Appalachians who were severed from their
parents, grandparents, and siblings through slave trading (Dunaway 2003a, 53–
62), these few households enjoyed the *white* racial privileges of *knowing* their
kin, of living with them in the same dwellings, and of constructing a shared
family history over several generations. Moreover, their status provided them
a "respectable reputation" that set them apart from free blacks who did not
enjoy their color-class position. In addition to this public advantage and to
preferential treatment by county courts, the males in these families were more

[23] Examination of family patterns in Bushman (1989).

FIGURE 19. This Reconstruction sketch of an ethnically mixed family demonstrates the sexual exploitation of enslaved women by white males. While a majority of enslaved and free black families were disrupted or removed from local communities, a tiny percentage of families who were as light-skinned as these children enjoyed close linkages to white elites and experienced the longest family persistence of all African-Americans in Appalachian communities. *Source: Harper's Weekly* (30 Jan. 1864).

literate and far more likely to practice a skilled trade than either poor whites or other free blacks.

Close ties to affluent white ancestry provided them public legitimacy that most free blacks did not enjoy. While that link to whiteness did not afford them any legal right to inherit property from the white patriarchal line, their racial identities were intertwined with the family histories of powerful local elites who felt obliged to provide them a cloak of community tolerance and non-intervention. One elderly informant in east Tennessee termed such liberated mulattoes "family retainers," to signify that they "retained" the white family's history as part of their own, at the same time that the white family carried the history of these black members of their families – even though they never publicly acknowledged them. In short, there was a shifting essence to "whiteness" and "blackness." Just as sexual and public misconduct caused affluent whites to question the "white racial purity" of impoverished Caucasians, a mulatto whose behavior reflected "whiteness" might be more respected in a local community than a landless, uneducated white male. In many court cases, a mulatto was defined to be a racially mixed individual who could be easily recognized "not solely by color, kinky hair, or slight admixture of negro blood ... but by reputation, by his reception into society, and by the exercise of certain privileges" that were not available to slaves or to darker free blacks (ASC Records, ADA, Thurman vs. State 1850).

Structural Interference into Slave Families

Southern novels (e.g., Randolph 1852) and slaveholder letters constructed a paternalistic mystique that claimed that owners very rarely separated slave families. Public affirmations by Appalachian slaveholders that "we only do what's best for our people" were *ideological camouflage* to shroud their oppressive practices with decency and morality. However, these cultural myths are called into question in the face of Appalachian slave recollections and of census data. In order to maximize labor productivity and slave-trading profits, most Appalachian masters sold, moved, and relocated slaves in reaction to economic pressures (Dunaway 2003a, 38–50). Thomas Jefferson's pragmatism with respect to slave family separations was typical of the attitudes of Appalachian masters. Because he was "endeavoring to purchase young & able negro men," Jefferson sold an older slave away from his family. He rationalized that while he was "always willing to indulge connections seriously formed by those people," he could only protect slave families "where it c[ould] be done reasonably" (Betts 1953, 21).

Regional slaveholders constructed "an ideological framework of oppressive humiliation" (Wallerstein 1983, 102) in which slaves were defined as weaker beings who did not cherish family bonds as whites did. Despite their own family ideals, Appalachian masters and mistresses constructed an ethnocentric ideology grounded in the assumptions that slaves did not desire permanent marriages, did not establish strong emotional ties to their children, or did not value extended kinship networks. In addition, the disadvantages to disrupted families were denied since the slave's "strongest affection" was purported to be "love of his master, his guide, protector, friend," not ties to black kin (Eastman 1852, 213–15). Like their southern counterparts, Appalachian masters dispassionately rationalized that any family disruption could be ameliorated by the slave's quick remarriage or pregnancy (Van Evrie 1853, 230–43). Perhaps most of the region's slaveholders shared the condescending ideology of the Appalachian mistress who assessed "darkey" marriages as "comical, mirthful and hilarious," not family connections to be respected (Sterret Memoir, IAT, 3). Given such dehumanizing and racist ideologies, we should not be surprised that the primary structural mechanism by which Appalachian slaveholders directly controlled the reproductive process was through their interference into slave marriages (see Table 49, Web site). In every instance reported in the Appalachian slave narratives, "the slaves were allowed to marry but were compelled to first obtain permission from the master" (Rawick 1972, 4: 80). Three-quarters were married "by de marster's word," usually in an informal ceremony in which the master had them step over a broomstick. Only about one-tenth of the Appalachian masters permitted their slaves to have religious services, and even fewer owners made any legal record of the marriages. One of every eight enjoyed no ceremony at all, like a Jackson County, North Carolina, slave who reported that "when a man wanted a woman, he went and axed the marster for her and took her on. That is about all there was to it" (Rawick 1972, 11:167).

Appalachian slaveholders had good reason to avoid church weddings and to keep slave marriages informal. So long as black unions failed to meet the marriage criteria of white religious and civil authorities, Appalachian masters could dissolve the kinship bonds of their slaves without moral or legal sanction. If masters extended to slave marriages the "sanctity" of the church and the legitimacy of public recording, they would throw into question their racist ideology that blacks did not construct families that were the moral and cultural equivalent of their white owners' families. Slave marriages were economically important to Appalachian masters, so few of them granted their slaves total independence in such crucial matters. Thus, many Appalachian masters took an active role in marriages that went far beyond granting permission to willing spouses. In fact, Appalachian masters strongly influenced about one-third of the spouse selection decisions and unilaterally matched spouses in about 1 of every 13 marriages. Coosa, Alabama, slave Penny Thompson remembered that "mos' times masters and misses would jus' pick out some man fo' a woman an' say: "Dis yo' man, an' say to the man 'Dis yo' woman.' Didn't make no difference what they want. Then they read some from the Bible to 'em an' say 'Now you is husban' an' wife'" (Rawick 1979, 9: 3873). In about 1 of every 21 marriages, the overseers matched up slaves arbitrarily. When Martha Showvely was age 13, her overseer tried to arrange her marriage to an older male she had never met. "I said yes," she recalled, "den after I got home, I got scared." Within a few months, however, she succumbed to her owner's pressure, and she delivered three children by the time she was 20 (*Weevils* 1976, 265).

While espousing fierce loyalty to their own kinship networks, Appalachian masters destroyed black families in great numbers. In order to maximize profits from their investments, the region's slaveholders routinely removed slaves through forced labor migrations. Using racial stereotypes to justify their ruthless actions, Appalachian owners terminated two of every five of the marriages among their slaves (see Table 47, Web site). When Appalachian masters emigrated, sold slaves, "gifted" slaves to their children, or hired out laborers, they disrupted one of every four slave marriages. In their disruption of slave families, Appalachian masters replicated national trends, for small slaveholders broke up families much more frequently than large plantations (Crawford 1992, 346). While smallholdings with fewer than 16 slaves contained 43 percent of the slave population in 1850, they accounted for nearly two-thirds of all slaves living in divided residences and for more than 60 percent of the slave children in one-parent residences (Fogel 1989, 179, 183). In addition to 15 percent of family disruptions caused by abroad marriages (spouses with different owners), Appalachian plantations threatened the persistence of slave families through five types of forced labor migration. Sales of slaves accounted for nearly

FIGURE 20. Through several forced labor migration strategies, Appalachian masters structured the absence of adult males from slave households. This father has been sold away from wife and children. After emancipation, almost none of the spouses separated by such interstate sales were able to reunite. *Source:* Library of Congress.

three-fifths of family disruptions while 16 percent of family separations resulted from long-term hireouts. The rest of the permanent disruptions were caused by laborer assignments to owners' distant work sites, gifts to children, and owner migrations.

Of the 205 Appalachian masters described in the Works Progress Administration (WPA) narratives as selling slaves, more than one-third of them disunited husbands and wives (see Table 9). Thus, Appalachian slaves were more likely to be sold away from their spouses than were their Lower South counterparts.[24] "So 'tis dat de womens have fust one, an' den tudder man," to apply the words of a middle Tennessee ex-slave (Rawick 1979, 5: 1791). In reality, most separated slave families permanently lost contact with their kin because their masters removed them too far away for contact to be maintained. "Don't worry you can get another one," a Laurel County, Kentucky, master quipped to a man

[24] Estimates of the proportion of all southern slave sales that caused spouse separations range from 13 to 23 percent (Fogel and Engerman 1974, 1: 48–52; Tadman 1989, 300).

TABLE 9. *Structure of Enslaved and Free Black Appalachian Families*

Household Residential Pattern	Slave	Free Black
Solitaire (1 person)	6.2	——
Decomposed nonnuclear (usually composed of adult siblings and/or other adult kin and nonkin)	3.3	14.6
Extended family	4.7	22.8
Married couple	8.5	6.2
Married couple with children	20.0	29.4
Single female with children	55.4	29.4
Single male with children	1.9	6.2

Sources and notes: Slave household composition was derived from analysis of 217 slave narratives and of slave lists in the manuscript collections of 52 Appalachian slaveholders. Free black household composition was derived from analysis of 1,690 entries in Registers of Free Blacks for Virginia Counties of Augusta and Washington and the West Virginia County of Kanawha. A *decomposed* unit was one in which adults who had lost parents, spouses, and/or children resided together; most of these households combined kin and nonkin adults.

whose wife had just been sold (Coleman Papers, UKY, Slave Interviews, 38). When mother and children migrated west with the wife's master, Ben Chambers "ain't never seed" his father "no mo' " (Rawick 1979, 1: 94). Appalachian slaves also lost contact with kin when they were given away to their masters' distant children. When the son of a northern Georgia master opened a frontier plantation in Florida, he selected the most valuable laborers and artisans, without any attention to preserving their kinship ties (Brown Papers, UNC, 26 Jan. 1853). In the 1820s, the Carr family (Papers, UVA, 5 Jan. 1822) separated several slave families by exporting them to different parts of the Lower South. A Staunton, Virginia, father "was trafficked away from his woman and children to another state" (Weld 1800, 179). Maggie Stenhouse and her two children never saw her husband again after he was sold (Rawick 1972, 10: 222). An Amherst Virginian soothed his conscience that he had not sought a higher price by separating a female slave from her young children. However, the slaveholder was not troubled that he had severed wife and offspring from an abandoned father (Wright Papers, UVA, 10 Nov. 1847).

Abroad marital relationships were particularly vulnerable to separations. One Appalachian slave recalled that his "uncle wuz married but he wuz owned by one master and his wife wuz owned by another." When the husband returned for one of his visits, "his wife had been bought by the speculator and he never did know where she wuz" (Rawick 1977, 5: 298). When he was arranging the separation of one married couple, the Buffalo Forge operator contrived to have a slave trader pick them up simultaneously. While the husband was to be hired out locally, the speculator assured the master that "if you wish your woman to go out of the country I will send her off" (Weaver Papers, DU, 27 June 1859). Similarly, a Winchester, Virginia, mistress wrote in her diary of the manner in which the owner ripped apart the family of the slave she was leasing.

In her diary, Mrs. McDonald recorded, "He does not tell her there is a negro trader coming for her." A week later, "Poor L. [w]as gone," leaving behind her husband and a child (McDonald 1992, 82–84).

Even when owners applauded themselves for preserving family units, they rarely sold fathers with their spouses and children. For instance, a western North Carolina slaveholder advertised his intent to market an "entire" family consisting of "a woman 27 years old, five children and another hourly expected...all one man's children" (Lenoir Papers, UNC, 4 Nov. 1847). The fate of the father is never mentioned when western Carolina planter Nicholas Woodfin smugly commended a neighbor who had "very properly directed that a woman and her four children be sold together" (Swain Papers, NCDAH, 21 Aug. 1843). A Franklin County, Tennessee, slave remembered that his mother had to remarry several times, "because they would carry her husband off to one state or another" ("Unwritten History," FUA, 141). When slaves were sold on the Rome, Georgia, auction block to settle an estate, numerous families "never seed their fo'ks after they was sold at the 'dividement' of the property" (Rawick 1979, 9: 3639). Maria Perkins wrote to alert her "abroad" husband that their family would be broken up if he could not find a way to prevent it. "My master has sold albert to a trader on Monday court day," she wrote in alarm, "and myself and other child is for sale also....I am quite heartsick" (Rose 1976, 151).

Most of the Appalachian slave narratives describe trading incidents. To justify their exploitation, slaveholders constructed an "ideological inversion of reality" that placed the blame for the actions of the masters upon the victims (Tadman 1989, 217). According to the mystique, "The negro and negress, with new partners and another marriage [we]re quite as happy as if they had never been separated" (Van Evrie 1853, 242–43). Appalachian masters may have comforted themselves with such self-righteous mythology, but the auction block and traveling speculators loomed like ever-present shadows over black Appalachians. Impending family separation was the underlying reason that Appalachian slaves verbalized most frequently for physical attacks on their masters or for running away. Southwest Virginia slaves originated a hymn entitled "Massa's Gwyne Sell Us Termorrer" to document the annual "shippin' the slaves to sell 'em" that occurred between Christmas and early January (*Weevils* 1976, 277). Jim Threat remembered that his Talladega, Alabama, kin "lived in constant fear that they would be sold away from their families." Maggie Pinkard of Coffee County, Tennessee, describes the recurrent trauma most poignantly: "When the slaves got a feeling there was going to be an auction, they would pray. The night before the sale they would pray in their cabins. You could hear the hum of voices in all the cabins down the row" (Rawick 1977, 12: 335, 257).

Owners structured the absence of fathers from two of every five slave households (see Table 46, Web site). Legally, offspring were the property of the mother's master, and fathers retained no legitimate right to maintain linkages with their children. Since either owner could terminate family visits, "abroad" fathers must constantly renegotiate this fragile privilege. When they were hired out or assigned to distant work sites, fathers maintained contact with their families at the will and whim of their masters. Ben Chambers recalled that his father belonged to another "plantation what ain' fur away." Like other abroad spouses, Chambers's father had to "git a pass eb'ry time he want[ed] to come see" his family (Rawick 1979, 3: 669). In one other important way, masters structured the absence of males from the lives of their offspring, for slave children were rarely disciplined by their fathers. Instead, the owner's family and overseers were the individuals who administered verbal or physical discipline to them most often. Consequently, less than 7 percent of the Appalachian ex-slaves perceived their fathers to be positive authority figures.[25]

Mothers and children were expected to retain their masters' names, further obscuring the identity of fathers. Very few Appalachian ex-slaves were able to maintain permanent surnames that reflected the identities of their biological fathers. Because "it was the custom for slaves to take the name of the man what owned them," almost all of the Appalachian ex-slaves had been identified with multiple surnames "from having different masters." As a result, spouses usually did not utilize the same names. For instance, Fannie Tippins's married grandparents had different surnames throughout slavery, even though they were part of an extended family. Joe Wooten was one of the few black Appalachians who was able to have "a long life name." Joe took his father's name, refused to change it when he was sold, and accepted whatever punishment the new master meted out for his disobedience (Rawick 1972, 19: 42; Rawick 1979, 9: 3878; "Unwritten History," FUA, 94; Rawick 1977, 4: 658).

The legal homes of slave fathers were their assigned *work sites* while their families lived in the *mothers' cabins*. As one Blue Ridge Virginia father expressed it, "De wife house was often eight or ten miles from de home house, and we would go there Saturday night expectin' to see de wife we had left" (*Pennsylvania Freedmen's Bulletin*, March 1867). The political and economic paradoxes of fatherhood were embodied in this legal and cultural definition of where the center of the family lay. In more than one-half of the Appalachian narratives, ex-slaves defined *family* in terms of the "mother's house." After a slave marriage or after the announced pregnancy of an unwed woman, Appalachian masters "fix[ed] up a house for de wife. He want[ed] to be sho' dere's a nice snug house and yard to take care of all de chillen" (Rawick 1979, 3: 672), that "natural increase" from which surplus laborers could be marketed. Appalachia's abroad wives "faced the challenge of rearing their children and addressing their families' needs without the daily attention or resources of their husbands or the fathers of their children" (Stevenson 1996, 179). Moreover, enslaved females who lived on small holdings most often grew up and later bore their own children in matrifocal households in which there was no stable male presence on a daily basis. As a result, Appalachian enslavement stripped men of legal and

---

[25] Slave child discipline estimated using 93 incidents from the Appalachian slave narratives.

social fatherhood and of their opportunities to participate in the maintenance of family households.

Conclusion

Separate spheres gender conventions idealized affluent nuclear families in which women had servants and could avoid the kinds of stigmatized labor outside their households that put them in regular contact with males who were not members of their own class and race. At the same time, elite gender conventions dehumanized and marginalized as "barbaric" or "savage" any family construct that appeared to

- give females too much economic or sexual autonomy;
- require women, rather than husbands, to be "breadwinners";
- challenge patrilineage for child identities and property transmission;
- be too poor to support itself and not become a public burden;
- be either racially mixed or prone to interactions across racial lines; and/or
- comprise racially inferior individuals.

As we have seen in previous chapters, nonwhite and many poor white families were structurally and functionally different in ways that violated affluent gender conventions. On the one hand, these "dangerous classes" developed alternative standards for acceptable behavior for women, and their family constructs were often too matrilineal or too matriarchal to keep them within the bounds of dominant gender conventions. On the other hand, the public income-earning labors of a majority of Appalachian women (as summarized in Tables 6 and 8) placed them outside the narrow constraints of separate spheres respectability. In addition, their diverse portfolios of household-based labors (see Table 10) challenged separate spheres gender conventions. For most of these women, the household was not a closed space in which they concentrated only on idealized reproductive roles. In reality, family survival and prosperity required them to merge motherhood duties with various forms of market-oriented and community service work in ways that "respectable ladies" did not.

When embodied with the authority of the state, the cult of domesticity caused structural contradictions and conflicts for

- nonwhite family constructs that diverged from the white patriarchal model,
- white female heads of household lacking the cultural and economic honor that derived from the presence of husbands,
- white women who crossed racial lines to form a family,
- poor white and free black families, and
- all enslaved families.

When we factor together the population statistics that these categories represent, what we discern is that a majority of Appalachian women – in fact, a majority of all southern women – were in family constructs that were at risk of public intervention or slaveholder disruption. It is not precise enough to argue

TABLE 10. *Nineteenth-Century Household Labors of Southern Appalachian Women: The Overlap of Productive and Reproductive Labors*

Type of Labor	Unpaid Labor	Paid Labors		
		Nonwaged	Waged or Contract	Enterprise Owner
Household subsistence and maintenance	Household maintenance Care of ill and elderly		Whites or free blacks taking in boarders	
Reproductive and sexual labors	Sexual intercourse Childbirth and child care	Midwife Prostitute Slave concubine	Waged white or free black or enslaved hireout as domestic servant, wet nurse, or child-care nurse Hired or owned slave in brothel	White or free black house of prostitution
Agricultural labors	Family garden plot Dairy management Small livestock tending Fieldwork and outdoor farm tasks	Production of dairy products, eggs, feathers, small livestock, and garden produce for household subsistence and marketing Laborer on tenant or sharecropping parcel	White operator of tenant or sharecropping parcel	Farm or plantation owner
Nonagricultural labors	Craft production for household subsistence	Production of crafts for marketing, particularly textiles	Putting-out systems: producing crafts under contract with merchants or industries	Operator of inn or tavern in home Other small business operation out of home, such as seamstress
Other public labors	Charitable or church work Slave religion Cherokee clan duties or conjuring			

that family was "a white privilege" (Solinger 2005, 38), for there were class and ethnic differences that prevented impoverished Caucasian female-headed households from being respectable. In reality, only affluent white families were as "sacred" as separate spheres advocates claimed. All female-headed poor white and nonwhite households were legally and socially defined as unacceptable aberrations. Consequently, elite and middle-class white males could rationalize – with support from the women of their classes – that public intervention or slaveholder destruction of these households did not represent disruptions of "real families."

8

Motherhood as Privilege

Patriarchal Interventions into Women's Reproductive Labors

> Our matrons, our mistresses of families contribute more than all other causes put together, to form the national tastes, opinions, principles and morals.... Our children derive from them their first lessons in every thing. Should they be incapable of giving them to good purpose, all their pupils will probably become instruments of evil rather than good.
>
> (*Southern Literary Messenger* 1838, 640)

Antebellum publications, such as *Godey's Lady's Book*, fostered the notion that "the true woman's place was unquestionably by her own fireside – as daughter, sister, but most of all as wife and mother." Women must "never forget that *home* is the very *center* of her sphere" because the wife who strayed away from domesticity would lose "that almost magic power, which, in her proper sphere, she w[ould] wield over the destinies of the world" (Butler 1836, 38–59). According to John Abbott's (1833, 5) manual, "The mother is the guardian and guide of the early years of life, from her goes the most powerful influence in the formation of the character of man." Similarly the 1835 *Ladies Magazine and Literary Gazette* (8: 94) declared that women were "born to train the sons and daughters of men," so they must have a solid "Christian education."

On the surface, nineteenth-century southern clerics and commentators make it appear that women's reproductive capacities lay at the heart of southern definitions of *family* and *honor*. Motherhood was idealized as the pinnacle achievement and life's labor for white women. However, their reproductive contributions to society were made at high cost. Southern white women married younger and bore more children than northern Caucasian females. Two of every five southern white women bore eight or more children while the majority of northern females had fewer than six offspring. While most northern white women delayed marriage until after age 21, two-fifths of southern white females wed in their teens. One of every 50 U.S. deaths was a mother's demise during or soon after childbirth. However, the maternal mortality rate for a southern female was 1.3 times greater than this national trend. In addition to the health risks of pregnancy and high fertility, southern white women faced years of grieving because 40 to 60 percent of their children died before age 10 (Savitt 1978, 40). Even elite white women "faced years of unending childbearing and caretaking" (McMillen 1990, 39). The reproductive history of Elizabeth Perry (Autobiography, UNC, 174) was typical. Her elite position as the wife of an Appalachian South Carolina planter who held 20 slaves and assets valued at $54,460 did not shelter her from the risks of motherhood. In the first decade of her marriage, she was pregnant every year, and she endured four miscarriages, two stillbirths, and four live births. Of a total of 13 childbirths, only 7 of her offspring lived into their teen years.

Clearly, the reproductive risks faced by affluent females were antithetical to the patriarchal ideals that defined reproduction to be the core value of "true womanhood." However, this was not the only disjuncture between cult of domesticity rhetoric and institutionalized practices. The ideals of sexual "virtue and purity" were institutionalized into laws to protect females from sexual exploitation and rape, but the benefits of those regulations were denied to poor and nonwhite women. Caring for and guiding children into productive adulthood were hailed by antebellum commentators as the reasons for a woman's existence, but elite males institutionalized practices that disrupted child rearing by women of the "dangerous classes" of poor whites and nonwhites. Despite the outpouring of gendered rhetoric, the reproductive capacities of nineteenth-century women were neither equally valued nor equitably protected. Because of the inferior racial and class positions of poor white and nonwhite females, southern states and Appalachian communities discriminated against them in ways that were a stark contrast to the cult of true womanhood. In the sections that follow, I will examine

- women's differential legal protection from sexual exploitation,
- disruption of nonwhite and poor white mothering and child rearing, and
- the gendered consequences of structural conflicts between productive and reproductive labors.

Differential Legal Protection of Women from Sexual Exploitation

While southern gender conventions touted wedlock as the only respectable condition for white women, social sanctions were placed on certain types of marriages. Laws declared slaves incapable of "lawful matrimony," criminalized interracial unions, and made formal unions between free blacks and slaves impossible. Moreover, laws about sexual behavior were aimed inequitably at constraining those "dangerous classes" of women whose "degraded" racial heritage and "base" work lives frequently led them to violate moral norms about cross-racial relationships. In addition to these racial constraints on women's sexual autonomy, a gender bifurcation is evident in southern laws about sexual exploitation. On the one hand, the legal rhetoric focuses on shielding the honor, virtue, and sexual purity of affluent white women who embraced cult of domesticity norms – thereby institutionalizing racial and class criteria that effectively excluded all poor white and nonwhite females from being defined as possible victims. On the other hand, these laws were grounded in fundamental *racialized gender privileging*. While white females could be prosecuted for violations of public restrictions on cross-racial liaisons, white males were never defined as perpetrators. Moreover, it was not legally possible for a nonwhite female to be sexually exploited by a white male. According to Thomas Morris (1996, 23–45), "Most whites who suffered for consensual interracial sexual relationships were women and their children." Because official history producers sought to conceal the sexual aggressions of men, I have found it nearly impossible to locate public documents in which the voices of poor white, free black, or Cherokee women describe sexual exploitation. Hidden in obscure, racist, sexist sources, however, are powerful clues that these groups of women were exploited to a far greater extent than manuscripts or public documents would lead us to believe.

Sexual Exploitation of Cherokee, Free Black, and Poor White Women

In the late 1700s, Euroamericans claimed that "all Cherokee women are public women in the full meaning of the phrase: dollars never fail to melt their hearts" (Becker 1977, 72). This stereotype was first applied in reaction to the independent trading of Cherokee women at colonial forts. Even though they continued to reside with their families, some of these females became enmeshed in informal unions with white soldiers. When there were food shortages, the women fulfilled their traditional wifely roles and carried provisions to males they defined to be their "husbands" (DeVorsey 1971, 102–4). During frontier conflicts, many of these women defied orders from town chiefs and continued to visit their mates at the forts, often providing them with advance warnings about Cherokee battle plans (Palmer 1875–93, 434–37). While these women may have been behaving in the same ways they normally acted with Indian husbands (Williams 1927, 89–90), it is highly unlikely that any but a tiny few of the white males viewed them as anything other than temporary sexual liaisons outside the bounds of respectable matrimony. Indeed, there were no formalized marriages between these men and women. White missionaries claimed that Cherokee women brought such sexual exploitation on themselves because they were often outside the confines of their homes. Thus, they depicted "respectable" Cherokee males as "those who "ke[pt] their women & children at home & in comfortable circumstances," away from situations in which they interacted autonomously with white males (ABCFM Papers, HUL, 25 July 1818).

White traders must have engaged in repeated instances of sexual abuse of indigenous women, but the British rarely made historical note of such complaints. On occasion, British trade records include a passing mention of a village complaint of a sexual assault that was "resolved" by offering bribes to Cherokee males. In 1756, for example, a white trader's packhorse man got a Cherokee woman drunk in the village of Keowee and "used her ill" (McDowell 1958–72,

231), the kind of assault that must have been reported numerous times without any official punishment leveled against offending males. Missionaries blamed whites for degrading Cherokee girls sexually, but they attempted to constrain such relationships by expelling female Indian church members for engaging in such cross-racial "criminal intercourse" (Payne Papers, NLC, 9: 81–83). In sharp contrast to rumors about Indian assaults on Caucasian women, rapes by whites occurred so frequently that the presence of male strangers in Cherokee villages was "in the highest degree alarming" to indigenous females (Mooney 1900, 209). An unusual missionary account provides us a fleeting reminder of the kind of white sexual exploitation that must have occurred routinely when British soldiers or American militiamen entered Cherokee communities. In the 1830s, six soldiers sexually assaulted two women at their home. "The women stood by a tree," the missionary recounted, "and the soldiers with a bottle of liquor were endeavoring to entice them to drink." Because her husband was "absent," the soldiers "caught [the married female], dragged her about, and at length, either through fear, or otherwise, induced her to drink; and then seduced her away, so that she is now an outcast among her relatives" (ABCFM Papers, HUL, 28 July 1826, 29 Mar. 1827, 19 Aug. 1829). Inherent in this report are four gender and racial biases of which we should take note. First, the writer blamed the attack ultimately on absent husbands, who were away to hunt and not at home to protect their wives. Second, the writer never directly states that the soldiers *raped* the women, and he implies that the women would not have "submitted" if they had not "decided" to imbibe alcohol. Third, the writer selectively excludes important facts from the women's perspective, at the same time that he employs rhetoric that shifts much of the blame away from the white attackers. Fourth, the assault on the unmarried female is silenced entirely, no doubt reflecting white stereotypes that single Indian women were "too public" in their affections.

In a rare instance in which we can hear female fear of sexual exploitation, a group of Cherokee women reported to a northern journalist that white men who entered their communities "ha[d] employed every art to raise and shorten [thei]r petticoats" and had left them "more wretched" (Mitchill 1818, 360). In the public records of Indian agents, we can also spot hints that white sexual exploitation occurred often. Benjamin Hawkins, U.S. agent to the Cherokees and Creeks, was convinced that poor whites formed linkages with indigenous women only as a means to acquire land and to earn livelihoods that they could not otherwise attain. As an example of such ruthless men, he described a Mr. Marshall, who "ha[d] resided twelve years in [Cherokee] towns, and ha[d] two Indian wives." Despite that, Marshall never interacted with the rest of the community, "saying that during the whole of his residence he had not entered 3 of the Indian houses." Hawkins claimed that northern Georgia and northern Alabama whites "who had Indian families took no care of them, neither to educate them or to teach them anything useful." Furthermore, Indian women "were always the slaves of the house and the fathers making money by any and every means in their power, however roguish, and using the children and the relations of the family as aids" (Weeks 1916, 54). In an 1838 petition to the National Council, Cherokee women expressed concern about the influence that white husbands would have in the decision-making process to cede lands to the U.S. government. The women complained that white males with Indian spouses were "only concerned how to increase their riches" and were not concerned with the living conditions "of their own wives and children" (Jensen 1981, 29). In recognition of such sexual exploitation by low-income whites, the Cherokee National Council prohibited disposal of a Cherokee wife's property by a white husband (Perdue 1998, 154). White sexual exploitation did not end after the forced removal in 1838. In a pattern that was more often documented in the postbellum South, a Cherokee woman "wandered from farm to farm" in 1850s southeast Tennessee, "and her and her children only got to work on the land when she let the man have his way" (oral history collected by author).

It is no easier to document the extent to which poor white and free black females were sexually exploited. While historical inclusion of information about their sexual exploitation is rare, poor white and free black prostitution received far more comment in antebellum primary sources. It is doubtful that prostitution was anything but an act of economic desperation for most of these women, who headed households with several racially mixed children and were among the poorest families. Despite the elitist ideology of domesticity, southern prostitution enjoyed its greatest period of openness and social tolerance between 1820 and 1870 (Walkowitz 1980, 43–46). The physical destructiveness of prostitution was minimized since it was viewed as an inevitable and useful outlet for "natural" male passions. Moreover, public perceptions were that prostitution was "immeasurably better than begging" because it was "honest work" that prevented these women from becoming burdens to the community (*New York Daily Times*, 22 Jan. 1853). Nearly 2 percent of white Appalachian women and more than 10 percent of free black women acquired income from prostitution, judging from the way in which they were described in census manuscripts (see Table 4). Advertisements for "gentlemen's houses of entertainment" appeared frequently in the region's antebellum newspapers (e.g., *Tennessee Gazette*, 15 Feb. 1804). "For the sole purpose of drinking and pandering to the lustful passions," reported one resident, strolling women worked the crowds that gathered on county court days (McClary 1960, 103). As her family traveled in southwest Virginia, a shocked young female traveler sighted "out in the public porch" of a tavern near Natural Bridge "the girls and the whiskers" (Buni 1969, 98).

Small brothels operated openly near the region's railroad depots and extractive industries. For example, northern Georgia's Etowah Mining and Manufacturing was a large company town that boasted its own bordello staffed by white and black women (Jackson 1989, 13). Free and enslaved prostitutes worked in the numerous saloons and gambling halls of gold mining boom towns (Green 1935, 222). In Fannin County, Georgia, the 1860 census enumerator listed "Lady of Pleasure" as the occupations of the two young Green sisters. With only $10 between them, the two prostitutes lived in a rented town house in order to service copper mine workers. As he traveled through the Appalachian South, Olmsted (1860, 508) observed candidly that "there must always be women among the lower classes of whites, so poor that their favors can be purchased by slaves." Western Carolina's Mary Yeargin was one such unmarried, landless female. In 1850, the county court required her to pay "a $100 bond against any assemblage of negroes at her house or her premises." Since she was probably unable to pay, Mary would have been ordered to the poor house, where her labor would have been auctioned to pay her fine (Bolton 1994, 48). So long as they served only white males, white women were rarely prosecuted for prostitution by towns and courts. When white prostitutes crossed racial lines, however, they legally committed "fornication," behavior that was criminalized for females but not for white males. When they were tried in court for infractions, white prostitutes were fined or jailed while free black prostitutes were typically whipped (Rothman 2003, 93–96, 110).

We also find indirect evidence of male sexual exploitation in divorce actions. Some women sought divorces on the grounds that their husbands were sexually brutal. Nancy Turner and Hannah Barr filed divorce petitions, claiming their husbands beat and raped them when drunk, even when they were pregnant (Stevenson 1996, 108–9). Civil War veterans also candidly mentioned sexual exploitation of their white and free black mothers. Like slave women, John Hank's unwed mother of seven was vulnerable to the sexual exploitation of landlords. Her son recalled that "the man that was said to be my father had negro property and never did anything for me." The cottage-tenant mother of another veteran bore seven illegitimate children by her landlords, some of whom "had negroes and property," but still "never did any thing" to help their poor white offspring (Dyer and Moore 1985, 996). The private correspondence of a western North Carolina upper-class teenager (Clark Papers, DU, 6 Aug. 1831) substantiates the pattern described by these two impoverished sons. After describing how he had become preoccupied with thoughts about sexual intercourse, this young man confided in a letter to a male friend his assault upon one of the poor white females who worked on his father's plantation. When he encountered a lone girl going to plow, "I was upon her before she knew it," he bragged, going on to pinpoint that she "had titties as big as your fist, as round as a butter ball and would have weighed a pound." Two entries in a county register of free blacks demonstrate how local courts applied a patriarchal double standard with respect to cross-racial sexual behavior. In these two instances, the court clerk rejects the daughter of a white woman who crossed racial lines, but he legitimates the offspring of an elite white male who exploited an enslaved female. Because she was "born free of a white woman in the County of Page," Lucinda and her four light-skinned offspring were undesirable and "not permitted . . . to remain" in Augusta County. Even if the clerk stereotyped Lucinda as sexually promiscuous, he was not consistent in rejecting mulatto females on this ground. Two entries below Lucinda's request is the registration of five-month-old Louisa Sheffey, described as "brighter than [her] mother," young mulatto slave Sophia Edwards. The new infant had just been emancipated by her owner, Hugh Sheffey, while Sophia remained in bondage (Bushman 1989, 80, 135).

Differential Protection under Southern Rape Laws

There were only 250 antebellum rape cases tried by courts in all the southern states, and only 11 of these cases were brought by females in upper- or middle-class households.[1] Even though so few affluent Appalachian women reported sexual assaults, many of them were preoccupied with fears of black strangers' assaulting them in their homes. In Augusta County, Virginia (Legislative Papers, VSL, 22 Dec. 1831 petition), for instance, a group of middle-class nonslaveholding wives petitioned the state to abolish slavery because they "kn[e]w not...the night, or the unguarded moment...which [would be] pregnant with [thei]r destruction." Rape laws focused upon African-American men as the most likely sexual predators while denying that nonwhite females could be victims of such assaults by white males. Every southern state legally defined rape to be an act that only could happen to a white female; thus, no white male could be prosecuted for raping a nonwhite female. Moreover, there were very few court cases involving attacks by free black males on free black women (Morris 1996, 304–6). In Wythe County, the color differences probably contributed to a jury's conviction of dark-skinned Henry Robinson for raping mulatto Mary Wilson (Brown 1996, 209).

The legal rule of thumb was that rape was a charge that could not be applied to slaves because the "intercourse" of these females was "promiscuous." Furthermore, an attack by a male slave on a female slave was nothing more than "mere assault and battery." Laws clearly specified that a black rape of a black woman "would not be punished with death" because it was "the white race of the victim that gave to the offense its enormity." An account in the slave narratives makes clear the vulnerability of enslaved females, who were not protected by rape statutes. To reproduce as many slaves as possible for export, Julia Brown's northern Georgia master encouraged forms of sexual exploitation that the slaves found unbearable, but they had no legal recourse to stop his extreme violations of white gender conventions. According to Julia, the slave community expected black males to adhere to taboos against incest, even when it was encouraged by masters. When one father impregnated his young daughter, the wife and her neighbors in the slave quarters demanded that the owner remove the male, or they would "kill him in the night" (Rawick 1972, 12: 142). Despite the lack of protection of enslaved females, it was a capital offense for a black male to rape or to attempt to rape "any white woman" or to have "carnal connexion with any white female child." Most states legally treated cross-racial advances and physical assaults on women as though they were rapes, so a high proportion of all cases were aborted confrontations or verbal offenses that did

---

[1] Four of those charges were lodged by women whose husbands were middle-class operators of small plantations in West Virginia and Appalachian Virginia (Sommerville 1995, 484, 494, 514n93).

not involve physical contact (Morris 1996, 304–7, 310, 320). While the vast majority of rape charges were brought by poor white women, conviction of white assailants was rare. When the alleged rapist was a white man, the court typically assumed female consent and attacked the character of the victim. Furthermore, court sentences for white males were far more lenient than those imposed on men of color (Brown 1996, 210). For instance, white tradesman Moyles Reiley was convicted in western Maryland because he "had abus'd Elizabeth Piper . . . in her own house . . . during the absence of her Husband." Yet his only punishment was that he must pay the court "Bond and Security . . . that he shall behave quietly and peaceably for the future" ("Proceedings" 1918, 237).

Strangely, enslaved black Appalachian males accounted for more than one-third of the rape convictions recorded in Alabama and Virginia.[2] Since they did not represent this proportion of the slave populations in those states, why would this have been the case? Compared to male slaves on large Lower South plantations, black Appalachians were more likely to be hired out on long-term contracts to distant employers; and they were leased more frequently than their female counterparts (Dunaway 2003a, 38–41). Consequently, black "men on the road" were likely to be viewed as "dangerous strangers" outside their home communities. In addition to the added risks of traveling without white supervision, enslaved and free black males interacted more often with white women, especially with poor female laborers with whom they shared workplaces (Dunaway 2003b, 140–47). Because of these two factors, black Appalachian males were more likely to be charged with "rape" for behaviors that were neither sexual nor criminal in orientation. Any act of verbal insolence or physical contact with white females might be labeled rape because of the amplified fears of the general public. Using profane language, asking a white woman for sex, urinating in public, or following too near a white woman could trigger rape charges. For example, Milly Holly charged a northern South Carolina slave with rape because he put his hand on her shoulder "very lightly" and asked her to "give [him] a little." Similarly, an east Tennessee woman charged a black man with rape after he grabbed her "by the back of the neck." In both cases, the women screamed, and the males fled (Morris 1996, 315–18).

Even though black Appalachians appear disproportionately in rape cases, they were neither consistently found guilty nor sentenced to capital punishment. In the previously mentioned cases, neither black male was convicted of rape. In the east Tennessee case, the court ruled that there was no attempt to rape because the male had made no attempt "to ravish her." In the South Carolina case, the court ruled that there was only an "assault on a white woman," for which the male was administered 500 lashes and sold out of the district. In Greene County, Virginia, the slave Jack was executed after a rape charge was

---

[2] Rape convictions calculated from PPC Files, ADA, 1821–53; from 158 death penalties in Johnston (1970, 257–59); and from slave condemnations in Virginia Executive Papers, VSL, Letters Received, 1750–1835.

lodged by impoverished Elizabeth Wright, a weaver who had one child and was "in a state of pregnancy," even though she "ha[d] never been married" (Morris 1996, 305). If rape statutes were intended to protect the honor and security of white women, why did courts fail to send clear signals that *all* cross-racial aggression by nonwhite males would receive extreme punishment? The complex explanations for this seemingly contradictory stance lay in

- sexist biases about rape,
- the economic value of slaves, and
- the inferior class of the female victims.

Courts took into account seven discretionary factors that were not mandated by the rigid laws. First, the victim must bring her charge immediately, for her lack of instantaneous "voluntary outburst" was evidence of consent. The male view of the "normal" reaction of a female to rape was that "a forcible violation of her person so outrages the female instinct, that a woman, not only will make an outcry for aid at the time, but will instantly and involuntarily . . . seek some one to whom she can make known the injury and give vent to her feelings." Second, juries were reluctant to determine that a rape had occurred unless there had been vaginal penetration in which the male had ejaculated. In one case, the illiterate female did not understand questions that were intended to determine whether the assailant had "entered her body," so the prosecutor addressed a query to her that was far beyond the limits of the gender conventions that he would have observed if the victim had been affluent. "In plain English," he shouted, "did he fuck you?" (Morris 1996, 317–20). Juries gave more weight to a charge when there was a credible witness, and they considered women to have given consent if they did not show active and extended resistance. For a jury to convict an attacker for rape, the victim or witnesses must provide evidence that the assailant's intent was sexual intercourse. There could be no rape unless the assailant used force or unless the victim resisted and screamed vigorously. Judges and juries also operated out of the myth that a woman could not become pregnant "if an absolute rape were to be perpetrated" (Sommerville 1995, 506n70).

The second explanation for disparate court reactions lay in the class position of the alleged victims. Most charges were brought by poor white women or girls, and a high proportion of them were illiterate (Sommerville 1995). It was common practice for prosecutors, judges, and juries to place heavy weight on the class and community reputation of the female who brought the charges. One North Carolina judge stressed that "the inference of [the male's] intent . . . is to be drawn from the character of the young woman whom he assaulted, and from the respective social conditions of the parties." In instances of rape charges against black males, full protection of the law "was reserved for white women of some social standing whose reputations were what Southern white men believed they ought to be. If a woman fell below these standards, her charges of sexual abuse by slaves might be disbelieved or the defendant might receive a fairly modest punishment" (Morris 1996, 321). Thus, there was no racial solidarity among whites in Appalachian courtrooms. Instead, affluent whites often spoke as character witnesses for the black male and assailed the morals and past sexual history of the poor female.

In 11 northern South Carolina cases over a 34-year period, almost all the complaints were made by illiterate women. In a majority of these cases, the testimony of these lower-class women was simply not sufficient to convict, so the slaves were whipped and released (Sommerville 1995, 502–4). When 11-year-old Rosanna Green charged a Wythe County slave with rape, his owner and a number of his affluent friends claimed that the youngster had a jaded reputation because she had "behaved badly with a black boy in the neighborhood." Even though the slave was convicted, the owner used his political ties to pressure the court to recommend leniency (Virginia Executive Papers, VSL, 1–20 June 1829). In order to protect their financial interests, owners sought to prevent execution of their convicted slaves. One strategy was to influence the governor to have the bondsmen "transported out of state" because an interstate sale would provide greater recompense than the fee paid by the state for an executed slave (Morris 1996, 505n48). Another slaveholder strategy was to seek clemency from the governor through political contacts and letters from affluent acquaintances. After the court found a black male guilty of raping Pleasant Cole, the slaveholder and his friends began a letter writing campaign to the governor to try to secure clemency for the slave. Working-class petitioners responded with concern that this black male was a danger to the community, especially to "females in the humble walks of life, who have not thrown around them the protection of wealth and influential friends." No doubt, the public outcry against inequitable application of the law along class lines led the governor to carry out the death sentence (Legislative Papers, VSL, Leesburg Petition, 1 July 1831). When free black Tasco Thompson was tried for raping a Frederick County, Virginia (FCSCO Book, VSL, 208, 210, 224), girl, the defense assaulted the "exceedingly disreputable character" of the white family in order to convince the jury to recommend "leniency" rather than the death penalty. The attorney made the case to the jury that the mother had caused the black male's attack upon her daughter by "acting colored." It was "disreputable," he insisted, that the mother had past associations with blacks. When the foreman delivered the jury's verdict, he commented that this low-income white family "yielded their claims to the protection of the law by their voluntary associations with those whom the law distinguishes as their inferiors." The *Richmond Daily Dispatch* (27 Apr. 1854) decried the rape charge against a respectable free mulatto because it was brought by a Shenandoah Valley white woman who associated with some of the "lowest and most debased free negroes." During the trial of an enslaved male for the rape of Elizabeth Smith, the defense attorney tried to have the charge dismissed because the victim was a female of "simple mind" and "weak character" (Virginia Executive Papers, VSL, 18 Oct. 1833). In short, white elites "were animated by notions of class and gender that permitted them to hold poor white women and girls in such low regard that they would ally with African-American men against white female accusers" (Sommerville 1995, 515–16).

It is important to stress two points about the class and racial contradictions inherent in rape cases. First, the court records are so shrouded in Victorian prudery that it is impossible to distinguish the cases that involved actual rapes or attempted rapes. What is clear, however, is that a high percentage of the cases were grounded in verbal or nonphysical violations of racialized gender conventions by black males. When they lodged rape charges for violations of racial etiquette, some poor complainants acted upon social ideologies that caused them to believe that courts would act in solidarity with them because they were white. In other words, they acted upon the *rhetoric of honor* that shielded affluent white women. However, courts never extended the respect and courtesy that the poor females believed they were guaranteed by elite gender conventions. In other words, these females expected the legal system to make literal interpretations of statutes that outlawed cross-racial sexual liaisons. But judges, prosecutors, and jurors reacted out of class, gender, and economic biases that limited the degree to which courts were willing to protect the "white honor" of "unrespectable" lower-class women. Second, there was never a declaration of "innocence" for the man of color. Accused black males almost always received severe forms of punishment, even when the charges and evidence were weak. A nonthreatening touch on the arm or shoulder or a verbal sexual innuendo resulted in a brutal whipping or sale out of the area, separating forever the male from his family.

Sexual and Reproductive Exploitation of Appalachian Slave Women

The Appalachian women who experienced the most severe degree of sexual exploitation were slaves. Once the international slave trade closed in 1808, the United States "no longer had an external arena to bear the bulk of the cost of slave breeding" (Wallerstein 1976, 1209). Of all the slave societies in the New World, only the United States reproduced a large internal slave population (Genovese 1974, 5). Between 1790 and the Civil War, African-American families were scarred by the forced migration of nearly one million slaves from nine Upper South states to six Lower South and Southwest states (Fogel 1989, 65). According to Tadman (1989, 122), the Upper South operated like a "stock-raising system" from which "a proportion of the natural increase of its slaves was regularly sold off." Slaveholders generated large numbers of Upper South human exports by exploiting the reproductive capacities of women. Consequently, Appalachian masters trapped their slaves in a vicious circle of frequent family breakups, structural pressures for mothers to remarry, and the economic reality that women must be fertile to prevent their own sale. To maximize the reproduction of surplus laborers for export, Appalachian masters systematically promoted high slave fertility rates through structural interference in the lives of slave families and women. The sexual autonomy of Appalachian slave women was threatened by three patterns of systematic reproductive exploitation:

- sexual exploitation by white males,
- owners' structural interference into pregnancy and childbirth practices, and
- owners' structural pressures toward high fertility.

FIGURE 21. To produce surplus laborers for export to the Lower South, Appalachian slaveholders engaged in reproductive exploitation in several forms. In addition to pressures toward high fertility and high infant mortality caused by premature weaning, mothers endured the horrors of having one of every three of their children sold away before age 15, as this family separation illustrates. *Source:* Library of Congress.

Nearly 15 percent of the Appalachian narratives describe acts of white sexual exploitation of enslaved women, and most of those instances involved acts of male force or physical violence. Moreover, 1 in 10 Appalachian slave families was headed by a woman whose children were the outcome of her sexual exploitation by white males (see Table 47, Web site). For instance, John Finnelly knew his father was one of the white males on their plantation, but his mother would never identify him. "I don't know him," John said, "'cause Mammy never talk[ed] 'bout him 'cept to say 'he am here.'" Most Appalachian masters did not force their attentions at random upon women in the quarters. Instead, selected women were taken to the "big house" and set up as cook, maid, or nurse in a room or cabin within easy reach of the exploiter. For instance, Loudoun County planter George Carter purchased teenage slave girls for sexual pleasure (Stevenson 1996, 239). About 5 percent of the slave narratives describe slaveholders who structured more long-term arrangements with enslaved women. When his sons married, one middle Tennessee master would give them "a woman for a cook, and she would have children right in the house by him, and his wife would have children too." Some white parents tolerated their sons' exploitation of house slaves, and, subsequently, they "would heartlessly sell [their] own offspring." Fearful that their sons would break community moral codes by "ruining the reputations" of the white girls they courted, some slaveholding women selected "good-looking" servants and "closed their eyes" to their sons' sexual exploitation and impregnation of enslaved teenagers. One owner taught his young son how to exploit enslaved females. Both males raped a teenage slave girl – "the father showing the son what it was all about." In another instance, the black bride "was her young marster's woman and he let her marry because he could get her anyhow." One slave explained that women endured such exploitation because "they had a horror of going to Mississippi and they would do anything to keep from it." Some owners kept slave mistresses throughout their entire lives, such as elderly emancipated "Aunt Millie" of middle Tennessee. As a young servant, she lived alone in "a home off from the [master's] house" and bore a son by the slaveholder. Among Appalachian masters, Thomas Jefferson engineered the most famous of these concubinage relationships with Salley Hemings (Blassingame 1977, 475–87). Even though his mother had a black husband, Noah Perry recalled that the elderly father of the master "always kept a claim on mother and us kids. He had a little house near the big house and when he was visiting . . . mother kept house for him. He usually stayed about six months and we'd get to live at the little house all that time." When he left, the family would "go back" to the slave quarters (Rawick 1972, 4: 35, 16: 31, 12: 239; "Unwritten History," FUA, 1–2, 8, 55–56; *Weevils* 1976, 300–301).

The second form of systematic reproductive exploitation was owner interference into pregnancy and childbirth. Masters denied to enslaved women the prenatal care they afforded to their own wives in the way of nutrients and rest, for owners assigned black women to work during pregnancy that they considered to be too taxing for their own wives and daughters when they were not pregnant. Antebellum planter manuals advised owners that pregnant women "must be treated with great tenderness, worked near home & lightly. Pregnant women should not plough or lift, but must be kept at moderate work" (McMillen 1990, 39–42). Even when masters espoused a "lighter" workload, their schedule of moderate work and shortened work hours was still too arduous. Southern doctors recommended that affluent pregnant women limit their physical exertion to activities no more strenuous than those conducted "in carriage," and elite women took regular afternoon naps (Smith 1997, 119–20). Because of the widespread medical myth that poor and nonwhite females "go through their pregnancy with little or no trouble" (Newell 1908, 535), owners structured work regimens that kept pregnant slave women at work right up until delivery. On average, an enslaved female was removed from fieldwork only about 20 days throughout her entire pregnancy, and there were few instances in which pregnant women were released from work assignments for extended periods. There was probably no letup in the pace of work during the first two trimesters, very little relief in the third trimester, and they continued to work at about three-quarters of their normal workload (Campbell 1984, 800–801, 811).

One Appalachian physician considered anything more than four days a month lost work time extravagant for pregnant slave women (Payne 1853, 204). Some babies "was born on a straw-pile in the fiel'" on Jordon Smith's plantation because his northern Georgia master made women stack hay late in their pregnancies. One middle Tennessee cotton planter kept pregnant women working so late in their pregnancies that they often had a "miscarriage right there in the field." George Jackson was born in "de weavin' room" because his pregnant mother was required to finish her nightly quota of back-breaking textiles production (Rawick 1979, 9: 3640; Rawick 1972, 19: 215, 16: 45). Hard work severely restricted the amount of weight gained by pregnant women because Appalachian masters provided little or no nutritional supplementation to compensate for physical labor. As a result of overwork and malnutrition of pregnant women, the black infant mortality rate was high (Gaspar and Hine 1996, 145), and more than half of black babies and children died before age five (Fogel, Galantine, and Manning 1992, 321). On Appalachian plantations, infant and child mortality rates were much higher than these southern averages (Dunaway 2003a, 141–45).

Appalachian masters followed birthing practices that were common throughout the U.S. South (Campbell 1984, 807; Fogel 1989, 28). For affluent women, antebellum medical guides recommended four to eight days of postpartum bed rest, no walking for two weeks, and no outdoor activity for three to four weeks after delivery (Meigs 1848, 315). In contrast, enslaved women were expected to be walking outdoors by the fifth day after delivery (Ewell 1817, 125). Within two to three weeks, slave women returned to their work schedules (Warrington 1853, 176), spending less than half as much time in their "lay-in" as their white slaveholding women enjoyed (Stevenson 1996, 104, 250).[3] Solicitous toward their own wives, Appalachian masters described postpartum slave women as malingerers (Rawick 1972, 1: 425–26, 3: 498, 796, 4: 75–76). At the Oxford Iron Works, women were viewed as "lazy" if they did not quickly return to their production duties (Ross Letterbook, VHS, 9 Jan. 1813). One Blue Ridge Virginia master complained that his female slaves would "hardly earn their salt" after childbirth. If a female resisted returning to the fields before she had physically recovered from childbirth, he dismissed her physical weakness, claiming that "she lays up till she feels like taking the air again, and *plays the lady* at your expense" (Olmsted 1860, 190). In addition to their early return to work, postpartum slave women were endangered by extended malnutrition. Already anemic and weakened from inadequate nutrient intake during pregnancy, more than half of all lactating Appalachian mothers did not receive the additional 500 to 1,000 calories needed daily to support breastfeeding.[4]

On average, U.S. enslaved males experienced a slightly higher mortality rate than females, and only 2 percent of all U.S. slave mothers died in childbirth or shortly after (Steckel 1985). However, the death rates for Appalachian slave women were 1.5 times higher than those national trends and 1.8 times higher than the risks faced by local white females. Black Appalachian women also died

---

[3] In similar fashion, poor white female waged laborers returned to work a few days after delivery (Falkner 1990, 4–6, 51).

[4] For greater detail about malnutrition on Appalachian plantations, see Dunaway (2003a, 100–113, 145–49).

nearly twice as often as the white males who so frequently exploited them sexually. In sharp contrast to national trends, 107 Appalachian slave women died to every 100 enslaved males. Only black children younger than 10 died more frequently than did Appalachia's childbearing slave women. Prior to their teens, enslaved females survived at higher rates than boys, but the situation reversed itself for Appalachian female slaves after they reached menarche. Malnutrition, pressures toward early and frequent childbearing, and overwork during pregnancy and after delivery increased the incidence of maternal mortality. However, higher mortality rates are also associated with pregnancy intervals of two years or less, the trend that typified the reproductive careers of Appalachian slave women (Stevenson 1996, Dunaway 2003a). As a result of hard work and malnutrition during pregnancy, 7.5 percent of the mothers of the Appalachian ex-slaves died during delivery or from physical complications caused by childbirth – a maternal mortality rate that was nearly four times higher than the national average.[5] Even when they survived pregnancy and childbirth, slave women were seriously weakened by their contradictory roles as productive workers and reproductive laborers. After giving birth to a four-pound baby, one 16-year-old slave mother "heard the doctor say [she] could not survive till morning." After several weeks, the woman finally "was able to leave [her] bed," but she "was a mere wreck of [her] former self. For a year there was scarcely a day when [she] was free from chills and fever," and her infant stayed weak and "sickly" (Jacobs 1861, 60–61).[6]

Appalachian slaveholders also pressured enslaved women toward higher fertility. One demographic measure of greater slave fertility is an assessment of the degree to which slaves too young for efficient labor were disproportionately represented in the population. Where agricultural laborers were in greatest demand, plantations were reproducing less than one slave child for every adult (Engerman and Genovese 1975, 181). In contrast, Appalachian slaveholders owned 1.3 to 1.4 times more children than adults. Appalachian owners ensured such high fertility by pressuring enslaved females to begin to bear children in their teens. In sharp contrast to national trends, three-quarters of the black Appalachian mothers endured their first pregnancy before the age of 19, and Appalachian slave women averaged only 17.2 years when they delivered their first baby. For example, Delia Garlic had "one baby in her arms, another in [her] pocket," before she was 21 (Rawick 1977, 1: 153). Moreover, the region's enslaved women averaged less than two years between their pregnancies. Appalachian reproduction strategies are startling when compared with fertility averages for other populations. For the U.S. South as a whole, the average age of enslaved women at the birth of their first child was about 21, and these mothers were spacing more than two years between pregnancies

---

[5] Slave mortality rates were calculated from U.S. Census Office (1855, 191–93, 249–51, 255–57, 259–61, 285–87, 289–91).
[6] For other examples, see Rawick (1972, 7: 138, 10: 100, 12: 136, 274, 16: 77), Rawick (1977, 1: 144, 8: 1221), Rawick (1979, 3: 914).

(Trussell and Steckel 1978, 504). Nearly 60 percent of the Appalachian mothers produced more live births than was typical of the reproductive history of U.S. slave women. In fact, nearly one-half the mothers averaged 13.2 offspring over the span of their childbearing years, compared to a national average of 9.2 live births. More than half of all Appalachian slave women endured more pregnancies and bore more children than other U.S. slave women. More than one-third of the women bore 15 or more children, and another one-quarter experienced 10 to 14 live births.[7]

Paradoxically, the high mortality rate of Appalachian slave children (Dunaway 2003a, 141–49) spurred increased fertility, a pattern that parallels contemporary population trends in parts of Africa and Asia (Mies and Shiva 2001, 277–95). When the first child died before age one, four-fifths of the Appalachian slave women were pregnant again within less than two years. The child mortality rate escalated during the historical period when the marketability of teen and adult slaves was rising. After 1800, infant and child mortality rates rose steadily on Appalachian plantations, in exactly the same historical era when the number of slave exports to the Lower South was peaking. As the market demand for slaves escalated, women's reproductive rates increased, as did the mortality rates among slave children (Stevenson 1996, 245–48). It is not coincidental that Appalachian slave women began to reproduce at younger ages or that they shortened the waiting periods between pregnancies. Far from being natural or the result of women's unilateral decisions, such high fertility was imposed on Appalachian slave women, to no less degree than frequent pregnancies were inflicted upon the wives of slaveholding males (Steckel 1985, 100–101). The rising mortality rate spurred significant declines in the mothers' average age at first birth and in the amount of time women spaced between live births. Consequently, the number of children born to slave women increased over time, as a result of earlier ages at first birth and shorter average spacing between pregnancies.

To offset the dampening economic effect of a high child mortality rate on their slave exports, Appalachian masters *externalized* to enslaved women the responsibility for producing adequate numbers of surviving children. While reeling under the emotional strains of childhood deaths in their own families, Appalachian masters burdened their enslaved women with repeated incidents of emotional and psychological distress associated with the loss and removal of their offspring. By blaming mothers, Appalachian masters denied the causative roles of malnutrition and overwork in the ill health or deaths of slave children. Because black women experienced a higher incidence of miscarriages than whites (Savitt 1978, 119), owners often accused expectant mothers of destroying the fetuses (e.g., Ross Letterbook, VHS, 9 Jan. 1813). If infants died prematurely of sudden infant death syndrome (Scholten 1985, 44–47), owners often indicted the mothers for murder (e.g., Hubard Papers, UVA, 15 Dec. 1841). When a new infant died "sometime in the night" on one Appalachian

---

[7] Reproduction patterns derived from analysis of Appalachian slave narratives.

plantation, the master reported in his journal that Matilda had "over laid" a baby that "was well and hearty when she went to bed." When her newborn died under similar circumstances, Marietta was found guilty of infanticide by the Loudoun County court and ordered deported to the Lower South (*Loudoun Democratic Mirror*, 11 Nov. 1858). By bestializing the mother in these ways, the master received community legitimation for his structural interference in slave reproduction. By violating the only areas of possible reproductive autonomy enjoyed by the enslaved mother, the owner cemented his structural dominance over the slave family.

Disruption of Nonwhite and Poor White Mothering and Child Rearing

In addition to being denied legal protection from sexual exploitation, poor white and nonwhite Appalachian women were not afforded the privileges of motherhood promised by separate spheres ideologies. While these gender conventions placed the affluent mother on a mythologized pedestal, enslaved women were dehumanized as biological producers of future black laborers. Similarly, poor white and free black women were stigmatized as unfit to rear offspring. Heavily influenced by intellectual fads in biological determinism (Spencer 1851), elite and middle-class clerics and parenting commentators were convinced that character weaknesses were imparted through the mother's milk by women who were morally and intellectually inferior as a result of their poverty or their inferior race (Scholten 1985, 61–63). Throughout the ante-bellum period, slaveholders and court systems systematically removed children from "dangerous class" females. Such interventions were certainly not humane, for the intent was to capture child laborers for affluent economic agendas. Consequently, the right to engage in the labors of mothering and child rearing was socially and legally restricted by the race, class, and marital status of the female parent.

Missionary Assaults on Cherokee Child Rearing

After the Revolutionary War, Indian agents and missionaries made it their goal to rescue "the savages from the filth of the smoky hut, from the naked and untamed state of the heathen, and from the idols of the pagan world" (ABCFM Papers, HUL, 24 Nov. 1824). Drawing their ideals from the cult of domesticity, missionaries and Indian agents considered Cherokee parents unfit because they reared children in nonpatriarchal households in which the mothers were "considered as having a right to the children in preference to the fathers." Because fathers "did not support or have the command of children" (Brainerd Journal, HUL, 20 Oct. 1818, 2 Feb. 1820, 9 Aug. 1818), Cherokee youngsters suffered from "want of parental government" (Gallatin 1822, 107). In short, parents did not function in "a family capacity" (Payne Papers, NLC, 8: 1, 20, 41). In addition, missionaries focused on the irresponsibility of indigenous mothers who were not setting the example of Christian piety for their children (Paine Notebooks, HUL, 2: 20 Dec. 1820). Rather than nurturing infants within the protected spheres of their homes, Cherokee women breastfed their babies publicly while working in clan groups (Royall 1830, 112–14). In the eyes of white civilizers, such child rearing methods were simply "not compatible with a more advanced state of civilization" (Gallatin 1822, 108).

Missionaries were convinced that "children should be removed as much as possible from the society of the natives," so they advocated training away from parents as "the best & perhaps the only way to civilize and Christianize" them (CM Papers, MA, 23 July 1809). Mission churches established strict rules against traditional feasts, divorce customs, "heathen" dress, and doctoring "after the wild Indian manner," and they preached that Cherokee "Language, Customs, Manner of Thinking, etc. should be forgotten." The schools sought to cleanse their students of every aspect of "savage life" by requiring them to adopt Anglo names, the English language, and "the etiquette of the table."[8] The missionary priority was to "raise the female character in the Nation" by teaching mothers and daughters domestic arts and appropriate sexual behavior. The second most important missionary goal was to train girls for the vocations of farmer's wife or teacher of "poor children who c[ould] not come to the Missionaries schools" (ABCFM Papers, HUL, 28 Jan. 1816, 21 Aug. 1824, 17 Oct. 1824, 9 Feb. 1825, 11 Aug. 1825, 19 Oct. 1827). The traditional autonomy of females (McLoughlin 1984b, 44) was particularly shocking to missionaries, who were convinced that the "heathenish sexual promiscuity" of Cherokee mothers prevented them from building moral character in their offspring. According to one account, "The intercourse between the young of both sexes was shamefully loose. Boys & girls in their teens would strip & go into bathe, or play ball together naked. They would also use the most disgustingly shameful language, without the least sense of shame." To overcome "the failures of their parents to raise moral youth," the missionaries created gender-segregated schools that interfered with the traditional right of young women to dominate mate selection and courtship. In an effort to constrain the "freedom" of cross-gender interaction between the sexes that had characterized their "savage" lives, missionaries taught boys and girls in separate buildings and locked bedroom doors at night (Brainerd Journal, HUL, 29 Oct. 1819, 14 Oct. 1821, 21 May 1822, 3 Aug. 1823). One female missionary attempted to convince Cherokee girls that they and their mothers behaved "like fallen women." No doubt with Victorian prudery, she "set a bad woman before them in the most horrid light [of which she] was capable." Appalled by the "looseness of manners prevalent" among Cherokee mothers and the "wearing of a profusion of ornaments in [their] ears," missionaries required Cherokee students to alter their dress and learn "proper hygiene and decorum" (Payne Papers, NLC, 8: 49). With respect to neat feminine appearance, one female missionary found Cherokee girls to be "in a deplorable situation," so she instructed them "how the young ladies of the North were taught to govern their manners and temper"

---

[8] According to Brainerd Journal (HUL, 28 Feb. 1823), one child was renamed *Boston Recorder*, after the church newspaper.

and to pay close "attention to personal appearance" (Paine Notebooks, HUL, 2: 20 Dec. 1820, 25 June 1824).

As a result of these sexist policies, mothers primarily sent boys to the schools while they kept their daughters at home in order to socialize them in the matrilineal rights of women. Even mestizo mothers frequently removed their daughters from school when missionaries began to proselytize white marriage and courtship customs. In one such instance, the missionary lamented, "We were very sorry to part with this child and have her taken back to the regions of darkness perhaps never to see the light." The missionaries complained that mothers "indulge[d] their children" too much when they complained about school rules (Brainerd Journal, HUL, 22 Mar. 1828, 28 Feb. 1823). "It is very painful to us," wrote a Moravian missionary, "that the children are taken from us often when they are just beginning" to be acculturated (CM Papers, MA, 28 Dec. 1806). In violation of school rules, children ran away or their mestizo mothers appeared to take their children to forbidden ceremonies. The two playgrounds near the Brainerd Mission enticed students into the "evil of ballplay," so "the welfare of the school" required extreme punishment or expulsion of transgressors. The children themselves engaged in civil disobedience when missionaries demeaned Cherokee customs, especially those associated with the Green Corn Ceremony (Brainerd Journal, HUL, 22 Nov. 1818, 15 Mar. 1830). A Moravian missionary recorded that student attendance at the Green Corn Dance "doesn't sit well with us, but we don't know how to prevent it" (CM Papers, MA, 22 Apr. 1806). In one instance, a missionary attempted to serve a group of students "green beans before they had their dance. Several immediately remonstrated, accusing him of great wickedness. He labored in vain to convince them of their error. As he and one of his old neighbors sat down to eat, the others all refused to partake, and left" (Brainerd Journal, HUL, 5 and 7 July 1820).

Because of missionary assaults on Cherokee family and gender conventions, offspring with white lineage were vastly overrepresented in schools. Indeed, the missionaries "fix[ed] their marks entirely beyond the reach of all the common Indians" to cater to the well-to-do mestizo families (ABCFM Papers, HUL, 4 Aug. 1824, 27 Mar. 1826). Most mothers socialized their children to ignore the white sexist assumption that manual labor was inappropriate for females. Young girls mirrored the resistance of their mothers by running away from schools where teachers indoctrinated them with the message that they must not continue the "uncivilized" work in which their mothers engaged (Payne Papers, NLC, 8: 51, 1). Little wonder that missionary teachers "[we]re complained of very much by the young people ... under their care for Education" (Brainerd Journal, HUL, 19 June 1818, 29 Dec. 1820, 2 June 1820). Most Cherokee women resented the racism that teachers showed toward traditional students. In addition to the language barrier, mothers were worried that several laws expanded missionary control over Cherokee schoolchildren, including the right of the missions to indenture apprentices for 7 to 12 years to nearby whites. The Brainerd mission (Journal, HUL, 26 June and 1 Nov. 1820) effected a method for ensuring dependable "apprentices to the blacksmith business" because the

National Council "gave it as their decided opinion that the boys should be bound to [the missionaries] for a certain time," instructing town chiefs that it was their responsibility to "see that they were not taken away within that time" (*Laws* 1852, 94). Because most Cherokee women saw the missionaries as threats to the preservation of traditional culture, they sent only a tiny percentage of their children to the church-sponsored schools. Moreover, the matrilineal clans repeatedly demanded the closure of missionary schools after 1822 (McLoughlin 1984b, 215–17, 180–238, 337).

Public Intervention into Poor White and Free Black Mothering

Like Cherokee mothers, poor white and free black women were stigmatized as unfit to rear offspring who could make positive contributions to society. Drawing from intellectuals who popularized biological determinism (Spencer 1851), elite and middle-class clerics and commentators were convinced that poor white and free black females were reproducing a "dangerous class" of workers, whose subculture was a potential threat to patriarchal gender conventions and to the rigid legal boundaries between the races. Because of the higher incidence of female heads of impoverished households, free black and poor white women lacked the protection of respectable males and worked at all sorts of manual labor outside their homes, often employed alongside male slaves. Because their income-earning activities required them to travel alone, these women were viewed as sexually promiscuous. Moreover, they lacked the economic resources and the social capital to meet the "moral mother" ideal. Affluent whites argued that impoverished white and free black women were inadequately prepared for motherhood because they lacked education, a form of social capital that was systematically denied them by prosperous whites who resisted taxation to support free public schools (Dunaway 2003b, 41–47). "If a mother have no education," an 1828 issue of *Ladies Magazine and Literary Gazette* (1: 24) warned, "her children will inherit her deficiencies of character and will prove either incumbrances or positive evils to the community." Even though separate spheres advocates idealized mothers who could instill "Christian education" in their offspring, a majority of southern women were illiterate. Indeed, women older than 21 were twice as likely to be unable to read and write as males of the same age cohort. There were very few free schools, and only girls between the ages of 6 and 13 attended them when they were available (U.S. Census Office 1841, 123). Like other southern free females, a majority of Appalachian poor white and free black women were illiterate (Dunaway 1996, 292). While traveling in western North Carolina, an educator reported: "Female education is verry much neglected. I am not of the opinion that more than one half can either read or Write, a much less proportion can do both" (Newsome 1929, 309). Similarly, a northern Georgia teacher was convinced that "the great expense that attends an education in the Southern states has placed it as an impassable barrier between the rich and the poor" (Burke 1850, 197). Obviously, then, these classes of women could not rear the kind of "offspring of refinement and gentility" that separate spheres advocates claimed as the southern women's reason to exist (Stevenson 1996, 40). Such ideology, however, pushed a majority of southern women outside the perimeters of "moral motherhood."

Most poor unmarried free women exhibited a visible degree of reproductive autonomy and deviance from respectable motherhood that was not acceptable in southern patriarchal society. About one-fifth of all nineteenth-century pregnancies occurred among free mothers who were not married, and there was a widespread myth that poor and nonwhite females bore most of these illegitimate children. Even though the illegitimacy rate among the poorest 20 percent was 1.5 times greater than that of the richest 20 percent, the highest incidence of illegitimacy occurred in the middle class. While there was a lower illegitimacy rate among church members, more than one-quarter of church members engaged in premarital sex (Smith and Hindus 1975, 542–46). Clearly, the more affluent classes engaged in ideological camouflage to conceal the degree to which they strayed from elite gender conventions. Despite their violations of public fornication laws, affluent females escaped court intervention into their lives because most of them were able to attract respectable husbands (McMillen 1990, 39–40). Nineteenth-century manuscript records and the federal census make it clear that teenagers were considered adults at age 15, and poor youth were expected to work outside their familial households to provide supplementary income. While poor families required independence of girls at an early age, more affluent females stayed in their parental homes until their marriages between ages 19 and 22, most of them never earning income. Because teenaged poor white and free black females worked outside their family homes much more often than affluent girls, this public visibility caused them to be stereotyped as being much more prone to premarital pregnancies, illegitimate births, and cross-racial sexual liaisons.

It was the failure of poor white and free black women to meet hypocritical standards of *moral motherhood* that drew the greatest regulatory attention from the legal system. County and state regulations criminalized poverty, fornication, and bastardy and removed children from prosecuted women (Howington 1986, 68–70). Two-thirds of the county court cases of sexual misconduct involved a cross-racial liaison by a white female, and one-fifth of the cases involved activities with a male of the female's own race (Bynum 1992, 105–10). While prosecution of white males for black or Indian liaisons almost never occurred, one western North Carolina official reported in 1860 that cases were brought against poor white female heads of household for bearing illegitimate children at almost every session of the county court. "By no means," he emphasized, were their offspring "exclusively white. Mulattoes [we]re not a rare article" (Hedrick Papers, DU, 7 Apr. 1860 speech). However, many women were prosecuted by county courts without being charged with either sexual violation. In one of every seven cases, poverty itself was criminalized for female heads of household who could not provide for their offspring (Bolton 1994, 123). Statutes specified five instances in which county courts should prosecute free mothers and indenture their children:

- white females who bore offspring out of wedlock,
- women deemed to be "unfit mothers,"
- women raising "orphans" who were either deserted by or without financial support from fathers for one year,
- mothers who did not have "sufficient estate" to ensure the support and education of fatherless children, and
- free black mothers who did "not employ their time in some industrious, honest occupation" (Graham Papers, NCDAH, 20 July 1848).

It was easy for courts to remove children from female heads of household because "women had no legal rights of guardianship over their children unless specifically endowed with them by courts." Southern states defined an orphan to be a "fatherless" child whose male parent was absent as a result of death, abandonment, or "illegitimate" relations with the mother. While courts routinely granted affluent widows legal guardianship over their children, officials frowned upon leaving orphans with impoverished white and black mothers (Coryell et al. 2000, 142).

Southern poor relief was structured around *compulsory labor by paupers* and temporary shelter for the elderly or disabled. By 1860, about two-thirds of the Southern Appalachian counties operated poor houses; but the only inmates residing in these facilities were elderly, insane, and physically or mentally handicapped whites. Able-bodied women and their children were institutionalized only long enough to indenture them to long-term labor with local employers. After court intervention, three categories of women passed through poor houses and lost control of their children: unmarried mothers, widows impoverished by the deaths of spouses, and mothers too ill to continue to work and support their households. In the 1850s, more than two-fifths of the poor house inmates processed by court order were unmarried mothers while 30 percent were their children younger than 15. Two-thirds of these individuals were auctioned away from their families within six weeks (Katz 1986, 88–90).

Archival records make it clear that indenturement was a routine occurrence and that this exploitative form of child labor did not subside throughout the antebellum years (Crowther 1981, 37–49). For instance, the poor houses of Bradley County, Tennessee; Staunton, Virginia; and the West Virginia counties of Raleigh, Summers, Marshall, Harrison, and Brooke bound out 100 to 300 children every year.[9] In the early stages of local government formation,

---

[9] Derived from analysis of these manuscript poor house records: Bradley County, Tennessee, Poor Commission Records; Staunton, Virginia, Poor Records, FHC; Raleigh County Archives, Overseers of the Poor, 1850–54; Summers County Archives, Record of Poor Funds, 1859; Marshall County Archives, Record of the Overseer of the Poor, 1835–57; Harrison County Tax Book, Poor Funds, 1831–32; Brooke County Archives, Overseers of the Poor, 1861.

FIGURE 22. By exhibiting public behaviors on the streets of Chattanooga, Tennessee, that demonstrated the poverty of his family, this six- to eight-year-old white bottle peddler was risking removal from his mother and indenturement to long-term service. *Harper's Monthly* (August 1858).

Appalachian county courts set up procedures for handling destitute children and offspring of unfit mothers. Before Tennessee was formed as a separate state, for instance, the Washington County Court was indenturing "fatherless" children.[10] Indigent or illegitimate children of northern South Carolina were never permitted to become paupers dependent upon the public; rather, they were apprenticed until the age of 21 (Taylor 1942, 86). From 1831 to 1835, the poor wardens of Rutherford County, North Carolina, indentured more than 100 orphans annually. In one western North Carolina county, the sheriff even bound out young children after the mother was accused of "abusing & beating her children in a barbarous & inhuman manner" (Johnson 1937, 257, 690–96, 704). Statistical analysis of court indenturement in four Appalachian counties of Maryland, North Carolina, and Kentucky provides stunning details about the extent and nature of the apprenticeship process.[11] Between 1800 and 1860, four county court systems indentured 14,612 children, on average annually

[10] For example, the Washington County Court indentured a nine-year-old fatherless boy to work as a servant and wheelwright apprentice until the age of 21 (Sevier Papers, TSL, 18 Nov. 1794 indenture).

[11] Child indenturement patterns were analyzed using these manuscript records: Apprentice Bonds and Records, 1800–1860, for Buncombe and Burke Counties, North Carolina, NCDAH;

binding out 110 youngsters, whose average age was only 7.3 years. Males were typically bound out until age 21, females until age 18. Two-thirds of the indentured children were identified as free blacks or mulattoes while only one-third were described as white. About 12 percent of the children had been removed from white mothers simply because they were racially mixed. Even when indentured through orphan courts, a majority of the children appeared to have living mothers, and they were most often removed from women who were described as being too poor to provide for them. Thus, poverty was criminalized more frequently than the sexual misconduct of mothers. Except for orphans whose male parents had died, fathers were almost never mentioned.

Of the 701 free blacks registered between 1801 and 1864 in the courts of Augusta County and Staunton, Virginia, nearly one-fifth were children "bound out by the Overseers of the Poor." The Monroe County, West Virginia, court disposed of nearly two-thirds of its registered free blacks in this manner.[12] In 1860, 17 western North Carolina counties indentured 160 free black youngsters to long-term apprenticeships (Franklin 1943, 227). Southern ordinances mandated that "free issue bastards" (the racially mixed children of poor white women) were to be assigned to poor houses for apprenticeship until adulthood (Crowther 1981, 152). The mulatto offspring of white mothers were particularly vulnerable not only to indenturement, but also to enslavement. For instance, free born mulatto James Merrick was "taken in possession" and sold as a slave when his western Maryland employer died (Rose 1976, 134).

At least 15 percent of 1860 free laborers employed by farm owners had been indentured by county poor houses, two-thirds of them children (Dunaway 1996, 114). As the result of such policies, one Calhoun, Alabama, planter reported among his work force three child laborers who had been "bound out by the poor house." In Wayne and Magoffin Counties, Kentucky, farmers included among their labor force 8-year-old and 12-year-old children who had been "bound out by the poor house to work." In Greene, Monroe, and White Counties, Tennessee (1860 census manuscripts, NA), 28 free black children were bound out so that none of them worked for the same employer as their siblings or parents. Only about half of free black parents resided with their children, indicating that a high proportion of youngsters were working away from their families (see Table 7). Empirical analysis of a sample of free black households provides a revealing view of the public treatment of the children of these families.[13] A high proportion of the region's free African-American children lived away from their families in the households of employers, and a majority of them had been indentured by local poor houses into upper- and middle-class households.

Guardian's Bonds Books, 1852–59, Clay County, Kentucky, KDLA; Indentures through the Orphan Court for Frederick County, Maryland, MSA.

[12] Derived from analysis of Bushman (1989) and Monroe County Free Negro Register, WVU.

[13] Derived from analysis of a sample of free black households from the 1860 Census of Population manuscripts, NA ($n = 1,200$).

FIGURE 23. Because of limited employment opportunities and biases against such "dangerous class" mothers, free black washwomen, like these residents of Rome, Georgia, often headed households from which children were removed by courts and indentured to long-term service by county poor houses. *Source: Harper's Monthly* (June 1857).

Indenturement was not limited to older offspring, for three-quarters of the bound children were younger than 10.[14]

Children were not usually indentured because their mothers had behaved in publicly unacceptable ways. After abandonment or death of a husband, a

---

[14] To determine whether free black children were residing with their parents, I first located and computerized the information for every free black household in the 1860 Census of Population manuscripts, NA, for the counties of Knox, Tennessee; Buncombe, North Carolina; Wythe, Virginia; and Washington, Maryland. Then I located every free black individual who was residing in a white household. I cross-checked the surnames of these individuals against the household surnames and estimated whether these were children missing from parental households.

mother's poverty or illness made her children vulnerable to court interference. For example, Catherine Slim's free mother died during childbirth, so the infant was bound out by the poor house to a middle-class farm owner. By the age of 10, she was working alongside slaves in the fields (Rawick 1972, 16: 78, 10: 211). Because freedwoman Phebe Grinten was poor and ill, the Wilkes County, North Carolina, poor house indentured her five young children until they were 20 (Brown Papers, UNC, 8 May 1840). "NEGROES FOR SALE by virtue of an order from the Orphans' Court" was a frequent newspaper advertisement in western Maryland, where "fatherless children" could be bound out from infancy to age 21 (*Cambridge Chronicle*, 24 Jan. 1835). The poor house might indenture one or more children to work off the debts a free black mother owed to whites (Brown Papers, UNC, 3 Aug. 1836 Indenture). Widowhood could also end the mothering of a poor white or free black woman. After his father's death, the son of a McMinn County, Tennessee, tenant farmer was bound out "from the time [he] was nine yeares of age." A Coffee County, Tennessee, veteran reported that, from the age of eight, he "plowed every day" for farmers to whom he had been bound. William Harrad's father was killed in the Mexican War, followed by his mother's death when he was three months old. Subsequently, the orphan was indentured until adulthood by the McMinn County Poor House to a middle-class farm owner. "I was left in the hands of a slaveholder," Harrad lamented, "and sure Did see one hard time." In order to circumvent court interference and loss of contact with their children, some poor white and free black mothers *contractualized* the labor of their own offspring. Unmarried women with several children often apprenticed their sons for seven years or longer "to learn a trade" from some artisan or farmer. As early as the 1820s, upcountry South Carolina parents indentured their children to work on annual contracts in the cotton mills (Wallace 1961, 382). Virtually slaves, two free black children were bound out by their grandmother to work for their "vittils and clothes and schoolin'." John Hank was removed from his impoverished mother of seven and hired out by the county poor house at $2.00 a month, and he was still an indentured child laborer when he ran away to join the Confederate Army (Dyer and Moore 1985, 1705, 996–97, 1560, 64, 33).

Long-term indenturement severed familial bonds between mothers and offspring, especially when the children were racially mixed. While such court actions violated all the tenets of idealized motherhood, they served four societal functions. First, such legal actions prevented the cost of rearing indigent children from burdening taxpayers. Second, court prosecutions socially constrained "dangerous class" children by placing them under the control of elite and middle-class landowners, who regulated them through the same methods they employed to monitor slaves. Third, such cases reallocated the labor of thousands of children to middle-class merchants and to slaveholders. The courts showed little concern about removing the valuable labor of children from poor mothers, who would afterward have even fewer resources to battle impoverishment. Fourth, the courts removed racially mixed children from white mothers in order to eliminate social embarrassments that contradicted the social and legal definitions of racial separation. Moreover, slaveholders were convinced that poor white females were unable to impart to ethnically mixed offspring the kinds of domestic arts and social graces that made "mulatto" servants valuable. Despite its social control functions, court removal of free children stood in stark contrast to the ideals of southern family honor. More importantly, such criminalization of mothering and childhood destroyed families and created an unfavorable public identity for the affected youth.

Owner Interference into Mothering by Enslaved Women

In order to capture most extensively the labor of mothers and their offspring, Appalachian slaveholders routinely employed four strategies that prevented black women from nurturing their offspring according to the gender ideals followed by white slaveholding women:

- attentuation of breastfeeding, leading to high infant mortality
- assignment of mothers to labor that interfered with parent/child bonding and child care,
- early work socialization of children, and
- owner disciplining of children.

Even though slaveholding women comprehended that their infants were healthier and less likely to die when they breastfed them well past their first birthday (McMillen 1985, 339–40), masters shortened breastfeeding of infant slaves. In the guides and periodicals written for elite women, male experts (e.g., Gunn 1834, 66–78) recommended weaning of babies over a one- to two-week period when they were 8 to 12 months old. After about the sixth month, affluent mothers combined personal breastfeeding with bottled breast milk or supplements from a wet nurse. On average, elite mothers weaned infants a few weeks after their first birthday. In their diaries and letters, elite mothers recognized that early weaning endangered infant health, and they favored longer breastfeeding because lactation delayed conception (Mead and Wolfenstein 1955, 153–55). Most experts advised upper-class women not to establish rigid feeding schedules, but to permit the baby to establish its own routine of nursing (Sigourney 1838, 29). Judging from archival sources, Appalachian elite and middle-class women continued breastfeeding well beyond the weaning age recommended by doctors (Stevenson 1996, 98). Already walking when weaned, one middle-class white male reported that his mother "allowed [him] to use her breast very late" (*Janney's Virginia* 1978, 15). Another slaveholding mother wrote, "I have not weaned a boy that is large enough to talk of horse-racing, can make a fire, and feed calves" (Lenoir Papers, UNC, undated from Mrs. L. E. Lenoir).

Infants need to be fed on demand 10 or more times daily in the first nine months, and they should be fed nothing but breast milk during the first six months. At nine months, two solid meals should be supplemented by breastfeedings (Lawrence 1994, 186). To maximize their own profits and to capture the labor of women, however, Appalachian slaveholders "rationalized" breastfeed-ing in ways that interfered with all these natural processes and rhythms. Women returned to their work schedules within the first three weeks of birth, placing their infants on a limited feeding schedule. In contrast to child-initiated breast-feeding (Riordan and Auerbach 1993, 476–80), nearly one-half the Appalachian slave women were called from the fields only two to three times daily to nurse their infants. Another two-fifths of the women carried their infants with them to work, feeding them at prescribed intervals between their tasks. More than 8 percent of the slave mothers did not nurse their own infants during the work-day.[15]

Affluent women correctly intuited that the safest weaning procedure was one that gradually replaced one feeding at a time with solids (Lawrence 1994, 314). However, Appalachian masters denied to enslaved women the breastfeeding regimen that was customary among the women in their own households (e.g., Lenoir Papers, UNC, 13 June 1844). After the 1830s, elite women could use bottles and nipples to continue to supplement weaned infants with their own breast milk (Riordan and Auerbach 1993, 109–11). This was not an option available to slave women, so they were forced to rely on food supplements, often mixed with contaminated water. Supplementary foods were introduced to enslaved babies by the sixth month, even though such a young infant lacks the digestive enzymes needed to process solid foods, and its tongue cannot move food around in its mouth. To complicate matters, slave weaning was usually abrupt, leading to loss of appetite, deterred muscular development, and malnutrition in infants and to postpartum depression and breast infections in mothers. When slave infants began cutting teeth, mothers were expected to decrease breastfeeding considerably or to end it entirely. Yet it was at this stage of development that the highest incidence of infant mortality occurred (Falkner 1990, 182).

Appalachian masters engaged in another form of structural interference in slave women's reproductive roles. Wet nursing claimed the benefits of breast-feeding for the offspring of white masters while denying or limiting those health advantages to slave infants. While masters required early weaning of slave chil-dren, they employed black mothers to serve as wet nurses and caregivers for white offspring. At the same time that slave women were weaning their own infants early, one-fifth of them worked as wet nurses in white families. Georgia Flourney was a "nu' maid" throughout her reproductive years, and she breast-fed every "las' baby" of her female owner. Chaney Mack experienced two generations of ill effects from wet nursing. Although she was an underweight "seven-months baby," her mother weaned her early, introduced solid foods, and put her "on a terbacco pipe." When Chaney became a mother, she and her new baby were moved into the master's house so she could wet nurse the

---

[15] Slave breastfeeding patterns were derived from analysis of Appalachian slave narratives. Regard-ing high infant mortality rate due to early weaning, see Falkner (1990, 4–7) and Dunaway (2003a, 134–44).

owner's infant. The mothers of Fannie Tippin and Sarah Allen wet nursed their masters' children, leaving their own youngsters in the care of elderly slaves. Even though she was a field laborer, Anna Lee wet nursed the babies of her east Tennessee mistress. While she cooked meals for her own children, she would have the white baby "in one arm." Wet nursing often broke the health of slave women. Andrew Goodman's "maw wus a puny little woman" as a result of repeated, long-term wet nursing. While her own babies were "comin' 'long fast," another wet nurse tended her master's 10 children. As an elderly woman, she lamented that she "don't do nothin' all [her] days but nuss." She served as wet nurse to "so many chillen it done went and stunted [her] growth," causing her to become "nothin' but bones." At some point during their enslavement, two-thirds of Appalachian slave women were employed as caregivers to white children, requiring them to leave their own offspring without adequate food and supervision. Sarah Patterson watched all her own children die except one while she nurtured the master's children. When asked why she did this, she responded perceptively: "I was a woman. I wasn't no man" (Rawick 1977, 1: 144, 9: 1421–22; Rawick 1979, 2: 45, 9: 3879, 6: 2275; Rawick 1972, 4: 74, 107, 10: 287).

If they survived the high risks of infancy, young slave children encountered the second form of owner circumvention of mothering. Very few Appalachian masters organized centralized child care, but they required women to manage their offspring in a manner that did not interfere with their productive work assignments. Unstructured, informal child care amounted to little or no adult supervision for more than two-fifths of slave children. Even when centralized child care occurred, the competence of the providers was questioned by many Appalachian ex-slaves. Jim Threat criticized his master's practice of assigning "the old decrepit women" to tend "the babies and small children while the mothers worked." The elderly male at Pierce Cody's farm watched children from "a tall lookout on the roof." To tend children at Sarah Wilson's farm, her "mighty old" grandmother "set on the front porch all the time." Simon Hare and other children on his western Carolina farm played on their own all day; they would "waller around in de ditch like a old sow; get sleepy, go ter sleep right dare till old lady come rustle [them] up." Pressured to work away from infants and youngsters, parents developed their own child care strategies within the limited options available to them. More than one-third of the ex-slaves reported that their parents carried them to their work stations. However, nearly one-fifth of slave children were left alone during the workday, and another 15 percent were left to play with slightly older siblings. Noah Perry was left to his own devices while his mother "run the plow." On Stephen Varner's farm, the children "all stayed under a big oak tree," and "the marser would come around to see about them and give them milk" (Rawick 1977, 12: 335, 8: 913; Rawick 1972, 12: 196, 240, 7: 345–47, 1: 426; *Weevils* 1976, 81). During his youth, James Pennington felt like "a helpless human being thrown upon the world without the benefit of its natural guardians" (Bontemps 1969, 207–8).

FIGURE 24. A majority of enslaved Appalachian females, like this Page County, Virginia, woman, worked as caregivers to white children at some point in their lives. While weaning their own children early and leaving them with limited supervision in the quarters, wet nurses often broke their own health and were unable to nurture their own offspring. *Source:* Page (1897, 98).

Because of risks and dangers they encountered before the age of 10, many Appalachian ex-slaves recalled the lack of adult supervision cynically. As an infant, Mary Tate was "left alone" in her cradle at the family cabin while her mother was "about tasks on the plantation." The master "became annoyed at [her] crying and as punishment placed [her] in a fence corner" while it was snowing (Rawick 1977, 5: 212). Owners severely punished childhood mischief. Morris Hillyer was frequently flogged because he would "ride de calves, chase de pigs, kill de chickens, break up hen nests, and in fact do most everything [h]e hadn't ought to do" (Rawick 1977, 7: 138–39). While their mother worked in the big house, two middle Tennessee boys "was burning one another with

FIGURE 25. As a result of attenuated breastfeeding, malnutrition, and inadequate child care, one-half of all Appalachian slave children died before age 10. While their mothers worked in the fields or were hired out, some youngsters were tended by elderly slaves, like this Rockbridge County, Virginia, woman. However, 40 percent of Appalachian ex-slaves reported they had almost no adult supervision before age 10. *Source: Harper's Monthly* (March 1856).

broom sage, and [one] caught fire and went running and hollering" ("Unwritten History," FUA, 155). On Sally Brown's plantation, a wild boar attacked an unsupervised black toddler, "dragging it along into the field" (Rawick 1977, 3: 110). However, the greatest "source of evil to slave children" was their masters' offspring. When Ben Chambers was left without adult care, his "young marsters cut [his] big toe off wid a hatchet." Because of a horse-riding prank of her master's teenage son, Sarah Patterson was "crippled all [her] life" (Rawick 1979, 3: 671).

The third form of owner interference into mothering resulted from two labor management strategies through which owners removed children. As a result of masters' interference, only a small minority of Appalachian slave children experienced unbroken bonds and daily interaction with one or both parents. Nearly two-thirds of all Appalachian slave sales separated children from their families – 70 percent of these forced migrations occurring when they were younger than 15.[16] William Johnson summed up the ideology of Appalachian slaveholders when he commented, "White folks in my part of the country didn't think anything of breaking up a family and selling the children in one section of the South and the parents in some other section" (*Weevils* 1976, 166). Experiences like the following cases were common. A western North Carolinian sold away from her enslaved parents a daughter that he "disliked very much" (Lenoir Family Papers, DU, 9 Feb. 1863). Tillie Duke never knew "nothin' 'bout [her] parents" because she was sold as an infant (Rawick 1979, 4: 1242). In middle Tennessee, a slaveholder sold to an itinerant trader "Aunt Phoebe's little baby that was just toddling along" ("Unwritten History," FUA, 130). One McDowell County, North Carolina, master sold 12 of the 16 children of one of his slave women "fas' as dey got three years old" (Rawick 1972, 16: 13). Dan Lockhart "was sold at five years of age" (Drew 1856, 46) while Jim Threat's father was exported out of state at age seven and "never saw his parents again" (Rawick 1977, 12: 328). At the age of nine, Martha Showvely and two cousins were sold to itinerant speculators (*Weevils* 1976, 264).

The second labor management strategy of owners was to socialize children to begin work very young, often removing them from their relatives. Nearly 90 percent of Appalachian slave children began their work assignments well before the age of 10. About two-fifths of them were assigned house chores while the rest worked in the fields or tended livestock. Well before the age of 10, one of every eight Appalachian slave children was already employed at an industrial site.[17] Lorenzo Ivy was put into the fields just as soon as he "was large enough to use a hoe." When Henry Johnson "was a little bit a fellow," he was assigned "to pack water to twenty-five and thirty men" in the fields. From there he progressed to the use of a short hoe to "dig weeds out of de crop." George Jackson helped his mistress in her garden. He could "remember cryin' " because she would "jump [him] and beat [him]" when he mistook a cabbage for a weed. "She told [him] she had to learn [him] to be careful." Hired out before age 10, Fleming Clark "dr[o]ve cows and work[ed] in de 'bacca fields, pickin' worms off de leaves." Henry Williams was "put to work at six years old . . . clearing off new ground" and "thinn[ing] corn" on his knees. By age nine, Silas Jackson was already at his adult work in the fields. By age 10, Catherine Slim "wuz doin' women's work" in the fields and in the big house. Sally Brown was "pickin' cotton and hoeing" at age five, and she was expected to "keep rat up with the others." Most young slave girls, and a few boys, lost their own childhoods to tend their

---

[16] Derived from analysis of Appalachian slave narratives.
[17] Derived from analysis of Appalachian slave narratives.

masters' offspring (Rawick 1972, 11: 205–7, 166, 16: 22, 29, 45–46, 78, 4: 36; Rawick 1977, 14: 354, 3: 98, 5: 231; Blassingame 1977, 737, 482). Mothers also lost control over their offspring when masters selected them to be child laborers in their houses. About 1 of every 10 lived with whites, away from their parents and away from community bonds with other African-Americans. Until he was old enough to work in the fields, Morris Hillyer thought of his mistress as "the only mother [he] ever knew." Little wonder that Morris "didn't know how to act when he was sent out there among strangers" in the slave quarters. The daughter of the master's son and the enslaved cook, Rachel Cruze was kept as a body servant for her white grandmother, whom she "looked upon as [her] mother" (Rawick 1972, 10: 192, 255, 7: 138–39, 16: 78, 12: 136: Rawick 1977, 11: 17, 5: 293).

The fourth form of structural interference in mothering by enslaved women occurred as owners assumed the role of disciplinarian of children, shifting their loyalty away from parents. Nearly three-fifths of the Appalachian ex-slaves identified the master, the mistress, and the owner's children as the individuals who administered verbal or physical punishment to them most often. Less than one-quarter of Appalachian slave children were disciplined most often by their mothers, only a few by their fathers. Part of their early work socialization was intended to teach slave children to obey white youth. So long as they were very young and playing in the yard together, Lunsford Lane (1842, 18) did not perceive the racial hierarchy. At about age 10, however, Lunsford "discovered the difference between [himself] and [his] master's children. They began to order [him] about, and were told to do so by [his] master and mistress." James Pennington recalled the "tyranny of the master's children." James and his brothers were "required to recognize the young sirs as [their] young masters." The white children were taught to feel superior, and "in consequence of this feeling, they sought to treat [black children] with the same air of authority that their father did the older slaves" (Bontemps 1969, 208). When black youngsters "got into a fuss" with their masters' sons, they paid the price for childhood "insolence" (Rawick 1972, 12: 240–41).

The complexities of discipline were dangerous when children found themselves in a tug-of-war between plantation authority and parental influence. When abolitionists appeared in the slave quarters to help families escape, young Penny Thompson was "'fraid dat dey am gwine to takes [her] away." Confused about what was happening, she "den goes to de marster's bed a cryin' an' says to him, Ise don' want to go away." Because of her misplaced allegiance, the master foiled the escape to freedom (Rawick 1979, 9: 3875). Sarah Wilson was more perceptive about the disciplinary conflict. Sarah's owner named her "Annie," after herself. Because her mother "hate[d] Old Mistress," she despised the imposed name but "was afraid to change it." Sarah was in a quandary when both women would call her. "If [she] responded when her mistress called 'Annie' [her] mammy would beat [her] for answering to that name, and if [she] didn't go old mistress would beat [her] for that" (Rawick 1972, 7: 34). Jacob Stroyer (1888, 119–21) supplies a family history that pinpoints the powerlessness of

FIGURE 26. Until they were old enough for fieldwork, youngsters were put to work at all kinds of unskilled tasks on small plantations. Working in the big house kept children away from their mothers much of the time and denied those youngsters familial bonding with their parents and siblings. *Source: Harper's Monthly* (March 1856).

women and the manner in which whites destroyed children's respect for their parents. When Jacob was repeatedly switched by an overseer, he ran to his mother for rescue. When the enslaved woman intervened verbally, the white male "took a whip and started for her, and she ran from him." Jacob thrust himself in the way to shield his parent "until he stopped beating her." Subsequently, the overseer gave Jacob "a severe flogging." Although his mother "failed to help [him] at first," the child hoped that "she would come and stop" the beating. "But I looked in vain," Jacob lamented, "for she did not come."

Conclusion

To be a respected and moral mother, a nineteenth-century female must abide by what I shall facetiously term the "seven commandments of gender propriety." First, a woman could not ever achieve *family honor*, gentility, or social standing if she operated autonomously outside the appropriate male and female spheres. According to the most popular antebellum proponent of biological determinism (Blakemore 2000, 181), the "civilized" woman desired no sphere other than domesticity. Pro-slavery intellectuals interpreted this tenet to mean that the "dependent classes" – women and slaves – were naturally intended to be "confined within households under the governance of masters" (Fitzhugh 1854, 59). The second gender stricture was that a moral mother should only devote herself to *reproductive* labors within the confines of her own household, avoiding external income-earning *productive* labors. White females who were remiss in this regard were viewed as "petticoated despisers of their sex...would-be men...moral monsters...things which nature disclaims," according to a southern female apologist for separate spheres philosophy (Palmer 1876, 69). An elite southern woman encapsulated the third gender propriety when she wrote that an appropriately behaving wife "is scarcely placed in any situation that *her weakness* does not require [her husband's] presence as her safeguard" (McCord 1852, 327–28). For that reason, women should not desire to be heads of household. The typical court ruling of the day was that a mother must be subject to a husband and that every household must be ruled by a man (Sommerville 1995). How else could children and property be passed through a father's lineage?

The fourth gender propriety was that a woman must have sufficient time and resources to "cultivate" her natural calling as a mother, so she could exhibit the religious characteristics and education needed for early socialization of children. It was the responsibility of the mother not only to provide moral instruction to children, but also to train them about the essentials of gentility and fashion and the complex etiquette of class and racial differences (Block 1978). The fifth gender propriety for any woman who hoped to be a respectable mother was constraint on her sexuality. The decent woman carefully behaved so as not to bring disgrace upon her family for inappropriate actions and so as to prevent community inferences that a nonsexual act had a hidden sexual intent. For instance, any woman who traveled alone, as did most Indian, poor white, and nonwhite females, was branded sexually promiscuous. According to William Byrd II (Commonplace Book, VHS), "A woman shoud not appear out of her house, til she is old enough for people to enquire whose mother she is, and not so young as to have it askt, whose wife she is, or whose daughter." So as not to associate with males of inferior class or racial positions during courtship, the respectable woman observed the sixth gender propriety by making fine distinctions among females and males of differing classes and races (Brown 1996, 259). According to elite periodicals like an 1838 *Southern Literary Journal* (3: 89–90, 94), the seventh gender propriety was female *chastity* before and during marriage that was so obvious that her community labeled her pure. In the minds of separate spheres advocates, poor white and nonwhite women could not possibly be chaste because they either worked at inappropriate occupations or were heads of their own families.

It is not likely that most antebellum women actually lived up to all these impossible gender proprieties. Culturally, motherhood was idealized as the appropriate sphere for women, but the same paternalistic system structurally assaulted the reproductive practices of poor white and nonwhite women. Only affluent Caucasian mothers retained reproductive rights that permitted them to nurture and rear their children without threat of having them removed by the courts. Slaveholding and middle-class white males were legally powerful enough to determine which women could reproduce legitimately and which women would retain the inalienable right to be mothers of the children they bore. The role of mother was neither idealized nor left unchallenged for poor white and nonwhite women, whose economically productive work contradicted separate spheres ideals about female reproductive purity. Consequently, the ties between free black, poor white, and enslaved women and their children were often severed permanently through court interventions and through slaveholder disruptions of families. Just as family was preserved only as an inalienable legal right of affluent white males, decisions about who would rear children and under what circumstances were ultimately made by slaveholders and by affluent public officials. Moreover, the right to engage in child rearing was socially and legally restricted by the race, class, and marital status of the female parent. While parenting was described as the most sacred duty of women, social respect for reproductive labors was withheld from the "dangerous classes" of poor and nonwhite females. Indeed, motherhood was a privilege that the legal statutes and courts sanctioned only for affluent married white women.

Bibliography

Archival Collections Utilized

Alabama Department of Archives and History, Montgomery

ASC: Alabama Supreme Court Records
PPC: Pardons, Paroles and Clemency Files, 1821–1853

Alice Lloyd College, Pippa Passes, KY

Transcripts of Interviews, Appalachian Oral History Project

American Baptist Historical Society, Rochester, NY

BFMB: Baptist Foreign Mission Board Papers

Appalachian State University, Boone, NC

Transcripts of Interviews, Appalachian Oral History Project

Duke University Library, Durham, NC

Alfred W. Bell Papers
William Bolling Papers, List of Slaves at Oxford Iron Works
Samuel, Richard, and Rowland Bryarly Papers
George W. Clark Papers
Martha Foster Crawford Diary
Alfred M. and John A. Foster Papers
Benjamin Sherwood Hedrick Papers
Thomas Lenoir Papers
John M. Orr Papers
Benjamin Pennybacker Daybook
George Junkin Ramsey Papers, Legal Documents and Petitions

H. I. Rhodes Memorandum Book
Samuel P. Sherrill Account Book
Ella Gertrude Clanton Thomas Diary
William Holland Thomas Papers
William Weaver Papers

Emory and Henry University, Emory, VA

Transcripts of Interviews, Appalachian Oral History Project

Family History Center, Church of Jesus Christ of the Latter Day Saints, Salt Lake City, UT

Bradley County, Tennessee, Poor Commission Records
Staunton, Virginia, Poor Records, 1770–1872

Fisk University Archives, Nashville, TN

"Unwritten History of Slavery: Autobiographical Account of Negro Ex-Slaves." 1945. Compiled by Ophelia Egypt, H. Masuoka, and C. S. Johnson, typescript.

Georgia Historical Commission, Atlanta

Springplace Diary, Translated Typescript

Georgia State Archives, Atlanta

Bark Camp Baptist Church Minutes
Cabin Creek Baptist Church Minutes
Jacob Scudder to Georgia Governor, 17 September 1831
Journal of Georgia Commissioners to the Cherokees, January 1803

Handley Public Library, Winchester, VA

Market Street United Methodist Church Records, 1842–1860

Harvard University Library, Cambridge, MA

ABCFM: American Board of Commissioners for Foreign Missions Papers
Brainerd Journal
Daniel Butrick Journal
William Chamberlain Journal
Ann Paine Notebooks, ABCFM Papers

Indian Heritage Association, Muskogee, OK

Cherokee Documents Collection
Cherokee Phoenix

Institute for Advanced Technology in the Humanities, Electronic Texts, Valley of the Shadow, University of Virginia, Charlottesville

Memoir of Alansa Rounds Sterrett

Kentucky Department for Libraries and Archives, Frankfort

Guardian's Bonds Books, 1852–1859, Clay County, Kentucky

Lees Junior College, Jackson, KY

Transcripts of Interviews, Appalachian Oral History Project

Library of Congress, Washington, DC

"Early Virginia Religious Petitions," American Memory, online at http://memory. loc.gov.

Maryland State Archives, Annapolis

Indentures, Orphan Court, Frederick County, Maryland, 1800–1860

Moravian Archives, Winston-Salem, NC

CM: Cherokee Mission Papers, 1820–1827

National Archives, Washington, DC

1835 Census Roll of the Cherokee Indians East of the Mississippi
Chapman Roll, 1851, Records Relating to the Enrollment of Cherokees
CIAT: Records of the Cherokee Indian Agency: Tennessee, 1801–1835
Return J. Meigs Journal, 1802
OIA: Letters Received by the Office of Indian Affairs, 1824–1881
SOW: Records of the Office of the Secretary of War: Letters Received, 1801–1870
U.S. Census of Agriculture, 1860, Manuscripts for Appalachian Counties
U.S. Census of Population, 1860, Manuscripts for Appalachian Counties
U.S. Slave Schedules, 1860, Manuscripts for Appalachian Counties

Newberry Library, Chicago

John Howard Payne Papers, 14 vols.

North Carolina Department of Archives and History, Raleigh

Apprentice Bonds and Records, 1800–1860, Buncombe County, North Carolina
Apprentice Bonds and Records, 1800–1860, Burke County, North Carolina
Walter Clark Papers
Gash Family Papers
Governor Graham Papers

Green River Baptist Association Minutes
Miscellaneous Petitions, North Carolina General Assembly Session Papers
Morganton Female Working Society Minutes, First Presbyterian Church
Mount Olive Baptist Church Minutes
NCSC: North Carolina Superior Court State Dockets
NCSSC: North Carolina State Supreme Court Manuscript Records
Pleasant Grove Primitive Baptist Church Minutes
John Scott Papers
David L. Swain Papers
Jonathan Worth Papers

Northeastern University Archives, Tahlequah, OK

Cherokee Advocate
The Cherokee Rose Buds

Tennessee State Library and Archives, Nashville

Governor John Sevier Papers
TSSC: Tennessee State Supreme Court Reports

Troy State University Library, Troy, AL

John Horry Dent Farm Journals and Account Books, 1840–1892

University of Georgia, Hargrett Rare Book and Manuscript Library, Athens

Telamon Cuyler Papers

University of Kentucky, Martha I. King Library, Lexington

J. Winston Coleman Papers on Slavery
Forsythe Family Papers
Graham Account Book
Wickliffe-Preston Papers

University of North Carolina Library, Southern Historical Collection, Chapel Hill

W. W. Avery and Company Records, George Phifer Erwin Papers
Hamilton Brown Papers
Juliana Margaret Conner Diary
Calvin J. Cowles Papers
Anne Beale Davis Diary
James Hervey Greenlee Diary
James Gwyn Papers
John DeBerniere Hooper Family Papers
Lenoir Family Papers
James Lee Love Papers
Benjamin F. Perry Autobiography, 1874

Pleasant Union Christian Church Minutes
Thomas George Walton Papers
Martha Ann Hancock Wheat Diary, 1850–1866
Wheeler's Primitive Baptist Church Minutes

University of Tennessee Special Collections, Knoxville

Penelope Johnson Allen Papers
Disbursements by Return J. Meigs of Account of the Indian Department, June 30–Oct. 1, 1810
Valuations under the Treaty of 1828 Emigrations 1833 and 1834

University of Virginia Library, Charlottesville

Aldie Memorandum Book, 1838–1850, Berkeley Family Papers
Benjamin Johnson Barbour Account Books, 1801–1806 and 1858, Barbour Family Papers
Barbour Diary and Memorandum, March 1851, Barbour Family Papers
William Berkeley Ledger, 1857–1868, Berkeley Family Papers
Broad Run Baptist Church Minutes, 1762–1859
BRR: Blue Ridge Railroad Receipts and Accounts, 1828–1829, Randolph Family Papers
Buffalo Forge Negro Book, 1855, Weaver-Brady Papers
Buffalo Forge Time Book, 1843–1853, Weaver-Brady Papers
Carr Family Papers
Chestnut Grove Baptist Minute Books, 1773–1860
Christ Episcopal Church, Parish Register, 1830–1865
William W. Davis Iron Manufacturing Company Papers
Goose Creek Baptist Church Records, 1775–1853
Holland Family Papers
Hubard Family Papers
Col. Benjamin Johnson Account Books, 1801–1806, 1858, Barbour Family Papers
McCue Family Papers
Massie Family Papers
Mount Ed Baptist Church Minute Book
New Hope Baptist Church Minute Book, Thomas S. Bobcock Papers
Sarah Fouace Nourse Diary, 1781–1783, Nourse Family Papers
Randolph Family Papers
Watson Family Papers
Wright Family Papers

Virginia Historical Society, Richmond

Broad Run Baptist Church Minutes
William Byrd II Commonplace Book, 1722–1737
Frances Ann Bernard Capps Diary
JRKC: James River and Kanawha Canal Company Papers
Occoquam Baptist Church Minutes
David Ross Letterbook, 1812–1813
Miss Weiseger Diary

Virginia State Library and Archives, Richmond

Battle Run Baptist Church Minutes
Beaver Run Baptist Church Minutes
Bethel Baptist Church Character Certificates, Garnett Ryland Collection
Byrd Presbyterian Church Minutes
FCSCO: Frederick County Superior Court Order Book
Kanawha County Register of Free Blacks
Legislative Papers, a Collection of 25,000 Petitions Sent to the Legislature of Virginia
Mountain Plain Baptist Church Minute Book, 1833–1869
Reveille Baptist Church Minutes
Roanoke District Baptist Association Records
William Henry Ruffner Papers
Shiloh Baptist Association Minutes
Tredegar Letterbook, Tredegar Company Records
VBPW: Virginia Board of Public Works, Annual Reports
Virginia Executive Papers, Letters Received, 1750–1835
Washington County Register of Free Blacks
Zion Hill Baptist Church Records

West Virginia University, West Virginia Collection, Morgantown

Avery Methodist Protestant Church Minutes, 1843–1855
John Bassel Papers
Bethel Methodist Church Records, 1804–1849
Bluestone Baptist Church Minutes, 1804–1820
Brooke County Archives
Joseph W. Browning Letter, 1845
Courtney Family Papers
M. J. Garrison and Company Records
Great Bethel Baptist Church Minutes, 1770–1860
Jacob Guseman Records
Harrison County Tax Book, 1831–1832
Hepzibah Baptist Church Minutes, 1861–1865, Louise Hornor Family Papers
Huntersville Methodist Episcopal Stewards Book, 1846–1852
Jones Run Baptist Church Minutes, 1831–1859
Frederick B. Lambert Papers
Lewisburg Methodist Episcopal Church Records, 1834–1843, Roy Bird Cook Papers
Isaac McNeel Papers, 1850–1860 Account Books
Marshall County Archives
Edward E. Meredith Papers
Monroe County Archives
Monroe County Free Negro Register
Morgantown Methodist Episcopal Church Minutes, 1847–1860
Raleigh County Archives
Summers County Archives
Samuel D. Thorn Ledger, 1858–1860, Samuel W. Shingleton Records
West Liberty Presbyterian Sunday School Register, 1830–1834, William B. Curtis Papers
Wilson-Lewis Family Papers

Published Primary Sources

Abbott, John. 1833. *The Mother at Home or the Principles of Maternal Duty.* Boston: Crocke and Brewster.

Adair, John. [1775]. 1930. *Adair's History of the American Indians*, ed. Samuel Williams. Johnson City, TN: Watauga Press.

Ambler, Charles, ed. 1918. *The Life and Diary of John Floyd.* Richmond: Richmond Press.

Anderson, Robert. 1927. *From Slavery to Affluence: Memoirs of Robert Anderson, Ex-Slave.* Steamboat Springs, CO: Steamboat Pilot.

Appalachian Oral History Project. 1977. *Union Catalog.* Pippa Passes, KY: Microfilm Corporation of America.

Archives of Maryland. 1883–1927. Baltimore: Maryland Historical Society, 42 vols.

Attmore, William. 1917. "Journal of a Tour to North Carolina, 1787." *James Sprunt Historical Monographs* 17 (2): 1–89.

Austin, Emily. 1882. *Mormonism or Life among the Mormons.* Madison, WI: M. J. Cantwell.

Bailyn, Bernard, ed. 1965. *Pamphlets of the American Revolution, 1750–1776.* Cambridge, MA: Harvard University Press, 2 vols.

Baldwin, Helene. 1982. "Down Street in Cumberland: The Diaries of Two Nineteenth-Century Ladies." *Maryland Historical Magazine* 77: 222–29.

Ball, Charles. [1837]. 1969. *Slavery in the U.S.: A Narrative of the Life and Adventures of Charles Ball, a Black Man.* Philadelphia: Negro Universities Press.

Bartram, William. [1792]. 1940. *Travels through North and South Carolina, Georgia, East and West Florida, the Cherokee Country.* Philadelphia: James and Johnson.

———. 1853. "Observations on the Creek and Cherokee Indians, 1789." *Transactions of the American Ethnological Society* 3: 22–49.

Battle, Kemp, ed. 1905. "Diary of a Geological Tour by Dr. Elisha Mitchell in 1827 and 1828." *James Sprunt Historical Monograph* 6: 1–74.

Becker, Stephen. 1977. *Louis-Phillipe, King of France, Diary of My Travels in America.* New York: Delacorte Press.

Beecher, Lyman, and Asabel Nettleton. 1828. *Letters of the Rev. Dr. Breeden and Rev. Mr. Nettleton on the "New Measures" in Conducting Revivals of Religion.* New York: Carvill Co.

Betts, Edwin, ed. 1953. *Thomas Jefferson's Farm Book with Commentary and Relevant Extracts from Other Writings.* Princeton, NJ: American Philosophical Society.

Bickley, George. 1852. *History of the Settlement and Indian Wars of Tazewell County, Virginia.* Cincinnati: Morgan Co.

Blair, John, ed. 1905. "Mrs. Mary Dewees' Journal from Philadelphia to Kentucky." *Kentucky Historical Society Register* 63: 195–217.

Blassingame, John, ed. 1977. *Slave Testimony: Two Centuries of Letters, Speeches, Interviews and Autobiographies.* Baton Rouge: Louisiana State University Press.

Bontemps, Arna, ed. 1969. *Great Slave Narratives.* Boston: Beacon Press.

Boudinot, Elias. 1826. *An Address to the Whites Delivered in the First Presbyterian Church on the 26th of May 1826.* Philadelphia: William F. Geddes.

Brabson, Estalena, comp. 1975. *John Brabson: Patriot of the American Revolution and Some of His Descendants.* Seymour, TN: Tricounty News.

Brownlow, William. 1856. *The Great Iron Wheel Examined.* Nashville: Author.

Bruner, Clarence. 1933. *An Abstract of the Religious Instruction of the Slaves in the Antebellum* South. Nashville: Peabody College for Teachers.

Buckingham, James. 1842. *The Slave States of America*. London: Fisher, 2 vols.

Buni, Andrew, ed. 1969. " 'Rambles among the Virginia Mountains': The Journal of Mary Jane Boggs, 1851." *Virginia Magazine of History and Biography* 77: 78–111.

Burke, Edmund. 1777. *Account of the European Settlements in America*. London: J. Dodsley, 2 vols.

Burke, Emily. 1850. *Reminiscences of Georgia*. Oberlin, OH: J. M. Fitch.

Bush, Florence. 1992. *Dorie: Woman of the Mountains*. Knoxville: University of Tennessee Press.

Bushman, Katherine, ed. 1989. *The Registers of Free Blacks, 1810–1864: Augusta County, Virginia and Staunton, Virginia*. Verona, VA: Midvalley Press.

Butler, Charles. 1836. *The American Lady*. Philadelphia: Hogan and Thompson.

Byrd, William. 1929. *Histories of the Dividing Line betwixt Virginia and North Carolina*, ed. William K. Boyd. Raleigh: North Carolina Historical Commission.

Carroll, B. R., ed. 1836. *Historical Collections of South Carolina*. New York: Harper and Brothers.

Catesby, Mark, ed. [1683–1749]. 1974. *The Natural History of Carolina, Florida, and Bahama Islands*. Spartanburg, SC: Beehive Press.

Chenault, John. 1937. *Old Cave Springs: A Story of the War between the States in Madison County, Kentucky*. Louisville: Standard Printing.

Chickering, Jesse. 1848. *Immigration into the United States*. Boston: Charles C. Little and James Brown.

Chipman, Luzene. 1852. *Earnest Entreaties: Appeals to the Unconverted*. Raleigh, NC: Weekly Post.

Conway, Alan, ed. 1961. *The Welsh in America: Letters from the Immigrants*. Minneapolis: University of Minnesota Press.

Davies, Alun. 1983. " 'As Good a Country as Any Man Needs to Dwell In': Letters from a Scotch-Irish Immigrant in Pennsylvania, 1766, 1767, and 1784." *Pennsylvania History* 50: 313–22.

DeBow, J. D. B., ed. 1853. *Industrial Resources of the Southern and Western States*. New Orleans: DeBow's Review Office, 4 vols.

DeVorsey, Louis, ed. 1971. *De Brahm's Report of the General Survey in the Southern District of North America*. Columbia: University of South Carolina Press.

Doddridge, Joseph. 1824. *Notes on the Settlement and Indian Wars of the Western Parts of Virginia and Pennsylvania from 1763 to 1783*. Wellsburg, VA: Author.

Drew, Benjamin. 1856. *A North-Side View of Slavery*. Boston: John P. Jewett.

Duance, William, ed. 1887. *Extracts from the Diary of Christopher Marshall Kept in Philadelphia and Lancaster during the American Revolution, 1774–1781*. Albany, NY: Joel Munser.

Dunn, Durwood, ed. 1997. *An Abolitionist in the Appalachian South: Ezekiel Birdseye on Slavery, Capitalism, and Separate Statehood in East Tennessee, 1841–1846*. Knoxville: University of Tennessee Press.

Dyer, G. W., and J. T. Moore, ed. 1985. *The Tennessee Civil War Veteran Questionnaires*. Easley, SC: Southern Historical Press.

Eastman, Mary. 1852. *Aunt Phillis's Cabin, or Southern Life as It Is*. Philadelphia: Lippincott-Grambo.

Ellett, Mrs. 1857. *The Practical Housekeeper: A Cyclopedia of Domestic Economy*. New York: Stringent and Townsend.

Embree, Elihu. [1820]. 1932. *The Emancipator.* Nashville: B. H. Murphy.

Evans, Louis. [1755]. 1953. *General Map of the Middle British Colonies and of the Country of the Confederate Indians.* Reprint. New York: Ethyl.

Evans, Raymond, ed. 1981. "Jedediah Morse's Report to the Secretary of War on Cherokee Indian Affairs in 1822." *Journal of Cherokee Studies* 6 (Winter): 60–79.

Ewell, Thomas. 1817. *Letters to Ladies Detailing Important Information Concerning Themselves and Infants.* Philadelphia: Author.

Featherstonhough, G. W. [1844]. 1968. *Excursion through the Slave States, from Washington on the Potomac to the Frontier of Mexico, with Sketches of Popular Manners and Geological Notices.* New York: Negro Universities Press.

Ferry Hill Plantation Journal: Life on the Potomac River and Chesapeake and Ohio Canal: 4 January 1838–15 January 1839. 1975. Shepherdstown, WV: American Canal and Transportation Center.

Fitzhugh, George. [1854]. 1969. *Sociology for the South, or the Failure of Free Society.* New York: Negro Universities Press.

Fitzpatrick, John, ed. 1944. *Writings of George Washington from the Original Manuscript Sources, 1745–1799.* Washington, DC: Government Printing Office, 39 vols.

Force, Peter, ed. 1963. *Tracts and Other Papers Relating Principally to the Origin, Settlement and Progress of the Colonies in North America from the Discovery of the Country to the Year 1776.* Gloucester, MA: Peter Smith, 4 vols.

Gallatin, Albert. 1822. "Synopsis of the Indian Tribes within the United States East of the Rocky Mountains, and in the British and Russian Possessions." *Archaeologia Americana: Transactions and Collections of the American Antiquarian Society* 2.

Gaustad, Edwin. 1974. *A Documentary History of Religion in America.* New York: Harper & Row.

"General Slade's Journal of a Trip to Tennessee." 1906. *Trinity College Historical Papers* 6: 37–56.

Goodrich, Frances. 1931. *Mountain Homespun.* New Haven, CT: Yale University Press.

Grant, James. 1933. "Journal of Lieutenant-Colonel James Grant, Commanding an Expedition against the Cherokee Indians, June–July, 1761." *Florida Historical Quarterly* 12: 22–51.

Gunn, John. 1834. *Gunn's Domestic Medicine; or Poor Man's Friend, Shewing the Diseases of Men, Women and Children.* Madisonville, TN: Author.

Hamer, Philip, and George Roger, eds. 1972. *Papers of Henry Laurens.* Columbia: University of South Carolina Press.

Hamilton, Kenneth, ed. 1971. "Minutes of the Mission Conference Held in Springplace, 1819." *Atlanta Historical Bulletin* (Spring): 29–61.

Hamilton, Milton, ed. 1921–62. *The Papers of Sir William Johnson.* Albany: State University of New York Press, 13 vols.

Hamilton, Stanislaus, ed. 1898–1903. *The Letters and Writings of James Monroe.* New York: G. P. Putnam's Sons, 7 vols.

Harvey, Katherine, ed. 1977. "The Lonaconing Journals: The Founding of a Coal and Iron Community, 1837–1840." *Transactions of the American Philosophical Society* 67 (2).

Haywood, John. 1828. *The Natural and Aboriginal History of Tennessee.* Nashville: George Wilson.

Hildebrand, Jacob. 1996. *A Mennonite Journal, 1862–1865: A Father's Account of the Civil War in the Shenandoah Valley.* Shippensburg, PA: Burd Street Press.

Hooker, Richard, ed. 1953. *The Carolina Backcountry on the Eve of Revolution: The Journal and Other Writings of Charles Woodmason, Anglican Itinerant.* Chapel Hill: University of North Carolina Press.

Hughes, Louis. [1897]. 1969. *Thirty Years a Slave: From Bondage to Freedom.* New York: Negro Universities Press.

Hundley, Daniel. [1860]. 1979. *Social Relations in Our Southern States.* Reprint. Baton Rouge: Louisiana State University Press.

Irish Immigrants in the Land of Canaan: Letters and Memoirs from Colonial and Revolutionary America, 1675–1815. 2003. New York: Oxford University Press.

Jacobs, Harriet. [1861]. 1987. *Incidents in the Life of a Slave Girl Written by Herself.* Cambridge, MA: Harvard University Press.

Jacobs, Wilbur, ed. 1954. *Indians of the Southern Colonial Frontier: The Edmund Atkin Report and Plan of 1755.* Columbia: University of South Carolina Press.

Janney's Virginia: An American Farm Lad's Life in the Early 19th Century. 1978. McLean, VA: EPM.

Jensen, Joan. 1981. *With These Hands: Women Working on the Land.* New York: Feminist Press.

Jones, Charles. 1837. *Catechism of Scripture, Doctrine and Practice for Families and Sabbath Schools, Designed Also for the Oral Instruction of Colored Persons.* Savannah: T. Purse.

"Journal of John Sevier." 1919. *Tennessee Historical Magazine* 5: 232–64.

Kemble, Frances. 1984. *Journal of a Residence on a Georgia Plantation in 1838 and 1839.* Athens: University of Georgia Press.

Kercheval, Samuel. [1833]. 1986. *A History of the Valley of Virginia.* Harrisonburg, VA: C. J. Carrier.

Klinck, Carl, and James Telman, eds. 1970. *Journal of Major John Norton.* Toronto: Champlain Society.

Krochmal, Arnold, Russell S. Walters, and Richard M. Doughty. 1969. *A Guide to Medicinal Plants of Appalachia.* Washington, DC: U.S. Department of Agriculture.

Lane, Lunsford. 1842. *The Narrative of Lunsford Lane.* Boston: J. G. Torrey.

Lanman, Charles. 1848. *Letters from the Allegheny Mountains.* New York: G. P. Putnam.

La Rochefoucauld-Liancourt, François. 1800. *Travels through the United States of America.* London: T. Gillet, 2 vols.

Laws of the Cherokee Nation Adopted by the Council at Various Periods. 1852. Tahlequah, OK: Cherokee Advocate's Office.

Lawson, John. 1967. *A New Voyage to Carolina.* Chapel Hill: University of North Carolina Press.

Logan, John. 1859. *A History of the Upper Country of South Carolina from the Earliest Periods to the Close of the War of Independence.* Charleston, SC: S. G. Courtenay.

Longe, Alexander. 1969. "A Small Postscript of the Ways and Manners of the Indians Called Charikees, 1725." *Southern Indian Studies* 21: 3–49.

Lossiah, Aggie. 1984. "The Story of My Life As Far Back As I Can Remember." *Journal of Cherokee Studies* 9: 87–90.

Love, Nat. 1907. *The Life and Adventures of Nat Love.* Los Angeles: Author.

Lowrie, Walter Lowrie, and Matthew Clarke. 1832. *American State Papers: Indian Affairs.* Washington, DC: Gales and Seaton.

Lumpkin, Wilson. 1907. *The Removal of the Cherokee Indians from Georgia.* New York: Dodd and Mead, 2 vols.

McClary, Ben, ed. 1960. "The Education of a Southern Mind: Extracts from the Diary of John Coffee Williamson, 1860–1861." *East Tennessee Historical Society Publications* 32: 59–103.

——— and LeRoy Graf, eds. 1959. "'Vineland' in Tennessee, 1852: The Journal of Rosine Parmentier." *East Tennessee Historical Society Publications* 31: 95–111.

McCord, Louisa. 1852. "Enfranchisement of Women." *Southern Quarterly Review* 21: 322–41.

McDonald, Cornelia. 1992. *A Woman's Civil War: A Diary with Reminiscences of the War, from March 1862*. Madison: University of Wisconsin Press.

McDowell William, ed. 1955. *Journal of the Commissioners of the Indian Trade, September 20, 1710–August 29, 1718*. Columbia: South Carolina Archives Department.

———. 1958–72. *Documents Relating to Indian Affairs*. Columbia: South Carolina Archives Department.

McKivigan, John, ed. 1996. *The Roving Editor or Talks with Slaves in the Southern States, by James Redpath*. University Park: Pennsylvania State University Press.

Maguire, John. 1868. *The Irish in America*. London: Longmans-Green.

Martin, Joseph. 1836. *A New and Comprehensive Gazetteer of Virginia and the District of Columbia*. Charlottesville: Author.

Meaders, Daniel, ed. 1997. *Advertisements for Runaway Slaves in Virginia, 1801–1820*. New York: Garland.

Meigs, Charles. 1848. *Females and Their Diseases: A Series of Letters to His Class*. Philadelphia: Lea and Blanchard.

"Memorandum of M. Austin's Journey from the Lead Mines in the County of Wythe in the State of Virginia to the Lead Mines in the Province of Louisiana, 1796–1797." 1899–1900. *American Historical Review* 5: 518–41.

Mitchill, Samuel. 1818. "Progress of the Human Mind from Rudeness to Refinement: Exemplified in an Account of the Methods Pursued by Colonel Benjamin Hawkins to Civilize Certain Tribes of Savages." *American Monthly Magazine and Critical Review* 3: 358–64.

Montgomery, Lizzie. 1924. *Sketches of Old Warrenton, North Carolina: Traditions and Reminiscences of the Town and People Who Made It*. Raleigh, NC: Edwards and Broughton.

Mooney, James. 1886. "Sacred Formulas of the Cherokee." *Bureau of American Ethnology Annual Report* 7.

———. 1900. "Myths of the Cherokee." *Bureau of American Ethnology Annual Report* 19.

Morrison, A. J., ed. 1922. *Travels in Virginia in Revolutionary America*. Lynchburg, VA: J. P. Bell.

Myers, Robert, ed. 1972. *The Children of Pride: A True Story of Georgia and the Civil War*. New Haven, CT: Yale University Press.

Nead, Peter. 1866. *Theological Writings on Various Subjects*. Dayton, OH: Brethren.

Newell, Franklin. 1908. "The Effect of Overcivilization on Maternity." *American Journal of the Medical Sciences* 136: 533–41.

Newsome, A. R., ed. 1934. "John Brown's Journal of Travel in Western North Carolina in 1795." *North Carolina Historical Review* 11: 284–313.

Olmsted, Frederick. 1856. *Journey in the Seaboard Slave States with Remarks on Their Economy*. New York: Dix and Edwards, 1856.

———. 1860. *A Journey in the Back Country, 1853–1854*. New York: Burt Franklin.

_____. [1861]. 1953. *The Cotton Kingdom: A Traveller's Observations on Cotton and Slavery in the American Slave States*. New York: Knopf.

Page, Thomas. 1897. *Social Life in Old Virginia before the War*. New York: Charles Scribner's Sons.

Palmer, Benjamin. 1876. *The Family in Its Civil and Churchly Aspects*. Richmond, VA: Presbyterian Committee on Publication.

Palmer, William, ed. 1875–93. *Calendar of Virginia State Papers and Other Manuscripts*. Richmond: State of Virginia.

Parker, Freddie, ed. 1994. *Stealing a Little Freedom: Advertisements for Slave Runaways in North Carolina, 1791–1840*. New York: Garland.

Payne, Alban. 1853. "Report of Obstetrical Cases." *Steth* 3: 204–5.

Pennington, James. 1849. *The Fugitive Blacksmith, or Events in the History of James W. C. Pennington, Formerly a Slave*. London: C. Gilpin.

Perdue, Theda, ed. 1983. *Cherokee Editor: The Writings of Elias Boudinot*. Knoxville: University of Tennessee Press.

Peyton, J. Lewis. 1894. *Memoir of John Howe Peyton*. Staunton, VA: A. B. Blackburn.

"Proceedings of the Committee of Observation for Elizabeth Town District, Washington County." 1918. *Maryland Historical Magazine* 1: 227–48.

Proceedings of the Convention of Delegates for the Counties and Corporations in the Colony of Virginia, 1775. 1816. Richmond, VA: Ritchie, Trueheart and Duval.

Randolph, J. T. 1852. *The Cabin and the Parlor or Slaves and Masters*. Philadelphia: T. B. Peterson.

Rawick, George, comp. 1972. *The American Slave: A Composite Autobiography*. Westport, CT: Greenwood Press.

_____. 1977. *The American Slave: A Composite Autobiography, Supplement I*. Westport, CT: Greenwood Press.

_____. 1979. *The American Slave: A Composite Autobiography, Supplement II*. Westport, CT: Greenwood Press.

Reed, Andrew, and James Matheson. 1835. *A Narrative of the Visit to the American Churches*. London: Jackson and Walford.

Reeves, James. 1870. *The Physical and Medical Topography, Including Vital, Manufacturing, and Other Statistics of the City of Wheeling*. Wheeling, WV: Daily Register Book Job Office.

"Reflections on the Institutions of the Cherokee Indians." 1818. *Analectic Magazine* 36: 41–45.

Report of the Indian Commissioner. 1884.Washington, DC: Department of the Interior.

Rivers, William. 1856. *A Sketch of the History of South Carolina to the Close of the Proprietary Government by the Revolution of 1719*. Charleston, SC: McCarter Co.

Rose, Willie, ed. 1976. *A Documentary History of Slavery in North America*. New York: Oxford University Press.

Royall, Anne. [1830]. 1969. *Letters from Alabama, 1817–1822*. Tuscaloosa: University of Alabama Press.

Royce, Charles. 1884. *Cherokee Nation of Indians*. Washington, DC: Bureau of American Ethnology.

Ruffin, Edmund. [1847]. 1933. *Slavery and Free Labor Described and Compared: Address to the People of West Virginia*. Bridgewater, VA: Green Bookman.

Salley, A. S., ed. 1911. *Narratives of Early Carolina, 1650–1708*. New York: C. Scribner's Sons.

———. 1928–47. *Records in the British Public Record Office Relating to South Carolina, 1663–1684.* Columbia: Historical Commission of South Carolina.

———. 1930. *Journal of the Proceedings of the Honourable Governor and Council, May 29, 1721–June 10, 1721.* Atlanta: Foote and Davies.

Saunders, William, ed. 1886. *Colonial Records of North Carolina.* Raleigh, NC: P. M. Hall.

Schaw, Janet. 1923. *Journal of a Lady of Quality; Being a Narrative of a Journey from Scotland to the West Indies, North Carolina, and Portugal in the Years 1774 to 1776.* New Haven, CT: Yale University Press.

Schoolcraft, Henry. 1851–57. *Historical and Statistical Information Respecting the History, Condition, and Prospects of the Indian Tribes of the United States.* Philadelphia: Lippincott-Grambo, 6 vols.

Scott, Winfield. 1864. *Autobiography of Lieutenant-General Scott, Written by Himself.* New York: Sheldon, 2 vols.

Shackelford, Laura, and Bill Weinberg, eds. 1977. *Our Appalachia: An Oral History.* New York: Hill & Wang.

Sigourney, Lydia. 1838. *Letters to Mothers.* Hartford, CT: Hudson and Skinner.

Silliman, Benjamin. 1837. "Remarks on Some of the Gold Mines and on Parts of the Gold Region of Virginia." *American Journal of Science* 32: 98–130.

Simms, William. 1852. *The Pro-Slavery Argument: As Maintained by the Most Distinguished Writers of the Southern States.* Charleston, SC: Walker-Richards.

Singleton, William. 1922. *Recollections of Slavery Days.* New York: Highland.

Stroud, George. 1856. *A Sketch of the Laws Relating to Slavery in the Several States of the United States of America.* Philadelphia: H. Longstreth.

Stroyer, Jacob. 1888. *My Life in the South.* Salem, NH: Salem Observer Book.

Sturtevant, William, ed. 1978. "Louis-Philippe on Cherokee Architecture and Clothing in 1797." *Journal of Cherokee Studies* 3: 198–205.

———. 1981. "John Ridge on Cherokee Civilization in 1826." *Journal of Cherokee Studies* 6: 81–83.

Sumner, Helen. 1910. *Report on Condition of Woman and Child Wage Earners in the United States.* Washington, DC: Government Printing Office.

Tambory, Robert. 1910. "Visits to the American Wilderness." In *America Visited: Famous Travellers Report on the United States in the 18th and 19th Centuries*, ed. Edith Coombs, 79–121. New York: Book League of America.

Thomas, William. 1839. *Argument in Support of the Claims of the Cherokee Indians.* Washington, DC: Government Printing Office.

Thompson, Kathy, ed. 1976. *Touching Home: A Collection of History and Folklore from the Copper Basin, Fannin County Area.* Orlando, FL: Daniels.

———. 1982. *In Touch with the Past: A Guide to Historic Places and Homes in Fannin County, Georgia and Polk County, Tennessee.* Blue Ridge, GA: Author.

Thorndale, William, and William Dollarhide. 1987. *Map Guide to the U.S. Federal Censuses, 1790–1920.* Baltimore: Genealogical.

Thwaites, Reuben, ed. 1904–7. *Early Western Travels, 1748–1846.* Cleveland: Arthur H. Clark, 32 vols.

Tilley, Nannie, ed. 1947. "Journal of the Surry County Agricultural Society." *North Carolina Historical Review* 24: 494–531.

Toulmin, Harry. [1794]. 1948. *The Western Country in 1793: Reports on Kentucky and Virginia.* Reprint. San Marino, CA: Castle Press.

Tucker, George. [1824]. 1970. *The Valley of Shenandoah or Memoirs of the Graysons.* Chapel Hill: University of North Carolina Press.

U.S. Census Office. 1791. *First Census of the United States, 1790*. Philadelphia: Childs and Swaine.

———. 1801. *Return of the Whole Number of Persons within the Several Districts of the United States in 1800*. Washington, DC: U.S. House of Representatives.

———. 1814. *A Statement of the Arts and Manufactures of the United States of America for the Year 1810*. Philadelphia: A. Cornman.

———. 1821. *Census for 1820*. Washington, DC: Gales & Seaton.

———. 1823. *Digest of Accounts of Manufacturing Establishments in 1820*. Washington, DC: Gales & Seaton.

———. 1841. *Compendium of the Enumeration of the Inhabitants and Statistics of the U.S.* Washington, DC: Thomas Allen.

———. 1854. *Compendium of the Seventh Census in 1850*. Washington, DC: Government Printing Office.

———. 1855. *Mortality Statistics of the Seventh Census of the United States, 1850*. Washington, DC: A. O. P. Nicholson.

———. 1863. *Report of the Eighth Census in 1860*. Washington, DC: Government Printing Office.

———. 1864. *Agriculture of the United States in 1860*. Washington, DC: Government Printing Office.

———. 1865. *Manufactures of the United States in 1860*. Washington, DC: Government Printing Office.

U.S. Senate. 1867. "Condition of the Indian Tribes." Report 165, 39th Congress, Second Session. Washington, DC: Government Printing Office.

"Valley of Virginia Notes." 1923. *Virginia Historical Magazine* 31: 245–52.

Van Evrie, John. 1853. *Negroes and Negro "Slavery": The First an Inferior Race, the Latter Its Normal Condition*. Baltimore: J. D. Toy.

Veney, Bethany. 1890. *The Narrative of Bethany Veney: A Slave Woman*. Worcester, MA: A. P. Bicknell.

Verplanck, G. C. 1832. "Report, 1831." *American Quarterly Review* 11: 89.

Vogt, Carl. 1864. *Lectures of Man: His Place in Creation and in the History of Earth*. London: Longman, Green and Roberts.

Warrington, Joseph. 1853. *The Obstetric Catechism: Containing 2,347 Questions and Answers on Obstetrics Proper*. Philadelphia: E. Barrington and G. D. Haswell.

Washington, George. 1892. *Journals of My Journeys over the Mountains*. Albany, NY: Munsell's Sons.

Weeks, Stephen, ed. 1916. *Letters of Benjamin Hawkins, 1796–1806*. Savannah: Georgia Historical Society.

Weevils in the Wheat: Interviews with Virginia Ex-Slaves. 1976. Charlottesville: University Press of Virginia.

Weld, Isaac. 1800. *Travels through the States of North America, and the Provinces of Upper and Lower Canada During the Years 1795, 1796 and 1797*. London: John Stockdale.

White, George. 1849. *Statistics of the State of Georgia*. Savannah: W. Thorne Williams.

Wiggington, Eliot, ed. 1972. *Foxfire Book*. Garden City, NY: Anchor Books.

———. 1973. *Foxfire 2*. Garden City, NY: Anchor Books.

———. 1975. *Foxfire 3*. Garden City, NY: Anchor Books.

———. 1979. *Foxfire 5*. Garden City, NY: Anchor Books.

———. 1983. *Foxfire 8*. Garden City, NY: Anchor Books.

Wiggington, Eliot, and Margie Bennett, eds. 1985. *Foxfire 9*. Garden City, NY: Anchor Books.

Williams, Samuel, ed. 1927. *Lieutenant Henry Timberlake's Memoirs*. Johnson City, TN: Watauga Press.

———. 1928. *Early Travels in the Tennessee Country, 1540–1800*. Johnson City, TN: Watauga Press.

Winslow, Hubbard, and Mrs. John Sanford. 1854. *The Benison: The Lady's Manual of Moral and Intellectual Culture*. New York: Leavitt and Allen.

Yeates, W. S., S. W. McCallie, and F. P. Kind. 1896. "A Preliminary Report on a Part of the Gold Deposits of Georgia." *Geological Survey of Georgia Bulletin* 4: 1–77.

Yetman, Norman. 1970. *Life under the "Peculiar Institution": Selections from the Slave Narrative Collection*. New York: Holt, Rinehart & Winston.

Secondary Sources

Abrahams, Roger. 1992. *Singing the Master: The Emergence of African American Culture in the Plantation South*. New York: Penguin Books.

Abramson, Rudy, and Jean Haskell. 2006. *Encyclopedia of Appalachia*. Knoxville: University of Tennessee Press.

Allen, Theodore. 1989. *The Invention of the White Race*. London: Verso Press, 2 vols.

Ambler, Charles. 1964. *Sectionalism in Virginia from 1776 to 1861*. New York: Russell & Russell.

Anglin, Mary K. 1995. "Lives on the Margins: Rediscovering the Women of Antebellum Western North Carolina." In *Appalachia in the Making: The Mountain South in the Nineteenth Century*," ed. Mary B. Pudup, D. Billings and Altina Waller, 189–205. Chapel Hill: University of North Carolina Press.

———. 2000. "Toward a Workable Past: Dangerous Memories and Feminist Perspectives." *Journal of Appalachian Studies* 6: 71–99.

———. 2002. *Women, Power and Dissent in the Hills of Carolina*. Urbana: University of Illinois Press.

Appleton, T. H., and A. Boswell, eds. 2003. *Searching for Their Places: Women in the South across Four Centuries*. Columbia: University of Missouri Press.

Ash, Stephen. 1991. *Past Times: A Daybook of Knoxville History*. Knoxville, TN: Knoxville News Sentinel.

Bacot, D. H. 1923. "The South Carolina Up Country at the End of the 18th Century." *American Historical Review* 28: 682–98.

Batteau, Allen. 1980. "Appalachia and the Concept of Culture: A Theory of Shared Misunderstandings." *Appalachian Journal* 7 (1–2): 9–32.

Bays, Brad. 1991. "The Historical Geography of Cattle Herding among the Cherokee Indians, 1761–1861." M.S. thesis, University of Tennessee.

Beaver, Patricia. 1999. "Women in Appalachia and the South: Gender, Race, Region, and Agency." *National Women's Studies Association Journal* 11 (3): ix–xxix.

Berg, Barbara. 1978. *The Remembered Gate: Origins of American Feminism, the Woman and the City, 1800–1860*. New York: Oxford University Press.

Berlin, Ira, and Philip Morgan, eds. 1993. *Cultivation and Culture: Labor and the Shaping of Slave Life in the Americas*. Charlottesville: University of Virginia Press.

Bernhard, Virginia, Betty Brandon, Elizabeth Fox-Genovese, and Theda Perdue, eds. 1992. *Southern Women: Histories and Identities*. Columbia: University of Missouri Press.

Billington, Louis. 1985. "'Female Laborers in the Church': Women Preachers in the Northeastern United States, 1790–1840." *Journal of American Studies* 19: 369–94.

Blakemore, Colin. 2000. *Gender and Society: Essays Based on Herbert Spencer Lectures Given in the University of Oxford*. London: Oxford University Press.

Blassingame, John. 1972. *The Slave Community: Plantation Life in the Antebellum South*. New York: Oxford University Press.

Blethen, Tyler, and Curtis Wood. 1998. *From Ulster to Carolina: The Migration of the Scotch-Irish to Southwestern North Carolina*. Raleigh, NC: Division of Archives and History.

Block, Ruth. 1978. "American Feminine Ideas in Transition: The Rise of the Moral Mother, 1785–1815." *Feminist Studies* 4: 101–26.

Boatwright, Eleanor. 1994. *Status of Women in Georgia, 1783–1860*. Brooklyn, NY: Carlson.

Bodenhorn, Howard. 2002. "The Mulatto Advantage: The Biological Consequences of Complexion in Rural Antebellum Virginia." *Journal of Interdisciplinary History* 33: 21–46.

Bolton, Charles. 1994. *Poor Whites of the Antebellum South: Tenants and Laborers in Central North Carolina and Northeast Mississippi*. Durham, NC: Duke University Press.

Booth, Stephanie. 2001. *Buckeye Women: The History of Ohio's Daughters*. Athens: Ohio University Press.

Boswell, Angela. 2001. *Her Act and Deed: Women's Lives in a Rural Southern County, 1837–1873*. College Station: Texas A & M University Press.

Bouquet, M. 1986. *Family, Servants and Visitors*. Norwich, England: Geobooks.

Bouwman, Robert. 1980. *Traveler's Rest and the Tugaloo Crossroads*. Atlanta: State of Georgia: Department of Natural Resources.

Bowman, Carl. 1995. *Brethren Society: The Cultural Transformation of a "Peculiar People."* Baltimore: Johns Hopkins University Press.

Boydston, Jeanne. 1986. "To Earn Her Daily Bread: Housework and Antebellum Working-Class Subsistence." *Radical History Review* 35: 7–25.

———. 1990. *Home and Work: Housework, Wages and the Ideology of Labor in the Early Republic*. New York: Oxford University.

Boylan, Anne. 1978. "Evangelical Womanhood in the Nineteenth Century: The Role of Women in Sunday Schools." *Feminist Studies* 4: 62–80.

Brown, John. 1938. *Old Frontiers: The Story of the Cherokee Indians from Earliest Times to the Date of Their Removal West, 1838*. Kingsport, TN: Southern Publishers.

Brown, Kathleen. 1996. *Good Wives, Nasty Wenches, and Anxious Patriarchs: Gender, Race, and Power in Colonial Virginia*. Chapel Hill: University of North Carolina Press.

Bruce, Kathleen. 1980. *Virginia Iron Manufacture in the Slave Era*. New York: Century.

Bryant, Keith. 1980. "The Role and Status of the Female Yeomanry in the Antebellum South: The Literary View." *Southern Quarterly* 18: 73–88.

Buckley, Thomas. 1995. "After Disestablishment: Thomas Jefferson's Wall of Separation in Antebellum Virginia." *Journal of Southern History* 61: 445–80.

Burnett, Edmund. 1946. "Hog Raising and Hog Driving in the Region of the French Broad River." *Agricultural History* 20: 89–118.

Butler, Anne M., and Ona Siporin. 1996. *Uncommon Common Women: Ordinary Lives of the West*. Logan: Utah State University Press.

Bynum, Victoria. 1992. *Unruly Women: The Politics of Social and Sexual Control in the Old South*. Chapel Hill: University of North Carolina Press.

Campbell, John. 1921. *The Southern Highlander and His Homeland*. New York: Russell Sage Foundation.

Campbell, John. 1984. "Work, Pregnancy and Infant Mortality among Southern Slaves." *Journal of Interdisciplinary History* 14: 793–812.

Cantwell, Robert. 1984. *Bluegrass Breakdown: The Making of an Old Southern Sound*. Urbana: University of Illinois Press.

Champagne, Duane. 1989. *American Indian Societies: Strategies and Conditions of Political and Cultural Survival*. Cambridge, MA: Cultural Survival.

Clark, Christopher. 1990. *The Roots of Rural Capitalism: Western Massachusetts, 1780–1860*. Ithaca, NY: Cornell University Press.

Clinton, Catherine. 1982. *The Plantation Mistress: Woman's World in the Old South*. New York: Pantheon Books.

———, ed. 1994. *Half Sisters of History: Southern Women and the American Past*. Durham, NC: Duke University Press.

Cogan, Frances. 1989. *All-American Girl: The Ideal of Real Womanhood in Mid-Nineteenth-Century America*. Athens: University of Georgia Press.

Collins, J. L., and Martha Gimenez, eds. 1990. *Work without Wages: Domestic Labor and Self-Employment within Capitalism*. Albany: State University of New York Press.

Conway, Cecilia. 1995. *African Banjo Echoes in Appalachia: A Study of Folk Traditions*. Knoxville: University of Tennessee Press.

Corkran, David. 1962. *The Cherokee Frontier: Conflict and Survival, 1740–1762*. Norman: University of Oklahoma Press.

Coryell, J. L., T. H. Appleton, A. Sims, and S. G. Treadway, eds. 2000. *Negotiating Boundaries of Southern Womanhood: Dealing with the Powers That Be*. Columbia: University of Missouri Press.

Coryell, J. L., M. H. Swain, S. G Treadway, and E. H. Turner, eds. 1998. *Beyond Image and Convention: Explorations in Southern Women's History*. Columbia: University of Missouri Press.

Coser, Lewis A. 1977. *Masters of Sociological Thought*. New York: Harcourt Brace.

Cott, Nancy. 1977. *The Bonds of Womanhood: "Woman's Sphere" in New England, 1780–1835*. New Haven, CT: Yale University Press.

———, ed. 1992. *History of Women in the United States*. Munich: K. G. Sauer, vol. 7.

Cott, Nancy, and E. H. Pleck, eds. 1979. *A Heritage of Her Own: Toward a New Social History of American Women*. New York: Simon & Schuster.

Crane, Verner. 1929. *The Southern Frontier, 1670–1732*. Ann Arbor: University of Michigan Press.

Craven, Paul, and Douglas Hay. 1994. "The Criminalization of 'Free' Labour: Master and Servant in Comparative Perspective." *Slavery and Abolition* 15: 71–101.

Crawford, Earle. 1980. *Samuel Doak: Pioneer Missionary in East Tennessee*. Washington College, TN: Pioneer Printers.

Crawford, Stephen. 1992. "The Slave Family: A View from the Slave Narratives." In *Strategic Factors in Nineteenth Century American Economic History*, ed. Claudia Goldin and Hugh Rockoff, 331–50. Chicago: University of Chicago Press.

Crowther, M. A. 1981. *The Workhouse System, 1834–1929*. Athens: University of Georgia Press.

Darwin, Charles. 1859. *The Origin of Species*. London: J. Murray.

Day, Marie, and W. C. Dickinson. 1988. "The Netherland Inn." *East Tennessee Histor-ical Society Publications* 60: 67–77.

Delfino, Susanna, and Michele Gillespie, eds. 2002. *Neither Lady nor Slave: Working Women of the Old South.* Chapel Hill: University of North Carolina Press.

DeVorsey, Louis. 1961. *The Indian Boundary in the Southern Colonies, 1763–1775.* Chapel Hill: University of North Carolina Press.

Drake, Thomas. 1950. *Quakers and Slavery in America.* New Haven, CT: Yale University Press.

Dublin, Thomas. 1979. *Women at Work: The Transformation of Work and Community in Lowell, Massachusetts, 1826–1860.* New York: Columbia University Press.

Du Bois, W. E. B. 1969. *The Souls of Black Folk.* New York: Signet Books.

Dunaway, Wilma. 1994a. "The Incorporation of Southern Appalachia into the Capitalist World-Economy, 1700–1860." Ph.D. diss., University of Tennessee.

———. 1994b. "The Southern Fur Trade and the Incorporation of Southern Appalachia into the World-Economy, 1690–1763." *Review of the Fernand Braudel Center* 17: 215–42.

———. 1996. *The First American Frontier: Transition to Capitalism in Southern Appalachia, 1700–1860.* Chapel Hill: University of North Carolina Press.

———. 2001. "The Double Register of History: Situating the Forgotten Woman and Her Household in Capitalist Commodity Chains." *Journal of World-System Research* 7: 2–31.

———. 2003a. *The African American Family in Slavery and Emancipation.* Cambridge: Cambridge University Press.

———. 2003b. *Slavery in the American Mountain South.* Cambridge: Cambridge University Press.

Ebert, Rebecca. 1986. "A Window on the Valley: A Study of the Free Black Community of Winchester and Frederick County, Virginia, 1785–1860." M.A. thesis, University of Virginia.

Engelhardt, Elizabeth. 2003. *The Tangled Roots of Feminism, Environmentalism and Appalachian Literature.* Athens: Ohio University Press.

Engerman, Stanley, and Eugene Genovese, eds. 1975. *Race and Slavery in the Western Hemisphere: Quantitative Studies.* Princeton, NJ: Princeton University Press.

Falkner, Frank. 1990. *Infant and Child Nutrition Worldwide: Issues and Perspectives.* Boca Raton, FL: CRC Press.

Faragher, John. 1981. "History from the Inside-Out: Writing the History of Women in Rural America." *American Quarterly* 33: 537–57.

Faulkner, Charles, and Carol Buckles, eds. 1978. *Glimpses of Southern Appalachian Folk Culture.* Knoxville: Tennessee Anthropological Association.

Faust, Alber. 1927. *The German Element in the United States.* New York: Steuben Society.

Fenelon, James. 1998. *Culturicide, Resistance and Survival of the Lakota ("Sioux Nation").* New York: Garland.

Fink, Deborah. 1992. *Agrarian Women: Wives and Mothers in Rural Nebraska, 1880–1940.* Chapel Hill: University of North Carolina Press.

Finke, Roger, and Rodney Stark. 1992. *The Churching of America, 1776–1990: Winners and Losers in Our Religious Economy.* New Brunswick, NJ: Rutgers University Press.

Fischer, David. 1989. *Albion's Seed: Four British Folkways in America.* New York: Oxford University Press.

Flanders, Ralph. 1933. *Plantation Slavery in Georgia*. Chapel Hill: University of North Carolina Press.

Flynt, Wayne. 1989. *Poor but Proud: Alabama's Poor Whites*. Tuscaloosa: University of Alabama Press.

Fogel, Robert. 1989. *Without Consent or Contract: The Rise and Fall of American Slavery*. New York: W. W. Norton.

Fogel, Robert, and Stanley Engerman. 1974. *Time on the Cross: The Economics of American Negro Slavery*. Boston: Little, Brown, 2 vols.

———, eds. 1992. *Without Consent or Contract: The Rise and Fall of American Slavery*. Vol. 1. *Markets and Production: Technical Papers*. New York: W. W. Norton.

Fogel, Robert, R. A. Galantine, and R. L. Manning, eds. 1992. *Without Consent or Contract: The Rise and Fall of American Slavery*. Vol. 3.*Evidence and Methods*. New York: W. W. Norton.

Fogelson, Raymond. 1990. "On the Petticoat Government of the Eighteenth-Century Cherokee." In *Personality and the Cultural Construction of Society*, ed. D. K. Jordan and M. J. Swartz, 161–81. Tuscaloosa: University of Alabama Press.

Fogelson, Raymond, and Paul Kutsche. 1961. "Cherokee Economic Cooperatives: The Gadugi." *Bureau of American Ethnology Bulletin* 180: 87–97.

Folbre, Nancy. 1991. "The Unproductive Housewife: Her Evolution in Nineteenth-Century Economic Thought." *Signs* 16: 463–84.

Fones-Wolf, Ken, and Ronald Lewis, eds. 2002. *Transnational West Virginia: Ethnic Communities and Economic Change, 1840–1940*. Morgantown: West Virginia University Press.

Foreman, Carolyn. [1954]. 1976. *Indian Women Chiefs*. Muskogee, OK: Zenger.

Foreman, Grant. 1953. *Indian Removal: The Emigration of the Five Civilized Tribes of Indians*. Norman: University of Oklahoma Press.

Fox-Genovese, Elizabeth. 1983. "Antebellum Southern Households: A New Perspective on a Familiar Question." *Review of the Fernand Braudel Center* 7: 215–54.

———. 1988. *Within the Plantation Household: Black and White Women of the Old South*. Chapel Hill: University of North Carolina Press.

Franklin, John. 1943. *The Free Negro in North Carolina, 1790–1860*. Chapel Hill: University of North Carolina Press.

Franklin, John, and Loren Schweninger. 1999. *Runaway Slaves: Rebels on the Plantation*. New York: Oxford University Press.

Frantz, John. 1976. "The Great Awakening of Religion among the German Settlers in the Middle Colonies." *William and Mary Quarterly* 33: 266–88.

Fraser, W. J., R. F. Saunders, and J. L. Wakelyn, eds. 1985. *The Web of Southern Social Relations: Women, Family, and Education*. Athens: University of Georgia Press.

French, Christopher. 1977. "An Account of Towns in the Cherokee Country with Their Strengths and Distance, 1742." *Journal of Cherokee Studies* 2: 34–46.

French, Laurence, and Jim Hornbuckle, eds. 1981. *The Cherokee Perspective: Written by Eastern Cherokees*. Boone, NC: Appalachian Consortium.

Friedenberg, Daniel. 1992. *Life, Liberty and the Pursuit of Land: The Plunder of Early America*. Buffalo: Prometheus Books.

Garrow, Patrick. 1979. "The Historic Cabin Site: The Last Trace of the Cherokee Town of Coosawatte." *Early Georgia* 7: 17–21.

Gaspar, David, and Darlene Hine, eds. 1996. *More Than Chattel: Black Women and Slavery in the Americas*. Bloomington: Indiana University Press.

Gearing, Frederick. 1956. "Cherokee Political Organizations, 1730–1775." Ph.D. diss., University of Chicago.

Genovese, Eugene. 1974. *Roll, Jordan, Roll: The World the Slaves Made.* New York: Random House.

Giele, Janet. 1995. *Two Paths to Women's Equality: Temperance, Suffrage and the Origins of Modern Feminism.* New York: Twayne.

Gilliam, Catherine. 1982. "Jordan's Point – Lexington, Virginia: A Site History." *Proceedings of the Rockbridge Historical Society* 9: 109–38.

Glickstein, Jonathan. 1991. *Concepts of Free Labor in Antebellum America.* New Haven, CT: Yale University Press.

Gomez, Michael. 1998. *Exchanging Our Country Marks: The Transformation of African Identities in the Colonial and Antebellum Period.* Chapel Hill: University of North Carolina Press.

Gray, Virginia. 1928. "Activities of Southern Women: 1840–1860." *South Atlantic Monthly* 27: 264–79.

Green, Fletcher. 1935. "Georgia's Forgotten Industry: Gold Mining." *Georgia Historical Quarterly* 19: 210–28.

Groneman, Carol, and M. B. Norton, eds. 1987. *"To Toil the Livelong Day": America's Women at Work, 1780 –1980.* Ithaca, NY: Cornell University Press.

Gross, Ariela. 1998. "Litigating Whiteness: Trials of Racial Determination in the Nineteenth-Century South." *Yale Law Journal* 108: 109–88.

Grossberg, Michael. 1985. *Governing the Hearth: Law and the Family in Nineteenth-Century America.* Chapel Hill: University of North Carolina Press.

Gutman, Herbert. 1976. *The Black Family in Slavery and Freedom, 1750–1925.* New York: Pantheon Books.

Gwin, Minrose. 1985. *Black and White Women of the Old South: The Peculiar Sisterhood in America.* Knoxville: University of Tennessee Press.

Hagler, D. H. 1993. "The Ideal Woman in the Antebellum South: Lady or Farmwife?" In *History of Women in the United States,* ed. Nancy F. Cott, 6: 43–56. Munich: K. G. Saur.

Hagood, Margaret. 1939. *Mothers of the South: Portraiture of the White Tenant Farm Woman.* Chapel Hill: University of North Carolina Press.

Hagy, James. 1896. "The Frontier at Castle's Woods, 1769–1786." *Virginia Magazine of History and Biography* 4: 410–28.

Hale, Will T. 1930. *Early History of Warren County.* McMinnville, TN: Standard Printing.

Hall, Jacquelyn Dowd. 1986. "Disorderly Women: Gender and Labor Militancy in the Appalachian South." *Journal of American History* 73: 354–82.

Hamer, Philip, ed. 1933. *Tennessee: A History, 1673–1932.* New York: American Historical Society, 2 vols.

Hanna, Charles. 1985. *The Scotch-Irish or the Scot in North Britain, North Ireland, and North America.* Baltimore: Genealogical.

Hansen, K. V., and I. J. Philipson, ed. 1990. *Women, Class and the Feminist Imagination: A Socialist-Feminist Reader.* Philadelphia: Temple University Press.

Harmon, George. 1932. "Benjamin Hawkins and the Federal Factory System." *North Carolina Historical Review* 9: 138–52.

Harris, J. W. 1985. *Plain Folk and Gentry in a Slave Society: White Liberty and Black Slavery in Augusta's Hinterlands.* Middletown, CT: Wesleyan University Press.

Harvey, Katherine. 1969. *The Best-Dressed Miners: Life and Labor in the Maryland Coal Region, 1835–1910*. Ithaca, NY: Cornell University Press.

Hawks, J. V., and S. L. Skemp, eds. 1983. *Sex, Race and the Role of Women in the South*. Jackson: University Press of Mississippi.

Henderson, J. Youngblood. 2000. "Postcolonial Ghost Dancing: Diagnosing European Colonialism." In *Reclaiming Indigenous Voice and Vision*, 57–76. Vancouver: University of British Columbia Press.

Henri, Florette. 1986. *The Southern Indians and Benjamin Hawkins, 1796–1816*. Norman: University of Oklahoma Press.

Hill, Samuel. 1983. *Religion in the Southern States: A Historical Study*. Macon, GA: Mercer University Press.

Hill, Sarah. 1996. "Weaving History: Cherokee Baskets from the Springplace Mission." *William and Mary Quarterly* 53: 115–36.

Hodes, Martha. 1997. *White Women, Black Men: Illicit Sex in the 19th-Century South*. New Haven, CT: Yale University Press.

Hofstadter, Richard. 1944. *Social Darwinism in American Thought*. Philadelphia: University of Pennsylvania Press.

Hofstra, Warren. 1998. " 'The Extention of His Majesties Dominions': The Virginia Backcountry and the Reconfiguration of Imperial Frontiers." *Journal of American History* 84: 1281–1312.

Holtzberg-Call, Maggie. 1989. *Living at Home in the North Georgia Foothills: Remnants of a Traditional Way of Life*. McMinnville, TN: White County Historical Society.

Hopkins, T. K., and Immanuel Wallerstein. 1987. "Capitalism and the Incorporation of New Zones into the World-Economy." *Review of the Fernand Braudel Center* 10: 763–80.

Horton, James. 1986. "Freedom's Yoke: Gender Conventions among Antebellum Free Blacks." *Feminist Studies* 12: 51–76.

Hoskins, Katherine. 1979. *Anderson County*. Memphis: Memphis State University Press.

Howington, Arthur. 1986. *What Saveth the Law? The Treatment of Slaves and Free Blacks in the State and Local Courts of Tennessee*. New York: Garland.

Hoyman, Michele. 1987. "Female Participation in the Informal Economy: A Neglected Issue." *Annals of the American Academy of Political and Social Science* 493: 64–82.

Hsiung, David. 1997. *Two Worlds in the Tennessee Mountains: Exploring the Origins of Appalachian Stereotypes*. Lexington: University Press of Kentucky.

Huddle, William. 1908. *The History of the Hebron Lutheran Church, Madison County, Virginia, 1717–1907*. New Market, VA: Henkle Co.

Hudson, Charles. 1976. *The Southeastern Indians*. Knoxville: University of Tennessee Press.

Ignatiev, Noel. 1995. *How the Irish Became White*. London: Routledge.

Innes, Stephen, ed. 1988. *Work and Labor in Early America*. Chapel Hill: University of North Carolina Press.

Jackson, Carlton. 1993. *A Social History of the Scotch-Irish*. New York: Madison Books.

Jackson, Luther. 1942. *Free Negro Labor and Property Holding in Virginia, 1830–1860*. New York: D. Appleton-Century.

Jackson, Olin, ed. 1989. *A North Georgia Journal of History*. Woodstock, GA: Legacy Communications.

Janiewski, Dolores. 1985. *Sisterhood Denied: Race, Gender and Class in a New South Community*. Philadelphia: Temple University Press.

Jennings, Francis. 1993. *The Founders of America*. New York: W. W. Norton.

Jensen, Joan. 1980. "Cloth, Butter and Boarders: Women's Household Production for Market." *Review of Radical Political Economics* 12: 14–24.

———. 1986. *Loosening the Bonds: Mid-Atlantic Farm Women, 1750–1850*. New Haven, CT: Yale University Press.

Johnson, Guion. 1937. *Antebellum North Carolina: A Social History*. Chapel Hill: University of North Carolina Press.

Johnson, Mary. 1995. "A Nineteenth-Century Mill Village: Virginius Island, 1800–60." *West Virginia History* 54: 1–27.

Johnson, Patricia. 1983. *James Patton and the Appalachian Colonists*. Pulaski, VA: Edmonds Printing.

Johnston, James. 1970. *Race Relations in Virginia and Miscegenation in the South, 1776–1860*. Amherst: University of Massachusetts Press.

Jordan, Ervin. 1995. *Black Confederates and Afro-Yankees in Civil War Virginia*. Charlottesville: University Press of Virginia.

Kahn, Kathy. 1974. *Hillbilly Women*. New York: Avon Books.

Katz, Michael. 1986. *In the Shadow of the Poorhouse: A Social History of Welfare in America*. New York: Basic Books.

Kerber, Linda. 1976. "The Republican Mother: Women and the Enlightenment – an American Perspective." *American Quarterly* 28: 187–205.

———. 1988. "Separate Spheres, Female Worlds, Woman's Place: The Rhetoric of Women's History." *Journal of American History* 75: 9–39.

Kierner, Cynthia. 1998. *Beyond the Household: Women's Place in the Early South, 1700–1835*. Ithaca, NY: Cornell University Press.

King, Andrew. 1995. "Constructing Gender: Sexual Slander in Nineteenth-Century America." *Law and History Review* 13: 63–110.

Kriedte, Peter, Hans Medick, and Jurgen Schlumbohm. 1981. *Industrialization before Industrialization: Rural Industry in the Genesis of Capitalism*. Cambridge: Cambridge University Press.

Lambert, Darwin. 1989. *The Undying Past of Shenandoah National Park*. Boulder, CO: Roberts-Rinehart.

Lander, E. M. 1953. "Slave Labor in South Carolina Cotton Mills." *Journal of Negro History* 38: 161–73.

Lawrence, Ruth. 1994. *Breastfeeding: A Guide for the Medical Profession*. St. Louis: Mosby.

Lebsock, Suzanne. 1982. "Free Black Women and the Question of Matriarchy: Petersburg, Virginia, 1784–1820." *Feminist Studies* 8: 270–92.

———. 1985. *The Free Women of Petersburg: Status and Culture in a Southern Town, 1784–1860*. New York: W. W. Norton.

Levy, Berry. 1991. "Quakers, the Delaware Valley and North Midlands Emigration to America." *William and Mary Quarterly* 48: 246–52.

Lewis, Helen, Linda Johnson, and Donald Askins, eds. 1978. *Colonialism in Modern America: The Appalachian Case*. Boone, NC: Appalachian Consortium Press.

Lewis, Johanna. 1991. "Women Artisans in Backcountry North Carolina, 1753–1790." *North Carolina Historical Review* 68: 212–34.

Leyburn, James. 1962. *The Scotch-Irish: A Social History*. Chapel Hill: University of North Carolina Press.

Little, Lewis. 1938. *Imprisoned Preachers and Religious Liberty in Virginia: A Narrative Drawn Largely from Official Records of Virginia Counties, Unpublished Manuscripts, Letters and Original Sources.* Lynchburg, VA: J. P. Bell.

Longenecker, Stephen. 2002. *Shenandoah Religion: Outsiders and the Mainstream, 1716–1865.* Waco, TX: Baylor University Press.

Loveland, Anne. 1978. "Domesticity and Religion in the Antebellum Period: The Career of Phoebe Palmer." *The Historian* 39: 455–71.

McClintock, Anne. 1995. *Imperial Leather: Race, Gender and Sexuality in the Colonial Contest.* London: Routledge.

McDonald, Forrest, and Ellen McDonald. 1980. "The Ethnic Origins of the American People, 1790." *William and Mary Quarterly* 37: 179–99.

McIlwaine, Henry. 1888. "The Struggle of Protestant Dissenters for Religious Toleration in Virginia." *Johns Hopkins University Studies in Historical and Political Science* 4 (4).

McKenzie, Robert. 1988. "From Old South to New South in the Volunteer State: The Economy and Society of Rural Tennessee, 1850–1880." Ph.D. diss., Vanderbilt University.

McLoughlin, William. 1969. "Massive Civil Disobedience as a Baptist Tactic in 1773." *American Quarterly* 21: 710–27.

——. 1984a. *The Cherokee Ghost Dance: Essays on the Southeastern Indians, 1789–1861.* Macon, GA: Mercer University Press.

——. 1984b. *Cherokees and Missionaries, 1789–1839.* New Haven, CT: Yale University Press.

——. 1986. *Cherokee Renascence in the New Republic.* Princeton, NJ: Princeton University Press.

McLoughlin, William, and Walter Conser. 1977. "The Cherokees in Transition: A Statistical Analysis of the Federal Cherokee Census of 1835." *Journal of American History* 64: 678–99.

McMillen, Sally. 1985. "Mother's Sacred Duty: Breast Feeding Patterns among Middle and Upper-Class Women in the Antebellum South." *Journal of Southern History* 51: 333–56.

——. 1990. *Motherhood in the Old South: Pregnancy, Childbirth and Infant Rearing.* Cambridge: Cambridge University Press.

McWhiney, Grady. 1988. *Cracker Culture: Celtic Ways in the Old South.* Tuscaloosa: University of Alabama Press.

Maggard, Sally. 1986. "Class and Gender: New Theoretical Priorities in Appalachian Studies." In *Proceedings of the Eighth Annual Appalachian Studies Conference,* 114–27. Boone, NC: Appalachian Consortium Press.

Malson, M. R., ed. 1990. *Black Women in America: Social Science Perspectives.* Chicago: University of Chicago Press.

Mann, Susan. 1989. "Slavery, Sharecropping and Sexual Inequality." *Signs* 14: 774–98.

Matthaei, Julie. 1982. *An Economic History of Women in America: Women's Work, the Sexual Division of Labor, and the Development of Capitalism.* New York: Schocken Books.

Matthews, Glenna. 1987. *"Just a Housewife": The Rise and Fall of Domesticity in America.* New York: Oxford University Press.

Mead, Frank, and Samuel Hill. 1985. *Handbook of Denominations in the United States.* Nashville: Abingdon Press.

Mead, Margaret, and M. Wolfenstein, eds. 1955. *Childhood in Contemporary Cultures*. Chicago: University of Chicago Press.

Medick, Hans. 1976. "The Proto-Industrial Family Economy: The Structural Function of Household and Family during the Transition from Peasant Society to Industrial Capitalism." *Social History* 1: 291–315.

Mehaffey, Karen. 1992. *Victorian American Women, 1840–1880: An Annotated Bibliography*. New York: Garland.

Melder, Keith. 1964. "The Beginnings of the Women's Rights Movement in the United States, 1800–1840." Ph.D. diss., Yale University.

Mendels, Franklin. 1972. "Proto-Industrialization: The First Phase of the Industrialization Process." *Journal of Economic History* 32: 241–61.

Meyer, Simon. 1972. *One Hundred Years: An Anthology of Charleston Jewry*. Charleston, WV: Author.

Mies, Maria. 1986. *Patriarchy and Accumulation on a World Scale*. London: Zed Books.

Mies, Maria, and Vandana Shiva. 2001. *Ecofeminism*. London: Zed Books.

Mills, Gary. 1981. "Miscegenation and the Free Negro in Antebellum 'Anglo' Alabama: A Reexamination of Southern Race Relations." *Journal of American History* 68: 16–34.

Mitchell, Robert, and Paul Groves, eds. 1987. *North America: The Historical Geography of a Changing Continent*. Boulder, CO: Rowman & Littlefield.

Morris, Richard, ed. 1976. *Encyclopedia of American History*. New York: Harper & Row.

Morris, Thomas. 1996. *Southern Slavery and the Law, 1619–1860*. Chapel Hill: University of North Carolina Press.

Nagel, Joane, and Matthew Snipp. 1993. "Ethnic Reorganization: American Indian Social, Economic, Political, and Cultural Strategies for Survival." *Ethnic and Racial Studies* 16 (2): 203–35.

Naragon, Michael. 1994. "Communities in Motion: Drapetomani, Work and the Development of African-American Cultures." *Slavery and Abolition* 15: 63–87.

Newby, I. A. 1989. *Plain Folk in the New South: Social Change and Cultural Persistence, 1880–1915*. Baton Rouge: Louisiana State University Press.

Newsome, A. R. 1929. "Twelve North Carolina Counties in 1810–1811." *North Carolina Historical Review* 6: 281–309.

Noe, Kenneth. 1994. *Southwest Virginia's Railroad: Modernization and the Sectional Crisis*. Urbana: University of Illinois Press.

Nolt, Steven. 1996. "A Spirit of Exclusivity: The Progress of Religious Conflict in Colonial Pennsylvania." *Pennsylvania Mennonite Heritage* 19: 2–16.

Olmstead, Clifton. 1960. *History of Religion in the United States*. Englewood Cliffs, NJ: Prentice-Hall.

Orren, Karren. 1991. *Belated Feudalism: Labor, the Law, and Liberal Development in the United States*. Cambridge: Cambridge University Press.

Osterud, Nancy. 1991. *Bonds of Community: The Lives of Farm Women in Nineteenth-Century New York*. Ithaca, NY: Cornell University Press.

Overdyke, W. D. 1950. *The Know-Nothing Party in the South*. Baton Rouge: Louisiana State University Press.

Penfield, Janet. 1977. "Women in the Presbyterian Church: An Historical Overview." *Journal of the Presbyterian Historical Society* 55: 107–23.

Perdue, Theda. 1977. "Rising from the Ashes: The Cherokee Phoenix as an Ethnohistorical Source." *Ethnohistory* 24: 207–26.

———. 1980. "The Traditional Status of Cherokee Women." *Furman Studies* 26: 18–39.

———. 1985. "Southern Indians and the Cult of True Womanhood." In *The Web of Southern Social Relations: Women, Family, and Education*, ed. W. J. Fraser, R. F. Saunders, and J. L. Wakelyn, 42–55. Athens: University of Georgia Press.

———. 1998. *Cherokee Women: Gender and Culture Change, 1700–1835*. Lincoln: University of Nebraska Press.

Perdue, William D. 1986. *Sociological Theory*. Palo Alto, CA: Mayfield.

Phifer, Edward. 1977. *Burke: The History of a North Carolina County, 1777–1920, with a Glimpse Beyond*. Morganton, NC: Author.

Phillips, Ulrich. [1908]. 1968. *A History of Transportation in the Eastern Cotton Belt to 1860*. New York: Octagon Books.

Pomfret, John. 1951. "A Quaker Society, 1675–1775." *William and Mary Quarterly* 8: 493–519.

Porter, Susan. 1996. *Women and the Commonwealth: Work, Family and Social Change in Nineteenth Century Massachusetts*. Amherst: University of Massachusetts Press.

Portes, Alejandro. 1983. "The Informal Sector: Definition, Controversy, and Relation to National Development." *Review of the Fernand Braudel Center* 7: 151–74.

Pudup, Mary, D. Billings, and A. Waller, eds. 1995. *Appalachia in the Making: The Mountain South in the Nineteenth Century*. Chapel Hill: University of North Carolina Press.

Raboteau, Albert. 1980. *Slave Religion: The "Invisible Institution" in the Antebellum South*. New York: Oxford University Press.

Rankin, Richard. 1993. *Ambivalent Churchmen and Evangelical Churchwomen: The Religion of the Episcopal Elite in North Carolina, 1800–1860*. Columbia: University of South Carolina Press.

Rawick, George. 1973. *From Sundown to Sunup: The Making of the Black Community*. Westport, CT: Greenwood Press.

Ready, Milton. 1991. "Forgotten Sisters: Mountain Women in the South." *Journal of Appalachian Studies Association* 3: 61–67.

Reid, John. 1977. *A Better Kind of Hatchet: Law, Trade, and Diplomacy in the Cherokee Nation during the Early Years of European Contact*. University Park: Pennsylvania State University Press.

Reid, Joseph. 1976. "Antebellum Southern Rental Contracts." *Explorations in Economic History* 13: 69–83.

Renner, Richard. 1974. "Conscientious Objection and the Federal Government, 1787–1792." *Military Affairs* 38: 142–45.

Richter, Daniel. 2001. *Facing East from Indian Country: A Native History of Early America*. Cambridge, MA: Harvard University Press.

Riley, Glenda. 1988. *The Female Frontier: A Comparative View of Women on the Prairie and the Plains*. Lawrence: University Press of Kansas.

Riordan, Jan, and K. G. Auerbach. 1993. *Breastfeeding and Human Lactation*. Boston: Jones & Bartlett.

Rippley, LaVern. 1976. *The German-Americans*. Boston: Twayne.

Rohrbough, Malcolm. 1987. *The Trans-Appalachian Frontier: People, Societies, and Institutions, 1775–1850*. New York: Oxford University Press.

Rothman, Joshua. 2003. *Notorious in the Neighborhood: Sex and Families across the Color Line in Virginia, 1787–1861*. Chapel Hill: University of North Carolina Press.

Ruiz, Vicki, and Ellen DuBois, eds. 2000. *Unequal Sisters: A Multicultural Reader in U.S. Women's History*. London: Routledge.

Russell, John. [1913]. 1969. *The Free Negro in Virginia, 1619–1865*. New York: Negro Universities Press.

Ryan, Mary. 1979. "The Power of Women's Networks: A Case Study of Female Moral Reform in Antebellum America." *Feminist Studies* 5 (1): 66–85.

_____. 1981. *Cradle of the Middle Class: The Family in Oneida County, New York, 1790–1865*. New York: Cambridge University Press.

Sanger, S. F., and D. Hays. 1907. *The Olive Branch of Peace and Good Will to Men: Anti-War History of the Brethren and Mennonites during the Civil War, 1861–1865*. Elgin, IL: Brethren Publishing House.

Sappington, Roger. 1973. *The Brethren in Virginia*. Harrisonburg, VA: Church of the Brethren Press.

Savitt, Todd. 1978. *Medicine and Slavery: The Diseases and Health Care of Blacks in Antebellum Virginia*. Urbana: University of Illinois Press.

Scholten, Catherine. 1985. *Childbearing in American Society, 1650–1850*. New York: New York University Press.

Scott, Anne. 1984. *Making the Invisible Woman Visible*. Urbana: University of Illinois Press.

_____, ed. 1993. *Unheard Voices: The First Historians of Southern Women*. Charlottesville: University of Virginia Press.

Scott, James. 1985. *Weapons of the Weak: Everyday Forms of Peasant Resistance*. New Haven, CT: Yale University Press.

_____. 1990. *Domination and the Art of Resistance: Hidden Transcripts*. New Haven, CT: Yale University Press.

Scott, Shaunna. 1990. "Gender among Appalachian Kentucky Farm Families: The Kentucky Farm Family Oral History Project and Beyond." *Journal of Appalachian Studies* 2 (1): 103–14.

Seals, Monroe. 1974. *History of White County, Tennessee*. Spartanburg, SC: Reprint Publishers.

Searight, Thomas. 1894. *The Old Pike*. Uniontown, PA: Author.

Sears, Richard. 1989. "Working Like a Slave: Views of Slavery and the Status of Women in Antebellum Kentucky." *Register of the Kentucky Historical Society* 87: 1–19.

Seitz, Virginia. 1995. *Women, Development and Communities for Empowerment in Appalachia*. Albany: State University of New York Press.

Sellers, Leila. 1934. *Charleston Business on the Eve of the American Revolution*. Chapel Hill: University of North Carolina Press.

Semple, Ellen. 1901. "The Anglo-Saxons of the Kentucky Mountains: A Study in Anthropogeography." *Geographical Journal* 17: 588–623.

Shadburn, Don. 1989. *Cherokee Planters in Georgia, 1832–1838*. Roswell, GA: W. H. Wolfe Associates.

Shapiro, Henry. 1978. *Appalachia on Our Mind: The Southern Mountains and Mountaineers in the American Consciousness, 1870–1920*. Chapel Hill: University of North Carolina Press.

Sharpless, Rebecca. 1993. "Southern Women and the Land." *Agricultural History* 67: 30–42.

Sheehan, Bernard. 1973. *Seeds of Extinction: Jeffersonian Philanthropy and the American Indian*. Chapel Hill: University of North Carolina Press.

Shinedling, Abraham. 1963. *West Virginia Jewry: Origins and History, 1850–1958*. Philadelphia: M. Jacobs Press.

Singleton, Theresa. 1995. "The Archaeology of Slavery in North America." *Annual Review of Anthropology* 24: 119–40.

Smith, Barbara. 1992. "Walk-Ons in the Third Act: The Role of Women in Appalachian Historiography." *Journal of Appalachian Studies* 4: 5–28.

————. 1999. " 'Beyond the Mountains': The Paradox of Women's Place in Appalachian History." *NWSA Journal* 11: 1–17.

Smith, Daniel. 1973. "Changing Patterns of Local Leadership, 1760–1820." *Essays in History* 18: 52–85.

Smith, Daniel, and Michael Hindus. 1975. "Premarital Pregnancy in America, 1640–1971: An Overview and Interpretation." *Journal of Interdisciplinary History* 5: 537–70.

Smith, James. 1982. "Historical Geography of the Southern Charcoal Iron Industry, 1800–1860." Ph.D. diss., University of Tennessee.

Smith, Margaret, and Emily Wilson. 1999. *North Carolina Women Making History.* Chapel Hill: University of North Carolina Press.

Smith, Mark. 1997. *Mastered by the Clock: Time, Slavery, and Freedom in the American South.* Chapel Hill: University of North Carolina Press.

Smith, Marvin. 1987. *Archaeology of Aboriginal Culture Change in the Interior South: Depopulation during the Early Historic Period.* Gainesville: University of Florida Press.

Smith, Marvin, and J. M. Williams. 1978. "European Trade Material from Tugalo, 9ST1." *Early Georgia* 6: 38–53.

Snell, William. 1972. "Indian Slavery in Colonial South Carolina, 1671–1795." Ph.D. diss., University of Alabama, Birmingham.

Solinger, Rickie. 2005. *Pregnancy and Power: A Short History of Reproductive Politics in America.* New York: New York University Press.

Soltow, Lee. 1975. *Men and Wealth in the United States, 1850–1870.* New Haven, CT: Yale University Press.

Sommerville, Diane. 1995. "The Rape Myth in the Old South Reconsidered." *Journal of Southern History* 61: 481–518.

"Special Issue: Appalachian Women." 1985. *Now and Then* 2 (1/ 2).

"Special Women's Issue." 1974. *Mountain Life and Work* 50 (6).

Speck, F. G., and C. E. Schaeffer. 1945. "The Mutual Aid Society and Volunteer Company of the Eastern Cherokees." *Journal of the Washington Academy of Sciences* 35: 169–79.

Spencer, Herbert. 1851. *Social Statics, or the Conditions Essential to Human Happiness.* London: John Chapman.

Spruill, Julia. 1938. *Women's Life and Work in the Southern Colonies.* Chapel Hill: University of North Carolina Press.

Starling, R. B. 1939. "The Plank Road Movement in North Carolina." *North Carolina Historical Review* 16: 13–36.

Starobin, Robert. 1970. *Industrial Slavery in the Old South.* New York: Oxford University Press.

Steckel, Richard. 1985. *The Economics of U.S. Slave and Southern White Fertility.* New York: Garland.

Stevenson, Brenda. 1996. *Life in Black and White: Family and Community in the Slave South.* New York: Oxford University Press.

Strickland, Rennard. 1975. *Fire and the Spirits: Cherokee Law from Clan to Court.* Norman: University of Oklahoma Press.

Sumner, William G. 1963. *Social Darwinism: Selected Essays of William Graham Sumner*. Englewood Cliffs, NJ: Prentice-Hall.

Swanton, John. 1946. "The Indians of the Southeastern United States." *Bureau of American Ethnology Bulletin* 137.

Sweet, William. 1954. *Methodism in American History*. New York: Abingdon Press.

Tadman, Michael. 1989. *Speculators and Slaves: Masters, Traders, and Slaves in the Old South*. Madison: University of Wisconsin Press.

Takagi, Midori. 1999. *"Rearing Wolves to Our Own Destruction": Slavery in Richmond, Virginia, 1782–1865*. Charlottesville: University Press of Virginia.

Taylor, Rosser. 1942. *Antebellum South Carolina: A Social and Cultural History*. Chapel Hill: University of North Carolina Press.

Taylor-Colbert, Alice. 1997. "Cherokee Women and Cultural Change." In *Women of the American South: A Multicultural Reader*," ed. Christie A. Farnham, 43–55. New York: New York University Press.

Thompson, Ernest. 1963. *Presbyterians in the South*. Richmond, VA: John Knox Press, 3 vols.

Thornton, Russell. 1990. *The Cherokees: A Population History*. Lincoln: University of Nebraska Press.

Tilly, Louise, and Joan Scott. 1978. *Women, Work and Family*. New York: Holt, Rinehart & Winston.

Trouillot, Michel-Rolph. 1995. *Silencing the Past: Power and the Production of History*. Boston: Beacon Press.

Trussell, J., and Richard Steckel. 1978. "The Age of Slaves at Menarche and Their First Birth." *Journal of Interdisciplinary History* 8: 477–505.

Tucker, Norma. 1969. "Nancy Ward, Ghighau of the Cherokees." *Georgia Historical Quarterly* 53: 187–208.

Turner, Charles. 1948. "Early Virginia Entrepreneurs and Personnel." *Virginia Magazine of History and Biography* 58: 325–34.

Van Benthuysen, Robert. 1951. "The Sequent Occupance of Tellico Plains, Tennessee." M.A. thesis, University of Tennessee.

Walkowitz, Judith. 1980. *Prostitution and Victorian Society: Women, Class and the State*. Cambridge: Cambridge University Press.

Wallace, David. 1961. *South Carolina: A Short History, 1520–1948*. Chapel Hill: University of North Carolina Press.

Waller, Altina. 1988. *Feud: Hatfields, McCoys and Social Change in Appalachia, 1860–1900*. Chapel Hill: University of North Carolina Press.

Wallerstein, Immanuel. 1976. "American Slavery and the Capitalist World-Economy." *American Journal of Sociology* 81: 1199–1213.

———. 1983. *Historical Capitalism*. London: Verso Editions.

———. 1989. *The Modern World-System III: The Second Era of Great Expansion of the Capitalist World-Economy, 1730–1840s*. New York: Academic Press.

———. 2000. "Writing History." In *Europa*, compiled by Carl DeKeyzer, 5–15. Ghent: Ludion Press.

Warren, Kim. 2006. "Separate Spheres: Analytical Persistence in United States Women's History. *History Compass* 4 (10): 1478–99.

Wayland, John. 1957. *Twenty-Five Chapters on the Shenandoah Valley*. Strasburg, VA: Shenandoah Publishing House.

Weber, Max. 1958. *The Protestant Ethic and the Spirit of Capitalism*. New York: Charles Scribner's Sons.

Weiner, Deborah. 1995. "The Jews of Clarksburg: Community Adaptation and Survival, 1900–1960." *West Virginia History* 54: 59–77.

Weiner, Deborah, and Maryanne Reed. 1996. "Contradiction, Compromise and Commitment: The Jews of Beckley, West Virginia." *Now and Then* 13: 3–36.

Weiner, Marli. 1998. *Mistresses and Slaves: Plantation Women in South Carolina, 1830–1860*. Urbana: University of Illinois Press.

Welter, Barbara. 1966. "The Cult of True Womanhood." *American Quarterly* 18: 151–74.

Williamson, Jerry. 1995. *Hillbillyland: What the Movies Did to the Mountains and What the Mountains Did to the Movies*. Chapel Hill: University of North Carolina Press.

Wood, Betty. 1995. *Women's Work, Men's Work: The Informal Slave Economies of Lowcountry Georgia*. Athens: University of Georgia Press.

Woodson, Carter. 1916. "Freedom and Slavery in Appalachia." *Journal of Negro History* 1: 132–50.

Woodward, Grace. 1963. *The Cherokees*. Norman: University of Oklahoma Press.

Wright, Gavin. 1978. *The Political Economy of the Cotton South: Households, Markets and Wealth in the Nineteenth Century*. New York: W. W. Norton.

Wust, Klaus. 1969. *The Virginia Germans*. Charlottesville: University Press of Virginia.

Index